ew Canadian Readings

LAWFUL AUTHORITY

READINGS ON THE HISTORY OF CRIMINAL JUSTICE IN CANADA

Edited by
R.C. Macleod

Copp Clark Pitman Ltd.
A Longman Company
Toronto

ISBN: 0-7730-4681-X

Editing: Camilla Jenkins
Design: Kathy Cloutier
Cover: Photograph courtesy of the Metropolitan Toronto Police.
Typesetting: Compeer Typographic Services Limited
Printing and Binding: Alger Press Limited

Canadian Cataloguing in Publication Data

Main entry under title:
Lawful authority

(New Canadian readings)
Bibliography: p.
ISBN 0-7730-4681-X

1. Criminal justice, Administration of — Canada — History.   2. Criminal law —
Canada — History.
3. Crime and criminals — Canada — History.   I. Macleod, R. C.,
1940– .   II. Series.
KE8813.Z85L39 1988   345.71′05   C87-094174-7
KF9223.L39 1988

Photo credits: p. 228, PG-K, 105–33, Kingston Picture Collection, Queen's
University Archives; p. 228, Bishop Barker Co./Public Archives Canada/PA-30472;
p. 232, PG-K, 105–54, Kingston Picture Collection, Queen's University Archives;
p. 235, 340.8 B25, Metropolitan Toronto Library.

Copp Clark Pitman
2775 Matheson Blvd. East
Mississauga, Ontario

Associated companies:
Longman Group Ltd., London
Longman Inc., New York
Longman Cheshire Pty., Melbourne
Longman Paul Pty., Auckland

Printed and bound in Canada

FOREWORD

New Canadian Readings is an on-going series of inexpensive books intended to bring some of the best recent work by this country's scholars to the attention of students of Canada. Each volume consists of ten or more articles or book sections, carefully selected to present a fully-formed thesis about some critical aspect of Canadian development. Where useful, public documents or even private letters and statistical materials may be used as well to convey a different and fresh perspective.

The authors of the readings selected for inclusion in this volume (and all the others in the series) are all first-rank scholars, those who are doing the hard research that is rapidly changing our understanding of this country. Quite deliberately, the references for each selection have been retained, thus making additional research as easy as possible.

Like the authors of the individual articles, the editors of each volume are also scholars of note, completely up-to-date in their areas of specialization and, as the introductions demonstrate, fully aware of the changing nature of the debates within their professions and genres of research. The list of additional readings provided by the editor of each volume will steer readers to materials that could not be included because of space limitations.

This series will continue into the foreseeable future, and the General Editor is pleased to invite suggestions for additional topics.

J.L. Granatstein
General Editor

CONTENTS

INTRODUCTION

Criminal behaviour fascinates us. It might not be too much to say that it obsesses us. Ever since newspapers began to cater, in the late nineteenth century, to the tastes of their readers rather than solely to the political interests of their owners, crime has been a staple of the press. The electronic media have continued the pattern without significant change. Since the nineteenth century, crime has also been a literary theme of major importance at every level from Dostoevsky and Dickens to Mickey Spillane. Agatha Christie has been a one-person publishing industry for sixty years. Hollywood and television would be lost without crime as a source for plots. It could be argued that this preoccupation is universal and timeless, and in one sense it is. The Greek tragedies and Shakespeare certainly have sufficient murder, lust, and mayhem to satisfy most tastes. But these classics focus on the individual act and its human consequences. From the nineteenth century onward, we find a number of completely new preoccupations. Writers become interested in the less serious but far more numerous crimes that the ordinary individual is likely to encounter. Speculation on the causes of crime becomes an important theme. Prisons, judges and juries, police and criminal lawyers, in short all the elements of the modern state devoted to dealing with the criminal, become familiar parts of both elite and popular culture.

Historians, until very recently, have paid almost no attention to this part of our past. In the last two decades, however, there have been significant studies of discrete aspects of the criminal justice system. These studies have widely different origins and perspectives. Historians of the *Annales* school in France, and their followers elsewhere, have begun to investigate criminal activity as a part of the everyday life of ordinary people.[1] Legal historians have produced useful histories of the criminal law and institutional studies of the development of the court system, but social historians are just beginning to investigate the impact of these institutions on those who pass through them.[2] The significant new interpretations of the history of prisons and penitentiaries have come from historians concerned with the impact of industrialization.[3] The most satisfactory histories of the origins and development of police forces are the work of the urban historians.[4]

Important as many of these works are, they share a common defect in that they examine elements of the criminal justice system more or less in isolation. Before the history of crime and criminal justice can emerge from its infancy, it is absolutely necessary that historians begin to treat crime, police, courts, and prisons as interdependent parts of a single entity and, moreover, as an entity that has a well defined location in time. The various elements began to come together in the eighteenth century in Western Europe and North America and by the middle of the nineteenth century the system was fully realized in most countries. Although few historians have noted the fact, an integrated system of criminal justice is one of the essential defining characteristics of the modern industrial state. Industrial society required standards of public behaviour that were more uniform and predictable than those tolerated by the pre-modern state. The day-to-day control of fractious individuals could no longer be entrusted to kinship groups, community pressure, and the church because the agencies varied in both time and place in their standards and effectiveness.

The pre-modern state had elaborate definitions of criminality but no reliable means of enforcing its criminal law. In most cases, apprehension of offenders was possible only with the active co-operation of the local community. The courts dealt with both civil disputes and criminal matters, with most of their time and attention devoted to the former. The training and experience of lawyers and judges was almost exclusively in matters of real property, contract, wills, and the like. There was little money and less prestige to be gained from the practice of criminal law until well into the twentieth century. Courts met frequently and the prisons were poorly equipped to retain the accused while he or she awaited trial. The penalties at the disposal of the court were also limited by the inadequacy of the prisons. Capital punishment was available for serious offences, corporal punishment and fines for minor ones. Without police forces and adequate prisons, a flexible and graduated response was out of the question. If the informal institutions of social control failed, the state had to fall back on the drastic alternative of calling in the soldiers. Governments were increasingly reluctant to take this step in the nineteenth century. Dead citizens worked no factories, paid no taxes, and their relatives tended to be unfavourably disposed towards the government.

The complex of institutions that developed in the nineteenth century solved most of these problems and, in the process, helped to create a society quite different from anything that had previously existed. All the various kinds of government intervention in the way people were educated, worked, and lived their daily lives were made possible by the control over individual behaviour provided by the criminal justice system. The system brought with it many economic advantages, but it would be a serious error to imagine that its creators operated from purely economic motives. The new society had many features that were seen as good in themselves. People could generally walk the streets free from the fear of assault or robbery. The new penalties that replaced torture and hanging were relatively rational and humane. The new approach to the criminal held out the possibility that whole sections of the community sunk in vice and crime could be redeemed through the penitentiary, either directly or by example. The pioneers of the system — Jeremy Bentham, John Howard, Henry Fielding, and Patrick Colquhoun in England, the Boston Prison Discipline Society in the United States, Hugh Thompson, the father of the Kingston Penitentiary in Upper Canada — all burned with missionary zeal. Victorians were intensely proud of what they had created. When they spoke of extending "civilization" to the less fortunate parts of the world, the criminal justice system was at least as important a part of that concept as religion and railroads, and more important than literature and art. Criminal law, police, courts, and prisons were usually the first institutions imposed on European colonies in Africa and Asia. They were the foundation of modern government, the best that Europeans had to offer.

Of all western countries, Canada accepted the new institutions of criminal justice and their accompanying ethos in the nineteenth century with the fewest reservations. Kingston Penitentiary, when it was built in the 1830s, was not only one of the most advanced designs of its day, it was the largest and most expensive public building in the country. Canadians retained their faith in the rehabilitative powers of the penitentiary long after prison experts in Britain and the United States had become disillusioned: to this day, we continue to lock up much higher percentages of convicted criminals. Montreal and Toronto seem to have copied London's police force at a very early stage, when they were scarcely more than large towns, although this is not well documented. The Fathers of the Confederation were careful to make the criminal law an exclusive federal responsibility in 1867, rather than follow the American example and leave it to the provinces. From the 1870s onwards, the North West Mounted Police were probably the most successful and innovative rural police force in the world. Canada was the first country in the British Empire to codify its criminal law and to rationalize the pretrial process by introducing crown prosecutors and eliminating the grand jury.

Canadian scholars and observers from elsewhere have often commented on the exaggerated respect for authority that forms part of the Canadian national character. Our collective enthusiasm for new developments in the criminal justice system is clearly related to this ethos in some fundamental way. The Canadian preference for "peace, order, and good government" over "inalienable rights" has more complex roots than the Loyalist tradition, powerful as that was. The fact that Canada passed under British control just as Bentham, Howard, and the other reformers were popularizing their ideas was certainly important. That the institutions of the old regime in Canada were French and became instantly obsolete with the conquest was equally so. While the French system of criminal justice was wiped out in the 1760s, the new colony proved to be stony ground into which the criminal law and courts of eighteenth-century Britain were not easily transplanted.[5]

The dominant ideology of Family Compact Toryism in Upper Canada never regarded the preservation of English society and government in their entirety as a possible or even desirable goal. Canadian political leaders throughout the nineteenth century consistently and deliberately adopted some elements of the English criminal justice system and rejected others as unsuitable. Where no usable English institutions existed to meet Canadian needs, they invented their own and disguised them in English forms and rhetoric. The goal of an ordered society on the English model remained constant. The means by which that goal would be achieved were necessarily different from those of the mother country. The most perceptive Canadian leaders were convinced that their own methods were much better, more modern and rational, free from the dead weight of the accumulated anachronisms of centuries. The whole process resembled remodelling an old house. The traditional design and furnishings were preserved, but the plumbing, wiring, and heating, the elements that made the structure work, were as modern and functional as possible.

Given the centrality of the criminal justice system in the Canadian experience, it might be expected that Canadian historians would pay a great deal of attention to it, but historical writing on the subject is recent and fragmented. Some good work has been done in some areas, as the papers reproduced in this book reveal. Vast gaps remain. Lacking anything approaching a synthesis, historians are dependent upon models adapted from criminologists whose theories rarely take account of the historical dimension. A specifically Canadian model that would provide a framework for analysing the differences and similarities between our own society and others seems even more distant. The other side of the coin is that the scope for new and exciting research in this area is almost without limit.

Notes

1. The best introduction to this rapidly growing body of literature is Alfred Soman, "Deviance and Criminal Justice in Western Europe, 1300–1800: An Essay in Structure," *Criminal Justice History: An International Annual*, vol. 1 (1980).

2. Legal historians tend to be much more interested in civil and constitutional law than in criminal law. The great English legal historians include a chapter or two on criminal law in their general histories for the sake of completeness. See, for example, Theodore F.T. Plucknett, *A Concise History of the Common Law*, 5th ed. (London, 1956). The same is true for the United States. See Lawrence M. Friedman, *A History of American Law* (New York, 1973). Social historians are mainly historians of labour and the working class. Their approach is best exemplified in the writings of E.P. Thompson and his students. See E.P. Thompson, *Albion's Fatal Tree: Crime and Society in Eighteenth Century England* (Middlesex, 1975).

3. See Michel Foucault, *Discipline and Punish: The Birth of the Prison* (London, 1977) and Michael Ignatieff, *A Just Measure of Pain: The Penitentiary in the Industrial Revolution* (New York, 1978).

4. The pioneering work in this field, and still one of the best, is Roger Lane, *Policing the City, Boston, 1822–1855* (Cambridge, Mass., 1967).

5. Douglas Hay "The Meanings of the Criminal Law in Quebec, 1764–1774" in *Crime and Criminal Justice in Europe and Canada*, edited by L.A. Knafla (Waterloo, Ontario, 1981).

SECTION 1

CRIMINALS AND CRIMINALITY

The historian who studies criminal behaviour in the past is confronted with the same difficulties facing the criminologist concerned with contemporary society: the problem of defining crime, the problem of measuring the extent of crime and the problem of explaining criminal behavior. The passage of time does nothing to make these questions more tractable. In fact, as the papers in this section demonstrate, it multiplies the barriers to understanding. The historian's subjects — criminals, victims, policemen, and judges — are all dead and therefore not susceptible to the interviews and self-report studies that criminologists have used to good effect. Formal definitions of crime in the form of statutes are easy enough to come by but attitudes to crime in periods before public opinion surveys can only be inferred indirectly. The basic institutions of the criminal justice system — police, courts, and prisons — were much more varied in the eighteenth and nineteenth centuries than they are today. Their effectiveness, even their existence, cannot be taken for granted and must be carefully investigated. For the historian, in other words, much, perhaps even a majority of the work involves getting to the point where the contemporary criminologist begins.

This is not to suggest that historians can evade the responsibility to confront the basic questions about crime. Properly done, investigations of crime in the past should provide comparisons that are as useful as contemporary cross-cultural studies. But if historical studies of crime are to serve this purpose, it is vital that the historian have some grasp of the major theoretical debates in the criminological literature. Unfortunately most historians do not bother to do this. They see the study of crime in the past only as an additional approach to analysing the history of a particular society. This is an entirely legitimate goal for historical studies but if it is the only one, it limits unnecessarily the scope of inquiry. Too many historians seem to think that once they have described criminal behaviour in a particular period, their duties have been fulfilled. In recent years, some historians have begun to realize the possibilities of placing their studies in the context of contemporary criminological research. These approaches remain tentative but the small quantity of work of this kind done so far in Canada has opened up exciting possibilities.

In his study of female crime in New France in the eighteenth century, André Lachance discusses the obstacles created by the nature of the official records of crime. Although the government of New France was very good at record-keeping compared with most other parts of the world in the eighteenth century, time has taken its inevitable toll. Lachance found that he was able to determine the outcome of trials in only 65 percent of the cases for the period he studied. The criminal justice machinery of the colony was primitive by twentieth-century standards. There was, for example, nothing like a police force in the modern sense and it seems likely that the quantity of crime unknown to the authorities was substantially larger than it would be today. Nevertheless, by comparing his findings with modern figures and with studies of similar eighteenth-century societies, Lachance is able to establish a measure of confidence in his findings.

Crime in New France followed a familiar pattern in that it was disproportionately a male activity. The crime rate for women was, however, about double that of their counterparts in modern Quebec and in some contemporary European societies. This variation is interesting but well within the range that can be accounted for by cultural differences. Curiously, Lachance ends the article with an explanation of why the crime rate for women was lower than that for men in New France, when it would have been surprising to find a different pattern.

John Weaver's approach in his article on the Gore District of Upper Canada is a useful model for any historian engaged in the study of crime in the past. He takes an integrated approach to the subject by carefully examining the institutional structure within which crimes took place and were recorded. There is a sophisticated awareness of the theoretical issues and a firm grasp of how the particular historical context must inform the debate. Weaver's point that the reluctance of local authorities to establish paid police forces was due almost entirely to considerations of cost is an important one. American and British historians have explained similar phenomena in terms of ideological objections to the police. Weaver's article suggests that the issue deserves to be re-examined in light of the financial constraints facing local governments.

The article by Michael S. Cross seeks to explain a particular set of violent episodes that took place in Bytown (the future Ottawa) in 1849. One man was killed, scores were wounded and a great deal of property was damaged in riots which broke out over a planned visit by the Governor General, Lord Elgin. Elgin had signed a piece of legislation called the Rebellion Losses Bill, thereby making responsible government in Canada a reality. His action infuriated Tories and delighted supporters of the Reform party throughout Canada, but the reaction was not as violent anywhere else in the country as it was in Montreal and Bytown.

As Cross demonstrates, political violence grew in this case from underlying class and ethnic tensions. Cross is able to make a convincing case for the primacy of class over ethnicity as a cause of the violence. The Irish and the French Canadians had been bitterly at odds in the Ottawa Valley throughout the 1830s and 1840s. But those ethnic differences were submerged relatively easily when the opportunity arose to challenge the control of the English Protestant gentry. The rioting occurred when the latter group, seeing its power slipping, made a desperate effort to retain control.

Political and ethnic violence are kinds of criminal behaviour that are relatively rare in modern democratic states. Before the twentieth century they were much more common. It is by examining differences of this kind that the historian attempts to explore the evolution of society.

One might suppose that it would be virtually impossible to find out much about the individual lives of criminals in the nineteenth century. Judith Fingard's article on the residents of Halifax jails in the 1860s and 1870s happily proves otherwise. Fingard traces the careers of a small group of individuals who repeatedly ended up in official custody for minor offences. Because they spent so much time before the courts and in the jails, the poorhouse and the insane asylum, their individual characteristics were well known to the police, the judges, and the newspaper reporters of the day. These are not statistics but unique human tragedies.

Although this article represents a preliminary report on a larger project, several interesting conclusions emerge. Those unfortunates who were chronically unable to cope with the harsh conditions of life often used the jails as places of temporary refuge. A more surprising finding is that the families of recalcitrant individuals did not hesitate to use the courts as an extension of family discipline. This is a phenomenon that clearly deserves further investigation.

The focus on individual criminal careers brings out some of the shortcomings of statistical studies. Fingard's jailbirds often gave false information concerning their ages. They also reported a variety of occupations. As the author points out, arguments about the relationship between crime and class based on reported occupations are largely meaningless. The real occupation of these individuals was petty crime, relieved occasionally by short spells of legitimate work.

WOMEN AND CRIME IN CANADA IN THE EARLY EIGHTEENTH CENTURY, 1712–1759†

ANDRÉ LACHANCE

In Canada very little research has been done so far on criminal justice for the period with which I am concerned at present, namely, the first half of the eighteenth century. In general, those who have manifested an interest in the archives of criminal justice have not consulted them for their own sake. The documents have been used by genealogists (both professionals and amateurs), and a few historians have extracted some picturesque anecdotes while pursuing research which had nothing to do with judicial institutions. Only a few people — a law historian, Professor André Morel; a penologist, Raymond Boyer; an ethnologist and historian, Robert-Lionel Séguin, and myself[1] — have seriously investigated these records of criminal justice. The excellent studies by André Morel are by far the best articles written to date,[2] especially his article on punishment in the bailiwick of Montreal (1666–1693), his biography of the king's Solicitor-General, Mathieu-Benoît Collet, and his commentary on the paper I delivered at the meeting of the Canadian Historical Association (which took place at Edmonton in June 1975), a study which was later published in the *Revue d'histoire de l'Amérique française* under the title *Réflexions sur la justice criminelle canadienne au 18e siècle*. The works of Raymond Boyer on the crime and punishment[3] and Robert-Lionel Séguin on witchcraft, licentiousness and defamation in New France[4] suffer from a similar lack of synthesis. Boyer and Séguin published their note-cards in a helter-skelter manner, with the result that their studies are collections of anecdotes and colourful trials, rather than serious analyses of crime and legal procedure. For example, Séguin published nearly 575 pages of minute details drawn from cases of immorality. In lending such importance to crimes of morality, he gave an altogether wrong impression of society in New France where these offences were not that significant.

My purpose is to present one aspect of Canadian criminality in the eighteenth century — crimes committed by women. In view of this purpose, the research was conducted in the royal criminal archives. My study, therefore, is based on the criminal records of the Superior Council, the *prévôté* and the admiralty of Quebec; the records of the royal jurisdictions of Montreal and Trois-Rivières; the *Collection de pièces judiciaires et notariales*, containing numerous criminal cases tried by different royal Canadian courts; the documents drawn up by the governors and the intendants; and the official correspondence between Versailles and the colonial administrators of Canada.

Though classified chronologically, these records have been only partially inventoried. Often, as in Montreal, for example, the interrogations, depositions

---

† L.A. Knafla, ed., *Crime and Criminal Justice in Europe and Canada* (Waterloo: Wilfrid Laurier University Press, 1981), 157–97.

of witnesses, summonses, sentences, and sales of confiscated property are mixed together in no special order. Thus findings presented in this study are fragmentary, owing to lacunae in the archives. For example, we know the sentences in only 65 percent of the trials; some cases left practically no traces at all. Many documents worked on were randomly selected. Consequently, the figures cited in this study indicate no more than approximate orders of magnitude — especially since we are well aware of the wide discrepancy between the total number of crimes committed and those which happened to be reported to the authorities. Under the French regime in Canada, many crimes and criminals escaped prosecution because of geographic factors or because of the extremely limited size of the police force. Despite these limitations, it is still justifiable to quantify the data, in an effort to illustrate general tendencies, and the conclusions are interesting.

The results can be outlined as follows. In a population between 21 000 in 1712 and 55 000 in 1759, I found 995 persons indicted by the royal courts. Of these 995, we know the sex of 977 persons (98.2 percent). Women accounted for 49 percent of the total population of Canada,[5] but only approximately 20 percent (19.7 percent) of total indictments. This ratio is comparable to that found in England,[6] and in Paris,[7] during the same era. However, this figure is 10 percent higher than the known total number of prosecutions in the colony of New York in the eighteenth century.[8] This rate of prosecution of women in eighteenth-century Canada is also higher than that which is revealed in the statistics for twentieth-century Canada and Quebec. In 1976, women charged with crime represented only 9.2 percent of the total number of persons apprehended.[9] It should be noted that, since the mid-nineteenth century, the rate of female crime has never exceeded 15 percent.[10] In Quebec, in 1967, this rate was only 11.5 percent.[11]

All in all, in spite of the relatively higher incidence of official female crime under the old regime of New France, as compared with female crime in our own times, the fact remains that during the eighteenth century female criminality is not high. Contrary statistics would be surprising because, under the old regime, women exercised very few functions outside of the home; the hegemony of society's standards belonged to the men. The values and duties of each sex were set by men. It was the prerogative of men to define acceptable social standards and to curb deviant behaviour. In short, under the old regime, power — that is, the authority to decide, to govern, to define, to set rules of conduct, and to punish — belonged solely to men.[12]

In fact, each sex had its own criminal pattern. Table 1 illustrates the resemblances and differences in these patterns. It is interesting to note here that, relatively speaking, women were involved in more crimes against property (31.3 percent female versus 21.4 percent male) and crimes against morality (6.8 percent to 5.4 percent) than men. Women were more often accused of theft (26 percent to 18.2 percent), of public scandals and prostitution (5.7 percent to 0.5 percent), of insults, calumny, slander, and defamation (13.5 percent to 7.1 percent), and of resisting a legal officer in the exercise of his office (12 percent to 4.3 percent).

However, in crimes involving offences against the king, men and women were indicted in roughly the same proportions. In the royal courts we find that men were prosecuted more frequently for crimes of violence against persons (male 56.7 percent, female 46.4 perecnt). One offence, however, seems to be attributed exclusively to women — namely, infanticide. The predominant role of women in these various offences does not seem restricted to Canadian society. Research done in Paris, England, and in the colony of New York for the same period, leads more or less to the same conclusion.

Crimes Against Persons

Table 1 shows clearly that the category of crimes against persons is dominated by men. This seems to corroborate the assertions of certain criminologists, who account for the less violent behaviour of women by calling it "natural." "Nature," by depriving women of the physical strength needed for certain offences and conditioning them against many other hardships, also makes them more resistant to criminogenic forces.[13] At first, these statements seem to be corroborated because the only categories of offences where women lead are closely related and of a certain type: insult, calumny, defamation and slander. These are all offences where verbal rather than physical violence is used. But how valid is the explanation advanced by criminologists for the behaviour of eighteenth-century Canadian women who, to survive, had to perform arduous tasks generally designed for men? Because men were frequently absent for military duty, or fur trading, women were placed in a position where they had to perform these tasks. We must dissent somewhat from this explanation of criminal scientists when we discover that 42 percent of the women pursued by justice committed physical violence on persons by assault and murder, or by resisting a legal officer in the exercise of his office, whereas only 13.5 percent of indicted women commit verbal violence.

After consideration of these figures, it becomes more difficult to stress the physical weakness of eighteenth-century Canadian women, especially when we read that they chased, with clubs, the law-enforcement officers who came to their home to deliver a warrant. These women went so far as to snatch the court order from the hands of the officer.[14] How can one invoke women's "weak nature" to explain the low crime rate of females, when a women by the name of Marie-Joseph Ethier, from Maskouche (a little village near Trois-Rivières), with an axe and shovel, clubbed her husband to death,[15] and when another one, Catherine Charland, a young servant twenty-two years of age, killed her mistress by striking her in the face and on the head with a pewter plate?[16] What can be said of another woman, Marie-Madeleine Cesar — nicknamed Levrard — who, "in a fit of anger," gave, with a right-hand punch, a magnificent black eye to the brother bursar of the Community of the Brothers Charon. Furthermore, Marie-Madeleine was severely chastised by her husband who, for that excess of anger, beat her in order to teach her that in his household, "he was opposed to all acts of violence," as he said to the judge.[17]

There is one kind of criminal violence exclusively attributable to women which claims our attention here. This is infanticide, the murder of a new-born babe. Four women were accused of this crime in eighteenth-century Canada. It should be remembered that, owing to the difficulty of proving such a murder, the State, in accordance with the edict of February 1556 by King Henry II, required all unmarried mothers to declare their pregnancy. The difficulty in proving infanticide accounts for the small number of women prosecuted for this crime in Canada. Two out of the four found accused for this crime were housemaids. It is not surprising to find such persons accused of this crime for, as Professor John Beattie says:

> women in service were, on the one hand, most commonly in their early child-bearing years and, on the other, in close and constant contact with men, both members of the family they worked for and their fellow servants. In addition, of course, a domestic servant was especially threatened by pregnancy, for apart from the ruinous blow it gave her character, it meant dismissal: if she had no family to turn to, an unmarried servant had little hope of keeping both her child and her job.[18]

In Canada, by and large, the working conditions of servants were similar. For example, Marie-Geneviève Gaudreau, a nineteen-year old maid, was gotten with child by a fellow servant. Having succeeded in hiding her pregnancy, she gave birth without any help in the cold night of 17 January 1726. She quickly flung the infant down from the verandah of her master's house in Quebec City into Cul-de-Sac Street, where she had just delivered herself of the child.[19] The next day the discovery of the baby's dead body near the house where the girl was working, and her extreme state of weakness, alerted the authorities and prompted them to arrest her. She was condemned to be hanged on 19 January 1726. However, "it's an ill wind that blows no good," for the child's father, Étienne-François Brocard, a young serving-man born in Paris, who had so far refused to marry her, changed his mind. The marriage took place in Quebec on 21 January 1726, and we hear no more of the couple afterwards.

With regards to another servant, Marianne Sigouin, it was not for her first child born out of wedlock that she was arrested. She admitted having given birth to a child which she had left in the care of the king's local prosecuting attorney. At her trial the girl testified that it was the cook of the king's ship that sailed to the colony in 1731 and left for France shortly afterwards who had given her the child which she had just been delivered of and which she had smothered at birth. For this "unnatural crime" the Superior Council of Quebec was merciless and condemned her first to public penance, and then to be hanged in the public square of downtown Quebec.[20] Marie-Anne Gendron, the third offender, was condemned to the same penalty but she was only hanged in effigy, having succeeded in escaping before she could be arrested.

The fourth person to be indicted for child murder, Madeleine Boin, was a married women whose husband had been away from the colony for over a year. With child by another man, afraid of being mocked and insulted, and shamed of the plight she was in, she hid her pregnancy and killed her child at birth. But in a small town such as Quebec was at the time, it was very hard to hide a child's body. Thus her crime was discovered and she was indicted. First she was tried by the prévôt of Quebec, where she was convicted. She then appealed to the Superior Council. In view of the fact that she already had two young children, the High Council of Canada commuted the hanging sentence previously delivered by the prévôt of Quebec and punished her by flogging, branding and perpetual banishment from the colony. In fact she was sent back to France, with her two children, to join her husband.

When one examines the penalties inflicted on women found guilty of crimes against persons one is struck by their great variety. They range from hanging to a dismissal of criminal charges. The murderers were hanged, the gossips who insulted people and spread ill-natured rumours were compelled to make public reparation for the harm they had done, and those who had committed assault had to pay damages, surgeon's fees and apothecary's bills. Moreover, they sometimes were admonished by the court and fined.

One interesting aspect worthy of note, which shows the limited sphere of action left to women in early Canadian society, is that the majority (92 percent out of 49 cases in which the place of perpetration is known) of murders, assaults and verbal offences committed by women took place at home or in the immediate vicinity of the home, whereas in the cases involving men, crimes against persons were generally committed in taverns. It is this, much more than women's "natural weakness," which accounts for the fact that only 16.7 percent of all individuals accused of crimes of violence against persons were women.

Crimes Against Property

In general, women committed a much greater proportion of crimes against property than men: 31.3 percent versus 21.4 percent. Of all crimes against property, theft is the offence which most often accounted for women's appearances in court: 26 percent of those summoned were indicted. Together with crimes against persons, theft was the crime for which eighteenth-century tribunals had to intervene most frequently in the case of women. The same is true of the New York colony.[21] Even today, theft is the feminine crime most frequently brought before the tribunals.[22] In 80 percent of the cases in the eighteenth century, the kind of theft commonly committed by women was without violence and without housebreaking and, in general, 82 percent of those took place in the daytime. Moreover, women were accused of domestic theft alone or with other women, but seldom with men (only 12 percent). Domestic theft accounted for 28 percent of female property crimes, and other thefts committed in broad daylight comprised the remaining 58 percent of non-violent theft cases.

Domestic theft was often facilitated by the easy access that women servants had to their masters' property. There is the case, for example, of Josephe Dumesnil (nicknamed Petitpas), a servant in the household of Jean-Baptise

Quenel, the captain of the coast at Lachine, near Montreal. Her masters had entrusted her with the care of the house while they were working in the fields. She took advantage of their absence to force open the lock of a cupboard, take a bill of exchange for 48 livres, one Spanish crown and a Carize sweater and flee with her booty. Her master, upon his return from the fields, discovered the theft, went after the girl on horseback, caught up with her and took her directly to prison.[23] Another servant, Françoise Laurent, purloined her master's purse — which she found lying on a chair — while her master, Jacques Pomereau, a bourgeois merchant of Montreal, was being shaved in the courtyard.[24] In general servants would steal various small objects such as utensils, napkins, aprons, ribbons, lengths of cloth, soap, etc., which they found within reach. It may be noted that these domestic thefts were more commonly urban than rural affairs.

As for shop-lifting, which was frequent in Paris and in England, there is not a single case, and only one instance of pick-pocketing is recorded. That involved Charlotte Martin-Ondoyer, mother of Françoise Laurent, who was found guilty in 1734. Under the effect of alcohol which "muddled her mind," she took a wallet from the pocket of Miss Godefroy de Linctot — a lady of good birth — who was strolling in the crowd in the market place of Montreal. Her husband, Antoine Laurent, drum major of the troops garrisoned at Montreal, gave her a flogging when he learned what she had done.[25] Likewise, there is only one known instance of a prostitute's robbing her client. This was the case with Françoise Duval (nicknamed Vinaigre), the wife of Joseph Tibault alias Bellerose, living in the suburb of Laurent. She had met Jean Nadeau, the master of the fishing boat "Saint-Jean," who had taken her on board his bark. After drinking wine and brandy with her, Nadeau made propositions to her. To pay for "her services" he gave her four bills of exchange, but as he was drunk, he gave her 250 pounds worth of them. Once sobered and realizing his error, he lodged a complaint against the woman, who fled in order to escape her husband's fury.[26] Lastly, a husband, Antoine Marsal (a merchant of Quebec), brought an action against his wife, Marguerite-Geneviève Gerbain, for theft. Not only did she appropriate furs and cloth which she found in her husband's store, but she also stole money from the till and went so far as to empty her husband's pockets while he was asleep.[27]

As was the case in Paris in the eighteenth century,[28] there were more women than men (4.7 percent of the total number of women as compared to 2 percent for the men) indicted for receiving stolen goods. Such an offence was attributed to Charlotte Duval (nicknamed Vinaigre), for instance. Charlotte was the sister of Françoise (whom we have already encountered) and wife of a day-worker, François Seizeville. She went out with her twelve-year-old nephew, who she pretended was her son, and begged for alms from house to house on the road between Boucherville and Varennes, meanwhile also offering for sale linen and clothes which a soldier, Joseph Obeuf alias Latreille, had stolen at René Phelippeau's store in Varennes.[29]

When one studies the actual statistics, it appears clearly that the number of crimes against property, at least as far as domestic theft and robbery committed by prostitutes are concerned, must have been much higher than those which happened to be recorded. One thing is certain: in the case of domestic theft many "enlightened" masters who were kind-hearted or who simply did not want to be deprived of their servants (rather scarce in Canada at the time),[30] preferred not to denounce them and arranged matters privately to settle the problems. The same is true of the victims of prostitutes: rather than lose face, they chose not to lodge official complaints of the alleged injustices which they had suffered.

In general, domestic theft was severely punished by Canadian judges. This attitude was due to a traditional mentality which considered a servant as a member of the household. In this context, when a servant stole an object which — like herself — belonged to the family patrimony, she dealt a blow to one of the most venerable bastions of traditional society, namely, the family. Her offence constituted a scandal akin to ingratitude and parricide.[31] For that reason, capital punishment was the customary sentence for such crime and in three instances a Canadian magistrate, imbued with these principles, condemned the thieves to be hanged. The judges also used flogging as an ordinary form of punishment for thieves — often in combination with branding and banishment. Some servants guilty of theft were sentenced to be placed in stocks.

For other offences against property, punishments varied according to the nature of the crime and the "social standing" of the victims. Two women offenders were hanged for having appropriated state property which had been entrusted to their care. A prostitute was banished from the colony for life. Two young adolescents aged thirteen and fourteen were confined in the General Hospital of Quebec (one for three months, the other for six years), and others were reprimanded or admonished by the judge in the court room. Those guilty of concealing stolen goods, on the other hand, were either sentenced to be flogged and confined in the general hospital, or were simply reprimanded. Finally, there is the case of a black slave, Marie-Joseph-Angélique, who was convicted of arson. She set fire to the house of her mistress in 1734, and the fire indirectly spread to forty-six houses in the town of Montreal. She was hanged in the market place, then burned at the stake, and the ashes of her body were scattered to the winds.[32]

Crimes Against Morality

Another category for which the actual number of crimes committed by women was much higher than the official statistics indicate is that of crimes against morality, which include such offences as adultery, bigamy, debauchery, pandering, concubinage, rape, incest, indecent behaviour, sodomy, bestiality, and prostitution.

Apart from crimes against God (viz., heresy and blasphemy) this kind of offence is less frequent than any of the five major categories of crimes; it even ranks after crimes of violence against the state. In spite of the fact that women were (relatively) more frequently brought to courts than men for these offences, the number of women accused of crimes against morality amounts to only 6.8 percent of all the offences for which women were indicted. On the other hand the percentage of accusations brought against men for the same kind of offence is only 5.4 percent. In this context these figures are quite low. Even at that, however, they are somewhat higher than for nineteenth- and twentieth-century Canada. "Prostitution and related offences never amounted to more than 1 to 4 percent of the general delinquency of women, married or unmarried," writes Marie-Andrée Bertrand in her work on *La femme et le crime*.[33]

In eighteenth-century Canada, crimes against morality for which women were prosecuted comprised offences which were a source of public scandal, such as adultery, bigamy, concubinage and prostitution. Prostitution was the most often prosecuted of these offences, representing 5.7 percent of all women indicted. This rate seems much lower than the actual crime rate, especially in the last decade of the French regime when there is not a single case of prostitution that is prosecuted. The silence of the archives seems contradictory because of the presence of more than six thousand soldiers in the colony.[34] Many were known as shady characters, debauched and licentious,[35] thus offering ideal conditions for the spread of prostitution. The latter certainly existed; the depositions of several witnesses reveal this fact. For example, the soldier Pierre Gouet (nicknamed Lalime), deposed against Marie-Louise Baudin, alias St Jean, that he spent two days in bed with "La Baudin" in abandoned houses. He added that she was known by the soldiers as "a top that spins, in the city of Montreal, with others of her kind."[36] Similar testimony was recorded concerning two sisters: Charlotte Dumesnil alias La Musique,[37] and Josephe Dumesnil alias Petitpas.[38] And we could cite the name of Marguerite Brusseau, alias La Vadeboncoeur, in whose lodging the soldiers spent noisy nights "making the floor shake" with their hopping and dancing. This latter description is from the evidence given by an officer of the Superior Council of Quebec.[39] So, in this era, prostitution seems to have been generally tolerated. In the other decades studied there seems to be the same amount of tolerance for prostitution, unless and until the threshold of scandal was crossed. At that point, arrests took place and the prostitutes were imprisoned in groups of two, three, and four. Once this public purge was accomplished, several years passed before the same scene was re-enacted.[40]

Concubinage was another morality offence prosecuted before the court in eighteenth-century Canada. In one instance, two women were arrested for this offence, but their cases were not prosecuted after they married their lovers in the church.[41] Finally, we find in the royal tribunals of Canada a case of adultery.[42] Such instances, however, were not particularly frequent. In summation, few women were prosecuted for crimes against morality; when they were, it was because they had created an exceptional scandal.

The court rarely dealt severely with violations against morality. The two trials for concubinage were settled amicably and no sentence was pronounced. Canadian judges occasionally handed down sentences for prostitution, condemning the accused to the full extent of the law, which was confinement in the Hôpital Général. But adultery was punished severely, probably because in this era, the offence threatened a fundamental institution of society — the family. The sole woman condemned for adultery during the eighteenth century, Geneviève Millet, wife of Pierre Roy, was sentenced to atone for the scandal she had caused. She had to appear in the ceremony of public penance, was flogged at the crossroads and public squares of Quebec City, and then was confined for three years with the prostitutes in the Hôpital Général.[43] In short, few women were brought before the royal courts for crimes against morality unless there was a public scandal. Canadian society of the eighteenth century seems to have become more and more tolerant of infractions of sexual morality.

Offences Against the State

In this fourth category of crime one finds proportionately as many accused women as accused men: 15.1 percent and 15.2 percent. This division includes counterfeiting, resisting a legal officer in the exercise of his office, desertion from the army, smuggling, building without royal permission, breaking a ban, escaping from prison, sedition and embezzlement of public funds.

Whereas men were chiefly charged with counterfeiting (7.6 percent vs. 2.1 percent), women were prosecuted especially for refusing to obey court orders (12 percent of the women vs. 4.3 percent of the men). This could be partially explained by the fact that women were often the first persons to face the law enforcement officer who came to the Canadian's home to seize chattels, or to deliver a sentence, summons or warrant of arrest. Women in traditional society were generally at home to rear the children, to prepare meals, to make and mend clothing,[44] while the men were often out working. As for women accused of counterfeiting, they were apprehended by the courts as accomplices of their husbands or of soldiers. They did not forge money themselves; male counterfeiters made use of the women's charm and supposed artlessness in order to trick the public and exchange their false bills and notes more easily.

No Canadian women, however, were accused of smuggling, breaking a ban, embezzlement of public funds, sedition or building without royal permission. Canadian judges punished more severely women who were accomplices in counterfeiting than they did women who attacked officers of the law. The accomplices were sentenced to the lash, branding, banishment and even to be hanged, while the attackers were reprimanded or admonished. Frequently, the magistrates merely imposed a monetary fine on female attackers and awarded damages and compensation to the victim.

Finally, only one woman was accused of an offence against God; she was charged with complicity in a case of witchcraft, but was acquitted.[45]

Even if the legal status of the Canadian woman under the French regime was that of a minor,[46] the Canadian judges did not tend to absolve her from responsibility for deviant acts. Because, in the Canadian context of that day, women were authorized, in the absence of their husbands, to assume responsibilities (legal and therefore social) more important than their official status would normally permit, the magistrates did not favour females with special treatment. On the contrary, they condemned women to equal if not more severe corporal punishment than men (table 4). The sole discrimination in the meting out of punishment to the respective sexes lay in sentencing to the galleys. Because of decency and the "weakness of their sex," women were condemned to flogging, branding, banishment, or confinement in a general hospital rather than to the galleys. In addition, the Canadian judges, when they used corporal punishment against women, resorted more frequently to the ultimate penalty: hanging (table 3). Considering the punishments inflicted on women by Canadian judges, we find that they sought to wound the pride of the accused women more than they did that of men. More women (14.3 percent) than men (5.2 percent) were condemned to public infamy.

Finally, contrary to contemporary Canadian[47] or French practices,[48] relatively speaking, eighteenth-century Canadian magistrates required more evidence for conviction, and less for acquittal of men (41.6 percent) than of women (26 percent). They seem to have taken a more severe attitude to delinquent women than to deliquent men, as if the female deviant irritated more than the male deviant and thus must be convicted more frequently.

TABLE 1

Men and Women Accused and the Main Categories of Offences

Categories of Offences	Number of Persons Accused			Percentage		Percentage of all		Percentage of Total Accused
	Men	Women	Totals	Men	Women	Men	Women	
Offences against God	11	1	12	91.7	8.3	1.4	0.5	1.2
Offences against the King	119	29	148	80.4	19.6	15.2	15.1	15.1
Crimes against persons	445	89	534	83.3	16.7	56.7	46.4	54.7
Crimes against property	168	60	228	73.7	26.3	21.4	31.3	23.3
Crimes against morality	42	13	55	76.4	23.6	5.4	6.8	5.6
Total	785	192	977	80.3	19.7	100	100	100

TABLE 2

Men and Women Accused of Major Crimes in Canada, 1712–1759

Crimes	Number of Persons Accused			Percentage		Percentage of all		Percentage of Total Accused
	Men	Women	Totals	Men	Women	Men	Women	
Counterfeiting	60	4	64	93.8	6.3	7.6	2.1	6.6
Infanticide	—	4	4	—	100	—	2.1	0.4
Verbal offences	56	26	82	68.3	31.7	7.1	13.5	8.4
Homicides	52	5	57	91.2	8.8	6.6	2.6	5.8
Assault	303	52	355	85.4	14.6	38.6	27.1	36.3
Prostitution, public scandal	4	11	15	26.7	73.3	0.5	5.7	1.5
Resisting legal officer in the exercise of his office	34	23	57	59.6	40.4	4.3	12.0	5.8
Theft	143	50	193	74.1	25.9	18.2	26.0	19.8
Receiving of stolen goods	16	9	25	64.0	36.0	2.0	4.7	2.6

Moreover, women also were treated less tolerantly in requests for release from prison.

We find that Canadian judges (as they did for men) punished stringently women who committed crimes against property. The court imposed corporal punishment, banishment or public infamy in 68 percent of the total sentences passed in cases of crimes against property, while for offences against the State and against persons, the same punishments are found in only 36.4 percent and 37.7 percent of the cases, respectively. Judges also pronounced severe sentences for those who committed offences against morality, especially when these crimes threatened the family. In short, Canadian judges were especially severe when women violated values that traditional society considered fundamentally sacred — that is, private property and family; otherwise they were generally lenient.

In conclusion, we may state first of all that women were apprehended especially for crimes against persons and property. They were prosecuted chiefly for assault, theft, verbal offences and resisting legal officers in the exercise of their offices. In fact, female crime was a daily occurrence and reflected the human relationships of the Canadian woman.

TABLE 3, PART 1

Categories of Offences and Sentences Against Women

Offences	Acquitted	Admonished	Banished (Perpetual)	Banished (Temporary)	Blame	Branding	Civic Trial	Confinement	Flogging	Hanged
					Sentences					
Offences against God	1	—	—	—	—	—	—	—	—	—
Offences against the King	3	1	1	—	3	1	—	—	1	1
Crimes against persons	4	—	1	—	3	1	2	—	1	1
Crimes against property	6	3	3	2	3	3	—	4	5	6
Crimes against morality	—	—	—	—	—	—	—	7	1	—
Total	14	4	5	2	9	5	2	11	8	13
Percent	10.4%	2.9%	3.7%	1.5%	6.7%	3.7%	1.5%	8.1%	5.9%	9.6%

TABLE 3, PART 2

Offences	Interdict	Payment of Damages	Pillory	Public Offences (Other)	Prosecution Abandoned	Public Penance	Settlement Out Of Court	Torture	Total	Percent
					Sentences					
Offences against God	—	—	—	—	—	—	—	—	1	0.7%
Offences against the King	—	5	—	—	—	—	—	—	22	16.3%
Crimes against persons	—	3	—	9	11	3	2	1	53	39.3%
Crimes against property	1	2	1	1	8	—	—	—	50	37.0%
Crimes against morality	—	—	—	—	—	1	—	—	9	6.7%
Total	1	10	1	10	19	4	2	1	135	70.3%
Percent	0.7%	7.4%	0.7%	7.4%	14.1%	2.9%	1.5%	0.7%		100%

TABLE 4

Percentage of Sentences Pronounced Against Men and Women

	Acquitted or Released	Public Infamy	Corporal Punishment	Other
Men	41.6%	5.2%	28.0%	25.2%
Women	26.0%	14.3%	28.7%	31.0%

Second, we should bear in mind the small percentage of women brought before the royal courts. Must we therefore conclude that female delinquency was relatively unimportant? No, because there is a wide discrepancy (especially in the fields of domestic theft and of morality) between recorded crime and the actual number of offences committed; the latter, instead of decreasing, must in fact have grown with the increase in the female population. Nevertheless, a reduction in the prosecution of crime, especially crimes against morality, may be the result of a change in the scale of values in Canadian society.

The low rate of female delinquency may be explained by the relative absence of women in active Canadian society as a result of the accepted traditional female role: domestic work carried on in the privacy of the home rather than in places of public gatherings.

In summary, the female criminality in eighteenth-century Canada reflects the role of the woman in Canadian society: wife and mother whose sphere of activity is the home.

Notes

1. André Lachance, *Le bourreau au Canada sous le régime français* (Quebec: Société historique de Québec, 1966); *La justice criminelle du roi au Canada au XVIIIe siècle* (Quebec, 1978); "Une etude de mentalité: les injures verbales au Canada au XVIIIe siècle," *Revue d'histoire de l'Amérique française* 31 (Sept. 1977): 229–38.

2. André Morel, "La justice criminelle en Nouvelle-France," *Cité Libre* 14 (Jan. 1963): 26–30; "L'imposition et le contrôle des peines au Bailliage de Montreal (1666–1693)" in *Études juridiques en hommage à Monsieur le juge Bernard Bissonnette*, 413–32; "Mathieu-Benoît Collet" in *Dictionnaire biographique du Canada*, 2: 156–68; "Reflexions sur la justice criminelle canadienne au 18e siècle," *Revue d'histoire de l'Amérique française* 29 (Sept. 1975): 241–53.

3. Raymond Boyer, *Les crimes et les châtiments au Canada français du XVIIe au XXe siècle* (Montreal: Le Cercle du Livre de France, 1966).

4. Robert-Lionel Séguin, *La Sorcellerie au Canada français du XVIIe au XIXe siècle* (Montreal, 1959); *La vie libertine en Nouvelle-France au dix-septième siècle* (Montreal, 1972), 2 vols; *L'injure en Nouvelle-France* (Montreal, 1976).

5. Jacques Henripin, *La population canadienne au début du XVIIIe siècle* (Paris: Presses Universitaires de France, 1954) 18–19.

6. J.M. Beattie, "The Criminality of Women in Eighteenth Century England," *Journal of Social History* (Fall 1974): 81.

7. P. Petrovitch, "Recherches sur la criminalité à Paris dans la seconde moitié du XVIIIe siècle," in *Crimes et criminalité en France sous l'Ancien Régime, 17e–18e siècles*, edited by A. Abbiateci, 234.

8. Douglas Greenberg, *Crimes and Law Enforcement in the Colony of New York, 1691-1776* (Ithaca, 1976), 51.

9. M.-A. Bertrand, *La femme et le crime* (Montreal, 1979), 64, 191.

10. Ibid., 104.

11. Bureau of Federal Statistics, *Statistique de la criminalité, 1967* (Ottawa, 1969), 40–43.

12. M. Johnson, "Histoire de la condition de la femme dans la province de Québec," in *Tradition culturelle et histoire politique de la femme au Canada, Études préparées pour la Commission royale d'enquête sur la situation de la femme au Canada*, no. 8 (Ottawa, 1975), 6; M.-A. Bertrand, *La femme et le crime*, 179–82.

13. Gisèle Halimi, *Le programme commun des femmes* (Paris, 1978), 165–66.

14. See, for example, Archives nationales du Québec à Montréal, (hereinafter ANQM), Documents judiciares, File January–June 1740, 20 Apr., ANQM, NF 25, PJN 1098.

15. ANQM, Documents judiciaires, File June–December 1746, 2 Nov. to 10 Dec.

16. Archives nationales du Québec à Québec (hereinafter ANQQ), NF 25, Pièces judiciares et notariales (hereinafter PJN), 621.

17. ANQM, Documents judiciaires, File July–December 1744, 4 Dec. to 15 Dec.

18. J.M. Beattie, "Criminality of Women," 84.

19. ANQQ, NF 25, PJN 730, 739; Tanguay, *Dictionnaire biographique du Canada*, 2: 477.

20. ANQQ, NF 13, Procédures judiciaires, Matières criminelles, 4: 435 ss.; NF 11–37, Registre du Conseil superieur 4, no. 37: 90v–92v.

21. Greenberg, *Crime and Law Enforcement*, 50.

22. Bertrand, *La femme et le crime*, 74.

23. Married in Quebec to Pierre Labadie, she had obtained from Governor La Galissonnière a separation of bed and board "cloth" in 1749. ANQQ, NF 25, PJN 1736.

24. ANQM, Documents judiciaires, File October 15–December 1750, 21 to 26 Oct.; ANQQ, NF 25, PJN 1570, 1645, 4176–39.

25. Ibid., File January–March 1734, 15 Jan. to 12 Feb.

26. Ibid., File January–May 1756, 21 Feb. to 10 May.

27. ANQQ, NF 25, PJN 1075.

28. Petrovitch, "Recherches sur la criminalité à Paris," 235.

29. ANQM, Documents judiciaires, File January–June 1757, 18 Feb. to 1 June.

30. Marcel Trudel, *Initiation à la Nouvelle-France* (Montreal, 1968), 155.

31. Petrovitch, "Recherches sur la criminalité à Paris," 212.

32. ANQM, Documents judiciaires, File April–June 1734, 4 June; ANQQ, NF 25, PJN 1036, NF 11–37, Registre du Conseil supérieur de Québec 4, no. 37: 24–26.

33. Bertrand, *La femme et le crime*, 177.

34. Gilles Proulx, "Soldats à Québec, 1748–1759," *Revue d'histoire de l'Amérique française* 32 (1978–79): 536–37.

35. Archives nationales, Colonies, Série CIIᴬ, vol. 95, 336; vol. 98, 83; vol. 99, 238v.

36. ANQM, Documents judiciaires, File January–May 1754, 8 Mar. to 21 May.

37. Ibid., File January–May 1753, 23 Feb. to 12 Mar.

38. ANQQ, NF 25, PJN 1736.

39. Ibid., PJN 1892.

40. Morel, "Reflexions sur la justice criminelle Canadienne," 252.

41. ANQM, Documents judiciaires, File August–December 1715, 7 Sept. to 2 Nov.; File January–June 1740, 25 June to 18 July.

42. Archives nationales, Colonies, Série C11ᴬ, vol. 60, 48v–49. See also Petrovitch, "Recherches sur la criminalité à Paris," 215.

43. Hocquart au Ministre, 3 Oct. 1733, Archives nationales, Colonies, Série C11ᴬ, vol. 60, 48v–49.

44. Peter Laslett, "Le rôle des femmes dans l'histoire de la famille occidentale," *Le fait féminin*, edited by Evelyne Sullerot (Paris, 1978), 454–59.

45. ANQM, Procès fameux, 1734–1756, Havard de Beaufort affair, 30 June 1742 ss., s.f.

46. Johnson, "Histoire de la condition de la femme," 6.

47. Bertrand, *La femme et le crime*, 96.

48. Halimi, *Le programme commun des femmes*, 171.

CRIME, PUBLIC ORDER, AND REPRESSION: THE GORE DISTRICT IN UPHEAVAL, 1832–1851†

JOHN WEAVER

Social disorganization was one of the most striking features of life in Upper Canada in the early Victorian period. The extension of the transportation network, the expansion of villages into towns and towns into cities, and the reception of immigrants displaced by economic and demographic crises in the United Kingdom produced a series of shocks felt throughout the colony. Few regions, however, were more vulnerable than the Gore District. Situated at the western end of Lake Ontario, this district included the present countries of Halton, Wentworth, Brant, Wellington, and Waterloo and was the site of massive canal and railway construction. It also received large numbers of the famine Irish.[1]

The complex realm of criminal justice provides a way of understanding the social upheavals of the period. To do so one must examine two closely related aspects of the system: the rates of crime and the responses of the criminal justice system to the crimes themselves. Annual crime rates and the conduct of the criminal justice system form interdependent indicators of social health, or to use a less value-laden term, social organization. Crime rates, for example, are often the product not only of crime itself but also of changes in what society considers to be acceptable behaviour. This is particularly true of lesser crimes against public order and morality, because attitudes towards these tend to fluctuate more than the attitudes towards more serious and violent crimes such as murder. At the same time, of course, crime rates reflect a real shift in behaviour and indicate the turmoil in the district that followed from the transatlantic movement of capital and people. Put in another way, the records of the criminal justice system reflect both sides of a complex process: social disorganization and the changes in the responses to that disorganization.

The study of crime and criminal justice are important parts of social history. As a discipline, social history entices the historian with appealing sets of categories, such as class and culture, community and conflict, work and leisure, family and ethnicity. Social history also benefits from an abundance of hypotheses framed in an exciting body of international literature. All these suggest new historical sources or new techniques with which to rework the old. At the same time social history can be a cause of frustration, because the sources never seem to answer essential questions with authority; new questions

† *Ontario History* 78, no. 3 (1986): 175–207. The author wishes to acknowledge the contributions of his research assistant, Helen Carson, the extremely helpful comments from two anonymous readers, and the dedication of the editors of *Ontario History*.

pull the inquiry toward demanding work. The results of long hours of toil too often do not live up to the original expectations. All of these qualities colour the study of crime and repression in the Gore District.

Historians of crime have devised certain ways to quantify the records of the criminal justice system and to set up categories that allow crime and society to be analysed over time and across a given space. American historians, for example, have used quantification to study the nineteenth-century system of criminal justice in South Carolina, Massachusetts, Philadelphia, and Columbus, Ohio. In Britain, J.J. Tobias, an historian of criminal justice, levelled an early attack against quantification, but recent controversies here now revolve around what the data actually measure rather than the usefulness of the data. In both countries, carefully constructed analyses of data serve as a measure both of crime and of the attitudes of authorities to crime.[2]

In Upper Canada the records of crime also reflect both crime and attitudes towards it. For example, it appears that drunkenness, prostitution, and vagrancy all increased in the late 1840s. This stemmed from both local and transatlantic forces that were changing the pattern of traditional social relationships. At the same time, the higher rates for these offences were partly due to a less tolerant attitude toward the rough pastimes of plebeian culture. Toleration of "immorality" in a largely agrarian and commercial society seems to have been giving way to more rigorous attitudes. "Reform" ideas also entered into the rate of increase. By mid-century the belief that poverty and crime could be alleviated by the forced reformation of the individual had become widespread and achieved an architectural expression in the house of industry and the penitentiary. These reforms also appealed to local authorities concerned with matters of economy. Clamping down on rootless new arrivals, dissuading them from staying in town, or punitively renovating their temperament promised savings to authorities who could no longer meet the escalating calls upon relief funds. And against all of these considerations was the background of railway and canal construction with its large pools of transient labour, strikes, and riots. Finally there was the jaundiced attitude toward the Irish who made up so much of the population that was involved in these processes, as immigrants and navvies. The records of arrests and court proceedings speak emphatically to this last point.

The collecting and the arranging of data on crime and punishment are as challenging as the attempt to interpret it. Indeed the form in which one places evidence and the meaning drawn from it cannot be separated; what is coded and how it is coded affect the analysis. The criminal justice system produced an abundance of material for the social historian; each stage in the system, from arrest to punishment produced specific information. Local jail records like those for the Gore District contained a different body of information from the records of the courts or the penitentiary punishment books. Jail records, for example, contained committals for both felonies and misdemeanours, for cases tried at the assizes and quarter sessions and before town magistrates. The recording of misdemeanour arrests is rendered only slightly imperfect by the fact that from 1840 on Hamilton maintained its own tiny cellar lock-up where drunks and vagrants were held until they could be brought before a magistrate.

If they could pay their fines they were discharged without ever having been placed in the district jail; if unable to pay, however, they were sent to the district jail.[3]

Measured by the volume of prisoners and remarks, the district jail functioned as a lowly lock-up used frequently by the town's high bailiff and justices of the peace. The real problem with jail records is that they say little about the circumstances of individual cases. What these records do provide, however, is information about prisoners, their alleged crimes, and their progress through the justice system (see table 1). Difficulties that arise from the use of jail records will be discussed as they are encountered.

TABLE 1

The Gore Jail Ledgers and Their Contents, 1831–51

Usual Sequence in Ledgers	Heading	Years Available	Remarks
1	Name	All	
2	Crimes	All	Usually same as no. 5.
3	Date of committal	All	
4	By whom committed	All	Used for determining area of arrest.
5	Crimes convicted of	All	
6	Sentence	All	
7	Date of sentence or discharge	All	Used with no. 3 to determine the length of wait in jail.
8	Age	All	Considerable clustering noted at ages 20, 25, 30, and 35.
9	Country	All	Assumed to be birthplace.
10	When bailed	All	
11	Remarks	All	States if there was no prosecution, or if prisoner was released for other reasons.
12	Occupation	1843–48	
13	Religion	1843–48	
14	Read or write	1848–51	Four categories: Read and write with superior education, read and write well, imperfectly, unable.
15	Temperance or moral habits	1848–51	

SOURCE: Data file based on Gore District Records.

To what extent is the story that these records reveal typical of Upper Canada as a whole? The province, as many historians have shown, was far from homogeneous. The Ottawa Valley, the Kingston area, and the West all had features that distinguished them from each other, and as a consequence generalizations are extremely difficult. Still, all parts shared a number of important features. Similar groups of social worthies dispensed justice as magistrates, and they all worked within the same system of judicial institutions. Most districts were exposed to immigrants and casual labour, especially these along Lake Ontario. In this sense the Gore District should been seen as an area in which these social developments were experienced with particular force. It was a unique transitional point for itinerant labourers and immigrants who left the lake vessels to begin their travel overland. All districts had construction and the problems associated with it; few had as much urban building or as many transportation projects as the Gore District.

Crime and Repression

Jail committals for the Gore District disclose slight fluctuations from season to season and year to year. The summers, with movements of immigrants and labourers, transformed Oakville, Dundas, Hamilton and Paris into lively towns packed with people seeking work and recreation. Assaults, horse thefts, and thefts of small articles rose slightly above average during July, August, and September. The seasonal levels prove less distinctive than other temporal patterns. A few years, for example, were exceptionally troubled. The mid–1830s, years of heavy immigration and rising costs, introduced high property crime rates (see table 2). Committals for property crime jumped again from 1842 to 1847. The trend then concluded and brought an expression of relief from the grand jury in April 1847: "It is gratifying to find that the number of persons of this description [felons] is much smaller than usual in the District, and the offenses which the unfortunate people stand charged with, generally of a less aggravated and serious nature."[4] During the early 1840s, strangers in large numbers arrived in or near the Gore District to labour on the Grand River navigation project and the nearby Welland Canal. Underemployed and embittered by labour practices and local bigotry, they had arrived just after the poor harvests of 1842 and the subsequent harsh winter. Rural distress affected farm labourers; canal projects introduced the exploited navvies with their direct actions to redress grievances.[5] In *Crime and Authority in Victorian England*, David Philips demonstrated a connection between periods of economic distress and trial committals for larceny.[6] Despite the risk of attributing a rash of any category of committal to a single set of factors, economic conditions surely affected crime in the Gore District. Immigration and public works, however, made for a different economy and society than Philip's "black country." Surges in new arrivals, harsh working conditions, and a rise in food prices may have pushed up the property crime rate. The gross measure of property crimes can be broken into many components. One ingredient has been chosen to suggest the plausibility of a connection between distress and theft. In 1846, the Gore District experienced by far its greatest number of arrests for stolen food and clothing. The previous high had been thirteen cases in 1835; there were thirty in 1846 (see table 3). Both years were ones of great immigration.

The annual rates for crimes against persons undulated in a pattern similar to that for crimes against property (see table 2). A jump in violence accompanied the hectic immigration period and boom growth around Burlington Bay in 1835. In the wake of the Rebellion of 1837, the region "settled down." Of course, the jail was so crowded with treason suspects in 1838 that it could not have held many transgressors of the commonplace laws, but the rates for crimes remained low in 1839 and 1840 and the treason suspects cannot

TABLE 2

Estimated Annual Rates of Crime per 100 000, Gore District, 1832–51[a]

Year	Population	Property Crimes[e] per 100 000	(N)	Crimes against Persons[f] per 100 000	(N)	Public Order Crimes[g] per 100 000	(N)	Miscellaneous Crimes[h] per 100 000	(N)
1832	27 225	113	(31)	40	(11)	4	(1)	18	(5)
1833	31 820	148	(47)	31	(10)	57	(18)	13	(4)
1834	34 618	80	(28)	84	(29)	38	(13)	6	(2)
1835	40 156	147	(59)	177	(71)	32	(13)	27	(11)
1836	43 920	125	(55)	100	(44)	7	(3)	30	(13)
1837	46 601	103	(48)	139	(65)	26	(12)	161	(75)[i]
1838	50 319	83	(43)	42	(21)	70	(35)	151	(76)
1839	51 527	83	(43)	35	(18)	27	(14)	132	(68)
1840	53 729	84	(45)	26	(14)	34	(18)	56	(30)
1841	42 577[b]	85	(36)	101	(43)	42	(18)	94	(40)
1842	45 059	129	(58)	49	(22)	27	(12)	73	(33)
1843	47 000[c]	153	(72)	138	(65)	94	(44)	38	(18)
1844	49 000	141	(69)	116	(57)	147	(72)	26	(13)
1845	50 000	164	(82)	148	(74)	122	(61)	102	(51)
1846	52 000	162	(84)	100	(52)	77	(40)	75	(39)
1847	54 000	133	(72)	69	(37)	161	(84)	26	(14)
1848	59 615	106	(63)	101	(61)	173	(103)	34	(20)
1849	—	—	(40)	—	(42)	—	(85)	—	(6)
1850	—	—	(85)	—	(59)	—	(176)	—	(26)
1851	42 619[d]	176	(75)	197	(84)	434	(185)	59	(25)

a Crime means committal to jail for an alleged offence. Discharges and the involvement of more than one party in a single crime were not taken into account. These considerations would have reduced the rate of all categories except public order and miscellaneous.
b Creation of the Wellington District.
c See note 1 in text.
d The creation of counties reduced the base population.
e Property crimes included all forms of theft, larceny, stealing, burglary, destruction of property, and offences involving guile or fraud. Theft and larceny were the most frequently cited charges.
f Crimes against persons included abduction, assault, beating, cutting, kidnapping, murder, shooting, and stabbing. Assault was by far the most frequently cited.
g Crimes against public order included abusive language, breach of by-laws, drunk and disorderly conduct, gambling, public nuisance, prostitution, vagrancy. Drunk and disorderly was by far the most frequently cited.
h Miscellaneous crimes included contempt of court, refusing to give evidence, breach of military law, suspicion of treason, high treason, and want of sureties to keep the peace. Except for the incidence of treason arrests in 1837–38, want of sureties was the most frequently cited. Lack of information on the context of these instances precluded their being placed with crimes against persons or public order.
i The Rebellion of 1837 produced 120 prisoners. Some were arrested in late 1837 and others in early 1838.

SOURCE: Data file based on Gore District Records.

account for that. Growth had slowed; public works and improvements faltered. Possibly, too, the suppression of the rebellion chastened, terrified, and exhausted the Gore District. Canal navvies and migrants attracted to the

TABLE 3

Absolute Number of Committals and Selected Rates for Specific Crimes, Gore District, 1832–51

	Murder, Accessory to Murder, and Rape (N)	Theft of Food and Clothing (N)	Want of Sureties to Keep the Peace[b] (N)	Drunk and Disorderly Conduct		Assaults	
				Rate per 100 000	(N)	Rate per 100 000	(N)
1832	3	3	—		—	(26)	7
1833	3	4	—		—	(28)	9
1834	3	4	—		—	(66)	23
1835	5	13	—		—	(167)	67
1836	5	1	—		—	(96)	42
1837	1	6	—	(11)	5	(129)	60
1838	9	9	—	(18)	9	(16)	8
1839	7	7	—	(15)	8	(14)	7
1840	1	1	1	(9)	5	(26)	14
1841	9	5	—	—	—	(75)	32
1842	3	4	1	—	—	(31)	14
1843	10	5	—	(15)	7	(110)	52
1844	4	4	7	(12)	6	(106)	52
1845	2	10	24	(70)	35	(100)	50
1846	8[a]	30	20	(56)	29	(85)	44
1847	7	17	5	(124)	67	(52)	28
1848	2	5	12	(136)	82	(82)	49
1849	3	1	3	—	72	—	35
1850	9	1	14	—	152	—	51
1851	6	5	12	(336)	143	(134)	57

a This figure definitely warns against reading the arrests for murder as reflecting incidences of that crime. Three suspects and several witnesses were arrested in one case. All other offences were less problematic in their linkage between number arrested and a rate or index of crime.
b See text for a definition.

SOURCE: Data file based on Gore District Records.

employment of town construction began to flow into the district in 1842–43, and with their arrival the rate for crimes against persons rose. In 1847, the violence began to diminish. The tumult of a sudden resurgence of growth passed; by 1845 the Welland Canal had been rebuilt, and the Grand River Navigation project wound down in 1849. In 1850 and 1851, however, railway navvies streamed into the Gore District, evidently bringing disorder in their wake. At Copetown, as on the Welland Canal a few years earlier, the labourers' camp split into two brawling factions of Irishmen, "Fardowners" (from Cork) and "Connaughtonians." The rate of crimes against persons now soared to its highest level, nearly double that of 1848.

Fluctuations in the rates for three specific offences, one drawn from the miscellaneous category and two from the crimes against persons group, locate the peaks and troughs of friction and violence around the dates of significant socio-economic occurrences (see table 3). The first offence, labelled "want of sureties to keep the peace," was a basis for committal to jail on the grounds of breaking a pledge, arising from prior complaint, not to abuse another party. The jail registers did not report the circumstances of individual cases; arrest might have involved domestic disputes, threats, or rowdy conduct in a neighbourhood. Significantly, the practice of invoking want of sureties was practically unknown before the troubled mid–1840s, when it became relatively common. A second category of offence, assaults, clearly showed very high rates from 1835 to 1837, followed by the remarkable drop noted for all crimes against persons. The assault rate bounced up strongly in the distressed growth years of 1843–46, declined thereafter, and rebounded in 1851. Finally, the offence of threatening, too, had risen steeply in 1844 and then fallen. In sum, periods conventionally seen as "good times," periods of large or numerous public works in the colony, contained comparatively alarming public disorders. Indeed, the character of building — the suddenness of turns in the economic cycle and the practice of attracting large pools of floating labour — contributed to the criminal disorders.

The fluctuations of property crimes and crimes against persons form a slightly distinct path from public order offences. The latter did not bounce about exceptionally. They tended to curve upward (see table 2). Before 1843, public order offences constituted 12 percent of all committals; from 1843 to 1851 they accounted for 35 percent. We can turn to several explanations: urbanization, moral reform, community anxiety, and the generation of truly greater "immorality" by social upheaval. First, let us dismiss urbanization. According to the ecological school of sociology, urban places were essentially destructive of primary relationships, leading to personal disorganization, mental breakdown, suicide, delinquency, crime, corruption, and discord. The Gore District Jail data could support this anti-urban ecological interpretation, for the towns of the Gore District were growing remarkably during the 1830s, 1840s, and 1850s and the share of committals for urban places far exceeded their proportion of the total district population. But the apparent correspondence between urbanization and increasing crime rates is deceptive. In contrast to a mechanistic linkage of urban growth with disorder, a behaviourist school of sociology that stresses the attitudes of law makers and enforcers brings research onto the humanistic plane, where conventional documentation provides the context. Following this approach, it becomes clear that, in defining and outlawing new offences, the authorities of Upper Canada shared with those of England and the United States a set of anxieties and theories about crime. The colony absorbed the reform tendencies of these jurisdictions. More emphatically, the ecological approach misses entirely the international context. Let us, then, consider both the attitudes of the authorities and the international forces. The former can be reconstructed or inferred from evidence on enforcement and from legislative and institutional history. The latter can be appraised by looking at the social traits of those arrested.

It is important not to confuse the modest public-order crime rate in the 1830s with a near absence of vice (see table 2). In the countryside, especially twenty or so miles from the jail, magistrates routinely avoided making inconvenient arrests. This was true as late as the 1850s. Memoirs, petitions, and town records, however, have described copious "wickedness." Upper Canadian society had a firm attachment to drink, and "taking the horn" was a custom that enlivened marriages, christenings, funerals, harvests, and daily labour. A trial report from 1843 described a wedding celebration ending in a homicide: "Friends and relations of the parties had been making the rounds nary for two or three days in succession at different inns in the town."[7] When the Dumfries Mills were being constructed, the workingmen demanded and received the usual daily ration of rum. At public entertainments like fairs and circuses, drink brought on the "rude and boisterous roar of riot."[8] The most unlikely locales for drinking and other vices were religious camp meetings. But, reminiscing about the 1820s and 1830s, Charles Durand recalled how "wicked people on the outside often attended meetings; carried on all kinds of games; even horse-racing, wrestling, fighting." The secular Sabbath was a recreational institution. Sunday revels began on Saturday night and lingered into Monday morning, bringing heavy traffic onto Hamilton's streets. On 27 July 1837, Hamilton magistrates described the Sabbath as "obviously the day on which offences against the Peace occurred: rioting, fighting in the streets, drinking, using foul and abusive language, and driving furiously in the streets." Along the waterfront the drinking, gambling, and whoring went on in taverns, hotels, and licensed stores. With a population of about three thousand in 1840, the town probably had twenty drinking establishments. A hastily created shanty selling rum and beer even served labourers repairing the Burlington Canal in the early 1840s. Drinks were also dispensed by houses of ill-fame. The number of these establishments is uncertain, but the following five ran into trouble with Hamilton authorities in the early 1840s: Marianne Ravelle's "bad house," Daniel Tolliver's "notorious house," Mr. and Mrs. Luckey's "disorderly house," Joe Case's grocery and beer shop, which kept "common women of the town," and Mary Lavill and May Lilly's "house of ill fame."[9]

Recreational occasions gave authorities hectic times. July, August, and September were favoured for the visits of circuses on the Erie Canal and Lake Ontario circuit; local fairs were held during these months as well. The liquor tents, petty swindles, and extra supervision laid on for the mass events augmented the jail population. The training of the militia — mustered either on the Queen's birthday or in late June — increased the turbulence. It not only brought young men and hard drinking together, but "it was a general belief that no law existed during training day so that all disputes during the year were put off and settled at that time."[10] Longer daylight, open doors and windows, and the ease of movement along the streets brought disorderly behaviour and assaults audibly and visibly to the attention of town dwellers.

Initially, in the small and scattered communities of the Gore District, the authorities tolerated moderate shades of vice and a sowing of wild oats. One early case of liquor sales being prosecuted illustrates a concern with revenue rather than probity. During a warm summer camp meeting at Mount Pleasant in 1824, a beer vendor, Asa Kebrich, sold a quart of whiskey to a "respectable carpenter" and was later summoned and fined. He had not violated a code of public morality, but he had failed to secure a licence. Licences were certainly a means of attempting to control drink, and in later years Reform magistrates favouring temperance clashed with Tory magistrates in the quarter sessions over the regulation of the liquor traffic. It is significant that in the Kebrich case the sole concern was revenue. Even twenty years later, the effort to stamp out low life could not proceed without community sanction. In Waterdown, for example, a zealous magistrate, Ebenezer Griffin, who endeavoured to ban turkey raffles and drinking in 1841, was ousted by community pressure. In the larger towns, however, this tolerance of coarse entertainment soon ended.[11]

The ground work for a lobby against vice had just begun when Kebrich sold the offending quart at Mount Pleasant. It began with the spread of Sunday schools and the formation of local temperance societies in 1829. By the early 1830s, moral tracts printed by the influential American Tract Society in New York had penetrated the Gore District under the aegis of the American Presbyterian Church in Hamilton. Founded in late 1832 or early 1833, the church had been formed on the temperance plan. An Upper Canada Religious Tract and Book Society was organized at York in January 1832, drawing inspiration from both the London and the New York movements. By 1834 its influence extended into the Gore District with the founding of the Mount Pleasant Auxiliary Tract and Book Society. The fusion of religious revival and reform messages was propagated in Hamilton's literary newspapers, the *Casket* and *Garland*.[12]

On their own, the reformers could not uproot custom. However, the moral tales that warned of rootless strangers and of the temptations present in the anonymous society of cities resonated with certain events of the 1830s and 1840s. Immigration was an obvious worry, especially in Hamilton, because in the words of Sheriff Cartwright-Thomas (1840), the town was "where the immigrant tide breaks."[13] It is likely that between 1829 and 1836 eighteen thousand immigrants came through or settled in the Gore District. Every society is suspicious of strangers, and the virtual tripling of the district's population from 1830 to 1842 supported a notion — well developed in the American Tract Society's publications — that newcomers possessed a dangerous anonymity that tempted them onto wayward paths descending to criminal activities, especially in towns and cities. As a gateway to other districts, Hamilton witnessed many thousands of transients, and, as the regional centre, it attracted the purveyors of vice. The upsurge in newcomers passing through Hamilton in the navigation season of 1843 on their way to and from the construction site on the navigation works of the Welland Canal and Grand River seemingly confirmed the equation of chaos with strangers. Order had collapsed at Brantford, where navvies' labour grievances and a dispute between leader of the Irish Catholics and the local establishment had sparked riots and a flagrant defiance of authority. In July 1843, a mob had driven several magistrates out of town.[14]

There were three ways that anxieties translated into higher rates of jail committals for offences against public order, particularly in Hamilton: fears were expressed through complaints; new by-laws were passed to reduce temptations or set examples; and the town strengthened the criminal justice apparatus. An apprehensive public did complain about public safety and vice. In November 1846, a public meeting in Hamilton advanced a petition to council that drew a connection between places of vice — "the excessive number of taverns and tippling houses" — and threats to the community. There had also been a series of fires.[15] Fire terrified the town, and, along with an extensive series of fire prevention by-laws, there came a fear of vagrants as arsonists. People wandering at night disquieted the town fathers.

Hamilton passed a series of by-laws in the 1830s and early 1840s that restricted bowling as a indolent recreation, prohibited roulette, established penalties for prostitutes and found-ins, and codified a sweeping measure against drunkards, vagrants, and rowdies. English law had long regarded public disorder and vagrancy as offences, and Upper Canadian justices of the peace could make summary convictions, but the magistrates and town bailiffs made few committals until 1843, when the Hamilton town council passed a directive: "[It is] [o]rdered that all vagrants, vagabonds, or other persons of ill fame, or persons who are drunk or so conducting themselves to be a nuisance and found wandering in the Town at night shall be liable to be arrested and upon conviction thereof shall be liable to a fine of 30 shillings for each offence or in non-payment, 30 days in the District Gaol."[16] The by-law, certainly the spirit it embodied, led to as many as 50 percent (516 of 1 105) of Hamilton's share of committals to the Gore Jail from 1843 to 1851. The mood of 1843 was sustained in 1846 by a new charter for Hamilton. Unlike the 1833 town charter, it gave the town the power to arrest vagrants, to appoint a stipendiary police magistrate, to establish and regulate a police force, and to use the Gore Jail as a city jail. Acts of incorporation for Dundas and Brantford in the following year empowered the town councils to suppress tippling, charivaris, and gambling and to control common showmen, circus riders, mountebanks, and jugglers. The Province of Canada in 1845 had passed an act to prevent profanation of the Lord's day; it forbade Sunday tippling, skittles ball, football, racket or any other noisy game and gambling or races.[17] Public order had achieved considerable legislative recognition.

The third way in which public-order concerns manifested themselves was policing. The town crept erratically but undeniably toward an active and vigilant system. Among its inaugural deeds in March 1833, the council of the newly incorporated Town of Hamilton appointed a high bailiff who had to report to some member of the Police Board (the official name for council) any breach of regulations established by the town. When making an arrest, the high bailiff had the authority to command any inhabitant to assist. Prisoners were to be brought as soon as possible before any two members of the five-member police board, and they would impose the fines or jail terms.[18] The arrangements worked poorly. During the first two years of the system, two high bailiffs were dismissed — one for the rough handling of a woman and three unspecified complaints. Moreover, the public did not always respond to calls for assistance.[19] In November 1835, the town appointed a second bailiff for the night watch. The turnover among bailiffs continued and, most important, the bailiffs worked part-time and awaited complaints.

In the summer of 1837 an outbreak of unsolved burglaries provoked demands for stronger policing, but the adverse economic conditions meant that the town could not obtain sufficient funds to support "a paid police."[20] Instead, ten men volunteered for rotating patrol duty. The organization of volunteer forces before professionals were finally accepted also occurred in American cities, whose historians have seen this as evidence of a republican reluctance to using an "army" to ensure order. British historians too have observed a persistence of voluntarism in policing. Some have attributed it to the English commitment to liberty, but a revisionist interpretation has stressed the desire of the gentry to retain local authority. But in Hamilton there were no paeans of republicanism and no evidence of a gentry favouring discretionary justice, only practicality, economy, and experiment. Arrangements for policing continued to shift virtually with every council or scandal. In 1842, the man who had been High Bailiff since 1839 was arrested for theft![21]

From the early 1840s onward, casual policing yielded to more vigilant practices, including the building of the lock-up in 1840. At least as early as 1843, council hired special constables to patrol the town when fairs, the quarter sessions, and the assizes brought strangers to town.[22] Under a city charter, Hamilton council formed a standing committee on police and hired a stipendiary magistrate to hear cases. The creation of this new office dedicated to minor offences likely served to encourage complaints and, therefore, arrests. The old system had burdened the municipal councillors, who may have avoided unpalatable duties. At about the same time that the city acquired its salaried magistrate, it experimented with policing by full-time employees. During 1847, Hamilton was served by a chief bailiff, a chief constable, and two salaried sub-constables. In 1848, however, the city replaced the two sub-constables with ten special constables — two to a ward — who received payment only on being called out for duty. In 1850 the city returned to four full-time employees, but the next April the influx of railway navvies led to remarkable and revealing additional arrangements in the interests of controlling labour, namely the creation of a special mounted police unit of no more than twenty-seven men paid by the contractor, the town of Dundas, and the City of Hamilton.[23] This arrangement had followed labour protests.

As Hamilton sought to increase its watchfulness yet nurse its expenditures, it gradually acquired the accoutrements of policing. To arm the special constables who patrolled during major events, the town purchased thirty "constables' staves" from a lumber yard in April 1843. The high bailiff applied in April 1845 to council for a "truck or Hand Cart to convey vagrants to prison."[24] Finally, after incorporation as a city, the council purchased distinctive caps and coats for its small force.[25]

Yet the policing reforms of the 1840s did not establish a professional police force, for as we have seen above, council back-pedalled in 1848 and 1849. The force remained small, and the 1847 complement of four only equalled that of 1837. In 1847 the ratio of police to the town population was 0.5 per

1 000; in 1920, by comparison, the Canadian national ratio was 1.2 per 1 000 and in 1975, 2.2 per 1 000. Except in the larger towns and cities, however, mid-Victorian police forces in England were small, so that Hamilton resembled contemporary English boroughs and counties, where the ratio was less than 1.0 per 1 000.[26] Nevertheless, the abandonment of voluntarism is reflected in the expenditures. While the population of Hamilton had tripled from 1837 to 1847, salaries for policing had increased at least sixfold (from £30 to £200), not including an additional £150 for the stipendiary magistrate.[27] More than ever before, Upper Canadians believed, though erroneously, they had a dangerous class among them. That a *heavily* policed society did not occur must be explained by the continued recourse to the military in emergencies, municipal frugality with respect to all but development projects, and the general strangeness of hired service as opposed to voluntarism.

Reform ideas and anxieties produced a strengthening of the laws and an extension of enforcement. But what about the related notion that social changes of these years had the effect of increasing crime rates? To answer that question, we need to consider the prisoners. Who they were tells us about privation. Over and above what the data convey about disorderly conduct and repression, they imply that the attacks on rough entertainment did not apparently reduce the incidence of truly vicious conduct, for public disorder did not necessarily conceive violent criminals or a dangerous class.

The Jail Population

Did the social characteristics of the people arrested differ in major ways from the rest of the population? For the years 1832 to 1851, information on a few variables including national origin, age, and sex allow limited contrasts with the population at large. Information also exists on occupations (1843–47), literacy (1848–51), and moral habits (1848–51). If the jail population differed from the rest of society in terms of those variables, is it legitimate to speak of a criminal class? Is it possible to find a pattern of degeneration in the lives of repeat offenders, beginning with a misdemeanour and ending with a felony? Or do we find, especially among the public order offenders, the unfortunate and the vulnerable? Finally, what international forces are indicated in the social traits?

The origins recorded for those detained must be treated with caution, since the prisoner could presumably declare whatever country of origin he wished. For example, the sudden decline of Americans from prominence in the jail cells in the mid–1830s may have originated when greater numbers of American settlers chose to call themselves Upper Canadians (see table 4). Nonetheless, the prominence of the Irish just before the rebellion has a substantial basis. The large Irish immigration to Quebec in 1831 (34 000) and 1832 (28 000) was not equalled until 1847. The famine migration of the late 1840s exacerbated the situation for the Irish, and once more large numbers of immigrants came to the Gore District, even if many merely passed through. From 1846 to 1851, 264 000 newcomers arrived at Quebec and the Irish constituted

TABLE 4

Most Frequently Cited Countries of Origin for Persons Committed to the Gore District Jail, 1832–51

Year	Country Most Cited	Percentage of All Committed	Country Second Most Often Cited	Percentage of All Committed
1832	United States	56.5	Upper Canada	15.2
1833	United States	39.2	Upper Canada	27.8
1834	United States	38.2	Ireland	30.0
1835	Ireland	35.3	United States	26.1
1836	Ireland	38.7	Upper Canada	29.8
1837[a]	Upper Canada	48.0	Ireland	26.5
1838[a]	Upper Canada	38.5	Ireland	25.9
1839	Ireland	40.0	Upper Canada	27.6
1840	Ireland	36.8	Upper Canada	23.6
1841	Ireland	34.3	Upper Canada	29.4
1842	Ireland	47.5	Upper Canada	15.6
1843	Ireland	53.3	Upper Canada	18.8
1844	Ireland	38.5	Upper Canada	27.9
1845	Ireland	48.9	Upper Canada	17.3
1846	Ireland	50.0	England	16.1
1847	Ireland	51.4	Upper Canada	15.6
1848	Ireland	54.9	England	18.3
1849	Ireland	53.1	Upper Canada	16.6
1850	Ireland	50.9	Upper Canada	18.0
1851[b]	Ireland	71.1	Upper Canada	10.3
Total	Ireland	44.8	Upper Canada	20.0

a Rebellions increased the Gore Jail population and biased it toward older men, yeomen raised in Upper Canada.
b The arrival of famine Irish and of Irish navvies for construction of the Great Western Railway may help to explain the extremely high percentage of arrests.

SOURCE: Data file based on Gore District Jail Records.

205 000, or 78 percent. Many thousands reached the head of the lake, landing at Hamilton and travelling overland into the surrounding townships and beyond. The fact that many passed through the Gore District renders suspect the attempt to estimate their proportion of the population and, hence, the exact level of their overrepresentation in the jail population (see table 5). Nevertheless, there is an interesting pattern in the charges against the Irish, who seem to have been singled out for moral order charges more than other national groups. Yet, judging by the committals for crimes against persons or property, they were no more criminal than Upper Canadians, Americans, Englishmen, or Scots.

Prisoners' occupations were reported only between 15 June 1843, and 30 December 1847 (1 094 cases for both sexes). Since there is no occupational distribution for the Gore population to act as a control, the analysis of this variable can only be descriptive. By far the largest category, accounting for 44 percent (457), were labourers and 47 percent of these were Irish. The second

TABLE 5

Comparison of Country of Origin of Jail Population with that of District Population

Country of Origin	Percentage Distribution of Jail Population, 1832–43	Percentage Distribution of District Population, 1842	Percentage Distribution of Jail Population, 1844–51	Percentage Distribution of District Population, 1851–52
England and Wales	14.0	13.1	14.5	11.9
Ireland	34.6	11.8	53.1	22.6
Scotland	5.7	12.1	7.7	10.0
Upper Canada	26.1	56.2	15.4	50.5
United States	16.8	6.8	8.1	6.8

SOURCE: Data file based on Gore District Jail Records; *Census of Canada* 1842 and 1851–52.

largest at 10 percent (109) was single women. Virtually all were Irish. The only other significant occupational groups were the following: farmers 3.7 percent (40), carpenters 3.6 percent (39), shoemakers 2.7 percent (30), blacksmiths 2.4 percent (26), masons 2.1 percent (22), and sailors 2.0 percent (20). There is a problem in establishing how this breakdown compares with the wider population. A faulty means exists. Roughly 75 percent of the committals from 1843 to 1847 originated in Hamilton. The distribution of Hamilton's population in 1851 as coded for Michael Katz's study of the city may be taken as a crude basis for comparison. In 1851, the proportion of unskilled and semi-skilled males in the city was 23.5 percent. The proportion of labourers among male prisoners was 52.0 percent. Labourers, then, were most likely overrepresented among prisoners.

In an exercise in rustic criminology, the jailor began to enter comments about literacy and drinking habits (temperate and intemperate) in 1848. From January 1848 until the end of this study, nine out of ten prisoners were considered intemperate. Given the high rate of public-order arrests, this is not remarkable. Interestingly enough, the estimates on literacy counter any supposition that Upper Canadians were better educated and hence less likely to be riff-raff than the Irish. Religion was not recorded for the years during which the literacy information was collected, so that it is impossible to separate the numbers of literate Irish Protestants from literate Roman Catholics. The general point remans that Irish male prisoners as a whole were more literate than their Upper Canadian counterparts. What Upper Canadians possessed, in greater proportion to the immediate newcomers, was a situation in a community. The standing of Scots as the most literate group in jail accords with impressions about Scottish dedication to education. The literacy rates were low for women prisoners from all four countries (see table 6).

A study of the traits of the female jail population affords a more complete insight into the social milieu of a new population that contributed to swollen arrest figures in the 1840s. About 60 percent of all women (427 of 715) in the jail from 1831 to 1851 were recorded as Irish; only 40 percent of all males (1 273 of 3 110) were Irish. In the category of public-order offences,

TABLE 6

Literacy among the Jail Population, by Sex and Country of Origin, 1848–51

	Country of Origin by Sex							
	Upper Canada		Ireland		England		Scotland	
Level of Education	Male (N = 129)	Female (N = 29)	Male (N = 465)	Female (N = 226)	Male (N = 135)	Female (N = 17)	Male (N = 81)	Female (N = 22)
Read and write with superior education	0.0	0.0	1.8	0.0	2.2	5.9	4.9	0.0
Read and write well	8.5	3.4	10.8	1.3	17.8	0.0	35.8	22.7
Read and write imperfectly	33.3	3.4	40.9	19.5	40.7	17.6	48.2	27.3
Unable to read and write	58.2	93.2	46.5	79.2	39.3	76.5	11.1	50.0

NOTE: This information is not available for the earlier years under consideration.

SOURCE: Data file based on Gore District Jail Records.

Irish women stood out even more. Three-quarters of the women taken in for drunk and disorderly conduct — a crime that had brought a dramatic increase in arrests after the arrival of famine Irish — were Irish. In the case of vagrancy, the proportion of Irish women among all women was four-fifths. The number of women arrested for crimes against persons and against property from 1844 to 1851 remained virtually the same as in 1832 to 1843, while the public-order arrests increased sevenfold. In suppressing vice and disorder, the constables probably found women easier to apprehend, subdue, and convey to jail. These actions affected relatively young women. Among the women, the sixteen to twenty-five age group accounted for half of the civil and moral order arrests and 60 percent of the sex offence committals. Underlying the moral order measures directed against women was the fact that rigid standards of feminine conduct were becoming established among the elite. Women were to be unassuming, happy in the home, tasteful, and tender. They were to be angels of mercy and the repositories of moral virtue. Transient women by their very lack of a home violated the standard. Again the social condition of the Irish, not the culture of rural Ireland, made them deviants from the norm in a booming young community that clutched at stability.

Moral campaigns, a shifting standard of punishment, and a concept of feminine virtue formed the general context for an overall rise in the committal rate for females, but a really sharp upturn beginning in 1848 calls for a more precise explanation. Much of the trend involved a considerable rise in the committal rate for drunk and disorderly behaviour. Until 1848, women made up only 20 percent of all those brought into the jail on that charge. In 1848 and subsequent years, they constituted just over 40 percent. There was an especially impoverished element in the female population after 1847, when single women cast up by the dislocations of the immigrations of the famine

Irish found their way to colonial cities. In relation to the total flow of immigration, their numbers appear infinitesimal, but they made easy prey for the police. A distressed female group of recent origin gravitated to towns and cities where railway navvies, transient machinists, and tradesmen had flocked in response to prospects for railway construction. The combination proved propitious for vice, especially in the spectacular Hamilton boom of 1850–51.

Much of the young Irish Roman Catholic overrepresentation in the data arises from the female repeat offenders. Women accounted for 18 percent of all committals but 28 percent (65 of 232) of all repeat committals. The female repeaters had arrest records far exceeding those of male counterparts (see table 7). Each of Hamilton's three most notorious women of the town had more than a dozen committals over relatively short periods. Jane Ellis, an English immigrant, was 21 when first arrested for being a public nuisance in June 1843. Within the next two years she was committed twelve more times under related charges: drunk and disorderly conduct and prostitution. Margret McMichael from Ireland was first taken in local custody when 25. All twenty-one of her arrests from July 1846 to 1851 were for drunk and disorderly conduct. Mary Ann Dickson, also Irish, was 22 when arrested for drunk and disorderly conduct in November 1850. By December 1851, she had gone to jail twelve more times on the same charge. Young and poor, these women also lacked subtlety in their relationship with community values. Consider one of the charges against Jane Ellis: "On Saturday [5 July 1884] about 7 p.m., Jacob Bishop swears he saw Jane Ellis walking through the streets with her breasts exposed and drunk. Henry Masiah was pointed out to him as the man who was walking arm in arm with her and playing with her breasts as they walked."[28] Whether or not these women had succumbed to alcoholism and prostitution from abandonment on the rigorous immigration trek, they could expect little sympathy from a community that had begun to revere women

TABLE 7

Pattern of Committals for Male and Female Repeat Offenders 1832–51

	Sex	
	Male	Female
Number of repeat offenders	167	65
Proportion of repeat offenders	72%	28%
Average number of committals per repeat offender	2.8	4.5
Committals for crimes against persons as proportion of all committals	34.7%	10.9%
Committals for crimes against property as proportion of all committals	29.5%	12.6%
Moral committals for public order crimes as proportion of all committals	33.7%	74.7%
Capital offences and other committals as proportion of all committals	2.1%	1.8%

NOTE: The repeat offenders were established by manual linkage of the records. Repeat offenders were defined loosely as all those committed twice or more.

SOURCE: Data file based on Gore District Jail Records. An alphabetic sort and merge program listed all cases by surname. First name, age, and country of origin occasionally help to confirm a linkage when surname spellings varied.

as the guardians of the family. They were condemned by their flagrant con-
travention of an expected female role and by the ease with which they could
be hauled in.[29]

Repeat perpetrators of public order offences — especially women — never
amassed records suggesting a descent from minor into serious transgression.
Nearly all had committed a cluster of repeat offences. For women it encompassed vagrancy, drunk and disorderly behaviour, and prostitution. For men
it widened slightly to include violence. A likely male combination was drunk
and disorderly conduct, minor thefts, and assaults. Generally, repeaters had
not perpetrated a wide assortment of crimes, nor did their records begin with
vice offences and culminate in a felony. Those convicted of capital offences
as a rule had no prior convictions. Of the eighteen persons convicted of capital
offences whose records could be traced in the period from 1832 to 1851,
only the convicted murderer Henry Van Pattern had earlier convictions in the
Gore District — twice for theft. No threatening subculture fed by booze and
raised on loitering matured into a vicious element. Between the two ends of
the criminal spectrum — minor offenders and felons — there was no striking
overlap.

Nevertheless, there were a very few men who occupied a middle ground
and pursued a course of petty violence and theft for years. Among them, the
virtual absence of any pattern of truly vicious criminality upsets simple descriptions about a criminal type. Extenuating circumstances explain a few of the
chronic "bad actors." Jesse Hickman had four convictions for assault and battery between November 1834 and May 1835, and he reappeared for two
convictions for threatening in 1843. A black barber from the United States,
in his mid-twenties when first convicted, it is possible to speculate on the racial
friction that led to his arrests. Old Daniel Gorman, a common labourer from
Ireland and fifty years of age when first arrested for stealing clothing, was sent
to Kingston Penitentiary in 1837. In 1839 stealing livestock earned him a
return stay as did a conviction for theft in 1840. Two more incidents of stealing
brought short local-jail terms in 1843. His age and the frequency of his petty
crimes suggest a state of impoverishment, physical disability, or underemploy-
ment leading to a willingness to accept the shelter of prison. A conceivably
more professional Upper-Canadian criminal, Caleb Swayze, was first arrested
in 1832 when in his early twenties and charged with robbery and forgery.
He was arrested twice in 1837 for theft and returned to jail in 1841 for
stealing. James Hall, a nasty drunkard and wife beater who turned to theft
on several occasions, compiled a criminal record from 1837 to 1849 that ranks
him as one of the truly vicious men whose career is an exception to the rule
that recidivists did not commit a variety of crimes. Other exceptions among
the 250 repeat offenders (8 percent of all those in the jail) can be cited in a
very short list: John Hyatt, an American arrested five times for assault and
once for theft between 1835 and 1837, and George Humphrey, a young
labourer from Ireland arrested for theft in 1845, for assault in 1846, and for
vandalism in 1847. No more than a score of comparable careers could be
cited to establish the existence of a dangerous criminal set. Of course, a regional
study misses the possibility of transient criminals with long and varied records

compiled in the colony and beyond. Mobile and professional counterfeiters, horse thieves, burglars, and pickpockets operated in Canada West, but their movements only surfaced in rare impressionistic accounts.[30]

The discursive analysis of prisoners — instructive in itself — registers strongly the point that the escalation of public order offences was a repercussion of international social uprootings. The shock waves of the Industrial Revolution and the crises in Ireland hit the shores of Lake Ontario. The mounting incidence of disorderly behaviour, in turn, augmented the anxiety of community leaders already sensitive to strangers because of occurrences of mass violence along nearby canal cuts. Fears spurred on repression, thereby increasing the number of public order arrests.

Trial and Punishment

Other indications of changing social attitudes are to be found in the modifications that Upper Canadians made in the period to criminal punishments. The reformation of punishment constituted a narrowing of the scope for community participation in matters of local justice and order. The deterioration of the local community as a bulwark for order and the edging forward of the bureaucratic state affected punishments. In the 1830s Upper Canada reduced capital offences, abolished corporal punishment, and built a reform penitentiary; it had moved more slowly than some British and North American jurisdictions and faster than others. However, before we examine punishment and incarceration, a few important subjects relating to trials are worthy of comment.

The duration of a prisoner's stay in jail awaiting trial was influenced by his or her wealth and local reputation because these considerations had a bearing on bail. Two magistrates could admit a prisoner to bail, or the prisoner could petition the Queen's (King's) Bench or one of its judges for an order to the magistrates to admit the prisoner to bail. The legal knowledge, community status, and wealth of a subject weighed in the process. Consequently, Upper Canadians had greater success in securing releases by bail than the Irish newcomers (see table 8). Common labourers seldom met bail, although exceptions arose when a bondsman or helpful countryman intervened. John Fennessy, leader of the Irish Catholics, was a likely agent in Brantford. In Ancaster, Bucklin Alderman was "a troublesome officious fellow," a bondsman in the 1830s. Magistrate John Haycock complained:

> [Alderman] sets bond for every scoundrel that requires it, and the more infamous the offender, the more fit for the interference of Mr. Alderman and who on all occasions arrays himself against the constituted authorities of the country, when he can do so safely to himself and give to the lower orders of the people (over whom he exerts considerable influence) an improper bias, upon every occasion that presents itself.[31]

The few "troublesome" characters did not affect the trend of outsiders being denied bail.

Economic and social distinctions were likewise reflected in the post-sentencing phase of public order offences. When there was a choice of paying a fine (usually thirty shillings) or serving a jail term (generally thirty days), the Irish often selected the latter whereas few Upper Canadians chose to remain behind bars. The payment of a fine was almost exclusively exercised by men. The most likely group to meet their fines were married Upper-Canadian farmers, while the least likely were single Irish women.

A great many prisoners arrested on suspicion of committing crimes against persons or crimes against property went free without a trial, either because the plaintiff dropped the charge or the grand jury found no true bill (see table 8). The fact that grand juries appear to have included many magistrates makes it unlikely that the institution reflected popular values and beliefs. Nonetheless, grand jurors, with their knowledge of local circumstances and personalities, may have given many prisoners the benefit of the doubt.

TABLE 8

Disposition of Inmates by the Courts: Most Frequent Charges, 1832–51

Crimes by Category	Percentage Committed Who Were Subsequently Convicted Receiving a Jail Term or Fine	Percentage Who Were Tried and Acquitted	Percentage Who Never Came to Trial: No Bill, Lack of Evidence, No Prosecution
Major crimes against persons			
Common assault (N = 492)	55.5	1.0[a]	43.5
Assault and battery (96)	47.8	6.3	45.9
Threatening (84)	14.4	3.6	82.0[b]
Murder (59)	21.7	25.8	52.5
Rape (36)	52.8	11.1	36.1
Major crimes against property			
Larceny (262)	59.6	13.5	26.9
Stealing (207)	51.0	12.6	36.4
Horse theft (99)	40.5	10.1	49.4
Theft of money (90)	51.0	12.2	36.8
Theft of clothing (88)	53.6	5.7	40.7
Theft of household goods (61)	60.6	6.5	32.8
Theft of food (38)	47.5	0.0	52.5
Public order offences			
Drunk and disorderly (481)	81.0	0.0	19.0
Disorderly (145)	87.4	0.0	12.6
Vagrancy (77)	96.1	0.0	3.9

a Since summary offences were brought before a magistrate, the phrase, "tried and acquitted" is not applicable. The committal rates were extremely high and rarely did a magistrate "discharge" anyone brought before him. Most common assaults were treated as summary offences.

b It is likely that a charge of threatening was used by a complainant or the authorities to hold someone in jail for a "cooling off" period with little intention of prosecuting.

SOURCE: Data file based on Gore District Jail Records.

During the grand jury hearings and the trials, bias may have come into play. For example, Irish men and women were underrepresented among those released either for want of indictments or from acquittals by trials, though it is unlikely that the Irish were more culpable or inept than people of other origin. As Donald Akenson has argued, ethnicity was not as significant a social fact in Upper Canada as the time of arrival. Moreover, the Irish were neither all destitute nor without eventual achievements as farmers. As a recent population, the Irish nonetheless lacked the community roots and hence the benefits of a magistrate's or juror's reference to extenuating circumstances or to knowledge of character (see table 9). If anything, the established community maintained a jaundiced view of the Irish. Writing about the Upper-Canadian perceptions of Irish immigrants, Joy Parr has documented the transition from an expectation of economic benefits to a recognition of the social costs.[32] Susanna Moodie, whose husband was an officer of the Belleville courts, gave a sketch of the criminal type that may well have had currency across Upper Canada. From a visit to Kingston Penitentiary, she concluded that "the convicts were mostly of a dull grey complexion, large-eyed, stolid looking men, or with very black hair, and heavy brows." The flaxen-haired peoples had tempers but seldom bore malice. "Not so the dull, putty-coloured sluggish man." As for Irish Catholics, Mrs. Moodie believed "they break and destroy

TABLE 9

Examples of How Cases Were Processed with Reference to Country of Origin, 1832–51

	Irish Inmates	
Disposition of Case	Percentage of Irish in the Category	Percentage of Irish Assuming an Even Distribution
Released on bail	27.6	45.2
No bill of indictment	37.1	45.2
Tried and acquitted	25.9	45.2
Sentenced to jail or paying fine with jail option taken	61.0	45.2

	Upper Canadian Inmates	
Disposition of Case	Percentage of Upper Canadians in the Category	Percentage of Upper Canadians Assuming an Even Distribution
Released on bail	27.6	20.5
No bill of indictment	32.3	20.5
Tried and acquitted	34.3	20.5
Sentenced to jail or paying fine with jail option taken	11.2	20.5

NOTE: The under- or overrepresentation of Irish or Upper Canadian inmates in certain categories of case treatment may well reflect differences in property or assets. Upper Canadians were obviously better able to obtain bail or pay fines.

SOURCE: Data file based on Gore District Jail Records.

more than the Protestants. . . . The principle on which they live is literally to care as little as possible for the things of today, and to take no thought at all for the morrow."[33] A belief that morphological features revealed inner character was common in the North Atlantic world at that time.[34]

In the 1830s punishments altered. During the district's first fifteen years, punishment was often public. During the 1820s, public instruments of punishment were often kept in readiness and called into requisition after almost all assizes — two hours in the pillory or stocks or thirty-nine lashes with the cat-o'-nine-tails were common sentences for minor offences. One perjurer in the late 1820s stood with his neck in a yoke for two days with "everyone gazing at him."[35] In the 1830s pain and humiliation were replaced with fines and incarceration, and in 1841 the pillory was abolished in Upper Canada. The last whippings in the Gore District were administered to two convicted thieves in January 1834, although the punishment remained on the statute books. Judges increasingly measured sentences in days or shillings rather than lashes or the suffering and unmeasurable mortification of the stocks. Public mortification had announced a community warning. Imprisonment, under some conditions, aspired to be reformatory. From the late 1820s to the late 1840s, a number of European countries and American states constructed penitentiaries whose architecture and rules sought to remould the inmates' character. Kingston Penitentiary was to have done likewise, though neither the administrative practices nor the sums committed for construction and personnel were sufficient to show a strong sense of purpose. As for local jails, they showed faint recognition of the reformatory objective. Essentially, they merely inflicted a slower and more invisible pain than corporal punishment.

The Gore Jail was dreadful. The four jail cells and six debtor rooms, several feet below ground level, received heat only from a hall stove. The jail lacked exercise room, and since a mere board fence surrounded the yard, prisoners seldom received physical activity. In 1832, each prisoner received seven pounds of bread a week, two blankets, and two sets of clothing. In later years, the food improved as meat and potatoes — lots of potatoes — were added. The district sheriff set the rules and appointed the jailor. In the 1830s difficult prisoners were chained. Sheriff Cartwright-Thomas, who held the office during the 1840s, was a strict disciplinarian and permitted visitors to speak to prisoners only through the grating in the cell doors between 9 and 10 a.m. and 1 and 2 p.m. Fortunately, the most common crimes did not result in long incarceration. Of those convicted of larceny, nine out of ten (88.7 percent) were sentenced to ninety days or less, and three-quarters to sixty days or less. All the same, a miserable jail diet and stagnation "below the ground where there is no fire, and where the light of the sun but seldom shines" affected the prisoners' health. In addition, there was overcrowding. During a crime wave in the spring of 1834, for example, the four criminal cells held eighteen prisoners.[36]

Reformatory punishment aimed to bend the prisoner toward a disciplined life. This meant excluding outside contact, the punishment of anyone who brought alcohol into the jail, the structuring of jail life by rules, and the provision of religious instruction. Prisoners had to be severed from the unwholesomeness of their usual society; they then had to be classified and segregated. Therefore, in 1848, jail ledgers began to include columns for literacy and moral habits. At the same time, Frederick Cumberland drafted plans for a new Gore Jail that included separate quarters for prostitutes, debtors, and felons.[37] All of these measures make Michel Foucault's assessment of a western European reformation in sentencing ring true in the colonial situation: "What was emerging no doubt was not so much a new respect for the humanity of the condemned . . . as a tendency toward a more finely tuned justice, toward a closer mapping of the social body."[38] The shame attached to a public punishment functioned in small stable communities. In the transient world of the nineteenth century, dynamic societies like industrial England or immigrant communities like Upper Canada found the old punishments impractical. The biased outcomes in judicial processes, the reformation of punishment, as well as the fluctuations in jail committals, betokened the fairly volatile development of a colonial society wanting in community stability. New institutions like policing and the penitentiary, the assault on plebeian culture, and criminal justice practices were reactions to a diminution of acquaintanceship and deference as bases of order. Local authorities willingly retreated from flexibility, toleration, and the warning of public punishment; however, they sometimes bridled at the expenditures and restrained the experiments in criminal justice.

Along with corporal punishment and public display, banishment was eliminated in the new tactics of order. Banishment constituted an interesting example of an Upper Canadian practice that ultimately devolved responsibility for enforcement of punishment upon a locality. In England, pressure on the penal system had introduced the transportation of prisoners first to America and later to Australia. Upper Canada's expedient had involved less expense and no organization. Judges had occasionally banished convicted felons from the colony. For the period covered by the jail records, there were seventeen banishments. Many arose from cases where the outcome of the trial could have gone either way. Was the horse stolen or borrowed? Was a thief goaded by bad company? Was the convicted rapist John Standish clearly seen by the women picking strawberries? Of the banishments, five were for horse-theft, none for other thefts, and one each for shooting, rape, and treason. In September 1831 the Gore District grand jury condemned the practice because the Crown did not punish those who returned. Some people were terrified of banishment, and when it was learned that the convicted rapist, John Standish, was being considered for banishment, his victim, Vashle Waterhouse, and her husband petitioned against the sentence, alleging that Standish would do them violence. The magistrate, William Holmes, supported their claim, branding Standish "a violent headstrong young man."[39] On the other hand, banishment allowed a community to retain and protect a worthy character that it believed to be falsely convicted.[40] Until the opening of the provincial penitentiary in 1835, banishment occasionally had been extended to prisoners convicted of capital offences. After 1835, judges could ration mercy in a more exact and less controversial form, by reducing the years with hard labour at Kingston (see table 10). Again, a new institution had taken the onus off the community.

TABLE 10

Disposition of Prisoners Convicted of Capital Offences and Sentenced to Death, 1822–50

Name	Year	Crime	Disposition
Joseph Nash	1822	Shooting	Mercy
Bostwich Forbush	1822	Riot	Mercy
Issac Dean	1822	Riot	Mercy
Phoebe Actley	1822	Shooting	Mercy
Ebenezer Allen	1825	Horsetheft	Mercy
Eli Swayze	1825	Horsetheft	Mercy
Michael Vincent	1828	Murdering wife	Executed
David Utter	1820	Shooting	Banished
John Standish	1831	Rape	Banished
Joseph Liquors	1832	Theft of steer	Mercy
John Rooney	1834	Murder	Banished
James Owen	1834	Murder	Died in jail
George Powis	1839	Shooting	7 years in K.P.
George Carmichael	1839	Shooting	5 years
George Asper	1843	Rape	14 years
Henry Van Patten	1843	Murder	Life
Joseph Thompson	1843	Murder	7 years
Courtland Travers	1843	Unnatural act	7 years
John Smith Carver	1845	Violent robbery	7 years
Patrick Martin	1845	Rape	7 years
Patrick Ellis	1846	Murder	Life
Andrew Davidson	1846	Murder	Life
George Noble	1847	Rape	7 years
George Beadle	1847	Rape	Life
William Dill	1849	Rape	Life
Lewis Miles	1849	Rape	Life
Joseph London	1850	Rape	Life
William Walker	1850	Embezzlement	Life

SOURCE: Data file based on Gore District Jail Records: Public Archives of Canada, RG 1, E1, Upper Canada Executive Council Minute books; RG 1, E3, State Papers; RG 5, A1, Upper Canada Sundries; RG 5, C1, Provincial Secretary's correspondence; RG 5, B28, Upper Canada fiats; RG 13, B1, Department of Justice, Official and semi-official correspondence.

Capital punishment was also touched by the reform of penal practices, and eventually, the occasions for local interposition declined. In 1833 the Upper Canadian assembly modestly revised the criminal code with respect to capital punishment. Until 1833 the criminal law of Upper Canada was the criminal law of England as it stood in 1792. Consequently, shooting at a person as well as horse and cattle theft — crimes committed in the Gore District — called for the judge to officially enter the death sentence, although the reality was far less severe.[41] In the Gore District, for example, at least nine capital sentences came down between 1822 and 1832, but convictions for riot, shooting, live-stock theft, and rape all resulted in the Crown's exercise of mercy. Revision of the Upper-Canadian criminal law trimmed the list of capital offences in a step toward a rationalized code. However, fifteen capital offences were retained; they included rape, arson, robbery, burglary, robbing the mails, and unnatural acts. The pursuit of mercy remained, along with its ritualized contact between the community and colonial executive as expressed by petitions. The Crown could manifest wisdom or compassion or signal an awful warning.

The activity that followed the sentencing of a criminal began with the drafting of petitions on behalf of the condemned by parents, friends, or in some instances by magistrates. When the parents initiated a petition, they established the family's loyalty to the Crown and proceeded to explain their dependence on the convicted person for support. The shame that had branded the family was also a basis for suggesting that punishment should not run its full course; the suffering had been real enough already. When friends and neighbours advanced a petition, they attested to the character of the prisoner and spelled out extenuating circumstances culminating in a single unfortunate lapse in a relatively blameless life. Alcohol and the influence of disreputable characters explained away horse thefts; insults or vicious threats had provoked a vicious attack or the threatening use of fire arms. In a few instances, magistrates made parallel statements or placed their names at the head of a petition. Normally the tone of these petitions was one befitting supplicants. Petitioners referred in contrition to a prior rashness or misdirection or a former miserable nature.[42] The circulation of a petition served the Crown by giving the friends and family of the condemned an occasion to reflect upon the wages of crime. Petitions usually resulted in an extension of mercy; they also generated a few public and political disputes. To function instructively by sending messages to the locale, or to work through channels of deference, thereby strengthening the authority of magistrates, the petitioning process required a stable population. Who could vouch for whom in the turbulent periods of immigration?

Petitioning declined by the 1840s, losing the prominence that it had had in earlier decades. This follows the trend of replacing practices that involved the community with less personal procedures, although reputation and references remained significant for bail and grand jury deliberations. Still, the colonial government and local elites seem to have been moving away from toleration, amateurism in enforcement, and discretionary conduct in juridical processes and punishments. Although more work must be done on who brought complaints and on juridical conduct and penal regimens in Upper Canada, the 1840s appear to have been a time when criminal justice and public order became less intensely personal. In their reformation of concepts and practices, colonial and municipal government adopted ideas from other societies but looked to these out of indigenous forms of anxiety arising from international disruptions. Colonial and local authorities sensed a rise in crime and largely attributed its origin to anonymous contacts among unattached strangers and the so-called vices of plebeian culture. Not surprisingly they misconstrued the sources of the rising numbers of felonies, because the circumstances that thrust unattached strangers into the colony could not be branded directly as evils. Immigration, transportation construction, and a general quickening of economic activity were too strongly associated with progress to allow any widespread critical review. Instead, relying on old-country beliefs and trends, the authorities in Upper Canada blamed cultures (Irish and plebeian) rather than socio-economic conditions.

Notes

1. Established in 1816, the Gore District encompassed the counties of Halton, Wentworth, Brant, Wellington, and Waterloo. The latter two formed the Wellington District in 1838, but until completion of the Guelph jail around 1840 prisoners went to Hamilton. In 1851, districts were abolished in favour of counties. These alterations mean that the same terrain cannot be compared over twenty years. Another difficulty must be acknowledged. District officials undertook annual population counts from 1816 to 1842; there was a census in 1848 and another early in 1852. Calculation of crime rates requires population figures. These have been estimated for several years by multiplying the number of dwellings reported in the annual assessment returns (published in sessional papers) by the average number of occupants per dwelling in 1842. The assessment returns excluded incorporated towns. However, Hamilton's annual population is known, and its growth rate was used as a surrogate for the growth of rates of Dundas and Brantford. Their 1842 population figures were then multiplied by the growth rate. The resulting population figures for incorporated communities were added to the populations calculated for the rest of the district. The total was rounded off to the nearest thousand. It should be borne in mind that, given periods of high transiency and immigration, it is likely that population estimates for the Gore District taken at a single moment will be lower than the total number of people that lived there in that calendar year. In other words, crime rates are imperfect measures of an imperfectly understood phenomenon.

2. Michael Stephen Hindus, *Prison and Plantation: Crime, Justice and Authority in Massachusetts and South Carolina, 1767–1878* (Chapel Hill: University of North Carolina Press, 1980); Eric Monkkonen, *The Dangerous Classes: Crime and Poverty in Columbus, Ohio, 1860–1885* (Cambridge, Mass.: Harvard University Press, 1975); Roger Lane, *Violent Death in the City: Suicide, Accident, and Murder in Nineteenth-Century Philadelphia* (Cambridge, Mass.: Harvard University Press, 1979). For the use of nineteenth-century data as indices for trends in criminal activity, see V.A.C. Gatrell, "The Decline of Theft and Violence in Victorian and Edwardian England" in V.A.C. Gatrell et al., *Crime and the Law: The Social History of Crime in Western Europe since 1500* (London: Europa Publications, 1980), 238–333.

3. McMaster University, Mills Library (hereafter ML), Hamilton Police Village Minutes, 20 Apr. 1840; 17 Apr. 1843.

4. Public Archives of Canada (hereafter PAC), RG 5, C1, 16784, The Report of the Grand Jury of the Gore District, 7 May 1847.

5. Thomas F. McIllwraith, "The Logistical Geography of the Great Lakes Grain Trade, 1820–1850" (Ph.D. dissertation, University of Wisconsin, 1973), 101–7. For an excellent account of the violence associated with the exploitation of canal navvies, see Ruth Bleasdale, "Class Conflict on the Canals of Upper Canada in the 1840s," *Labour/Le Travailleur* (Spring 1981): 9–39.

6. David Philips, *Crime and Authority in Victorian England: The Black Country, 1835–1860* (London: Croom Helm, 1977), 143–47.

7. For the evidence of relatively modest enforcement of the moral order, see PAC, RG 5, B20, Clerks of the Peace, Extracts of Fines, 1811–1833, file on Gore District. On the widespread use of alcohol see John Young, *Reminiscences of the Early History of Galt and the Settlement of Dumfries in the Province of Ontario* (Toronto: Hunter, Rose, 1880), 68; the homicide is reported in RG 5, C1, 1515, Report on the Case of the Queen vs. Hugh W. McCulloch, 9 May 1843.

8. Young, *Reminiscences*, 101.

9. The quotation is from ML, Police Village Minutes, 27 July 1837; PAC, RG 11, A2, Board of Public Works, vol. 94, Correspondence Book, Canals, 1839–46, William Shaw, "Report on Grog Shop," 30 Apr. 1845; ML, Police Village Minutes, 11 Aug. 1834; 25 Aug. 1835; 1 Sept. 1835; 6 Aug. 1835; 6 Aug. 1838; 5 Oct. 1840; 6 Oct. 1840; 5 Jan. 1844.

10. ML, Police Village Minutes, 25 July 1838; Wright, *Pioneer Days in Nichol* (Mount Forest, 1932), 161–62; HPL, *Hamilton Spectator Carnival Edition* (1902), n.p.

11. PAC, RG 5, A1, 5049–51, The Petition of Asa Kebrich, 3 Jan. 1829; RG 7, G14, vol. 9, Ebenezer Griffin to James Hopkirk, 18 Mar. 1842.

12. *Christian Guardian*, 5 Dec. 1829; Allan Greer, "The Sunday Schools of Upper Canada," *Ontario History* 68 (Sept. 1975): 169–84; William Gregg, *History of the Presbyterian Church in the Dominion of Canada* (Toronto: Presbyterian Printing and Publishing Company, 1885), 535; Toronto Public Library, *The*

Second Report of the Upper Canada Religious Tract and Book Society (Toronto: Christian Guardian, 1834); Charles Durand, *Reminiscences of Charles Durand* (Toronto: Hunter, Rose, 1897), passim.

13. PAC, RG 5, vol. 250, Cartwright-Thomas to Sir George Arthur, 16 Dec. 1840.

14. PAC, RG 5, C1, 6137, Petition of the Catholic Inhabitants of the Town and Vicinity of Brantford, 19 July 1843; 6124, John Wetenhall to Civil Secretary, 2 Aug., 1843; 6190, Nathan Gage to Civil Secretary, 3 Aug. 1843.

15. ML, Hamilton Police Village Minutes, 17 Nov. 1846.

16. ML, Police Village Minutes, 9 Oct. 1837; 25 May 1840; 21 Sept. 1840; 19 Sept. 1842. The by-law appears on 29 July 1843.

17. ML, Hamilton Police Village Minutes, 27 July 1837; 8 Vict., c. 45.

18. ML, Police Village Minutes, 16 Mar. 1833.

19. ML, Police Village Minutes, 2 June 1835; 15 Aug. 1835.

20. ML, Police Village Minutes, 25 July 1837.

21. The arrest of the High Bailiff was reported in ML, Police Village Minutes, 25 Aug. 1842.

22. ML, Police Village Minutes, 13 Mar. 1843.

23. ML, Police Village Minutes, 17 May 1847; 10 Jan. 1848; 6 Mar. 1850.

24. ML, Police Village Minutes, 3 Apr. 1843; 21 Apr. 1845.

25. ML, Police Village Minutes, 22 Mar. 1847; 22 Oct. 1849.

26. F.H. Leacy, ed., *Historical Statistics of Canada*, 2nd ed. (Ottawa: Statistics Canada, 1983), series Z63–65; Carolyn Steedman, *Policing the Victorian Community: The Formation of the English Provincial Forces, 1856–80* (London: Routledge and Kegan Paul, 1984), 39–51.

27. ML, Police Village Minutes, 29 May 1837; 10 Jan. 1848.

28. ML, Police Village Minutes, 29 July 1844.

29. Michael Katz, *The People of Hamilton, Canada West: Family and Class in a Mid-Nineteenth-Century City* (Cambridge, Mass.: Harvard University Press, 1975), 56–58. According to Michael Katz, a madam with finesse could avoid routine arrests, pay her fines when arrested, and even manage to amass property.

30. The telegraph allowed the Toronto authorities to inform their counterparts in Hamilton about the movement of "well-known thieves." See *Hamilton Gazette*, 8 Jan. 1849. Concerning early organized crime and the movement of criminals by steamboat and rail, see Metropolitan Toronto Library, Baldwin Room, L'Armitage, *The Great International Confederacy of Thieves, Burglars, and Incendiaries on the Canadian Frontier* (n.p., 1865).

31. For the background on Fennessy see PAC, RG 5, C1, 6875, John Fennessy to Governor Metcalfe, 18 Dec. 1843. For his probable intervention on behalf of Irishmen see RG 5, C1, 6124, Cartwright-Thomas to Harrison, 7 July 1843. For Alderman, see PAC, RG 5, A1, 73847–48, John Haycock to Col. Rowan, 29 Oct. 1833.

32. G.J. Parr, "The Welcome and the Wake: Attitudes in Canada West during the Irish Famine Migration," *Ontario History* 55 (June 1974): 101–13; Donald Akenson, *The Irish in Ontario: A Study in Rural History* (Kingston and Montreal: McGill-Queen's University Press, 1984), chaps. 1, 4, 5.

33. Susanna Moodie, *Life in the Clearings*, by Robert L. McDougall. (Toronto: MacMillan, 1959), 9, 155–56.

34. Louis Chevalier, *Labouring Classes and Dangerous Classes in Paris during the First Half of the Nineteenth Century* (Princeton: Princeton University Press, 1981), 351–72, 409–17.

35. Durand, *Reminiscences*, 85; 4 & 5 Vict., c. 4, s. 9.

36. PAC, RG 5, A1, 63518–19, Return of the Gore District Gaol 1832; 76498–500, Petition of the Magistrates of the District of Gore in April, General Quarter Sessions of the Peace, 11 Apr. 1834; 8143–44, Petition of John Wirick, present prisoner within Gaol at Hamilton, 10 Jan. 1835; RG 5, C1, 6441, Report of the Grand Jury of the District of Gore, 27 Apr. 1843; 19987, Report of the Magistracy of the Gore District, 6 May 1848; PAC, RG 13, B1, Department of Justice, file on criminal cases for 1850, Cartwright-Thomas to Attorney General, 27 May 1850; Report to Grand Jury, 10 Oct. 1842; *Journal of the Proceeding of the Municipal Council, Gore District* (Hamilton, 1842), 43.

37. Archives of Ontario, Maps and Illustrations Division, Architectural Drawings, Frederick Cumberland, Gore District Courthouse and Jail (1848), existing plan and new design, (52), 1, 2, 3.

38. Michel Foucault, *Discipline and Punish: The Birth of the Prison* (New York: Pantheon, 1978), 78. Foucault's discussion is remarkably suggestive, but for a more historical account of penitentiary architecture

CRIME, PUBLIC ORDER, AND REPRESSION   47

and reformation in a jurisdiction closer to Upper Canada, see the account of reform penitentiaries in Robin Evans, *The Fabrication of Virtue: English Prison Architecture, 1750–1840* (Cambridge: Cambridge University Press, 1982).

39. PAC, RG 5, A1, 62204, petition of John and Vashle Waterhouse, his wife, of the Village of Brantford, 17 Oct. 1831; 62208–9, Report of the Grand Jury, 1 Sept. 1831; 62217, William Holme to John Colborne, 17 Oct. 1831.

40. PAC, RG 5, C1, 13500, The Memorial of John R. Douglas, 13 Apr. 1846.

41. PAC Library, Upper Canada, Statute 3 Will. 4, c. 4, Relating to Capital Offences: With an Explanation of its Provisions in charge of Chief Justice Robinson, to the Grand Jury of the Home District (York, 1833).

42. The following were consulted: RG 5, B28, Fiats, Fiat dated 4 Feb. 1822; Fiat dated 15 Mar. 1832; RG 5, A1, 29737–88, Petition to Hon. William Campbell on the Case of Joseph Nash, 6 Sept. 1822; 39161–68, Petition of Eli Swayze, a condemned criminal in the Gaol of the District of Gore, 31 Aug. 1825; 62208–9, Petition of John Standish, 13 Sept. 1831; RG 5, B3, Petitions, 1112, 11352–53 (n.d.).

STONY MONDAY, 1849:
THE REBELLION LOSSES RIOTS
IN BYTOWN†

MICHAEL S. CROSS

In 1849 the Province of Canada was torn by the political crisis which followed the passage of the Rebellion Losses Act. The riots in Montreal — the attack on the Governor General, the burning of the Parliament Buildings — and the subsequent annexation movement in Lower Canada have frequently been described.[1] Less well known are the violent outbursts which took place in some Upper Canadian centres. One place in which bloodshed accompanied the Tories' denunciation of Governor General Elgin and his government was Bytown. Still a brawling lumber town, with much growing to do before it reached the status of city and gained the new name of Ottawa, Bytown was certainly more unruly than most communities in the province, and to that degree untypical. Yet its experience in 1849 is instructive for the way in which local animosities, ethnic tensions and economic unrest combined with political differences to produce large-scale social violence.

Rioting broke out in September 1849, over an address to be presented to Lord Elgin when he visited Bytown. But Stony Monday, as the first riot was known from the most common weapon used, was in fact only the culmination of long-building tensions in the community. Between 1835 and 1837 a group of rebellious Irish timberers, known as Shiners, had terrorized Bytown. Their violence originally had been aimed at driving the French Canadians from the timber camps and thus assuring themselves of jobs. Carried to Bytown, however, it had become a deliberate attack on the leadership structure of the town, the gentry establishment which for so long dominated Bytown and surrounding Carleton County. The gentry, however, showed their vitality by their resistance to, and eventual defeat of, the Shiners.[2] By the 1840s changing political and economic realities weakened the grip of gentility and left a leadership void in the community. When turmoil came again, their firm hands would not be there to soothe it.

Politically, the fall of the gentility was signalled by the rise of a strong Reform party to challenge the traditional Tory hegemony. While Carleton County stayed firmly in conservative lands, Bytown went Reform in the provincial election of 1847–48, when John Scott was elected member for the town. After incorporation of Bytown in 1847, Tories and Reformers were returned in near equal numbers to the town council until 1850 when the Reformers began an extended dominance over municipal politics. The gentility no longer could control politics, or other aspects of community life, because they had

† *Ontario History* 63 (1971): 177–90

lost the social utility which had marked their rule. Educated, trained in the arts of government, financially secure enough to enjoy the leisure necessary for leadership, the gentleman and merchants who made up the elite had received deference in politics and in social life; in return, they had provided the services desperately needed by this pioneer community. They organized emigrant aid societies and distributed food to the poor; they served as magistrates; they organized churches; they lobbied the government on behalf of the area's dominant economic activity, the timber trade. In the 1840s, the growth of the town had carried it beyond its reliance on the old aristocrats. The professional middle class was growing. These were new men capable of leadership, capable of meeting many of the social needs of the population, men who removed by their services some of the justification for the gentility's hold on power. Economic conditions also played a role. The unsettled condition of the timber trade in the forties drove many small operators to the wall and consolidated control in the hands of a few great timber kings. Wealth and leisure accompanied loss of competition for the lucky few. Men such as John Egan and Daniel McLahlin no longer needed the gentry to act as their intermediaries with government or to maintain social stability by aristocratic leadership. They were ready to assume that leadership themselves.[3]

At the other end of the social scale, the leadership of the gentility also was challenged. As the Shiner troubles of the 1830s had shown, the aristocrats had never been totally successful in gaining the trust of sections of the working class. And in the next decade they were substantially replaced, their services to the lower orders taken over by a new group of social leaders, the Catholic clergy. Balancing between the French Canadians and the Irish, the Church had found Bytown a difficult community. As Bishop Macdonnell had lamented in 1835, "I consider the honor and credit of our Holy Religion more exposed there than any other Mission in the Diocese. . . ."[4] The ministry of Rev. Patrick Phelan, between 1842 and 1844, had done much to improve the situation. Irish-born, bilingual and a skilled diplomat, he helped bring the two ethnic groups together within the Catholic Church. His work was completed by the Oblate Fathers and the Grey Nuns, who assumed responsibility for the parish after Phelan's promotion to bishop at Kingston. With new efficiency the Church provided for the needs of the community, building schools, an orphanage, and a hospital and establishing relief agencies. These services contributed to the declining influence of the gentility and to the widening gulf within the community.

Bytown had always been two communities, respectable Upper Town and the Lower Town of the poor. What was different now was the increasing self-awareness of the Catholic masses in Lower Town, their feeling that they no longer needed the services or the goodwill of the Upper Towners. That the divisions were along religious as well as social lines only made them more pronounced. While hostility remained between the two chief ethnic groups who made up the lower class, the *Canadien* and Irish increasingly formed a united front. In part, this unity came from the positive pull of a vigorous Catholic Church; in part, it came from the negative push of Protestant hostility.

Politics divided the town largely on religious grounds. Part of the self-consciousness of the Catholic working class majority in Bytown was its separation from the gentility's politics, as well as from its social services. With the Tory party so closely associated with the old order, Catholics naturally gravitated to Reform. Lower Town, where the poor, the Catholics, the French Canadians and the Irish lived, came under the control of the liberals. The 1851 municipal elections saw Reformers elected to all six seats in the East and Centre wards. East Ward, as well, was an excellent example of how Protestant-Catholic strife produced a sense of unity among French Canadians and Irish. Despite Tory attempts to play on ethnic animosities in this ward, which had a French-Canadian majority, Catholics remained united and returned two English-speaking and one French-speaking Reformer, all by large majorities.[5] The West Ward, encompassing well-to-do Protestant Upper Town, saw only Tories running. Two of the three members elected, W.F. Powell and Nicholas Sparks, were representatives of the old Bytown, of the pre-canal migrants who had so long held sway.

The waning power of the gentility can be read in the rejection of its leadership by the Catholics of Bytown. It also can be distinguished by the drift into Protestant extremism which took place in the former ruling group itself. As the Irish, during the Shiners' War, had reacted to their alienation with violence, so too the gentry of Carleton, losing their control over the community, turned to an organization as violent and lawless as the Shiner movement had been — the Orange Order.

The Order had existed in the Carleton County since 1825.[6] But at that time, and for the next decade and a half, Orangeism had been repudiated by the gentility as an obnoxious and vulgar manifestation of fanaticism.[7] In the 1840s this attitude changed dramatically. As W.J.S. Mood has pointed out, the essential elements for the success of the Orange Order in a community were religious tensions and religious balance.[8] Such conditions certainly existed in this area. In Bytown, Catholics predominated, with 57.9 percent of the population in 1848. In Carleton County, however, 66.7 percent of the population was Protestant. Ethnically, Irish and French Canadians represented 54.7 percent of the town's population, while Scots-Irish were the largest group in the County.[9] The mixture of increasingly self-aware Catholics and Protestant Irish produced an explosive atmosphere, especially in a time of economic stress.[10]

By 1844 an Orangeman, G.B. Lyon, could contest the Bytown seat in the legislature without provoking opposition from the gentility. As a scion of the Lyon family of Richmond, one of the founding families of the gentry group, his open espousal of Orangeism was a measure of the tension already being felt by the Carleton aristocrats. Other prominent families, like the Letts of Richmond and the Rochesters of Bytown, added their strength and their respectability to the forces of arch-Protestantism. Most important in the rapid rise of the Order, however, was the influence of William F. Powell. The Powell family had long been prominent in the area, since William's father, Major J.A.H. Powell, had taken land in the Perth military settlement in 1818. First sheriff of the Bathurst District, J.A.H. Powell had been followed in public office and social leadership by his three sons.[11] William Frederick Powell was already an ardent Orangeman when he moved to Bytown in the early 1840s. He assumed the editorship of the *Bytown Gazette*, long the voice of the gentility, and made it a powerful organ of the Protestant cause, a scourge of Popery in the midst of a predominantly Catholic community. Joined by the *Orange Lily*, founded by Dawson Kerr and William Pittman Lett in 1849, the *Gazette's* diatribes helped keep tensions high in the town.

Aided by the power of his newspaper and even more by the tensions of the time, Powell assumed a dominant position in local Tory ranks; he became the spokesman for the gentility. It would have been unthinkable a decade earlier for the gentlemen of Carleton to take their lead from an Orangeman. But in 1849 William Powell was the moving force in the Carleton League, part of the province-wide British American League, a desperate attempt by Tories to find a solution to the twin threats of free trade and responsible government. Powell forged a strong organization in Bytown and Carleton, including among its officers a number of former elite members. Powell was among the four delegates from Carleton to the League convention at Kingston in July 1849, the only one of the four not of the pre-1841 gentility.[12]

The old leaders of the community allowed their course to be plotted by Powell and the Orange Order. How much this was due to the conversion of a bitter gentility to the principles of Orange extremism and how much to a simple recognition that the Carleton public would more readily follow Powell than themselves is difficult to assess. If the gentility needed any proof of the latter point, it would come in 1854. Edward Malloch, the long-time MLA for Carleton and associate of the aristocrats, refused to step aside when Powell decided to run for parliament. Powell decisively defeated Malloch, his extremist views counting for more than Malloch's decades of faithful service. Powell lost only two townships: Nepean, which had the largest percentage of Catholics in its population; and Goulburn, which had the smallest.[13] Not only do these returns indicate Powell's victory over the gentility, they verify Mood's thesis. Orangeism was weak not only where Catholics were decisively strong but also where they were so few in number as to provide no threat to Protestant hegemony.

An incident which paved the way for the violence of 1849 demonstrates how the factors in the Bytown equation fitted together: Protestant extremism, Catholic self-awareness, Catholic independence from the social services of the older community. In 1847 Bytown was inundated with Irish immigrants passing through on their way west. Between 1 June and 17 July, some 3 100 emigrants arrived at Bytown, many of them infected with the typhus already raging in Quebec.[14] The Grey Nuns' Hospital was soon overcrowded with victims and on 5 June a temporary hospital was opened, built by the emigration agent, G.R. Burke, but staffed by the Grey Nuns. There they treated 619 patients, of whom 167 died.[15] In the town as a whole, 314 people died of typhus that terrible summer.[16] Of twenty-one nuns and novices serving in the emigrant hospital, seventeen contracted typhus and three priests also came down with the disease.[17] The tragedy, and their pride in the bravery of the Grey Nuns, helped knit French and Irish together. So too did the religious controversy which began in the autumn of 1847. Despite their efforts, the nuns came under severe attack from the Bytown Board of Health. It was charged that they ran their hospital inefficiently, that they frequently over-charged patients and that religious discrimination applied in admissions. The truth of these charges is impossible to confirm or deny. But Father Telman, head of the Oblate mission in Bytown, was certain that the criticisms were religiously motivated, that the Board was simply a mouthpiece of its dominant member, the able but quarrelsome Anglican minister, Samuel S. Strong.[18]

The dissension over the Grey Nun's administration of the hospital contin-ued intermittently over the next two years. In 1849 the disgruntled Protestants decided to establish their own hospital, amid violent attacks on the Catholic hospital. Led by the fanatically anti-Catholic *Orange Lily*, the Tory press repeated the old charges of maladministration and added more damaging new ones. The Grey Nuns, it was claimed, were using their hospital to proselytize, to convert Protestant patients. Denials from Mother Thibodeau on behalf of the nuns did nothing to quiet the storm of the controversy.[19] A new hospital was formed, incorporated in 1851 as the County of Carleton General Prot-estant Hospital, which became in 1924 the Ottawa Civic Hospital. This petty crisis had helped divide the community further on religious lines, had com-pleted the separation of social services, and had laid the ground for violence of September 1849.

Violence and disorder were nothing very new in Bytown and Carleton. Nor were they unique in the Ottawa Valley of the 1840s. Western Carleton and Lanark County were suffering by mid-decade from organized crime, with a gang of horse thieves raiding farms in the area. At Aylmer, Lower Canada, in 1850 the Customs Department had to call on the aid of troops to suppress a band of smugglers. And further upriver the same year gangs of men, as many as fifty to a side, were engaged in pitched battles along the Bonnechère River in clashes over property boundaries.[20] In this region, far from the sway of provincial authority, with no adequate local police and with a dominant eco-nomic activity — the timber trade — which encouraged ruthless and reckless pursuit of profit, social disorder was an everyday fact of life. A description of Peter Aylen, the Shiner chieftain, a decade earlier, could still be applied to many individuals in the Ottawa Valley: "he neither respects himself, nor fears God, or Man. The laws are like cobwebs to him."[21]

In this violent milieu, the pattern of the disorder in Carleton and Bytown was particularly interesting. It was clearly related to religious strife and to economic distress. It also saw the old ruling group come into direct violent conflict with the Catholic-dominated lower class of Bytown. Orange and Green clashes had centre stage in the 1840s, rather than the Irish-*Canadien* savagery of the previous decade. The high points of the religious troubles coincided with periods of depression: in 1843 during the first brutal collapse of the timber trade under the impact of reduction of imperial preferences; in 1846, when panic spread over the removal of British preferences; and in 1849, when at the low point of the depression the decade's frustrations boiled over. The relationship between religious conflict and economic distress cannot be established in any clear way. But it would be a "chicken and egg" exercise to attempt to unravel it, at any rate; there were two major causes of strife, and they both sprang from psychological pressures on the population. Finally, the class relations are significant. Even under the Shiners, the Irish lower class had only sniped at the gentility, aiming the greater part of their warfare at their fellow proletarians, the French Canadians. In the 1840s, however, the battle was drawn with the gentility and its new agency, the Orange Order, on one side and the Catholic masses on the other. And, to add another difference, it was the Orangemen who took the violent offensive, not the Catholics.

The first major outburst of the period came in 1843. The Governor General, Sir Charles Metcalfe, visited Bytown on Saturday, 19 August. As was usual on such occasions, elaborately decorated arches were erected at various points along his route. After he left town, however, the Orangemen decided not to remove an arch they had erected on Rideau Street in Lower Town. It was not simply that they felt the tiger lily decorations too lovely to disturb; built on a bridge, the arch was so positioned that Catholics on their way to church the next day would have to pass under it. The next afternoon, a full-scale battle threatened, as Catholics and Orangemen gathered by the hundreds in the vicinity of the arch. It was eventually torn down on the orders of a magistrate, the volunteer demolition crew working under a barrage of rocks from the angry Orangemen. Only diligent efforts by Judge Christopher Armstrong and Edward Malloch, a magistrate, succeeded in preventing a bloodbath. That evening they persuaded several heavily armed gangs of Catholics to disperse, rather than to take the revenge they had planned to levy on the Protestants. It was fortunate that the arch riot had passed off with only minor injuries: in Malloch's words, "several persons got their faces bruised, but not serious."[22]

The town was less fortunate in 1846. Orange-Catholic strife was a regular part of life in Bytown and Carleton after 1843, but it only rose to fever pitch with the onset of a serious depression three years later. That summer the Protestant farmers were hard-pressed, with markets difficult to find and a drought so severe that, in late summer, a boy could wade across the Ottawa River at the rapids above the Chaudière.[23] The timber trade was depressed, because of the removal of British preferences and the drought, which made it difficult to transport timber. As a result, Bytown was full of idle men, most Catholic timberers.[24] The tension mounted in the town until 12 July. A grand Orange procession, with lodges from throughout Carleton County, wound its way through Bytown, until it was attacked by a large Catholic mob. There followed a bloody riot, with fighting that tore Bytown for a day and a half.[25] It was the beginning of a violent summer. Magistrates were obstructed in their attempts to arrest lawbreakers; prisoners were rescued from jail. On 25 September the troops had to be called out when a group of magistrates, delivering a warrant, was assaulted by a gang of fifty men.[26]

When the Rebellion Losses Act, coming on the heels of responsible government, set off Tory violence in the Province of Canada, one place where the government expected trouble was the perennially disaffected Bytown. It was well-known that the Tories there were furious with what one conservative paper called "that miserable apology for a governor."[27] The new commander of the Bytown garrison, Brevet Major F.W. Clements, was under orders to keep the situation there under close surveillance and to inform the government of any threatening developments. Clements was not a particularly astute observer and he did little to prepare the authorities for what was to happen in September 1849. But his reports are interesting because they help to explain his behaviour during the riots. The Major made little attempt to conceal his own feelings about recent political developments. However much Irish and French-Canadian Reformers at Bytown might support the governor, Clements warned at one point, "there exists amongst her Majestys loyal subjects a strong feeling of dissatisfaction at the late Government Measures."[28] It required little interpretation to determine that Clements did not consider the Reformers "loyal subjects."

Beyond angry words from the Tory Carleton League, the early summer of 1849 passed with relative peace. Major Clements confidently reported on 11 August that, "nothing has occurred to induce one to think that any Riots or Disturbances are likely to occur in this part of the Country,"[29] But he had spoken too early. Less than two weeks later news arrived that Lord Elgin was planning a September visit to the area. A sharp division of opinion was soon apparent in the community. A bipartisan committee, under the chairmanship of Bytown MLA John Scott, was formed to prepare a non-political address to Elgin, to be presented on his arrival in the town. When William Stewart, MLA for Bytown from 1844 to 1848, was approached to associate himself with the address, he insisted upon taking the proposal to a meeting of his Tory compatriots. The meeting was dominated by the Orange extremists, William Powell, Roderick Ross and William P. Lett. It was decided "that the Conservative Party should abstain from lending their sanction" to any greeting for Elgin. More ominously, they agreed that the Tories should turn out at any public meeting held to adopt an address and assure that their opinions on the governor's behaviour were heard.[30]

Even Major Clements now saw the signs. He warned against Elgin's visit because it would provoke "a most serious and fatal collision . . . between the parties called Conservatives and Radicals; the former of whom are by far the most numerous and respectable portion of the community here."[31] The Reform newspaper, the *Packet*, was busy attempting to calm feelings, pointing out the disastrous results of any violence during the governor's visit. It was necessary to make a good impression on him for, the *Packet* pointed out, the riots in Montreal had reopened the question of the capital of the Canadas. If Elgin liked Bytown he might well recommend its choice as the seat of government.[32] The committee charged with drawing up the welcoming address took the same line. Lord Elgin's visit would be the ideal occasion, their draft resolutions said, to direct "his attention to our Staple Trade, — our noble River — . . . the position of Bytown, and its claim to be the future seat of government. . . ."[33] These appeals to reason convinced the ever-optimistic Major Clements, if not the Tories, for he reported on September 8 that the crisis had passed. "No disturbance or appearance of anything likely to affect the public peace" was apparent to him.[34]

Clements misread the situation. The determination of the Reformers to press ahead with the adoption of an address to Lord Elgin renewed the tension. When the mayor, Tory Robert Hervey, refused to call a meeting of the citizens, the Reformers decided to proceed themselves. The mood was ominous. Tories warned they would not permit a complimentary address to be adopted; Reformers, while claiming a desire for peace, nevertheless announced they would hold their ground against any Tory obstruction.[35] The conservative *Ottawa Advocate* later charged that the liberal MLA John Scott had publicly provoked violence. According to the *Advocate*:

> Mr. John Scott . . . repeatedly invited the Conservatives to a trial of strength, and with that superabundant stock of what the Yankees term *gas*, so proverbially his own — threatened to drive the Conservatives root and branch, lock, stock and barrel into the Ottawa — and to use his own words, if necessary to H-L.[36]

Undaunted by the mayor's refusal, the Reform town councillors Charles Sparrow and Joseph Turgeon called, on their own authority, a town meeting for Monday, 17 September. Mayor Hervey retaliated by announcing a rival meeting to be held on Wednesday, 19 September. Leaving nothing to chance, the two parties had arranged their gatherings in the hearts of their respective strongholds: the Reform meeting would be in the Lower Town market, the Tory meeting in Upper Town. The setting established, both sides began to prepare for the conflict ahead. On Sunday an already nervous Bytown buzzed with rumours of huge armies of Orangemen marching from Huntley, Goulburn, Fitzroy, North Gower, Marlborough, Nepean and Gloucester, marching fully armed, marching to attack the Catholic townspeople. The rumours proved well-founded, according to the *Packet*. It reported that, "During Sunday night and Monday morning waggon loads of Farmers continued to pour in, and about ten o'clock the main body, consisting of about five hundred men, headed by leaders from the Town, arrived, and about half-past One, P.M., proceeded to the place of Meeting."[37] On the other hand, the Tory press charged that the Reformers imported raftsmen from the Gatineau, "an armed and well organized band of ruffians brought there for the express purpose of creating a riot. . . ."[38]

After the riot, of course, both sides pleaded their innocence. The Tories denied that rioters had been brought in from the townships. "It is certainly the fact," the *Advocate* facilely explained, "that Monday was a greater market day than usual, which accounted for the presence of several of the Farmers in Town, but these 'good men and true' attended that meeting as became peaceable citizens." The Reformers claimed to be equally lamb-like. Their group at the meeting was made up purely of unarmed inhabitants of Bytown, who had no thought of trouble and were shocked "to see the orange ruffians flocking in from the country in hundreds."[39] Whatever the disclaimers, it is clear that when the meeting convened at two o'clock on the afternoon of Monday, 17 September, the opposing factions were supported by large numbers of men brought in from outside the town, and it is equally clear that both sides were heavily armed with stones and guns. The Tories, however, were better organized and had a decided majority on the market square.

The platform was erected at the southern end of the North Ward market, looking out over Lower Town's York Street.[40] A large, tense crowd of nearly 1 500 men milled about, already exchanging jibes and shoves, when Charles Sparrow climbed the stairs to the platform and declared the meeting open. Above a cacophony of shouts and oaths and party hurrahs, a red-faced Sparrow tried to make himself heard as he read the proposed address to Lord Elgin. The futile reading done, Sparrow nominated John Scott for chairman of the meeting, to a furious roar from the conservatives. Joseph B. Turgeon, a blacksmith of radical inclinations, leaped on a bench to second the nomination, only to have his harangue come to an abrupt end when a Tory partisan pulled the bench from under him, tumbling Turgeon to the ground. Edward Malloch was next to speak, while the Tories were still guffawing over the unceremonious departure of Mr. Turgeon. As Malloch shouted his preference for Dr. Hamnett Hill as chairman, the first stones were thrown.

The fight started in front of the platform provoked, the Tories said, by an attack on a farmer by a group of raftsmen. In seconds the air was full of stones. The outnumbered Reformers were driven back, to regroup in front of Leamy's tavern, where some foresighted gentlemen had stockpiled a supply of stones. They charged back into the market, where blood soon mixed with the dust. The battle spread into street and alleys. Guns appeared; the Tories obtained theirs from Rideau Street merchants, the Reformers from nearby houses. In the next quarter hour, dozens were wounded in the sniping which seemed to come from every doorway.

A new sound was heard, the sound of marching feet. Under the urgings of town officials, Major Clements had agreed to call out the garrison. As might be expected from his political opinions, the troops did not play an entirely impartial role in the proceedings. Ignoring the demands of Turgeon and Sparrow that the soldiers be directed to the market, Clements sent them through the by-streets in the area, where the Reformers were entrenched. Not surprisingly, almost all of the fifteen to twenty rioters arrested in this sweep were liberals. It was later claimed that the troops even passed by some Orange snipers to arrest the party of towns-people contending with them.[41] Arriving at the market, the soldiers guarded the Tories who placed Doctor Hill on the platform and held their own meeting. They passed an address disapproving of the course pursued by the government whose approach to policy "from the day of their assumption of power to the present time, we must unhesitatingly and emphatically condemn."[42] After Mayor Hervey had read this address the Tories celebrated their victory. As the *Packet* bitterly recounted it.

> The special constables sworn in by the Major then placed themselves at the head of the mob, and four deep they paraded the streets. After being harangued by the Leaders, and receiving instructions to come in upon Wednesday fully armed and equipped for war, the waggons were procured, and those poor unfortunate misguided Irish dupes left Town, exulting over the crimes and enormities of the day.[43]

The *Ottawa Advocate* described the events rather differently, in an article entitled "Glorious Conservative Triumph."

> It is with mingled feelings of regret and gratification we take up our pen to record the events of Monday last — Regret that our hitherto peaceful Town should be the scene of riot and bloodshed — Gratification that in the midst thereof and while apparently surrounded by insurmountable difficulties, we were able to defeat the Hellish designs of the reckless and cowardly leaders of the Radical party in this District, and teach them a lesson, by them to be remembered so long as there is a Shinor [sic] left to throw a stone or a Frenchman
> "Who yells and runs away
> That he may live to howl another day."[44]

Tuesday was spent mustering forces, gathering arms, readying for the Tory meeting on Wednesday. By 9:30 Wednesday morning, a liberal reported, "The town even at this hour . . . is full of people from the country and every face wears a sinister aspect."[45] Aware the situation was out of hand Mayor Hervey ordered the cancellation of the Tory meeting. It was far too late. At least a thousand men were in the streets, ready for battle. The Reformers were mustered in the market, armed with guns, bayonets and even two small cannon. The Tories, led by William Powell, controlled Upper Town. Powell was determined to go ahead with the Tory meeting and, to prevent the Reformers disrupting it, decided upon a preventative attack on the Lower Tory market. Orange banners waving, the Protestant army marched toward the canal which separated the two sections of Bytown. At their head were Powell, his henchman Alexander Gibb and, to assure that a heavenly hand would aid their earthly arms, the Anglican priest S.S. Strong. The 1840s here had reached their logical climax: scores of men, it seemed, would lay down their lives for the hatred and bigotry born of tradition and depression.

An unlikely hero emerged at the crucial moment — Brevet Major F.W. Clements. Rushing his troops into position, Clements seized the Sappers' bridge over the Rideau Canal. The Royal Canadian Rifles were thus stationed between the belligerent parties, standing ready with fixed bayonets to resist any attempt by either group to cross the bridge. It is undoubtedly true, as an observer noted, that if an attack had been launched the small body of soldiers "would have been but a feeble barrier."[46] However their presence was of crucial psychological importance. The rioters were given pause, they were forced to consider the seriousness of their actions. Both sides retreated to their strongholds, for much earnest debate on how to proceed, and even more aimless milling about. Over the next three hours a few stones were shied over the heads of the soldiers, but there was only one dangerous moment. Under the urging of Sparrow and Turgeon, the Reformers decided to disband. As they left the market, a few boisterous fellows, in a spirit of bravado, discharged their guns into the air. Thinking an attack had begun, the nervous Tories poured down from their rallying point on Barracks Hill. All they met were the bayonets of the troops. The conservative leaders managed to stop their men before anyone assaulted the troops. When word finally came that the

Reformers had dispersed, the country people formed up in ranks and marched off Barracks Hill. Led by a fife, a drum, and an Orange flag, they swung out onto Wellington Street. Firing their guns in the air, they paraded west and out of Bytown. The war was over.

For some, however, the affair was not quite finished. For young David Borthwick, a Tory, it ended on 24 September when he died of gunshot wounds received in the fighting on Stony Monday. His funeral the next day was a grand affair. Since he was of their faith, twelve Methodist clergymen then in conference in Bytown led the procession.[47] It was a grand affair, indeed, but it hardly compensated for David Borthwick's sacrifice on the altar of intolerance. The affair was not yet over, that afternoon of 19 September, for Major Clements, either.

That night special constables patrolled the town, rounding up potential troublemakers. A number of those apprehended were found to be carrying weapons clearly marked as government property, from the armories at Hull, Lower Canada. The armory there was under the control of the Wright family, who were apparently supplying the Reformers with guns. This casts an interesting light on the causes of the Bytown riots. It has been contended that the leaders were impelled primarily by political motives.[48] If so, the role of the Wrights becomes very puzzling. As a family they shared strongly conservative political views. The patriarch and founder of Hull, Philemon Wright, supported the Chateau Clique as a Lower Canadian Assemblyman, while his grandson Alonzo sat in Parliament as a Conservative for three decades. Presumably, then, politics were not central for the Wrights in this crisis. Personal considerations, and old animosities, were more important. Family ties had something to do with it, for the Reform leader John Scott was married to a Wright girl. The most plausible explanation, however, rests in the resentment the Wrights felt over the many snubs they had received, for so many years, from the gentility of Carleton. Never considered quite respectable because of their rough manners and Yankee origins, the Wright clan was now repaying the haughty gentlemen across the river.[49] How many other personal vendettas underlay the troubles of 1849?

To prevent more guns from falling into radical hands, Major Clements led a detachment of the Royal Canadian Rifles to Hull on the afternoon of Thursday, 20 September.[50] On the way they made a distinguished catch. Henry J. Friel, editor of the Bytown *Packet*, future mayor of both Bytown and Ottawa, was arrested while on his way to Hull to warn the Wrights. According to Friel, Clements was still showing his partisanship. He bullied and insulted Friel, calling him "a damned Scoundrel and ruffian," and insisted, "You and that damned Scoundrel Scott are the cause of all this."[51] Friel was dragged along with the troops to Hull.

Riding ahead of their men, Clements and two lieutenants arrived at the arsenal to find three men wheeling a cannon out of the building. The three were Joshua Wright, Ruggles Wright junior, and the one-time Shiner leader, Andrew Leamy. After a scuffle, in which the Wrights attempted to fire the cannon on the soldiers, the three were subdued and arrested. Somewhat implausibly, if ingeniously, the Lower Canadians later explained that they had been at the arsenal to protect the weapons *against* the rioters. When they saw the officer coming, they had thought them rioters disguised as soldiers.

This unconvincing argument did not impress Major Clements. The prisoners were marched back to Bytown. At the suspension bridge over the Ottawa, Friel was freed but the others were taken on into town, abused the whole journey by the troops. After holding the men at the barracks for three hours, Clements found to his embarrassment that he had no authority to detain them in Upper Canada. The weary prisoners were paraded back to Hull, charged before a magistrate and finally, five hours after their arrest, were released on bail. Except for the months of court proceedings which lay ahead before the matter was settled, the Rebellion Losses riots in Bytown were over.

One man dead, scores wounded, much of the central section of the town damaged, the physical results of the events of September 1948 were evident. But what did it all mean? What had caused the riots and what were their implications? Brault has explained the trouble in terms of politics, adding that religious differences heightened the feelings. The Catholic historian Father Alexis de Barbezieux, saw Stony Monday as the culmination of hostilities between the Orangemen and Catholic Irish.[52] Charles Mair, in his reminiscences on the Shiners, claimed the riots sprang from an Orange campaign to suppress the Shiners.[53] There is merit in all these views although Mair should have spoken of Irish Catholics rather than the defunct Shiner movement. The politics of which Brault speaks did provide the occasion, the excuse, for the battle. And certainly the opposing sides were ranged largely on religious lines. What these analyses fail to establish is why religious differences, which had always existed, should have erupted only in 1849 and why Catholics, French-Canadian and Irish, could put their differences aside to fight as allies after so many years of conflict. We come closer to a satisfactory explanation in a contemporary analysis, that given by the Montreal *Herald*. The newspaper contrasted the inhabitants of the country and the citizens of the town. The former were sturdy Scots Irish farmers, but:

> On the other side, you have the loose, rowdy, ruffianly population, from the rafts and shanties of the Ottawa and the Gatineau. Between these classes the old feud, which they have brought with them from their native country, has been heightened by political differences, and the personal misunderstandings which must always occur between settled thriving farmers and wandering uncivilized hordes like the Bytown "Shiners."[54]

The *Herald* exaggerated both the evils of the Bytonians and the virtues of the farmers. However it points to several significant factors. The migration patterns of the area had imported factionalism and bigotry from the United Kingdom, tumbling together Scots-Irish Orangemen and Catholics from Tipperary and other disaffected areas of Ireland. Widening ethnic and religious differences between county and town had given these imported tendencies fertile ground in which to grow. Equally significant, the newspaper indicated the importance of differing attitudes and interests between Bytown and Carleton.

These differences lay not only in religion and ethnic origin. The depression in the 1840s had hurried along what the geography of the timber trade was accomplishing already — the departure of the commercial frontier from Carleton County. Bytown, however large it was growing, was still on that commercial frontier in spirit if not in location. Its business and its population still depended on the timber trade. For Carleton, on the other hand, the depression had worked to weaken its ties to the timber frontier. The economic link was strained by the declining market the lumber community provided for Carleton farmers during the hard years of the forties. The development of demographic pressures within the county, as available land filled up, focussed Carleton's attention on other concerns, concern for opening new land to agriculture, concern for settlement roads rather than river improvements, concerns that brought the interests of the county into conflict with those of the timber trade and of Bytown.[55] Combined with the increasing independence of the lower classes of Bytown from the traditional county gentility, an independence fostered by the Catholic Church and differing interests, these factors helped create the climate for the riots of 1849. For French Canadian and Irish, language barriers were now less important than their common hostility to the religion, the politics, and the social outlook of the farmers of Carleton County.

A postscript to 1849. Lord Elgin, the catalyst of events, postponed his visit to Bytown after the riots. He did not come until the prosperous year of 1853, when he was warmly welcomed by all sections of the community.

Notes

1. See for example: Cephas D. Allin and George M. Jones, *Annexation, Preferential Trade and Reciprocity* (Toronto, n.d.); D.G. Creighton, *Empire of the St. Lawrence* (Toronto, 1956); M.S. Cross, *Free Trade, Annexation and Reciprocity, 1846–1854* (Toronto, 1971); Gilbert Norman Tucker, *The Canadian Commercial Revolution, 1845–1851*, edited by Hugh G.J. Aitken (Toronto, 1964).

2. On the Shiners see: Miller Stewart, "The King of the Shiners," in *Flamboyant Canadians*, edited by Ellen Stafford (Toronto, 1964); An Old Ottawan, "The Ottawa 'Shiners,'" *Toronto Week*, 18 Aug. 1893. On the Bytown gentry, Michael S. Cross, "The Age of Gentility: The Creation of An Aristocracy in the Ottawa Valley," Canadian Historical Association, *Historical Papers* (1967).

3. For example, see Walter Shanly's description of the timber barons in Frank Norman Walker, ed., *Daylight Through the Mountain: Letters and Labours of Civil Engineers Walter and Francis Shanly* (n.p., 1957), 186, 197.

4. Kingston Diocesan Archives, Macdonnell Letterbook, 1834–1839, Macdonell to Rev. Patrick MacDonagh, 6 July 1835, 140.

5. Bytown *Packet*, 11 Jan. 1851.

6. Nicholas Flood Davin, *The Irishman in Canada* (Toronto, 1877), 323–24.

7. See, for instance: Public Archives of Canada (hereinafter PAC), Upper Canada Sundries, vol. 225, Donald Fraser to S.B. Harrison, 31 July 1839; *Bytown Gazette*, 5 Nov. 1840.

8. William James Sale Mood, "The Orange Order in Canadian Politics, 1841–1867" (M.A. thesis, University of Toronto, 1950), 105.

9. Canada, *Census 1871*, vol. 4; *Census* of 1848.

10. This was a fact recognized by some contemporaries: Bytown *Packet*, 22 Sept., 6 Oct. 1849.

11. On the Powell family see: Andrew Haydon, *Pioneer Sketches of the District of Bathurst* (Toronto, 1925), 76–77; *Illustrated Historical Atlas of the County of Carleton* (Toronto, 1879), p.v.; Mood, "The Orange Order in Canadian Politics, 1841–1867," 114–22.

12. Bytown *Packet*, 12 May, 21 July 1849.

13. PAC, Carleton County Records and Poll Books, poll books for 1854; Province of Canada, Journals of the Legislative Assembly, 1852–1853, Appendix C, Census of 1852.

14. PAC, Provincial Secretary's Papers, Canada West, vol. 273, E. Van Cortlandt to the Provincial Secretary, Sept. 1849, no. 264.

15. Lucien Brault, *Ottawa Old & New* (Ottawa, 1946), 228.

16. Dr. H. Beaumont Small, *Medical Memoirs of Bytown* (Ottawa, 1903), 6.

17. Brault, *Ottawa Old & New*, 228; P. Alexis de Barbezieux, *Histoire de la Province Ecclésiastique d'Ottawa* (Ottawa, 1897), 1: 230–31; Quebec *Morning Chronicle*, 13 Sept. 1842.

18. Kingston Diocesan Archives, Bishop Phelan Miscellaneous Correspondence, Envelope 1, Telman to Phelan, 12 Dec. 1847. Strong's anti-Catholicism was also demonstrated in an 1853 dispute over schools in Bytown: Province of Canada, Journals of the Legislative Assembly, 1845–1855, Appendix B, "The Separate Schools Question in Upper Canada," W. Lochead to E. Ryerson, 28 Mar. 1853, 19 Feb. 1855; Petition of the Protestant Inhabitants of Bytown, 14 Mar. 1853. His abrasive personality later split his congregation: Ontario Archives (hereinafter OA), Strachan Papers, Strachan's Letterbook, 1854–1862, Strachan to Strong, 18 Mar. 1854, 13; Strachan to James Fitzgibbon, 26 Apr. 1854, 19.

19. Bytown *Packet*, 8 Sept. 1849. The controversy can be followed in the *Packet* for August and September, which reprinted the charges of the Tory press and gave its own rebuttals. The first charges appeared in the *Orange Lily*, 1 Aug. 1849.

20. Bytown *Packet*, 24 Apr. 1847; PAC, Governor General's Civil Secretary, Papers, no. 5281, Francis Hincks to Col. R. Bruce, 6 Feb. 1850; Bytown *Packet*, 5 Oct. 1850.

21. PAC, Upper Canada Sundries, vol. 175, James Johnston to Lieutenant Governor Head, 14 Mar. 1837.

22. PAC, Provincial Secretary's Papers, vol. 114, Malloch to Provincial Secretary, 12 Sept. 1843, no. 6370. This is the best account, but also see, Brault, *Ottawa Old & New*, 70–71.

23. Bytown *Packet*, 5 Sept. 1846.

24. PAC, Provincial Secretary's Papers, vol. 189, James Hopkirk to Christopher Armstrong, 7 Sept. 1846, no. 14758.

25. Ibid., and Brault, *Ottawa Old & New*, 71–72.

26. Brault, *Ottawa Old & New*, 71.

27. *Ottawa Advocate*, 19 Sept. 1849, quoted in *The Elgin-Grey Papers*, 4 vols., edited by Sir Arthur G. Doughty (Ottawa, 1937), 2: 507.

28. PAC, British Military Records, vol 616, Clements to Captain Kirkland, 10 July 1849, 123.

29. Ibid., Clements to Major Talbot, 11 Aug. 1849.

30. Bytown *Packet*, 25 Aug. 1849.

31. PAC, British Military Records, vol. 616, Clements to Talbot, 25 Aug. 1849, 304–5.

32. Bytown *Packet*, 8 Sept. 1849.

33. Ibid., 22 Sept. 1849.

34. PAC, British Military Records, vol. 617, Clements to Talbot, 8 Sept. 1849, 14.

35. Bytown *Packet*, 15 Sept. 1849.

36. *Ottawa Advocate*, 19 Sept. 1849, in Doughty, *The Elgin-Grey Papers*, 2: 503.

37. Bytown *Packet*, 22 Sept. 1849.

38. *Ottawa Advocate*, 19 Sept. 1849, in Doughty, *The Elgin-Grey Papers*, 2: 505.

39. Ibid.; PAC, Bytown, 1849, two letters, "Robert" to "Jessie," 18 Sept. 1849. The unidentified author of these two letters took part in the fighting on the Reform side.

40. This account of the events is reconstructed from a number of often conflicting sources: Bytown *Packet*, 22 Sept. 1849; *Ottawa Advocate*, 19 Sept. 1849, in Doughty, *The Elgin-Grey Papers*, 2: 502–5; PAC, Bytown, 1849, two letters, 18 and 20 Sept. 1849; OA, McLachlin Papers, Hugh McLachlin to Neil Robertson, 18 Sept. 1849; PAC, Hill Collection, vol. 20, Hugh McLachlin, to Daniel McLachlin, 20 Sept. 1849, 4959–60; PAC, British Military Records, vol. 617, Clements to Talbot, 17 Sept. 1849, 33–35.

41. PAC, Hill Collection, vol. 20, Hugh McLachlin to Daniel McLachlin, 20 Sept. 1849, 4960.

42. Bytown *Packet*, 22 Sept. 1849.

43. Ibid.

44. *Ottawa Advocate*, 19 Sept. 1849, in Doughty, *The Elgin-Grey Papers*, 2: 502.

45. PAC, Bytown, 1849, "Robert" to "Jessie," 18 Sept. 1849, postscript dated 19 Sept.

46. Ibid., 20 Sept. 1849.

47. Bytown *Packet*, 29 Sept. 1849.

48. Brault, *Ottawa Old & New*, 77.

49. On the gentry attitude to the Wrights, see Cross, "Age of Gentility," 112, 113.

50. The raid on the Hull armory is treated in a number of sources, which give all sides of the question: Bytown *Packet*, 22 Sept. 1849; PAC, British Military Records, vol. 617, Clements to Talbot, 22 Sept. 1849, 47–48; ibid., Hamnett Hill to Talbot, 29 Sept. 1849, 55–57; ibid., deposition of Major Clements before James Wadsworth, J.P. Hull, L.C., 20 Sept. 1849, 79; PAC, Hill Collection, vol. 20, Clements to Talbot, 20 Oct. 1849, 4967–70; PAC, Governor General's Civil Secretary, Papers, vol. 48, Talbot to Civil Secretary, 28 Sept. 1849, no. 5221; ibid., Clements to Colonel Young, 22 Sept. 1849, no. 5223; ibid., Clements to Talbot, 29 Sept. 1849, no. 5223; PAC, Provincial Secretary's Papers, vol. 274, memorial to H.J. Friel, 24 Sept. 1849, no. 1968; ibid., memorial of Ruggles Wright, Andrew Leamy, and Joshua R. Wright, 22 Sept. 1849, no. 1924; ibid., deposition of Ruggles Wright, et al., 22 Sept. 1849, no. 1924; ibid., deposition of Sexton Washburn, 22 Sept. 1849, no. 1924.

51. PAC, Provincial Secretary's Papers, vol. 274, memorial of H.J. Friel, 24 Sept. 1849, no. 1968.

52. P. Alexis de Barbezieux, *Histoire de la Province Ecclésiastique d'Ottawa*, 166.

53. Toronto *Week*, 18 Aug. 1893, 897.

54. Montreal *Herald*, quoted in Bytown *Packet*, 6 Oct. 1849.

55. The population of Carleton had reached nearly 25 persons to the square mile by 1851, virtually the saturation point for a marginal agricultural area. As a result the population was static over the next two decades. *Census 1871*, 4: 136.

Jailbirds in Mid-Victorian Halifax†

JUDITH FINGARD

The social history of crime and criminal justice in the nineteenth century has recently tended to emphasize two themes: first, attitudes towards crime and punishment, and the administrative reforms of institutions which grew out of those attitudes; second, the nature of criminality, particularly of serious crime and long-term trends, as revealed in case studies of offences in particular localities, including computer-based, statistical profiles of criminal populations. Both these approaches have their strengths, but it must be recognized that they are heavily weighted in favour of the theoretical, the institutional, and the statistical; they are also predominantly concerned with the view from the top down. Little is revealed about the criminals themselves. Among offenders, only the "social" criminals, bent on resisting authority or protecting customary rights, have attracted historical inquiry. Yet to study popular resistance and civil strife at the neglect of more prosaic "common" offences is to overlook the delinquents who kept the criminal courts and the prisons in business.[1]

I am proposing an approach to the common offender that we would call personal history or life-cycle history. By analyzing the careers of the criminals themselves, we can come to appreciate that the most prominent offenders — those who were most frequently caught and incarcerated and best known in their community — led lives that were nasty, brutish, and, if not short, then certainly unfulfilled. Their criminal careers cannot be romanticized, and to dismiss their criminality merely as a by-product of the rise of industrial capitalism, as some historians have done, seems to me to beg the question.[2]

The evidence for this study is based on a tiny proportion of the exceptionally rich records of courts and "carceral" institutions that are housed in the Public Archives of Nova Scotia. Drawing on this evidence, I want first to provide a brief overview of the penal and criminal geography of the city of Halifax. Second, I will illustrate, with examples, the types of repeat offenders who went to city prison in the mid-nineteenth century. Third, I will suggest, in the light of the case histories of my recidivists, some questions which merit investigation. While the specific case histories are drawn from the sources of one North American city, I contend that the human experiences they reveal, and the analysis they require, should be as relevant to every small nineteenth century city in western society as to Halifax.

On 30 October 1865, Mary Slattery, an illiterate woman of twenty-one or twenty-two went to city prison for thirty days after having been found guilty in Halifax Police Courts of lewd conduct. This was one of the thirty-one offences for which she went to jail between 1862 and 1873. Many similar

† Peter Waite, Sandra Oxner, and Thomas Barnes, eds., *Law in Colonial Society: The Nova Scotia Experience*, The Dalhousie/Berkeley Lectures in Legal History (Toronto: Carswell, 1984), 81–102.

offences were undoubtedly undetected; for others she was let go by the police or brought to court and either acquitted or admonished or dismissed. Most of her offences like those of other repeat offenders occurred in an area adjacent to Citadel Hill, the high point of land rising above the downtown core of the city on which were located the major military installations. The "wickedest" streets were Barrack (Brunswick) and Albemarle (Market), just east of the Citadel, and City (Maynard) running north from the hill into the expanding north suburbs. These "upper streets" were for most of the nineteenth century the tavern, brothel, and slum areas of the city, frequented in the middle decades by the resident "residuum," the semi-permanent military rank and file, and visiting seafarers, prospectors, and popular entertainers. They were quite distinctively "rough" neighbourhoods, densely populated, ramshackle, unsanitary, and the natural focus for policemen and military pickets.

Arrested, then, in the "low-life" areas of the city, Mary Slattery went to jail in a city abundantly endowed with carceral institutions, especially in the mid-Victorian period. From the overnight lock-up at the police station beneath the city court, detainees went to the inferior and superior courts which included the police court, the city court, and the Supreme Court. Once sentenced or remanded, they went variously to the commodious city prison (rebuilt in a new location in 1860), or to the much smaller county jail (rebuilt in 1865, complete with an execution yard), or to the provincial penitentiary (erected in 1845 and used until 1880). In addition, military offenders, who might find themselves in any of the civilian jails, could be sent by courts martial to the district military prison located in the Citadel or, after 1856, on Melville Island which the Royal Navy also used. Other jail-like institutions to which offenders were sent from time to time were the poorhouse, that proverbial catch-all for the helpless, which mid-Victorians preferred to call the "poor's asylum"; homes for juvenile delinquents, though most went to the separate reformatory wing of the city prison, established in 1845; and various short-lived, small-scale rescue homes for prostitutes.

The century-old city of some 30 000 permanent and 2000 to 4000 military and transient inhabitants in the late 1860s to early 1870s occupied, with its suburbs, a peninsular site of 4500 acres in the shape, roughly speaking, of a triangle, surrounded on two and one half sides by water and ringed round with the above-mentioned prisons. In the midst of the old town, located on the harbour side of the triangle, were the police station lock-up practically on the water's edge, the Citadel prison commanding the heights above the rough areas of the town, and the county jail, south of the Citadel but still within the downtown core. The shortest side of the triangle, to the north, was dominated on the high ground over Bedford Basin by Rockhead Prison, a massive pile of granite thrown up in the best asylum tradition. In the south, on the third side of the triangle which bordered on the Northwest Arm, was the provincial penitentiary. At the northend extremity of this third side of the triangle, where the broad isthmus joins the city to the mainland, the Melville Island prison was located close to the mainland side of the Arm. If the would-be offender was not overwhelmingly impressed with all this jail space, any lingering doubts he might have about society's responsibility towards him would have been removed as he gazed across the harbour from downtown and espied the stern red brick of the insane asylum, opened in 1859, optimistically called Mount Hope, on the opposite shore. Since it was the age of asylums, and particularly of corrective institutions, Halifax was obviously keeping pace with modern fashions. This bird's-eye view of the penal geography of the city should also convince us that, while the majority of the civilian, military, and transient population might have avoided incarceration in the multifarious cells of the city, they could not avoid the presence of the prison. Prison accommodation was readily available to those who needed it, a comforting thought, no doubt, to those on the outside. A comforting thought also, I would argue, to those who were on the inside about as often, if not more often, than they were in the streets, tenements, taverns, and brothels beneath the Citadel.

Since most crime took the form of petty offences, the "notorious" criminals of the day appeared most frequently in the police court for summary trials from which they were usually committed to Rockhead, the city prison. If the magistrate wished to send an offender to the penitentiary, he had to elevate the case to the city criminal court. Those who sent to jail repeatedly were, of necessity, persistent residents of the city, a fact which made them unusual within the geographically mobile society of the nineteenth century. The identification of these habitual jailbirds involves a painstakingly slow linkage of names in extant registers. The problem of compiling a jail record for such a population is that, unless the recidivist has an uncommon name, it is difficult to be sure that we are dealing with one and the same offender. Unfortunately, of the few clues available, age identification is an unreliable way of distinguishing between what might in fact be two or three people of the same name, since offenders were adept performers and enjoyed aggravating the clerks by reporting their ages promiscuously, even in court. A press reporter heard Mary Slattery declare her age in 1868 to be eighty, not long after she gave her age on a previous occasion as sixteen. She was in fact about twenty-four.[3] But the margin of error in identification narrows the more we consult supplementary sources, both quantitative and literary.

Although I have cast my net over the thirty-year period from 1854 to 1884, I have used the middle decade, 1864 to 1873, as the focus for compiling a profile of ninety-two recidivists. The list includes offenders who were imprisoned on average at least twice a year for at least five consecutive years, years which fall either completely or substantially within the decade in question. This population accounts for 1506 or almost 32 percent (31.7 percent) of the 4749 committals in that period. The remaining 3243 committals belong to the other 1748 individuals who went to city prison. Whereas jailbirds, therefore, averaged 16.4 committals each, the rest of the jail population averaged 1.9 each. What we have then is 5.3 percent of the offenders responsible for 32 percent of the committals.[4] While such habitual delinquency obviously cries out for investigation, we cannot unfortunately establish with reasonable certainty the number of court appearances which occurred over and above those that resulted in imprisonment. The jail registers for city prison begin in 1854 but cannot be checked against extant court registers until 1880. Any correlation between court appearance and jail sentences must instead depend on incomplete police court minutes and erratic court reports in the daily press.

My decision to deal with those who were imprisoned for what were considered minor offences against property, person, morality and the city charter, rather than the larger population of those arraigned before the police court has been determined, then, partly by the sources. And yet the jail population was a distinct one which merits special treatment. It represents those individuals who did not pay their fines at a time when most jail sentences handed down by summary trials could be avoided by such a payment. On the whole, we can assume that the offenders sent to jail could not afford the requisite fine. Sometimes, however, they wanted to go to jail, and other times the magistrate denied the option of a fine, particularly under the vagrancy laws. Yet the universal release from jail of prisoners long before they had completed their sentences confirms that commitments for vagrancy too were escapable either through subsequent payment of fines or easily obtained pardons.

Important though the city prison records are, my recidivists appear also in the county jail registers, the poorhouse registers (missing for 1871 to 1875), the public hospital registers and case books, the coroner's court inquests, as well as in newspapers and vital statistics. Very few of the habitual offenders in this period ended up in the penitentiary or the insane asylum. In contemporary nineteenth-century terms, their crimes were not considered sufficiently serious nor their deviant behaviour certifiable. Since my group is a civilian one, the military prisons do not figure in this study.

Eventually my analysis of the recidivist population will be based on my file of ninety-two.[5] On this occasion, however, I propose to illustrate the patterns of incarceration with six of the ninety-two biographies. They offer insights into both the unique personalities and the common patterns of crime and punishment. Andrew Doyle, Eliza Munroe, John Killum, Mary Ford, Thomas Norbury, and the Mary Slattery with whom I began. What they shared in mid-Victorian Halifax, above all, was an unenviable reputation for notoriety.

Andrew Doyle's name appears on the registers of city prison twenty-nine times between 1863 and 1874.[6] Like most male recidivists of the day, over half of his committals were for drunkenness and drinking-related offences. He conforms to the norm for criminal behaviour in Halifax and other cities in that he began his life of crime at an early age, in this case, seventeen. His first term in jail was in July 1863 when he was committed for drunkenness and using abusive and threatening language towards his father, Matthew. Doyle's relationship with his father and other kinfolk provides the key to his jail career because without his family he might not have gone to prison nearly so often. At least twelve of his first twenty-nine terms in city prison resulted from family violence in which Doyle was the assaulter and members of the family his prosecutors. From his father, he next turned to his brother, whose butcher stall windows he broke in 1864 and for which he languished in jail for another thirty days. Over the next ten years and beyond he continued to assault or threaten his principal relations: not only his father and brother, but his mother, sister, sister-in-law, and brother-in-law. Usually given in charge by his father and always convicted, Doyle was at first given short sentences and bound over to keep the peace. In 1867 the magistrate resorted to the one catch-all sentence available under the law, that of vagrancy, which enabled the court to imprison him for twelve months. On this occasion Doyle proclaimed that he did not care if he got ten years for which the magistrate cited him for contempt of court. Since it was the practice in the city for a considerable part of most jail sentences to be remitted, Doyle's first year for vagrancy was a five-month one and it did nothing to alter the pattern either of his drunken violence or his punishment. If he was not bashing the authority figure represented by his father, he was taking on the city policemen. Tired of trouncing his vulnerable female relations, he turned in 1883 to a six-year-old girl whom he criminally assaulted. While this offence resulted in a trial in the Supreme Court, with the Society for Prevention of Cruelty (SPC) prosecuting, the sentence he received of one year in the county jail was not particularly novel for him. But it was combined with the infliction of twenty lashes with a cat-o'-nine-tails, thought to be only the second time in the new nation's judicial history that the lash had been used on a civilian prisoner.

Contemporaries might have wished that the lash had been applied by his shoemaker father twenty years earlier. Yet Andrew was legally an adult by the time he served his first sentence. It was too late for family punishment of a corporal nature. The resort of Doyle's family to the courts was an important feature of family discipline in the mid-nineteenth century. The court co-operated with the family to seek a definitive solution. The way of resolving the problem both for Doyle's family and the city was thought to be banishment. Encouraging the offender to leave the city was frequently tried in the case of incorrigibles. In Doyle's case, like that of the other recidivists, it was unsuccessful. In common with other male jailbirds in the port city, he had some experience as a sailor which removed him from the city at least temporarily. In April 1870, for instance, we find him deserting from the coastal steamer *City of Halifax* and spending three days in the county jail until his vessel sailed. He does not appear in the records again until November, which seems to suggest that he did indeed go to sea. In 1872, however, his family, harassed afresh, made a concerted attempt to evict him from the city. Released from jail in April, after having served only a few days of a ninety-day sentence for disorderly conduct, on condition of leaving the city, his father made arrangements for his departure and paid for his passage. On 1 May Doyle prevaricated. He expressed his opposition to the scheme by assaulting his sister-in-law and creating a disturbance in his father's house. When his father told the magistrate about this intransigence, Doyle said "he refused to go because the papers had reported that he was being transported, and he would not go under such circumstance, and moreover, that he was not as bad as the papers represented him to be." Unimpressed, the mayor sentenced him to a year's imprisonment as a vagrant, to which sentencing Doyle, ever mindful of his dignity, responded, "All right, I'll serve the year out, and then I can walk the streets as free and independent as you can."[7]

Since it is unlikely that his family was conspiring against Doyle — certainly he never charged any of them with assaulting him — we are probably dealing with a seriously flawed personality, further aggravated by alcoholism. But what a personality: Irish blarney, loquacious charm, deviousness, and arrogance — all these traits emerge from the record. He commanded enough respect from Halifax street people for them to rescue him from the police in 1869 after he assaulted his brother. In November 1870 he sufficiently ingratiated himself with a Major Kidd, a former United States army officer, who considered him such "a jolly good fellow" that he invited him to Brown's restaurant in Hollis Street and, in the course of the meal, Doyle repaid his hospitality by allegedly picking $60 from the major's pocket. A reporter from the *Acadian Recorder* who knew his record well showed no sympathy for Doyle after his famous lashing in the county jail execution yard in October 1883:

> Doyle [he pronounced] is an arrant humbug. To hear him talk before the Police Court, one would think him to be not a fallen individual, but a fallen saint. He is most plausible with his vows of reformation, and has great power of bathos and glibness. . . . He was probably only imposturing yesterday when affecting to be suffering from the blows — in fact is reported to have said so; and the whipping has resulted in nothing practical.[8]

In the meantime by the mid-seventies, Doyle's health had begun to deteriorate under the ravages of his dissolute life. In 1876 he was treated in hospital for primary syphilis. In 1879 and 1880 his alcoholism took him to the medical ward of the hospital. By 1881 his delirium tremens had reached a critical stage: he could not eat or sleep, he suffered violent pains in his head and had well marked tremors. He was described in his medical history as "a worthless idle fellow. And though of good family and apparently well educated," in a state of intoxication all the time. His normal condition over the previous fifteen years was summed up in one word: "tight." The week he spent in hospital in October 1881 gives us some idea of what his family usually had to contend with. Admitted on 25 October, he was described as a "bummer" whose delirium tremens was so bad that he was locked up. Shortly thereafter he used this eloquence on the surgeon who obligingly freed him. Once liberated he escaped from the hospital through a kitchen window, attired only in his shirt and drawers. The next morning he was returned to the hospital, still in shirt and drawers, but now complete with beaver hat. On 31 October he again talked his way out of confinement into a hospital ward where he contended himself this time with wheedling enough brandy from a fellow patient to get drunk and turbulent. Locked up again, he kept up a horrible row all that night and in the morning expressed his displeasure by relieving himself all over the floor. The casebook concludes with the comment: "He seems to be more a subject for Mount Hope than for this institution."[9]

But to Mount Hope Insane Asylum he appears not to have gone. After prison terms in 1883 and 1884, he spent his time in the poorhouse and avoided a supreme court trial for larceny by dying there in January 1889, shortly after his last visit to the hospital, where he was treated for hemorrhaging from the lungs. Like many of his contemporary jailbirds, he fulfilled the prophecy of a city missionary who in one of his annual reports coined the motto: "Raised in Rockhead. Died in the Poorhouse."[10]

The nature of Doyle's pathological aggressiveness is beyond the scope of this paper. To some extent his problems, including his alcoholism, may have been exacerbated by physical problems. In 1875 a newspaper reported that while in city prison, he got hold of an axe and chopped off the four fingers of his right hand. While the report proved to be wrong, it did reveal that Doyle had lost all the fingers of his left hand in a saw-mill accident some years earlier.[11] Hence his inability to secure and retain work may have been the result of physical as well as behavioural reasons. Usually described as a labourer in the detailed registers of the late 1870s and early 1880s, he was also recorded as a tinsmith, a pauper, a peddler, a butcher, and as having "no trade." We know he worked both as a sawyer and a sailor. We must therefore allow that this physical disability may have adversely affected his quest for a livelihood as much as his drinking affected his mind and made him wish, in 1875, "for a knife to cut his throat." A suicidal nature, whatever its motivation, was a common feature of mid-nineteenth century recidivism.[12]

Eliza Munroe (Munro, Monrow)'s biography is much shorter than Doyle's because her life was considerably shorter.[13] Unlike his jail career, hers pertains mostly to the period before 1864. Imprisoned for the first time in 1858 at the age of fifteen, Eliza spent the bulk of her life between 1860 and 1867 either locked away or lying in the street. The jail records reads like this: 1860, five months on three convictions; 1861, four months on two convictions; 1862, nine months on five convictions; 1863, six months on four convictions, the last of which kept her in jail into 1864 when her confinement totalled nine months on the basis of four additional convictions. In 1865 she spent half the year in jail for four convictions, the last of which, combined with four further convictions the next year, gave her nine months in jail in 1866. She was released for the last time on 17 January 1867. Thirteen of her convictions were for vagrancy, the charge used to deal with her drunkenness and her prostitution as well as with her homelessness. As a result of a dissolute, hopeless life, she became an inmate of the poorhouse for six and a half months from 1864 to 1865 and returned there for two and a half months in 1866. She was incarcerated, then, for nothing more serious than vagrancy, for forty-seven and one-half of the final eighty-four months of her life. One of the months in the city prison was secured at her own request, self-sentencing being a frequent characteristic of recidivist life. Known as an "old offender," she differed from many of the street walkers in that she usually worked without female companions. Often she was found with her male customers in street, barn, stable, or yard. Six weeks after her final release from jail, Munroe died naked, plying her trade underneath a drunken soldier on 1 March 1867 in a backyard in Albemarle Street. The soldier was allowed to escape, and the coroner's inquest failed to cite assault as a cause of death. Instead it was ascribed to "the effect of alcohol and a depraved life." As she was "constantly intox-icated and one of the worst prostitutes on the hill." What more was needed by way of explanation?[14] Poor Eliza had been given little chance to escape from her desperate life. Her jail sentences were never longer than three months, and the most she spent out of harm's way was six months in the poorhouse. She died too soon to encounter the stipendiary magistrate who replaced the mayor and alderman in the police court in 1867. Perhaps the more vigorous sentences associated with his delivery of summary justice might have protected this helpless person.

Her helplessness derived not only from her status as a woman trying to support herself in a largely pre-industrial military town but also from physical handicaps. For one thing, she was black. While black persons were somewhat overrepresented among both the jail population in general and the recidivists in particular, they were vastly overrepresented among the convicted prostitutes. Blacks constituted 3 percent of the recorded civilian population in the 1860s and 1870s; whereas 40 percent of incarcerated prostitutes were black. If the meanest form of prostitution is seen as the bottom of the inadequate range of jobs available to women, then prostitution on the street in racially conscious Victorian Halifax afforded one of the few kinds of work open to black women. Like black men, they had to seek their employment in the dirty areas shunned or inadequately filled by poor whites.[15] The other handicap Munroe suffered was lameness. She had apparently lost the heel of one foot and toes of the other, perhaps through the frostbite that frequently afflicted the poor in the cruel climate of northern North America. Certainly she worked out of doors in all seasons. Whatever the cause of the amputations, the affliction probably disqualified her for both domestic service and marriage as possible escapes from her plight as an alley prostitute.[16]

The other black I have included in my case histories is a man named John Killum (Kellum, Killam).[17] Killum's long jail career stretched from the late 1850s to the turn of the twentieth century. He differed from Munroe and Doyle in one important respect: He came from a family of repeat petty offenders. Although his convictions were the earliest and most frequent, other members of his immediate family, including the women, went to jail on their own account or joined forces with him from time to time, especially his father Charles and his brothers Charles and Henry. It was not unknown for the whole family to be arraigned in court for creating a disturbance in their dwelling. While the idea of family crime might conjure up the picture of a professional criminal class, it more accurately reflects the victimization which a stable and independent but exposed minority unit experienced over time. People in marginal, self-employed occupations like the Killums — they were whitewashers — were not subject to the discipline of a master or manager. When they overstepped the bounds of propriety and deference, they were reminded of the limits placed on lower-class independence and initiative by the police, the magistrate, and the jailor. Accordingly, Killum's record of convictions is extremely broad and varied. Between 1864 and 1873 it includes petty larceny (the archetypal watch and chain robbery, for example), gambling, drunkenness, disorderly conduct, common assault, assaulting the police, throwing stones, soliciting charity under false pretences, and vagrancy. The conviction for obtaining money under false pretences reveals that the illiterate Killum had somehow contrived to draw up a petition in which he and his accomplice, John Willis, solicited aid from benevolent citizens, allegedly to bury Killum's lately departed mother. Brought before the presiding alderman in the police court, Killum was described as "a notorious character," and given ninety days at hard labour, while his chum was dismissed and told to keep better company.[18] The jail register indicates that, despite his notoriety, Killum was released by the mayor twelve days later.

Usually Killum went to jail for periods of twenty to ninety days (with one twelve-month conviction) between two and four times a year. Sometimes he pleaded not guilty. In October 1872, for example, he was tried for stealing several bottles of liquor from a dealer named Patrick Meagher. Killum's friends provided him with an alibi. Unfortunately, he had acted in concert with Richard Hobin, a sometime resident of Rockhead over the previous five years, who had just up and died. When the police claimed that on his death-bed Hobin had named Killum as the thief and that several bottles of Meagher's booze had been found in Killum's possession, the alibi was blown. As Killum left the dock to go to Rockhead for forty days, he protested his innocence and declared that "when he got out of prison he would sue Meagher for his character."[19]

By the late 1870s, though only in his thirties, Killum's ability to survive in the hostile environment waned, and he began to seek out the prison as a refuge. Sometimes he was awarded short sentences at his own request. He also became belligerent. In the early 1880s the magistrate court records indicate that members of the Killum family were charging John with assault, but his discharges from court were more frequent than his committals to prison. The 1880s and 1890s sometimes found him in court charged in conjunction with his son, as he and his own father had been charged in the 1860s. He also brought his own prosecutions in the police court, charging a woman with assaulting him in 1899, for example. Having spent considerable stretches of his youth in jail, he began in the 1880s to go also to the poorhouse. In 1884, at the age of forty, he visited that institution for the destitute, aged, and helpless seven times. By the turn of the century he seems to have been a semi-permanent resident. When in 1903 the governor of the city prison referred to the solid worth and unrealized potential of many of the well-known prisoners, he included John Killum, by then known to be failing in health. Prison governor Murray described Killum as "one of the most widely known characters in Halifax. Everybody gave John a bad reputation, but," said the governor, "he is one of the most trustworthy men that has ever been at the prison. He never will attempt to escape and has frequently been given charge of one of the teams. He was a good worker, an artist with the white wash brush."[20] Since the governor's comments referred to the way in which lack of opportunity produced and perpetuated criminal behaviour, Killum's career indicates the despair and uncertainty that became the lot of illiterate people living on the margin of society in a progressive age. The one opportunity certainly available to them was to work at Rockhead and die in the poorhouse.

Mary Ford is another jailbird whose family connections were vital to her career.[21] She was not only born into crime, she married into it. She was a young girl when she first went to jail in 1864 — allegedly sixteen, possibly as young as twelve. Her jail career stretches from 1864 to 1883. She died in 1885. Her life outside the prison appears to have been one long drunken debauch, characterized by family violence and family crime. While her record of incarceration surpasses that of her brother, Cornelius (Curly) Ford, it does not quite match up to that of her husband, James Prendergast (Pendergast).

Altogether Mary Ford went to city prison twenty-five times between 1864 and 1873. The first year of her jail career includes four sojourns in Rockhead and one in the county jail. Four of the five court cases involved other members of her family. Her first conviction in June for being drunk and disorderly was with her mother, Honora (Nora) Ford, and the aforementioned Mary Slattery. Nora Ford had been imprisoned several times since 1860, on one occasion for ill-treating her child, possibly Mary.[22] Mary Ford's second conviction in July involved drunkenness with Margaret Ford, her sister or sister-in-law. They were imprisoned under vagrancy legislation. The third conviction in November was for keeping a disorderly house with her father, Michael Ford, who, like Nora, was familiar with Rockhead. The fourth court appearance in mid-December, for which she was held in county jail, did not result in a conviction. She appeared in the dock with her mother, Nora, and her sisters, Ellen and Johanna, charged with keeping a common bawdy and disorderly house in Albemarle Street. Her mother went to prison, sister Ellen was discharged, and Mary and Johanna were sent to the poorhouse. Poorhouse notwithstanding, a couple of days later Mary was found drunk and sent to Rockhead for ninety days as a common vagrant. By the time she next appeared in police court in July 1865, she was described as "young in years but old in crime."[23] By now she had extricated herself, at least temporarily, from her family and was working as an independent prostitute in the brothel district. John O'Brien, a tavern keeper of doubtful respectability in Barrack Street, gave her in charge on this occasion for assaulting himself and his wife, Catherine. Unwilling to languish in Rockhead for ninety days, Mary tried to take her revenge on the O'Briens by charging them with keeping a brothel. Her evidence tells us something about her working life. Claiming to be eighteen, Mary testified that she frequented the O'Briens' establishment where she used rooms for her liaisons with sailors. For the room she paid Catherine O'Brien bed money: 2s.9d. on one occasion, 5s. on another. Her resort to the court to settle her score with the O'Briens proved to be unsuccessful. They were acquitted, and she continued on her drunken road to ruin. In June 1869, her unhappy state led to a suicide attempt in the verminous police cells below the courtroom where she was being held overnight for arraignment on one of her frequent drunkenness violations.[24] The magistrate took pity on her to the extent that he allowed her to choose between banishment from the city and imprisonment. She could leave town immediately or go to jail for twelve months. Both her suicide attempt and banishment are further illustrations of common patterns in the careers of recidivists.

By the early 1870s other forms of violence had become a feature of Mary Ford's life. In 1872, a year in which she went to jail five times, she also charged two men with assault on different occasions. One was her father, Michael, the other was her n'er-do-well husband, James Prendergast, whom she married that very year. In May her father claimed that her injuries had been sustained by falling down the stairs, and Mary failed to carry through with the prosecution.[25] There were witnesses to the other assault in August.

James Prendergast, described as usual as "a notorious rough," celebrated one of his frequent releases from prison by quarrelling with Mary in an Albemarle Street tavern, during which confrontation he stabbed her twice in the head with a knife. The law scarcely noticed such plebeian family violence at this period, sentencing Prendergast to a mere forty days in prison.[26] In 1874 Mary was subjected to more physical abuse and stabbing for which she gave James in charge in August and had the satisfaction of seeing him receive and actually serve a ninety-day sentence. Between her own terms and during James' terms in jail and absences from the city, either as an escaped convict or a sailor, Mary continued to engage in prostitution to support herself. In 1875, while the escaped convict-husband was out of town, Mary encountered a brutal client in a house in North Street who beat her on the head with a poker and left her badly cut and bleeding in the street to be rescued by the police.[27] In 1880 she was thought to be a fit object for reformation in a house for fallen women but expressed her gratitude by escaping and securing admission once more to Rockhead. Undaunted by the experience of middle-class rescue efforts, one of her last periods of incarceration was for being an inmate of a house of ill fame in 1883. In the meantime she continued to be battered by James. Recorded assaults occurred in 1878, 1879, 1881, and 1882. Even her father and brother began to intercede on her behalf, resulting in their own violent confrontations with James. When her father took her to court in 1881 for breaking his furniture, Mary was described as "a scarred, ugly looking caricature of what she was ten years ago."

In 1884, after her jail career had come to an end, Mary graduated to the poorhouse. In July of the following year, five months after the SPC prosecuted James for his last known assault on her, Mary was considered a fit object for that more modern institution, the hospital. Described as a domestic servant, married and thirty-three years of age, she entered hospital in July in severe pain with frequent vaginal bleeding. The physicians looked in vain for evidence of venereal disease. Her childlessness, her intemperance, her recidivism, and her destitution were not, however, in doubt. Discharged in late August, she returned a month later after "a prolonged debauch" which ended in paralysis. Entered in the record this time as "a rather stout fat woman," a hard drinker like her brothers and sisters, with irregular habits, and the wife of "a notorious 'Rockhead bird,'" Mary died on 18 October 1885 and was given a Catholic burial in Holy Cross Cemetery.[28] Mary left her brother Cornelius, and her husband, James, to carry on the family traditions of drunkenness, violence, and frequent incarceration.

Thomas Norbury represents the rough-and-tumble, frequently illicit world of the marginal tavern keeper in disreputable Barrack Street.[29] Most of his contemporary publicans avoided jail by paying their fines. Norbury was not always so lucky at his appearances before the court between 1868 and 1888. His ultimate fate is unknown and his origins are somewhat obscure, but we do know that, unlike the other five who figure here, he was not a native of the region. An Englishman, he ended up in criminal Halifax by a route familiar to many lumpen citizens of the garrison town in the nineteenth century: He was an ex-soldier. Sergeant Norbury's army career ended when he met Mrs.

Eliza Kane (Cain) with whom he set up house. She purchased his discharge from the army and he obliged her by buying from Mr. Kane "all the right, title, and interest in the latter's wife for $6."[30] This informal variety of divorce may have been in conformity with tradition, but it did not in this instance produce marital bliss or prevent confrontation with the legal husband. In February 1868 Kane successfully turned against Norbury and charged him with assault and keeping a disorderly house. Thereafter Norbury was frequently in court. In April 1868 Norbury and Eliza Kane were discharged after two separate charges of stealing customers' property in their tavern, a resort apparently for soldiers and gold prospectors. When he then lost a charge against keeping a disorderly house, Norbury served fifteen days of his ninety-day sentence before Eliza came to the rescue. He rewarded her in May by assaulting her, but she decided to drop the prosecution. Instead she hired Hugh Griffiths as a barman and bodyguard, much to Norbury's displeasure. Norbury, with whom Eliza Kane lived in "adulterous intercourse," as she put it, threatened the new barman who countered by taking him to court.[31] As a result both Norbury and Eliza Kane were fined $20, as much for their illegitimate relationship as for the assault on Griffiths. Norbury alone went to jail, again, we assume, until Eliza decided to pay his fine. A month later Norbury and a female servant were convicted of stealing $5 from Benjamin Bailey during a Sunday morning drinking and card-playing session in the Norbury establishment. Norbury appears not to have gone to jail, but the next charge against him, for selling liquor without a licence, which resulted in a fully served jail term of twenty days, was on information given by the same Benjamin Bailey whom he had recently robbed.

Two of Norbury's court appearances in 1868 and 1869 centred on his own prosecution of men who had threatened to stab him. He himself was next convicted in February 1869 when he and Eliza went to jail for larceny. He served his ninety-day sentence, while she secured an early release on payment of her fine. For the next three years he stayed out of jail and was still living in the same household as Eliza when the dominion census was taken in 1871. When he returned to Rockhead in 1872, he did so as a vagrant. Following four terms in jail for assaults and selling liquor without a licence in 1873, he again joined forces with Eliza in April 1874 to sell liquor illegally. Andrew Doyle was one of the witnesses in the case who claimed that he had obtained rum in Thomas' and Eliza's house on a Sunday. Norbury went to jail, and Eliza was discharged. Later that year, Norbury's deteriorating status was reflected in the first of several incarcerations for drunkenness and drinking-related offences.

By 1876 Norbury had parted from Eliza and entered into a more conventional relationship, which he soon proceeded to destroy by refusing to support his wife and babies. First in 1880 and again in 1883, after the family had been forced to return to the city from their refuge with Mrs. Norbury's mother in the country, Norbury refused to provide for them. Found destitute in the streets on the second occasion, the wife and children were rescued by the SPC which intervened with Norbury on their behalf, but to no avail. Consequently, the society took Norbury to court for neglecting his family for which he received ninety days at hard labour. When a local commentator remarked that Norbury would enjoy "a warm bed, comfortable food, medical and religious attendance, easy work for the winter in Rockhead, while his family was left destitute," the secretary of the society explained that the family had been admitted to the poorhouse. The proceeds of Norbury's stone-breaking labour in jail would pay for their support.[32] In the spring the family left the poorhouse just as Norbury arrived. His legacy to his children was chronic neglect, a charge brought in 1888 against him and his wife once again by the vigilant SPC. This time his children were taken away; the son was sent to the Protestant Industrial School and the daughter to the St. Paul's Home for Girls. Given his domestic failures, one wonders if Norbury rued the day Eliza wooed him and bought him from the army, where he was at least assured of room and board without ignominy.

Finally, let me tell you about the career of Mary Slattery.[33] As I mentioned earlier she went to jail thirty-one times between 1862 and 1873. She was murdered in April 1874, one day after her release from prison, where she had served eight months of a twelve-month sentence for vagrancy. The daughter of Mary Barry, another of the ninety-two recidivists, one of Slattery's earliest discharges in court occurred after she had been given in charge by her husband for drunkenness. About two-thirds of her convictions were for lewd conduct and vagrancy, the most common ways of locking away a prostitute. Like Eliza Munroe, Slattery was frequently incapable of taking care of herself. Homelessness led her to the police station for protection and it encouraged the magistrates to find alternatives to imprisonment for a woman whom they clearly considered incorrigible. They tried giving her second chances. In late September 1864, for example, she was arraigned in police court charged with wandering in the streets. She was excused on the understanding that she would be severely dealt with if found in the streets again. The next day, predictably, she was picked up and sent to jail for six months for vagrancy. The fact that she served only one week of this sentence is further evidence of the aldermanic disposition to give petty offenders the opportunity to reform themselves. Mary eluded the police for about three months this time. Then the *Morning Chronicle* reported her being found drunk in the street for the "fiftieth" time in mid-December and sent up for ninety days.[34] Somewhere between the court and the jail she managed to escape this sentence, but when she was discovered lying drunk in Albemarle Street on 29 December, she was put behind bars for three months, someone remembering that she had not served her previous sentence.

Slattery not only failed to make good her many second chances, but she also did not respond positively to the couple of attempts to banish her from the city. In January 1866 she was discharged after an arraignment for drunkenness on condition that she should go to Dartmouth across the harbour and stay there. The next month she was arrested with five other women in a house of ill repute. She received six months; some of the others, considered more hardened, got twelve. The net term of imprisonment ended with her being sent by steamer to Antigonish where she apparently had friends or relations. That was in November 1866. Yet she was back in jail again in early February

1867 to begin a three-month sentence for lewd conduct. In February 1871, having served four months of a twelve-month sentence, Slattery was again sent to Antigonish, this time with her jailbird mother Mary Barry. Although she stayed off the jail register until July 1872, police court minutes indicate that her sojourn in Antigonish could not have been much longer than two months, since she was in court for plying her trade in the Grand Battery guard room in May in company with Catherine Shea, a fellow jailbird. While Shea went to prison, Slattery was sent to the poorhouse. She was enumerated as one of the inmates in the census of 1871.

Like many recidivists, Mary Slattery's familiarity with the police court encouraged her to take her own grievances to court. In 1868 she charged Eliza Green with stealing her ring and money. Given her criminal record, the court did not lean over backwards to give her the benefit of the doubt in circumstances where the evidence conflicted. The case was dismissed. In 1870, however, she was assaulted and her assailant went to jail. This was not apparently his first conviction for this offence. Unfortunately for Mary, it was not her last experience of violent men.

Mary and another of her recidivist friends, Ann Mahoney, came out of jail on 31 March 1874 in company with John Keily, a somewhat less frequent resident of Rockhead whose record included convictions for assault on women in the street, one of which was described as "grievous."[35] The three ex-jailbirds made their way to Annie Foster's house in City Street where Slattery took a room and, according to her own deathbed deposition, Keily "attempted to take liberties with me when I resisted and he set me on fire with a lighted match by putting it to my skirt. I rushed into the room of Annie Foster when some soldiers of the 87th [regiment] who were there put it out. I believe said John Keily set on fire my clothes with intent to do me some serious bodily injury."[36] Mary died of burns and shock in the hospital on 2 April 1874, age twenty-nine. Her mother commemorated with a drunken binge.

While the evidence in the case emphasized the part played by alcohol, the incident was also the result of a quarrel concerning a picture frame which contained a likeness of Mary's child. Keily's violent reaction to the discussion of the mother-child relationship was triggered by his recollection of his own relationship with his mother. He was reported to have concluded the fatal argument by telling Mary, "I have burned my mother and I'll burn you, you bloody whore."[37] Subsequently Keily's indictment for murder was reduced to manslaughter, and he received a token sentence of four years in the provincial penitentiary. Halifax's public prostitutes, mothers, or not, were clearly not considered important enough to murder. No wonder imprisonment seemed benign compared to the harsh world around them. For Mary Slattery, a mid-Victorian prostitute, jail provided one of the few opportunities to live in safety and comfort.

Not very pretty stories these, but personal histories typical of the recidivists of the period. On the basis of this analysis of a particular criminal population, we can identify a number of areas which require further investigation by social historians of crime and criminal justice. First, we need to give more critical attention to what was described in the nineteenth century as minor or petty crime. Otherwise we are in danger of letting the past impose its values on us. So-called minor offenders, who frequented the summary courts and municipal jails, were often a serious threat to themselves and to others, especially the people with whom they were most familiar. Quite apart from the cases of assault, many of their convictions for drunkenness as well as for vagrancy arose out of incidents involving violence. Since much of the crime that was categorized as minor concerned violence not only within the lower classes but also against women and girls, legal historians need to analyze more closely the extent to which the courts tolerated "common" assaults, especially, though not exclusively within the context of the family. Many female victims were in almost continual danger. It is inconceivable to imagine more serious male aggression than that represented in the brutality meted out to Eliza Munroe, Mary Ford, and Mary Slattery. Yet their assailants were seldom indicted.[38]

Second, it seems to me we have no choice but to challenge some aspects of the recent revisionist portrayal of the criminal population put forward by social historians who use statistical evidence as their major source.[39] In their haste to dispose of the nineteenth-century concept of a criminal class, they overlook the ways in which repeat offenders did differ from the society around them. They miss the frailties of mind and body, especially alcoholism, that disadvantaged the Andrew Doyles and the inescapable handicaps that complicated the lives of the Eliza Munroes and made them more prone to excess and deviance. They are also inclined to apply concepts to the criminal population which are entirely unsuitable for recidivists. For example, offenders are assigned marketplace occupations when their only real occupation was a jail career interrupted by the occasional job or bout of unemployment. If Mary Ford is counted as a domestic servant, which the evidence allows, what does that tell us about a woman who was clearly a low-class prostitute? If Andrew Doyle is described as a butcher, what do we make of the five other types of known jobs that he performed over the years? If we describe Thomas Norbury as a tavern keeper, we admit him to a much higher occupational status than he in fact had, situated as he was at the very bottom of the illicit world of booze and entertainment. Later in life he claimed to be a cooper.

Nor do the numbers and categorization which mesmerize the quantifiers explain the interrelationships between members of the criminal population. Prostitutes, for example, interacted with brothel keepers and other prostitutes. In the case of the Fords it was mother with daughters. Mary Slattery followed her mother's example, had dealings with the Fords and, over the years, was also associated at work, in the street and in jail with at least seven other well known prostitutes who figure in my jailbird population of ninety-two. Outside city prison repeat offenders lived cheek by jowl in a very limited area of the city with other people on the margin of respectable society, some of whom had the luck, intelligence, and financial resources to avoid incarceration. Irrespective of their jail records, these people co-operated with each other, fought with each other, robbed each other, went to court together, informed on each other, rescued each other from the police — in other words, performed a whole range of distinctly interdependent activities. If they were not a criminal class, then they were most certainly a distinct social class.

The jailbirds and many of their associates shared characteristics assigned by contemporaries to the disreputable poor. When they were not in jail for their sins, they were in the poorhouse, particularly as premature old age descended upon them. They drifted aimlessly from one to the other but their problems appear to have been more pathological than economic. Time and again they cried out for help by smashing windows or attempting suicide, cries which society of the mid-nineteenth century was incapable of interpreting. And yet we are told they were the victims of industrial capitalism. If quantification produces such facile explanations, it is time to re-introduce qualitative standards to the study of social history.

The final point I want to emphasize relates to the well-documented use of the nineteenth-century jail as a place of refuge.[40] People used the jails to protect themselves against the harsh realities of life: winter, unemployment, enemies, and aggressors. Their frequent self-sentencing must, however, be examined in conjunction with the increasing resort by the poor to prosecutions in the police court. As we have seen, people as incorrigible as Ford, Norbury, Killum, and Slattery appeared as plaintiffs in the very institution in which they were usually being tried and found guilty. In addition, the Doyles and Killums looked to the court as a means of disciplining family members. If the nineteenth-century system of justice revealed social control, it was familial, not state-sponsored. The state was drawn into the disputes of the lower classes very reluctantly. Its agent, the magistrate, found that the criminal side of his work came to involve more and more family and neighbourhood quarrels, many of which resulted in magisterial arbitrations rather than formal prosecutions. The people's jail of the mid-nineteenth century was therefore a natural outgrowth of what we might call the people's court. The police court was also a popular institution in another sense. The "great unwashed," as the Halifax press described them, crowded into the court daily to cheer or boo, discreetly of course, the sentences handed down to their street associates.[41] We must investigate how long the lowest courts and the major jails remained popular institutions. To argue that during the mid-century people controlled them in any real sense would be going too far. But access to formal justice and institutional protections was undergoing a transformation. Further, views from the bottom up, stripped of romanticism and respectful of human individuality, should provide fruitful insights for the analysis of nineteenth-century crime and criminal justice.

Notes

1. For institutional studies, see D. Rothman, *The Discovery of the Asylum* (Boston, 1971); M. Foucault, *Discipline and Punish* (New York, 1978); M. Ignatieff, *A Just Measure of Pain* (New York, 1978). For statistical studies, see E. Monkkonen, *The Dangerous Class: Crime and Poverty in Columbus, Ohio, 1860–1885* (Cambridge, Mass., 1975); M. Katz, M. Doucet, and M. Stern, *The Social Organization of Early Industrial Capitalism* (Cambridge, Mass., 1982), chap. 6. For social crime, see G. Rudé, "Protest and Punishment in Nineteenth Century Britain," *Albion* 5 (1973): 1–23. On the need for and difficulty of providing criminal biographies in the nineteenth century, see V. Gatrell, "The Decline of Theft and Violence in Victorian and Edwardian England," in *Crime and the Law: The Social History of Crime in*

Western Europe since 1500, edited by V. Gatrell, B. Lenman, and G. Parker (London, 1980), 335; H. Graff, "Crime and Punishment in the Nineteenth Century: A New Look at the Criminal," *Journal of Interdisciplinary History* 7 (1977): 477–91; Monkkonen, *The Dangerous Class*, 74.

2. On the need for the history of the individual, see the review "Ourselves, As We See Us" by T. Zeldin in the *Times Literary Supplement*, 31 Dec. 1982. The most recent study of the relationship between crime and industrial capitalism is chapter 6 of Katz et al., *The Social Organization of Early Industrial Capitalism.*

3. *Morning Chronicle* (Halifax), 28 Sept. 1868.

4. Given the problem of identification by name, it is impossible to verify the accuracy of these figures, particularly the certainty that the 4749 committals were accounted for by 1840 different individuals. Nonetheless, the figures are roughly accurate, and the overwhelming predominance of the recidivists among those committed is not in doubt.

5. This is attempted in "Petty Offenders in Mid-Victorian Halifax," a paper presented to the Canadian Historical Association, Vancouver, June 1983.

6. For information on Doyle, see: City Prison Records, Registry of Inmates, Public Archives of Nova Scotia (hereinafter PANS), RG 35–102, Series 18B, vols. 2 and 3, and Registry of Visitors, RG 35–102, Series 18H, vol. 1; County Jail Registers, PANS, RG 34–312, Series J, vols. 12 and 18; Police Court Minutes, PANS, RG 42, Series D. vols. 18–24; Stipendiary Court Records, PANS, RG 42, Series D, vols. 18–24; Stipendiary Court Records, PANS, RG 42, Series D, vols. 28–31; Poor House Records, PANS, RG 35–102, Series 33A, vols. 6 and 8b; Victoria General Hospital Papers, PANS, RG 25, Series B, Sect. 2, vol. 45, Sect. 3, vol. 4, and Sect. 4, vol. 18; *Census 1881*, Halifax, Ward 4, Subdivision 2; *Morning Chronicle*, 11 and 15 Oct. 1864; 9 Mar. 1865; 26 Feb., 19 Apr., 7 Sept., and 13 Oct. 1866; 16 Sept. 1867; 13 Mar. 1869; 23 and 26 Nov. 1870; 22 Feb., 9 and 30 Mar., and 2 May 1872; 3 Apr. 1873; 25 May 1874; 1 Feb., 3 and 4 Aug. 1875; 1 and 6 July, 2, 4, 17, 18, and 19 Oct., 3, 4, and 21 Nov. 1882; 6 Jan., 2, 3, 19 Oct. and 14 Dec. 1883; 2 May and 8 Oct. 1888; *Acadian Recorder* (Halifax), 2 Oct. 1883.

7. *Morning Chronicle*, 2 May 1872.

8. *Morning Chronicle*, 13 Mar. 1869, 23 and 26 Nov. 1870; *Acadian Recorder*, 2 Oct. 1883.

9. Medical Case Book, Victoria General Hospital, PANS, RG 25, Series B, Sect. 3, vol. 4, pp. 423, 452, and 469.

10. North End City Mission, *Report 1896–1897*, 25, Special Collections Pamphlet Box F5, Killam Library, Dalhousie University.

11. *Morning Chronicle*, 1 Feb. and 3 Aug. 1875.

12. *Morning Chronicle*, 1 Feb. 1875.

13. For information on Munroe, see: City Prison Records, Registry of Inmates, PANS, RG 35–102, Series 18B, vol. 2; Police Court Minutes, PANS, RG 42, Series D, vols. 10, 12, and 14–21; Poor House Records, PANS, RG 35–102, Series 33A, vols. 1a and 2; Coroner's Inquests, PANS, RG 41, Series C, vol. 41; *Morning Chronicle*, 3 Aug., 1 and 30 Nov. 1865; 5 and 16 June, 24 Sept. and 22 Oct. 1866; 4 Mar. 1867.

14. Coroner's Inquest, 1 Mar. 1867, PANS, RG 41, Series C, vol. 41.

15. J. Fingard, "The 'Social Evil' in Halifax in the Mid-Nineteenth Century," a lecture presented to the History Society, University of New Brunswick, Fredericton, Nov. 1977.

16. See descriptive entry in the jail register for 6 June 1860, PANS, RG 35–102, Series 18B, vol. 2.

17. For information on Killum, see: City Prison Records, Registry of Inmates, PANS, RG 35–102, Series 18B, vols. 2 and 3, and Registry of Visitors, RG 35–102, Series 18H, vol. 1; County Jail Registers, PANS, RG 34–312, Series J, vols. 12 and 14; Police Court Minutes, PANS, RG 42, Series D, vols. 19–24; Stipendiary Court Records, PANS, RG 42, Series D, vols. 28–31; Poor House Records, PANS, RG 35–102, Series 33A, vols. 6 and 18; *Census 1881*, Halifax, Ward 1, Subdivision 2; *Morning Chronicle*, 28 June 1864; 10 Apr. 1865; 5 Oct. 1866; 3 July and 3 Aug. 1868; 6 Dec. 1869; 21 Dec. 1870; 20 Mar., 22 Apr, 18 June, and 15 Oct. 1872; 7 Nov. 1874; 9 Aug. and 21 Oct. 1875; 6 May, 31 Oct., 30 Nov. 1878; 19 Mar. and 25 Aug. 1883; 22 July 1885; *Acadian Recorder*, 8 Apr. 1867; *Evening Mail* (Halifax), 7 Aug. and 27 Nov. 1895; and 21 Apr. 1903; *Evening Echo* (Halifax), 26 May 1899.

18. *Acadian Recorder*, 8 Apr. 1867.

19. *Morning Chronicle*, 15 Oct. 1872.

20. *Evening Mail*, 21 Apr. 1903.

21. For information on Mary Ford, see: City Prison Records, Registry of Inmates, PANS, RG 35–102, Series 18B, vols. 2 and 3; County Jail Registers, PANS, RG 34–312, Series J, vol. 12; Police Court Minutes, PANS, RG 42, Series D, vols. 19–24; Stipendiary Court Records, PANS, RG 42, Series D, vol. 28; Poor House Records, PANS, RG 35–102, Series 33A, vol. 6; Victoria General Hospital Papers, PANS, RG 25, Series B, Sect. 2, vol. 45, Sect. 3, vol. 5, and Sect. 9, vol. 3; PANS, Halifax Marriage Registers, 1872, p. 249, No. 606; *Census 1881*, Halifax, Ward 4, Subdivision 1; PANS, Holy Cross Cemetery Records; *Morning Chronicle*, 21 June, 28 July, 22 Oct., and 24 Dec. 1864; 24 July 1865; 19 Jan. 1866; 4 Sept. 1868; 4 June 1869; 16 May, and 28 and 29 Aug. 1872; 7 and 8 Aug. 1874; 9 Sept. and 11 Dec. 1875; 29 and 30 Nov. 1876; 7 and 11 Dec. 1878; 29 Apr. and 5 Aug. 1879; 6 Sept. 1881; 2 Feb. 1885. For proof of her illiteracy, see Coroner's Inquests, PANS, RG 41, Series C, vol. 54 (Johanna Power).

22. See entry in the jail register for 5 Sept. 1861, PANS, RG 35–102, Series 18B, vol. 2.

23. *Morning Chronicle*, 24 July 1865.

24. *Morning Chronicle*, 4 June 1869.

25. *Morning Chronicle*, 16 May 1872.

26. *Morning Chronicle*, 28 and 29 Aug. 1872.

27. *Morning Chronicle*, 9 Sept. and 11 Dec. 1875.

28. Surgical Case Book, Victoria General Hospital, PANS, RG 25, Series B, Sect. 9, vol. 3, p. 109; Medical Case Book, Victoria General Hospital, PANS, RG 25, Series B, Sect. 3, vol. 5, p. 281.

29. For information on Thomas Norbury, see General Order No. 1, 12 Sept. 1867, PANS, MG 12, Series HQ, No. 64; City Prison Records, Registry of Inmates, PANS, RG 35–102, Series 18B, vols. 2 and 3, and Registry of Visitors, RG 35–102, Series 18H, vol. 1; County Jail Registers, PANS, RG 34–312, Series J., vols. 12, 14, and 18; Police Court Minutes, PANS, RG 42, Series D, vols. 22–24; Stipendiary Magistrate Court Papers, RG 42, Series D, vols. 28; Poor House Records, PANS, RG 35–102, Series 33A, vols. 5 and 6; Victoria General Hospital Papers, PANS, RG 25, Series B, Sect. 2, vol. 45 and Sect. 4, vol. 18; PANS, Halifax Marriage Registers, 1876, p. 152, No. 221; *Census 1871*, Halifax, Ward 3, Division 2; *Census 1881*, Halifax, Ward, 4, Subdivision 2; *Morning Chronicle*, 3 and 9 Apr., 6 May 1868; 27 Feb., 1 Mar., and 23 Aug. 1869; 20 Apr., 6 and 27 May 1870; 19 Apr. and 5 Nov. 1873; 27 Jan. 1883; 9 Jan. 1888; *Acadian Recorder*, 3 July 1868; *Morning Herald* (Halifax), 26 and 30 Jan. 1883.

30. *Acadian Recorder*, 3 July 1868.

31. Police Court Minutes, 2 July 1868, PANS, RG 42, Series D, vol. 23.

32. *Morning Herald*, 16 and 30 Jan. 1883.

33. For information on Mary Slattery, see: City Prison Records, Registry of Inmates, PANS, RG 35–102, Series 18B, vols. 2 and 3, and Registry of Visitors, RG 35–102, Series 18H, vol. 1; County Jail Registers, PANS, RG 34–212, Series J, vol, 14; Police Court Minutes, PANS, RG 42, Series D, vols. 19–23; Poor House Records, RG 35–102; Series 33A, vols. 1a and 2; *Census 1871*, Halifax, Ward 1, Division 1; Victoria General Hospital Papers, PANS, RG 25, Series B, Section 4, vol. 18; Coroner's Inquests, PANS, RG 41, Series C, vol. 50; Convict Register, Halifax Penitentiary, 1873–1880, PANS, miscellaneous microfilm 'P'; *Morning Chronicle*, 21 June, 22 Sept., and 15 and 29 Dec. 1864; 31 Oct. and 2 Dec. 1865; 5 Jan. and 20 Feb. 1866; 28 Sept. 1868; 19 Jan. 1870; 3 July 1873; 2, 4, and 30 Apr., 4 and 19 May 1874; *Acadian Recorder*, 5 May 1874.

34. *Morning Chronicle*, 15 Dec. 1864.

35. *Morning Chronicle*, 5 July 1864; Police Court Minutes, 14 Dec. 1868, PANS, RG 42, Series D, vol. 23.

36. Deposition of Mary Slattery, 1 Apr. 1874, Coroner's Inquests, PANS, RG 41, Series C, vol. 50.

37. Deposition of Annie Foster, 2 Apr. 1874, Coroner's Inquests, PANS, RG 41, Series C, vol. 50.

38. See N. Tomes, "A 'Torrent of Abuse': Crimes of Violence between Working-Class Men and Women in London, 1840–1875," *Journal of Social History* 11 (1978): 329–45.

39. For example, see Monkkonen, *The Dangerous Class*; Katz, Doucet, and Stern, *The Social Organization of Early Industrial Capitalism*.

40. Graff, "Crime and Punishment in the Nineteenth Century," 483; Katz, Doucet, and Stern, *Social Organization*, 237.

41. *Morning Chronicle*, 22 Aug. 1868. See David Phillips, *Crime and Authority in Victorian England: The Black Country 1835–1860* (London, 1977), 127–29; Gatrell, "The Decline of Theft and Violence in Victorian and Edwardian England," 244; Katz, Doucet, and Stern, *Social Organization*, 228–29.

SECTION 2

THE POLICE AND ENFORCEMENT

We are so accustomed to the presence of police that it is difficult to imagine government, particularly at the local level, functioning without them. Yet the police are a sufficiently recent innovation in the history of western civilization that a country as young as Canada could produce important developments in the evolution of this institution. There were no models for many aspects of the North-West Mounted Police beyond the basic structure that came from the Royal Irish Constabulary. Once established, the NWMP evolved largely on its own. Its success in producing creative solutions to the problems of policing vast areas of western and northern Canada led to widespread copying of its structure and methods in other parts of the British Empire in the early twentieth century.

It would be tempting to suggest that it was Canada's French-English background that created the conditions for innovation in the area of police. France in the eighteenth century was one of the earliest European countries to experiment with police. The French legal system proved much more hospitable to the organization of a permanent body of armed men at the disposal of the state than did the English common law. The French Revolution at the end of the century only improved the efficiency and accelerated the development of the police. Under Napoleon, the notorious Joseph Fouché made the French police universally feared and laid the foundations of the modern police state.

In England no such developments occurred, in part at least because the English reacted against the French example. The English were conditioned by their legal tradition and their political history to distrust the centralized and efficient use of power. Even the determined efforts of the Fielding brothers to popularize the notion of an effective police in mid-eighteenth-century London, although attracting much favourable public attention, failed to make any headway in Parliament. London, Europe's largest city in the eighteenth century, had only part-time, unpaid constables. This led to bizarre expedients on the part of those who suffered from the lack of enforcement, such as the private prosecution societies of the period whose members contributed to a fund for the purpose of taking thieves to court.

It was not until 1829, after a decade of skilful political manoeuvring, that Robert Peel was able to get Parliament to pass the Metropolitan Police Act. This piece of legislation was extremely influential, serving as a model for urban police forces throughout the English-speaking world. By placing control in the hands of an appointed commission, the police were effectively removed from the realm of local politics. Fears about the police as a threat to individual liberties subsided with the success of the new system. Outside London, however, the situation remained largely as before.

For a country like Canada in the nineteenth century there was not much in the British experience that was useful as far as police were concerned. Canada had no large cities like London. The largest urban centre, Montreal, had its own unique set of problems, which were quite unlike those of any English city. Montreal was a city divided between English and French, Protestant and Catholic. The tensions of race and religion frequently erupted into violence, as the article by Elinor Kyte Senior shows. Civic authorities in Montreal relied on the large British garrison in times of trouble. But the troops were an exceedingly blunt instrument, as several bloody incidents demonstrated.

Soldiers by the nature of their organization were outsiders, not part of the community. This was true even in later years when British troops were replaced by Canadian militia. As outsiders, injected into the situation only in times of crisis, the military could not perform several of the most useful functions of the police. They could not provide the authorities with intelligence from the street. They could not act as a constant deterrent by their presence throughout the city. They could not investigate acts of crime and violence after they happened. Only when citizens gathered in large groups to break the peace could the soldiers be deployed. The advantages of police seem so overwhelming that it is difficult to understand why they were not introduced for so long.

In the case of Montreal the traditional concerns about civil liberties and cost were reinforced by the political situation. French and English mistrusted each other so much that neither group could tolerate the idea of a police force controlled by their opponents. This suggests that policing requires some minimum degree of consensus to be successful. The article by Patricia E. Roy on Vancouver's 1887 riot supports such a conclusion. The appointment of special constables by the British Columbia government to replace the Vancouver police created widespread public resentment. The move came perilously close to creating more violence than it prevented.

The North-West Mounted Police understood very clearly the relationship between public acceptance and success as a law enforcement agency. As Carl Betke points out, they cultivated their relationship with the public in a variety of ways that had little to do with crime. Regular patrols that visted farms and ranches rarely produced any evidence of or complaints about crime. Yet the police went to considerable lengths to maintain them because they engendered trust. The police were also heavily involved in welfare activities in the late nineteenth and early twentieth century. They acted as public health officers and did a great deal of essential work in preventing the spread of communicable disease among livestock. Betke's article suggests that we need to know more about what police actually do as opposed to what their formal job descriptions say.

With the creation of police forces in the nineteenth century it was inevitable that governments would attempt to test the limits of what could be done with this new institution. The various attempts to introduce prohibition of alcohol in Canada and the United States constituted one such test. The efforts of the police to cope with perceived threats to the political order by militant labour were another. The question in the latter case was the precise location of the boundaries between criminal activity, legitimate political action, and economic protest. The police have usually been seen, especially by Marxist historians, as more or less willing tools of the capitalists in labour disputes. No doubt they were in many times and places but, as S.W. Horall demonstrates, the situation could be more complex. In the case of the Winnipeg General Strike of 1919, perhaps the most serious incident in Canadian labour history, the Mounted Police attempted to play a mediating role. This was consistent with their previous experience in such disputes. Since the 1890s the police had recognized the ambiguities and moral dilemmas inherent in strike situations. They strove to remain neutral and to prevent employers from manipulating the law for their own ends, not always successfully.

THE INFLUENCE OF THE BRITISH GARRISON ON THE DEVELOPMENT OF THE MONTREAL POLICE, 1832 to 1853†

ELINOR KYTE SENIOR

The frequent use of the imperial troops as an aid to the civil power in Montreal in the years from 1832 to 1853 led British military authorities to take the initiative in encouraging the development of rural and municipal police systems in the 1840s. This encouragement extended all the way from proposing police ordinances to providing officers and men to train a mounted constabulary in 1849 as well as supplying arms, ammunition, and saddlery to equip the police. In addition, former military officers and soldiers made up the top personnel of both rural and municipal police.

In the Montreal of the 1830s and 1840s no group in the city was more anxious than the British military command to see the creation of an efficient police ready and able to maintain internal order and thus relieve the garrison of this unpopular duty. And civil authorities agreed. But the steadily deteriorating civil situation of the late 1830s and the continued unsettled state of Montreal after the rebellions of 1837 and 1838 put the burden for the maintenance of public order largely on the garrison.

From as early as May of 1832 when imperial troops were engaged in the first fatal encounter between soldiers and townsmen during a Montreal election, military authorities became increasingly apprehensive about requests for troops as an aid to the civil power. In this 1832 incident, soldiers of the 15th East Yorkshire Regiment had been properly summoned by a magistrate. Their action followed precise military procedure for the use of troops at riots. They were commanded by commissioned officers, and were in the charge of a magistrate. They fired only after the Riot Act had been read by the magistrate who then ordered the commanding officer to quell the riot. Firing was accomplished with perfect discipline, the soldiers firing man by man, and ceasing to fire instantly upon order.[1] As three French Canadians were killed by the soldiers' fire, the leaders of the radical "Patriote Party" of Louis-Joseph Papineau succeeded in persuading the coroner to arrest the colonel and captain who had commanded the East Yorkshires at the time of the incident. These officers were kept in jail for over a week before their release on bail was secured, and they were committed to stand trial on charges of murder.

As was usual in such cases the charges were eventually dropped, but the lessons learned made the military command reappraise procedures for assisting the civil power in quelling disturbances, if such aid could so easily involve officers and soldiers in serious criminal charges including arrest, imprisonment, harassment, and heavy financial outlay for legal counsel. For the civil authorities, the encounter was a portent of their inability to cope with increasing

† *Military Affairs* 43, no. 2 (Apr. 1979): 63–68.

civil disorders. They had made extensive preparations to ensure order at the polls. Thereafter, they tended to press for military aid as soon as there was any sign of serious trouble, while the military regarded with increasing reluctance such requests insisting that, during elections, returning officers as well as magistrates sign the requisitions for military aid.

Over the next five years, from 1832 to 1837, Montreal experienced a disintegration of civil order that included the suspension of both municipal and provincial government. By April of 1938, the twenty-nine-man police force ceased to exist when funds ran out.[2] Thus, as tension erupted into public disorder, the city of just under 40 000 was devoid of any police establishment whatever. It is not surprising, then, that the military command, apprehensive at this breakdown of police arrangements and the increase in local disturbances, should issue new general orders with respect to the use of troops as an aid to civil power. These specified that no request for military aid would be complied with unless accompanied by a written requisition from the magistrate, stating that the ordinary civil force was insufficient to maintain peace. Troops were to be commanded by a commissioned officer, and as soon as the service was over, the officer was to send a detailed report of the service to the military secretary.[3]

By the autumn of 1837, as both rural and urban tension increased, the Commander of the Forces, Sir John Colborne, urged the Governor General, Lord Gosford, to lose no time "in establishing an armed police. . . . Montreal is the grand point to attend to . . . the leaders of the disturbances, if arrested, can only be taken by the armed mounted Police,"[4] Lord Gosford's decision to send Attorney-General Charles Richard Ogden to Montreal in early November with secret instructions to "enquire into the present state of the police force with a view to place it on an efficient footing"[5] was a result of pressure from the military command. Ogden's immediate solution to the lack of municipal police was to use the volunteer Royal Montreal Cavalry as mounted police and to organize a secret service to gather intelligence on the plans and activities of disaffected elements. Funds for the secret service and the makeshift mounted police were provided from the military chest.[6] The ease with which these financial arrangements were made was an indication of the immediate rapport which Ogden established with Sir John Colborne, a harmonious relationship that continued throughout the rebellion period.

Out of these extemporized measures agreed to by Colborne and Ogden on the eve of open rebellion in the Montreal district grew the nucleus of the police systems of the 1840s. From the ranks of the Royal Montreal Cavalry came several of the post-rebellion chiefs of police — Captain Charles Oakes Ermatinger and Thomas McGrath — while regular officers who were posted on "particular service" in the countryside were merged into the new rural police. Still others such as Lieutenant Colonel William Ermatinger, Captain Charles Wetherall, and Color Sergeant Thomas Wily formed the top personnel of the Montreal police for most of the 1840s.

The man to whom the secret service was entrusted in the fall of 1837 was Pierre Edouard Leclère. Leclère and Ogden drew on the services of the "Doric

Club," a physical force wing made up of the younger sons of loyalist Montrealers. The Dorics claimed that they were instrumental in "putting down the malcontents in the city before the outbreak . . . and rendered services of a secret nature to the Government . . . in the apprehension of the seditious and suspected, in obtaining information of their proceedings for Sir John Colborne, conveyed though the Attorney-General."[7] This close co-operation between civilians and military during the rebellion created a bond of sympathy and common interest which was to last throughout the forties, giving the military command in Montreal influence in areas such as the police which normally would have been beyond the reach of an imperial military force.

As soon as the first rebellion was suppressed, the military command was anxious to relieve the regulars of duties of a purely police nature. It was doubly anxious to ease troops out of their role of auxiliary to the civil power in suppressing internal disturbances. With Ogden's help. Sir John Colborne, who, by March of 1838 held both military and civil command, proposed a police ordinance which suggested that "in towns with large military establishments, a small force of police would be sufficient for the summer months . . . . It could be increased without much additional expense in the winter when the price of labour is low and crime is on the increase." It was assumed that the presence of a large garrison in Montreal would be a deterrent to serious disturbances. However, the Special Council governing the province refused to pass the ordinance, considering it "too arbitrary for this free country."[8]

Colborne then awaited the arrival of the new Governor, Lord Durham, before pressing another police ordinance on the Special Council. Durham agreed with Colborne on the need for efficient police. He was scarcely in the city a month when he implemented a police ordinance, largely the work of Colborne and Ogden, that created an imposing force of 102 men and four mounted patrols,[9] with Pierre Leclère as superintendent. Supplementing the city police was a new rural police under the bilingual loyalist militia officer, Lieutenant-Colonel Augustus Gugy. Gugy worked with fourteen stipendiary magistrates, all drawn from loyalist ranks, many of them regular army officers. In towns that had been centers of disaffection, such as St. Denis, St. Remi and Napierville, the rural magistrates were aided by a number of paid, armed constables who were lodged in police barracks, much on the style of the Royal Irish Constabulary. The main job of the rural police was to report on the state of the country, keep an eye on strangers, and observe any fresh grievances or suspicious behaviour of disaffected elements.[10]

The paid rural magistrates were Colborne's answer to the situation he had found the previous year when he complained that the local government was ignorant of the character of the rural population and of the extensive preparations made for revolt. In forming the new police, Colborne drew on the experience of Colonel George Cathcart of the First King's Dragoon Guards. Cathcart's recommendations on a rural police were drawn partly from his experience with a system set up in Jamaica after the slave revolt there,[11] an example of how developing institutions in one colony could be influenced by those of another by way of ubiquitous British regular officers.

This elaborate city and rural police establishment, organized largely at the instigation of the military and partly manned by British officers, had scarcely begun to operate when the second insurrection broke out in early November of 1838, catching the military somewhat off guard, which suggests that the rural intelligence system had not begun to function effectively. This well-organized conspiracy faced a well-prepared government and a greatly enlarged British garrison that promptly suppressed the uprising.

With the lessening of border tension and the return of disaffected elements to conventional politics by 1840, the new Governor, Charles Poulett Thomson, took a close look at the police establishment and expressed his displeasure at its size and cost. A three-man commission, including two British officers, was appointed to see "if the force was too large, the rate of pay more than sufficient for the duty performed and [whether] a great reduction may not be effected."[12] The result was retrenchment in both city and rural police.

Lieutenant Colonel Gugy was removed as inspecting magistrate of rural police, his force reduced, and its budget cut from £24 867 to £14 452.[13] One of the rural magistrates to survive the reduction was Captain Charles Wetherall, who was to become one of the key men in the Montreal police, serving as magistrate in the city itself and in 1843 taking on the difficult post of magistrate at Beauharnois after canal labour riots there. Perfectly at ease in French and English, Wetherall organized a police force for service on public works, and it was his success in raising this force that made Lord Elgin turn to him in 1849 to raise a mounted constabulary.

In Montreal itself the stringent economy measure of the new governor in 1840 reduced the police from an establishment of 120 to half that number while the budget was reduced from £10 046 to £3 504. In the shuffle of personnel, the man who had headed the secret service and organized the post-rebellion police, Pierre Edouard Leclère, was edged out. A year later the man who was to become the most important man in the Montreal police establishment for the next fourteen years — Lieutenant Colonel William Ermatinger — became police commissioner.

Ermatinger was the son of a Montreal fur trader and an Ojibway Indian princess. He began his military career in the Royal Montreal Cavalry, and, after studying law, served with the British Legion in Spain during the Carlist wars. Ermatinger, whose wife was a member of the prominent French-Canadian loyalist family, the Duchesnays, thus linked imperial and colonial forces and families in a way perhaps unique.

Working with Ermatinger and Wetherall for most of the forties was another British regular soldier, Thomas Wily, the color sergeant of the 83rd Regiment. Son of an indigent British officer, Wily had worked his way through the ranks, and when he arrived in Quebec City with his regiment, being proficient in French, he soon found himself promoted as adjutant of a provincial regiment. Upon the disbanding of this unit, he was made Montreal's chief of police in 1844 at the height of an election crisis in which a French Canadian was bayonetted to death by troops.

The British garrison in Montreal in the forties and early fifties numbered about 1 500 men, among whom were senior staff officers whose service dated back to the rebellion era. These were officers who knew the city, its temper, and its people intimately, none more so than the deputy quarter-master general, Colonel Sir Charles Gore. He became Commandant of Canada East in 1846 and, as such, was the man to whom the city magistrates had to apply for military aid. The other major link between the civil and military hierarchies in times of trouble was the town major, Ensign Colin Macdonald, a peninsular veteran of the 79th Cameron Highlanders. A forerunner of the modern public relations man, Macdonald's job was to keep things running as smoothly as possible between soldiers and townsmen, an unenviable task when troops confronted rioters.

Such a task faced the garrison in the spring of 1844 when soldiers were called out during election disorders. Under the direction of city magistrates, the troops formed lines to and from the polls so that voters could approach without fear, but in spite of this, fighting broke out. Reserve troops of the 89th Regiment were ordered to advance into the crowd. All went well until they neared a spot where a fight was in progress. One of the combatants, Julien Champeau, grabbed the bayonets of two soldiers, was stabbed by a third and died three days later.

The military command, harassed again by the arrest on a charge of murder of the young officer who had commanded the troops, determined never to allow troops to get near enough to hostile crowds for rioters to close in on them. Secret instructions were issued that "special care must be taken not to [allow] the Troops to come into contact with the people — they must be held at arms' length. The Bayonet is very good when opposed to a regular Enemy, but it would be sacrificing much to attempt to use it when Hundreds are opposed to Thousands." These instructions emphasized that "Officers must at all times recollect that the two most important advantages possessed by Regular Troops over a Mob are Discipline and Fire."[14] The new policy put additional strain on the military command. Requests for troops in aid of civil power in the future meant that the infantry would resort to fire in the face of hostile action from the crowd, for the practice of firing blanks as a warning was also discarded.

Mindful of the tension and bitterness surrounding the spring by-election of 1844, military authorities took the initiative in preparing for trouble as the general elections to the assembly approached in the autumn. A troop of the Provincial Cavalry was brought in from the border, and a strong body of regulars with a piece of field artillery was posted in Custom House Square. Overnight troops were stationed at various polls. So securely guarded was the city that the defeated reform candidate complained that Montreal "Bore all the appearance of being a state of siege," and charged that the troops acted "under magistrates known to be active and violent partisans of the opposing candidates."[15] The charges were neither unusual nor unexpected.

In their operations, the military had been aided by Police Magistrate Captain Charles Wetherall and by the newly appointed Chief of Police, Thomas Wily. But the police were stringently limited in what they could do. Precise instructions had been worked out early in the decade for the conduct of police during elections. Police magistrates were warned to "prohibit all interference on the part of Police Magistrates or Police Force, direct or indirect . . . at elections, . . . and every precaution should be employed on your part to remove even the appearance of interference." Police were to be permitted at the Poll only if an "emergency should arise and such requisition be made by the Returning Office . . . the men to be provided with no weapons save constable staves."[16]

These instructions had been devised to avoid the charge of party bias, just as military authorities tried to restrict the use of troops to avoid similar charges. Yet the restrictions on the police during elections put the burden of keeping order on the military, and it is not surprising that officers complained that during riots they did not observe "a dozen policemen on duty," and remarked on the "utter inefficiency of the few policemen who were visible . . . the force alluded to rather kept out of sight until the people dispersed, and the troops were withdrawn."[17] Discretion was, perhaps, the better part of valour, as the police were neither trained nor equipped to deal with riots of a grave nature.

In 1849 serious attempts were made by the provincial government under the reform administration of Louis-Hippolyte La Fontaine to organize a riot control police, armed and equipped from Ordnance stores of the garrison and trained by British officers. This attempt to create a mounted constabulary arose out of the civil turmoil connected with the passage of the Rebellion Losses Act, a measure to provide compensation to those who had suffered during the rebellion era. As La Fontaine and his provincial secretary, James Leslie, had little rapport with the senior army command in Montreal and both shared a distaste to "calling out troops,"[18] they at first tried to maintain order with local forces. At their disposal was a police establishment of seventy appointed and paid for by the city, and two police officials, paid by the provincial government. In an emergency they could swear in civilians as special constables.

When disorder erupted into riots that ended with the burning of the parliament building itself, La Fontaine urged the mayor and Police Superintendent William Ermatinger to "enrol a sufficient number of citizens to act as Police Officers." When this proved unsuccessful, La Fontaine undertook to have the adjutant-general of militia, Lieutenant-Colonel Étienne Pascale Taché, who had led a minor uprising in 1837, organize "a special police . . . to be furnished . . . with arms," an unusual step in a city which had never had an armed police. Taché set about mobilizing reliable members of the Montreal militia as special constables, and his force was supplemented by other Montrealers friendly to the reform government.

News of the arming of the special constables so infuriated the disaffected elements in the city that they marched to Bonsecours Market where Colonel Taché was "drilling them by lamplight . . . [and] so full of martial ardour was he, that it was difficult to persuade him that it was better to house them, armed as they were with cutlass and pistol . . . than to provoke an attack on them by the opposing party, all ready for a fight as they were."[20] Military authorities were far from sanguine that the crowd could be controlled and took the initiative in turning out the garrison. A guard was thrown across Notre Dame street, and Government House was barricaded. At Quebec Gate Barracks, the entire garrison was under arms, ready to move with artillery.

For Police Superintendent William Ermatinger it was a fearful time. "The slightest collision with troops or with the newly-armed [police] force," he wrote, "must have produced the most dreadful results. Masses numbering two or three thousand advanced as far as the Old Court House where they halted and were harangued by some gentlemen [Lieutenant Colonel Gugy of the militia and Mayor General Sir Charles Gore of the regulars] who, after great trouble, dispersed them gradually and by midnight the town quieted down,"[21] La Fontaine, under pressure from both the military who spoke out against "arming one portion of the people against the other,"[22] and from leaders of the opposition party, backed down and disarmed the special police.

The militia and leaders of the opposition party now faced grave responsibilities. The latter had given La Fontaine their word that the crowd would be controlled if the new police were disarmed. The former took no chances. The 71st Highland Light Infantry was ordered to the city along with the Provincial Cavalry. Privately, the Commander of the Forces alerted the governor of Nova Scotia to hold the 97th Regiment ready to move to Montreal if need be.

It was evident to the governor, Lord Elgin, and his first minister, La Fontaine, that if order was to be maintained without the constant use of troops, there must be a local force to take the place of the dismissed gendarmerie. At the suggestion of the Police Magistrate Captain Charles Wetherall, La Fontaine decided to raise a fifty-man armed mounted force on the model of the Royal Irish Constabulary, and to supplement it by a foot police of one hundred men, all to be paid for by the provincial government. Captain Wetherall was appointed to take charge of the security of the city and faced the task of organizing the new force. The anxiety of the military authorities to ensure that this new force was really in the hands of a person they trusted was evident in a letter to Wetherall from the military secretary. He wrote, "Warned by the two apparently abortive attempts by the authorities of Montreal recently to form a foot Police, the Commander of the Forces would have assuredly paused upon the issue of arms and equipment . . . [had he not trusted] to your well known Judgement and discretion that you will not suffer them to be delivered to any persons whom you do not feel confident or duly qualified to be entrusted with them."[23]

The training and arming of the new mounted constabulary was not without difficulties. Wetherall insisted that the force not be provided with arms until such time "as they are sufficiently well instructed in the use of them and are able to act so efficiently in a body as to resist any attempt by the mob to disarm them." He urged that the force be allowed to occupy the military barracks and stables at La Prairie, outside the city, and "that an Officer and a few N.C.O.'s of Cavalry be permitted to instruct the force in the usual cavalry exercises and stable duties."[24]

From the start, the new provincial police force seemed ill-starred. Its creation provoked the resignation of Montreal's chief of police, Thomas Wily, who "would not allow myself to be made use of in forming a purely partisan force . . . to be amalgamated with the City Police — a force which it has ever been my pride to make strictly impartial."[25] The conservative press lampooned the force unmercifully, and by mid-June, when it was announced that the foot portion of the new police would be disbanded, the Montreal *Gazette* demanded, "Let them dismiss the horse portion too ... the men were fools to enlist in such a service."[26] Despite the attacks, the mounted constabulary continued its training at La Prairie all summer while Montreal was in the throes of almost constant upheaval. Government authorities, including Elgin, wanted to bring the fifty-man force into the city, but Captain Wetherall considered it unwise. The government press, the *Pilot*, berated authorities for not doing so. "Had the Horse Police been in Montreal" when La Fontaine's house was attacked in August, the editor wrote, "they could have been moved promptly to the spot and captured the assailants in the very act."[27]

That government police could have acted more promptly than troops in an emergency civil situation was undoubtedly true. From the time that the police magistrate received La Fontaine's note asking him to be on the alert until troops arrived at La Fontaine's house, three hours elapsed. The police magistrate had alerted the garrison as soon as he received the note, but a request for military aid was not made until the rioters headed towards La Fontaine's house itself.[28] By the time the troops arrived, the crowd had attacked the house with stones and gunfire, and had been repulsed by gunfire from within the darkened house where La Fontaine and several friends had calmly awaited the crowd, rifles in hand and buckshot near by.

In spite of constant vigil by the police magistrates and preparedness on the part of the military, a crowd in motion could confound the best laid plans, and the leader of the Canadian government thus found his most dependable source of protection was personal friends. The delay in getting troops in motion meant that they arrived too late, yet had they been ordered to La Fontaine's house before the crowd moved towards it, likely no attack would have been made, and the magistrates would have been criticized for calling out the troops unnecessarily.

Wetherall was convinced that only martial law could save the city from a fratricidal *émeute*, but unable to persuade Lord Elgin of this, he resigned as police magistrate after he had been assaulted by the crowd. By the end of August of 1849, Elgin's efforts to persuade civil authorities to assume responsibility for the peace of the city bore fruit. Tranquility returned after the city corporation began swearing in "upwards of 200 Gentlemen, many of the highest respectability and of every shade of political opinion" who pledged themselves to maintain public order. With the return of order, the mounted constabulary was moved into barracks in Montreal in November "without any casualty or disturbance."[29] Yet within a year, the force was disbanded, either because of retrenchment in public spending or possibly because it never overcame its image as a partisan force.

During the year that the mounted police was being organized, trained, and disbanded, the regular city police suffered internal disorganization. Demoralized by the resignation of their chief, the police were without a permanent chief for some of the most turbulent months in Montreal's history. The uncertainty about the leadership of the force, combined with bitter newspaper attacks and devastating criticism from regular army officers, debilitated the force. The *Gazette* did not fail to observe that "no Police were present [at the burning of the parliament building] until the work of destruction had irretrievably commenced."[30] The commandant of the garrison complained that a "considerable force of police, say forty, were close at hand [when one of the riots erupted] but not the slightest effort was made by them to maintain order."[31] Whether the police remained inactive because they were unsure of their role when troops intervened in civil disturbances, they had to suffer such criticisms in silence, for the police had yet to acquire press agents.

The year of riots resulted in the election of a new city administration pledged to put an end to riotous proceedings. As provincial elections neared in 1851, the new mayor vigorously undertook measures to avoid disturbances. Three hundred special constables "from among respectable householders" were sworn in to assist a body of two hundred men hired to "act in two divisions with the regular police." The British garrison agreed to have reserves of artillery and other troops under arms if these measures failed to preserve order. Every citizen was exhorted "to consider the Honour of the City in his hands and to aid instantly in putting down disorders."[32]

City authorities took the initiative in arresting "several well-known rioters and driving them off to jail . . . until the election was over." The *Gazette* observed with wonder and approval that "it was a new thing to see a few policemen dash into the crowd, seize the leading bully, tie his hands behind his back if he resisted, pitch him into a sleigh and bear him off to jail in the face of his friends."

The novelty of a general election in Montreal at which citizens could approach the polls without danger of assault or violence led the editor to exclaim. "For the first time . . . in a quarter of a century . . . the authorities were master of the town,"[33] and Montreal's police began to acquire its police agents.

This burst of praise for the police was accompanied by a patronizing rebuke for the military. The *Gazette* commended the city fathers for not leaving the "peace of the city to the chance responsibility of a magistrate with a regiment of soldiers," and reminded readers that "this was the system we insisted on the Mayor adopting during the riots of 1849, but unfortunately at that time, the city authorities were of the *gens d'arme* order who had no idea of preventing or quelling tumult except by the bayonet. The consequence was that the soldiers failed to put down rioting."[34]

This somewhat gratuitous rebuff was forgiven but not forgotten by military leaders in 1853 when Montreal experienced its most tragic encounter between troops and townsmen in riots that broke out when the apostate Roman Catholic priest, Alessandro Gavazzi, lectured on the "errors of Popery" in the largely Roman Catholic city. Trouble was not unexpected. Gavazzi's lecture a few days earlier in Quebec City had ended in riot, and government authorities had warned the Montreal police superintendent to "make every arrangement for the preservation of peace."[35]

A combined police-military operation was prepared. Fifty men of the regular city police were to be posted outside the church where Gavazzi was to lecture.

These were commanded by a new chief of police, Captain Charles Oakes Ermatinger, older brother of the police superintendent. The new chief had had ample experience of Montreal rioters during the thirteen years he had served as captain of the Royal Montreal Cavalry. The city police were supplemented by eighteen men of the Water Police, a force recently organized to protect wharves and shipping and composed largely of discharged soldiers and former Royal Irish Constabulary.[36]

On the very day that Gavazzi was to lecture in Montreal, the garrison was undergoing a change of regiments, the 26th Cameronians arriving from a three-year tour of duty at Gibraltar. It was with some surprise and uneasiness, then, that the commandant received a visit from Police Magistrate Ermatinger and Mayor Charles Wilson with a request that troops be ready to turn out to aid the civil power by 6:30 that evening. To make matters worse, all the senior staff officers, including the commander of the forces, were at the wharf bidding farewell to the headquarters staff of the departing regiment. Yet one hundred men of the 26th Regiment were on the move by 6:30 p.m. and put under cover in a small engine house not far from the church where Gavazzi was lecturing.

In this operation, there was no indecision or hesitation on the part of the combined police force of seventy-eight men to try to control the crowd. For over an hour, as the crowd, estimated at between two and three hundred, tried to gain entrance to the church, the police held them off. It was not until both their chiefs were stunned with stones and the police were caught in an exchange of gunfire between the attacking party and an armed party from within the church, that the police withdrew to reform their ranks.

It was then that Mayor Wilson ran towards the engine house shouting to the military to "turn out the men." As the Cameronians fell in, the commanding officer, on the advice of the mayor, ordered the men to load and prime,[37] an unusual step as the act of loading and priming in front of a riotous crowd was often effective in dispersing it. Commanded by their colonel, a captain, and two lieutenants, the troops moved nearer the church on the orders of the mayor, Here they were divided, one division facing the church, the other facing towards the engine house where the crowd had rallied after being driven from the church.

The soldiers stood back to back, about fifty paces apart, their colonel standing midway between them. The men were at ease, their arms sloped. With the appearance of the troops, the police rallied and quiet prevailed until the congregation began to leave the church. Then stones were hurled and shots fired towards the church, and members of the congregation began to move towards the troops, presumably for protection. Simultaneously a disturbance broke out near the engine house, and a crowd began to rush towards the troops firing shots.

Mayor Wilson, without informing the commanding officer, quickly read the Riot Act, a five-line proclamation that can be read in two minutes. Scarcely had he finished than he heard the words, "Fire! Fire!" To his astonishment, the lower division of troops fired into the crowd.[38] Within a second or two, the upper division began an uneven file firing, even though their officer, Captain Cameron, was standing directly in front of them. Cameron rushed along the division, throwing up the firelocks to stop the fire, bullets flying under his arm and over his head. The firing killed four men and mortally wounded five, while many others were seriously wounded.

The Commander of the Forces, General William Rowan, in his first report of the incident to the Horse Guards, protested that, "It was greatly to be regretted that from insufficient police arrangements, the Queen's Troops have been constantly called upon by the magistrates to aid in putting down tumultuous assemblages. . . . Every precaution has been taken by myself and my predecessors to guard against the actual collision between the troops and . . . inhabitants, so much so, as to have incurred the reproach of unwillingness to resort to extreme measures, even when considered to be necessary."[39]

Rowan's charge of inadequate police arrangements was, of course, true. Yet Montreal civil authorities had been taking their police responsibilities seriously since Wilson had become mayor. Some seventy-eight police were stationed near the church, and military aid was asked for only after the police had been overpowered and gunfire exchanged between the contending parties. City fathers tended to protect the police, asserting that "they acted nobly, but their numbers were insufficient."[40]

Criticism of the troop action by both civil and military authorities and by the press was far more severe. Making every allowance for the fact that the regiment had only arrived at the station from Gibraltar, "a very quiet place where there were no riots," as their commanding officer recalled somewhat wistfully, the firing of the soldiers had been a gross breach of discipline, "a bungling act" as Town Major Macdonald described it. At the inquest, both the military officers and the mayor denied having given an order to fire, though soldiers testified that they distinctly heard the order to fire. The probable explanation came from a witness who claimed the order was shouted by a man in the crowd who stood near her. Captain Cameron testified that even had their colonel given the order to fire to the lower division, "My division would, most decidedly, not have been entitled to take up the firing from them."[41]

The *Gazette* and *Transcript*, both newspapers that had invariably championed the British soldier in the city, lashed out against the troops, and so intense were feeling against the soldicry that men of the 26th Regiment were waylaid and beaten. Demands for a gendarmerie-type police, which presumably would make military intervention during riots unnecessary, were pressed upon the city authorities from several directions. The *Gazette* commented tartly, "if we required an example, one has been furnished which the present generation is not likely to forget, showing how imperfectly troops can be made to perform the duties of the Police."[42] Under the impression of the riot, the police committee of the City Council recommended that the size and pay of the police be increased and that the force be provided with firearms and bayonets. The Council agreed to the increase in size and pay, but ordered that the police by "supplied with fusées or light muskets and bayonets, to be used in cases of great emergency."[43]

In the years from 1832 to 1853, the Montreal police developed under the aegis of the imperial garrison from a defunct force in 1837 to a one hundred-man armed police in 1853. With the rise of the city's population and the declining strength of the garrison, it is not surprising that the troops who kept nearly perfect discipline in 1832 and 1844 were less effective in 1849 and wavered in their discipline during the Gavazzi riot of 1853. Throughout this period, the city fathers showed an understandable reluctance to increase the police budget while they had an alternative source of security close at hand. In this sense, the presence of the garrison may have retarded the development of municipal police. Against this can be placed the high quality of the services which the garrison supplied in the staffing, training and equipping of the Montreal police. The discipline of the garrison set the tone of the force, imposing standards of service and conduct where standards were needed.

Notes

1. Public Archives of Canada (hereafter PAC), MG11, Q202, 1, 105.
2. Jean Turmel, *Police de Montréal* (Montreal 1971), 1:35.
3. PAC, RG8, C317, 123–26.
4. PAC, RG8, C1272, 21.
5. PAC, RG7, G15D, I22.
6. PAC, RG8, C1272, 23, and C1271, 81.
7. PAC, RG8, C803, 24.
8. PAC, MG24, B4, viii, 549, 565.
9. Newton Bosworth, *Hochelaga Depicta* (Montreal 1839), 180–81.
10. PAC, MG24, A40, 8327.
11. Ibid., 8103–8.
12. PAC, MG24, B4, 1x, 924.
13. Canada, *Appendix to Journal*, Legislative Assembly (1841), no. 1, i, app. Z; ibid. (1850), no. 1, A-Z, ix, app. X, 4.
14. Confidential instructions for troops having occasion to act against an insurgent mob in streets, or elsewhere (5 May 1849), in McCord Museum, Montreal; see McCord papers, Queen's Light Dragoons box.
15. *Montreal Gazette*, 30 Oct. 1844.
16. Instructions to Police Magistrates (18 Feb. 1841), in *Appendix to Journal* (1850), no. 1, ix, app. X, 5.
17. PAC, RG8, C317, 95 and C616, 253.
18. *Montreal Evening Pilot*, 27 Apr. 1849.
19. PAC, RG1, E1, 72, 67.
20. Sir James Alexander, *Passages in the Life of a Soldier* (London, 1857), 1: 21.
21. PAC, RG4, B25, i.
22. *Montreal Transcript*, 3 May 1849.
23. PAC, RG8, C1304, 1–12.
24. Ibid., C80, 15.
25. *Gazette*, 8 June 1849.
26. See in particular *Punch in Canada*, Montreal, 30 June 1849, 95–96. See also *Gazette*, 15 June 1849.
27. *Pilot*, 24 Aug. 1849.
28. Ibid.
29. PAC, RG4, B25, i.
30. *Gazette*, 27 Apr. 1849.

31. PAC, RG8, C616, 250–53.
32. *Gazette*, 1 and 3 Dec. 1851.
33. *Gazette*, 10 Dec. 1851.
34. *Gazette*, 15 Dec. 1851.
35. *Transcript*, 20 June 1853.
36. *Evening Pilot*, 17 and 19 Jan. 1859.
37. Captain Cameron's testimony at coroner's inquest, *Transcript*, 21 July 1853.
38. Mayor Wilson's testimony, *Transcript*, 21 June 1853.
39. PAC, RG8, C1282, 163–64.
40. *Gazette*, 11 June 1853.
41. *Transcript*, 29 and 21 June 1853.
42. *Gazette*, 13 June 1853.
43. PAC, RG7, G20, 55, 5909.

Pioneers and Police on the Canadian Prairies, 1885–1914†

CARL BETKE

In the preface to his impressive historical analysis of the North-West Mounted Police, R.C. Macleod marvelled at the "consistent popularity" of the mounted police, "particularly in western Canada,"[1] His book goes on to support the proposition that their popularity was based upon their success at maintaining law and order. Rather than follow the traditional emphasis on stories of spectacular individual heroism in quelling desperate Indians and criminals alike, Macleod has stressed the mounted police capacity for crime prevention in their military style, discipline, and prestige; their regular system of patrols; and their service to minimize active illegal expression of general or individual animosities against vulnerable minorities such as Indians and immigrants. That the incidence of crime was rare is obvious from the lists compiled in annual reports or from patrol reports.[2] Macleod's conclusion, that the peaceful situation was a result of the police presence, cannot altogether satisfactorily be demonstrated because the police were in the North-West Territories before almost all of the settlers, preventing any useful before-and-after contrast.

In any case, settlers did not, in the main, see any police heroics, whether or not their systematic patrols were effective deterrents to crime. It seems a sensible question to ask what the early settlers did see the police doing. There are at least two possible approaches to finding an answer: to study pioneer correspondence, reminiscences, and local histories; and to study the day-to-day reports of policemen in the rural West. A rapid glance through several local histories in search of references to North-West Mounted Policemen confirms the impression that they were for the most part not linked to dramatic criminal chases in community memories. What follows, then, is derived from the second approach, a study of police records for the period of rapid western settlement.

In a nation which reveres its police force, it is particularly important to probe the origins of the police image. At issue might be a conception of social order or the rule of law. If actual exploits did not create the reputation, then the nature of normal, peaceful service cannot be overlooked, dismissed, or reduced in significance. If the major impression the police created was of benevolent assistance in a host of important areas, that has implications for an assessment of the collective national character. Rather than a people riddled with criminal tendencies or overly acquiescent to repressive police authority, Canadians may have been a people particularly susceptible in their pioneer conditions (as were the Indians in their altered circumstances) to the first agents of government welfare. It can hardly be surprising that so mundane an appreciation would be expressed more colourfully in the popular literary imagi-

† Canadian Historical Association, *Historical Papers/Communications historiques* (1980): 9–32.

nation. But for the majority of original prairie settlers, there is striking evidence that the police may have been most noticeable for their visits, their assistance to those who were struggling or who felt alien in a strange, new land, their control of quarantine procedure during periods of disease epidemics, their veterinary contributions, or their usefulness in combatting the menace of prairie fires.

The first factor in the esteem enjoyed by the North-West Mounted Police was their great visibility. This was not so much a function of numbers as of deployment. Indeed, after the excitement of the North-West Rebellion in 1885 temporarily boosted the establishment of the force to one thousand, its size actually declined, even though the Klondike gold rush in the Yukon drained off several hundred to the North for a few years around the turn of the century. The mounted policemen were well known because of their commitment to regular, systematic patrols, summer and winter.

The patrol system of the police appears to have originated in response to escalating horse stealing in Canadian territory by American gangs after 1884.[3] In 1886 the previous custom of sporadic patrols was replaced by a much more rigorous program, not without occasional reaction on the part of ranchers unaccustomed to mounted policemen roaming their lands and grazing police horses on their valuable grass.[4] Commissioner Lawrence Herchmer immediately saw a general value to patrols beyond only the border region, and had them extended throughout the West from the numerous, scattered, small police detachments. That Herchmer's primary objective was to prevent horse stealing and other crime by maintaining an obvious police presence and a fund of knowledge about settlement conditions cannot be doubted. Information on "the state of the country, condition of crops, presence of strangers, travellers met" was to be obtained casually, since, of course, the police had no special right to pry. The concentration on crime prevention was all the more notable in occasional admonitions to secrecy stressing, as one confidential order put it, that some "patrols are to be made at uncertain times, so that those intending to smuggle may not be able to make out plans to get through."[5] Just before the turn of the century, Commissioner Herchmer was fond of describing his "outpost and patrol system" as "the great cause of the absence of crime on our side" of the border, or of crediting it with convincing "foreigners that law and order must be respected in this country."[6]

It is equally clear, however, that patrol instructions included far more than the requirement to watch for "doubtful characters." The legendary Superintendent Sam Steele issued orders with quite a different emphasis at Macleod in 1889:

> You will collect all the information you can about the settlers in the
> vicinity of your Detachment; how many new ones have arrived during the
> past year, how much stock they have and what kind, where they are
> settled, what crops good or bad are generally raised, quantity of hay put
> up, general feelings amongst them as to the fitness of the country for
> settlement, and if any have suggestions to make as to the revising of any of
> the Ordinances for the better Government of the District, their feelings on
> the Prairie Fire law and powers given under it. . . .[7]

Even the "small flying patrols" of a commissioned or non-commissioned officer and two constables, the purpose of which in some cases was to provide a surprise factor in the watch for desperadoes, were often made to isolated ranches and settlements not covered by regular outpost patrols in order to ascertain the same ordinary details of the settlement process.[8] To some extent the continuation of this emphasis was dictated by periodic requests of the Department of the Interior for copies of patrol maps, for crop information to encounter detrimental reports circulating in Britain and the United States on crop prospects in light of the growing season and weather, and for detailed information about numbers of settlers moving into and out of the North-West Territories. The last demand was ongoing, formalized after 1896 by the new Liberal Minister of the Interior, Clifford Sifton, who desired to know the details of sex, age, and location of origin or destination for the migrants.[9]

Whatever the purposes for patrol reports, the usual effect of the procedure was to provide regular visits to settlers which constituted the only alleviation of monotony not just for many pioneers, but also for the policemen themselves. Many patrol reports perfunctorily listed the observations required but, even among those which contain quite full descriptions of the experience, only occasional incidents broke the tedium of the ride. Difficulties for the police to handle were rarely registered; the police normally received "no complaints" and rode on. References to stray horses, stolen cattle, crop and stock conditions, dotted the thousands of patrol reports which were submitted throughout the Territories.[10] A rancher might complain of a homesteader cutting hay on his land; a settler might report his important lumber stolen; the constable might notice poor grain yields and the possibility of future distress at next year's seeding time.[11] These were the limits of most policemen's excitement. Some remembered in their retirement that the frontier farming situation itself promoted very little criminal tendency. "You take when people had come in there and taken up land," reminisced one, "they were too busy to get into trouble." The settlers, pointed out another, "were all in a small way and they were all looking out for their own business — they were just quiet decent people." His detachment "was the easiest place to work you could ever want. . . . You kept riding your district, you were interested in people in it, you were welcome where you went — it wasn't regarded as police surveyals."[12] In the early years the welcome was conditioned by isolation; in later years it was fostered by the fund of police experience which made their advice good on farming conditions, soil, climate, and winter survival.[13]

The lack of incident is aptly illustrated by some senior officers' reprimands about patrol reports which came in "very scant and uninteresting." The assistant commissioner was moved to enjoin his divisional commander at Battleford in 1900 "not to let your detachments go to sleep, and have the reports sent in promptly." One commanding officer, Inspector Begin, responded to another such missive with the comment that "if nothing at all occurs, and there is [sic] no complaints, he [the patrolman] will have no information to give only regarding the weather, condition of cattle, state of trails and river and whether there are any American cattle in the sub-district or not, whether any strangers are passing through. . . ."[14] Not to report much was less serious than not to patrol properly. A commanding officer for a district might notice a paucity of families visited, or a concentration in one favoured direction, or failure to keep up patrolling on Sundays. The occasional complaint from settlers on this last deficiency before the turn of the century would bring a stern response. Superintendent Burton Deane at Macleod, on receiving one of these reports, wanted an immediate investigation by a detachment sergeant. "Send me a complete list of all the settlers in this section, and place against the name of each the date of the last visit paid by a police patrol."[15] Patrols, whether or not significant crime threatened, were not to be neglected, and the settlers evidently derived comfort from them.

After 1900, with the population multiplying rapidly, new conditions reduced the possibility of complete coverage. The development of towns apparently distracted policemen from proper attention to more isolated areas, causing civilian complaints which came to Commissioner A. Bowen Perry's attention. It was no part of the "mounted constabulary's" role to protect small towns, ordered Perry in 1901; his was not a "municipal body" but one intended to provide geographically broad protection. The retort by Superintendent Morris at Prince Albert in 1902, that unprecedented expansion of settlement made regular visits to all settlers an impossibility, did not prevent Perry from continuing to insist on patrol efficiency. Despite orders to officers inspecting detachments to detail patrol activities meticulously, Assistant Commissioner McIlree still observed in the Prince Albert district in 1891 a tendency of the detachment men to "hang around the town too much." Patrol slips, which had been regularly signed by settlers along the routes of patrols in 1890s, were reinstated.[16]

The point is not so much the growing failure just before World War I to maintain the process for every last settler, as it is the insistence on making the effort, so that some proportion of the pioneers undoubtedly did continue to see mounted policemen from time to time. This was so even though the settlement frontier shifted northward. Extended northern patrols taking several weeks each were initiated, and a new division was created at Athabasca Landing. Here distances were greater and even local patrols were matters of at least several days' journey, but the substance of patrol reports was much the same as for those of the earlier settlements.[17] The pattern which had been well established on the prairies by the early 1890s would make the North the most notable scene of this particular part of the mounted police legend after the First World War.

Rural patrols in a period of immigration encountered many ethnic minorities among the settlers, some quite alien to the Canadian experience. That most of them were treated well had little to do with any individual propensities among policemen for tolerance. It seems reasonable to suppose that most constables and officers would have expected newcomers to adopt the English-Canadian way of life according to its basic British traditions.[18] The requirement of tolerance was dictated by first the federal Department of Agriculture and, after 1892, the Department of the Interior, in their capacities as colonizers of the Canadian prairie west. During both the Conservative and Liberal periods of government before and after 1896, the singular official demand was for immigrants who would enhance western agricultural production: "capitalists, farmers with capital, farm-labourers, and domestic servants," as Sir Charles Tupper put it in 1893. This was a business-like economic venture, but one inseparable from the prevailing nationalist dream. The Deputy Minister of the Interior, A.M. Burgess, quoted Tupper again in 1896 on the priority which should be given to the proper filling of the "vacant lands" of Manitoba and the North-West Territories.[19]

The well-known emphasis of the new Liberal Minister of the Interior after 1896, Clifford Sifton, and of his Manitoba colleague, Deputy Minister James A. Smart, hardly needs comment. The department's policy, stated Smart at the turn of the century, "was based upon the assumption that it is highly desirable that at the earliest possible moment all the fertile lands of the West should be located, and the country enriched by the general production which will be sure to follow the settlement of a hardy class of settlers." Commerce, other industries, and the general citizen would benefit from "the consequent lightening of our national burdens, such as they are, by the presence of a great number of shoulders to carry them." Smart even transformed the oft-repeated term, "desirable class" of immigrants, into "desirable agriculturalists." This concentration on competent agriculturalists would sanction the acceptance of many East-European immigrants thought by many Canadians to be culturally marginal or unsuitable, and it would condition the response of the police as well.[22]

The combination of cultural preference with official economic objectives brought British, American, Scandinavian, and German settlers the best general acceptance (and the least ethnic reference) in police reports. They came with sufficient capital and farming knowledge (especially the Americans), were in most cases accounted thrifty and hard-working (notably the Germans and Scandinavians), and therefore brought themselves almost immediately to reasonably prosperous circumstances. In addition, they shared acceptable cultural values, emphasizing cleanliness and neatness, following similar Protestant religious traditions (for the most part) and, in striving for the comfortable life, accepting the virtue of self-sufficiency. Canadian laws were not very alien to the British and Americans; Germans and Scandinavians respected the authorities. When mounted police officers contrasted alleged American disorder with Canadian law and order, the object seems to have been more to enhance the prestige of the Canadian police force than to complain about lawless American immigrants.[21]

Alien habits, however, could also be overridden by evidence of economic success. There are several striking examples of this phenomenon. The Mennonites established self-contained communities which sometimes seemed exclusive and vaguely threatening. One Sergeant St. George regretted in 1890 the "immense power" of Mennonite elders: ". . .so long as they remain so these people will be what they are today — foreigners in language, customs and sentiments" among whom "the rising generation is growing up as ignorant of the language of the Dominion as those who came some eighteen years ago from Russia." But their prosperity, contentedness, and peacefulness overcame these criticisms. A new Mennonite settlement at Duck Lake in 1891 immediately showed promise of the traditional farming ability and good behaviour; the police therefore discounted critical reports about them by neighbours as a mere reaction to their isolationism.[22]

When Mormons began arriving in southern Alberta in the late 1880s, the moral risk of their presence was at the outset discounted by the Interior Department in favour of their experience with irrigation which would, it was thought, provide an example to far more settlers beyond themselves.[23] Though they quickly established themselves as major food provisioners for mounted police posts, especially at Lethbridge, yet Commissioner Herchmer and Superintendent Steele at Fort Macleod felt constrained to place police detachments among them on watch for titillating evidence of polygamy, their zeal compounded by the "distrust and contempt" of surrounding settlers for the Mormon newcomers.[24] Though Steele's men by 1899 produced a few reports of suspected polygamy, no one in Canadian officaldom appeared to take an interest. In fact, Department of the Interior Deputy Minister Burgess confided to the Minister, Edgar Dewdney, his opinion that not only was "the evidence on which Mr. Steele's conclusion are based . . . of the most flimsy and unsatisfactory character," but what Steele's reports indicated should be dismissed as merely "a low condition of morality among the Mormons, . . . a matter which it is beyond the power and province of the Government to deal with." Furthermore, "if the progress of a settlement is not the measure of both the intelligence and industry of the settlers, I confess that I do not know what can be," and the great potential value of Mormon irrigation projects had to be kept in mind. The government, and therefore the police, simply accepted a statement by local Morman leader, Charles O. Card, denying polygamous activity.[25]

Subsequent attempts by Commissioner Herchmer to revive investigation by surveillance were discouraged by Fred White, North-West Mounted Police comptroller in Ottawa, as "unnecessary irritations" to the Mormon people. Thereafter, police records concentrated on the admirable agricultural example shown by the Mormons (particularly in developing irrigation systems and mills) within a peaceful and law-abiding community life. Ironically, most of the police dealings with the Mormons were in the nature of defusing the ill-feeling held for them by neighbours, ostensibly because of sharp or doubtful business practices.[26] When a local constable heard and excitedly reported another embarrassing rumour of polygamous arrangements in 1899, Superintendent R. Burton Deane quickly undermined his enthusiasm: "the less interest we appear to take in the Mormons' customs the better."[27]

While the fascination with Mormons focused on but one aspect of their tradition, the picture presented by the Doukhobors, after more than seven thousand of them arrived in 1899 in what would eventually be east-central Saskatchewan, was much more completely strange to Canadians. It was not just a matter of clothing and language, but also a religious understanding which stressed non-compliance with those government regulations which might restrict their communal commitment (individual land ownership) or register their personal information (births, deaths, marriages).[28] Early efforts to resist these Canadian government requirements, and attempts to understand and follow the curious leadership of Peter Verigin, included a series of protest marches by ever diminishing proportions of the Doukhobor people. The first, in the late fall of 1902, involved nearly two thousand Doukhobors, unprepared with proper food or clothing to withstand the cold, who got as far as Minnedosa, Manitoba, on foot before being turned back. Later Saskatchewan demonstrations rarely involved as many as one hundred, but their effect was dramatized by the highly embarrassing tactic of public nudity and by occasional violent internal clashes between those determined to maintain a communal lifestyle and the majority reconciled to individual homestead registration and other Canadian laws. The police attitude in all this was unbelievably patient, again not because of any exceptional sympathy for or insight into Doukhobor problems, but because the Department of the Interior desired to retain the remarkable agricultural finesse of these people. The troublesome few were most often escorted back home after their marches, only their most stubborn leaders occasionally being jailed briefly.[29]

The nature of the Interior Department's policy, with its ramifications for the police, was most clearly illustrated by the response to the thousands of Ukrainian immigrants who streamed into the North-West Territories after the mid-1890s. Immigrations officials saw the "primitive" lifestyle and "generally ignorant" condition of a "very modest, thrifty and hard working" people to be the formula they were looking for to wring Canadian prosperity from the newcomers' struggles to survive. The same observations, however, led police officers to the conclusion that many would not only have to be fed, but would require assistance in the form of seed and cattle to begin their farming operations. The perspectives were strikingly different: the Department of the Interior expected Canada to benefit from the very desperation of the new alien settlers; the police could not imagine leaving so destitute a people their own.[30]

The police received their education at the hands of the Interior Department at the Edna settlement north-east of Edmonton. During 1896, the police were providing limited assistance to destitute "Galician" pioneers there, mainly in the form of clothing in exchange for such work as clearing brush. When a police corporal with the aid of an interpreter reported extensive distress in August of 1897, immigration officials accused the police of meddling and of allowing themselves to be naively exploited by shrewd immigrants whose normal living conditions might easily appear as destitution to Canadian observers.[31] Following reception of a stiff reprimand to leave the Ukrainian settlers to their own devices, the mounted police reduced their alleviation of distress, and concentrated on educating a people of alien habit to cope with the unusual dangers of prairie fires in the new land and with the quarantine approach to epidemic disease. In the meantime, of course, the police acquired a much more benevolent reputation among Ukrainian immigrants than did immigration officers.[32]

Subsequent mounted police reports reaching the Department of the Interior must have been gratifying, stressing as they did the commendable speed with which young Ukrainian men and women went out from their homesteads to work as railway construction navvies and domestic servants in order painfully to raise the money to launch successful farms. As early as 1902 they admired the fine buildings which were replacing the earliest huts of the Ukrainians. They were not to be moved by unfounded criticisms from English-speaking neighbours, who found the alien newcomers' lifestyle distasteful, even on the occasion when those complaints were registered through the member of Parliament for the Edmonton area, Frank Oliver. Oliver claimed in 1899 that "Galicians" were responsible for rampant theft, but a special investigation by Inspector J.O. Wilson concluded that a fundamental anti-Galician prejudice underpinned the rumours.[33] The initial police dismay at the poor prospects of Ukrainian immigrants was transformed into a positive response first by Interior Department policy and then by evidence of agricultural success.

It was certainly not engendered by first impressions of Ukrainian social habits. Police reports early associated Ukrainians with violent acts, many of them in connection with their entertainments which allegedly featured heavy drinking. Confirmation for the police of the reputation for violent crime among the "Galicians" (generalized on occasions to apply to all East Europeans) was the incidence of murder arising from family quarrels. To commissioned officers of the police, the simple explanation in that era was that "some of these foreign races hold life very cheaply and will commit murder on slight provocation," particularly when, in 1912–13, mounting unemployment increased the "large floating population" mainly composed of out-of-work railroad construction navvies. Violence was, like the "shocking depravities" of "incest and defiling girls under 14," simply associated with ethnic character compounded by idleness in time of unemployment.[34] There was no calculation of the connection between the pressures leading to family quarrels on the one hand and the causes of transience among East-European job seekers on the other; even as there was no insight into the reasons why "foreign labourers" crowding into Edmonton in 1912 should be susceptible to the militant industrial unionism of the Industrial Workers of the World.[35] Though their understanding was not sophisticated, however, from first to last the police paid close attention, some of it kindly, to what they could only consider worrisome difficulties of adjustment by a most alien immigrant population. Perhaps the police constituted too much the first agency to be contacted about those problems ever to accept without reservation the Department of the Interior's complacent self-satisfaction with the remarkable agricultural advances against substantial economic and cultural odds of East-European peasant immigrants.

The contrast which proves the economic basis of mounted police approval for certain alien immigrants is to be seen in their disparagement of those groups which were not only foreign, but agricultural failures to boot. A collection of "old country French" settlers who entered the St. Louis de Langevin district near Duck Lake from 1893 through 1895 never received police accolades for their farming ability. Inspector D'Arcy Strickland labelled them from the beginning "a very undesirable class of people" because they arrived "with little or no money and are quite unable to buy machinery or make improvements on their locations." Two years later, a pair of patrolling sergeants still did not consider them "a class intended to be much of an acquisition to the country" for, although they had built "very fair houses," yet "they had not the least idea of farming in this country." The superintendent commanding the Prince Albert district concluded that their previous experience did not suit them for frontier trials.[36] There are several unfavourable references to the lifestyle and lack of progress among Jewish settlers. Some Romanian Jews at South Qu'Appelle in 1902 were characterized as a "lazy, dirty and lousy" people who would "not do a hands turn to help themselves." A neighbour attributed their troubles to the financial cheating of the New York agent for the colony but, whatever the reason, the combination of strangeness and ineptitude deprived them of police sympathy.[37] Interestingly enough, another group judged equally inept, the English Barr colonists, were nevertheless accounted desirable acquisitions whose survival should be ensured to encourage more of the same immigration.[38] Point of origin did count, but negatively only if accompanied by failure at the essential western business of farm production. The majority of settlers, therefore, were in good position to benefit from mounted police help.

Although Clifford Sifton was eager to induce agriculturalists to settle in prairie Canada, he was loath to provide them much material assistance once they arrived, lest the result be a new nation of subsidized paupers.[39] This official reluctance to guarantee the welfare of farmers who ought to be independently establishing their own security and Canada's wealth left the North-West Mounted Police as the sole agency available in the early settlement stages to supply at least the services which were deemed unavoidable. That the Department of the Interior conscientiously eschewed being soft on the pioneers actually helped to create a situation in which the police gained the glory along with the work. This can be understood by reference to urgent problems of great collective concern to prairie settlers: contagious animal diseases, contagious human diseases, destitution, and prairie fires.

Of crucial importance to western agriculturalists, whether homesteaders or cattle ranchers, was the veterinary service of the police, and the medical work performed had a far vaster significance for everyone whose domestic animals were thus protected from epidemic disease. Until 1896, when total responsibility for domestic animal health was given to the federal Department of Agriculture, both the Territorial and the Dominion governments relied heavily on police veterinarians, and on the force itself, to fend off potentially disastrous contagious diseases.[40] There were two branches of this work. One was quarantine and inspection of immigrant and domestic animals at the Canadian-American border, and the other was identification and eradication of disease which despite border precautions appeared within the country.

At the particular locations (five after 1893) where cattle could legally enter Canada and be subjected to quarantine procedure, special police detachments, which might have removed some fifty men and four officers from regular duty, were required to labour on behalf of the Departments of Agriculture and the Interior. This peaceful cowboy work for policemen was justified on the basis of its lesser cost than the alternatives and at the same time its provision of an extra reserve force of police available for emergencies which might arise, say, with respect to Indians. Before the turn of the century, presiding veterinary surgeons were for the most part police personnel. In order for the quarantine system to work, of course, the police detachments undertook daily border patrols to ensure that it was evaded as little as possible. Department of Agriculture delight with the arrangements was matched by Commissioner Herchmer's unhappiness. At the Wood End quarantine station near Estevan, he complained in 1895, not only the police veterinarian but also most of the "police herders" were doing no other but quarantine work: their salaries might just as well be paid by the Department of Agriculture. Nevertheless, police stationed at those detachments continued to have far more contact with "lumpy jaw" (actinomycosis) in cattle and with "sheep scab" than with criminals.[41]

Rather than being reduced, the police role in both border quarantine and general detachment detection of animal diseases was formalized by the 1896 legislation consolidating the service under the federal Department of Agriculture. The commissioner of the North-West Mounted Police became the chief veterinary official of the Department of Agriculture and his veterinary surgeons automatically became inspectors of contagious animal diseases. As for the involvement of the regular policemen, in 1897 the public was informed that "in all suspected cases of contagious diseases, such as Glanders among horses, Tuberculosis and Lumpy-Jaw among cattle, scab among sheep or Hog-cholera, the nearest Mounted Police Constable should at once be notified, when the necessary steps will be taken to prevent spread of the disease."[42] While the ultimate authorities were the commissioner and his veterinary surgeons, first resort was to the multitude of constables on detachment. After several years of experience with this "excellent system," Agriculture officials found control of animal contagious diseases "performed much more economically and effectively than would be possible under any other arrangements" by a police force distinguished by its mobility and "knowledge of the country and its conditions."[43]

Even before the 1896 changes, however, regular detachment procedures became quite as systematic as border quarantines. All detachments were instructed to watch for diseases as part of normal patrol duty, no small order considering that Commissioner Perry's list of most significant diseases after the turn of the century included mange, tuberculosis, anthrax, actinomycosis, and eye disease among cattle; scab in sheep; swine plague and hog cholera in hogs; and glanders, typhoid fever, and *maladie du coît* in horses. Veterinarians, who could not possibly conduct this kind of close supervision alone, were therefore dependent on the perceptiveness of the policemen, even though on occasion settlers themselves were unwilling to trust a constable's judgement. The reason was simple: identification of disease meant at least a quarantine corral on the spot, and perhaps immediate destruction of animals, something settlers were unwilling to accept needlessly. They wanted a veterinarian's judgement in every case, something for which neither level of government would provide extra funds. Usually, though, neighbouring farmers who first reported such cases had good reasons to appreciate police intervention, especially if the owners might "contend that their respective beasts are not afflicted with lumpy jaw and that the animals have either defective teeth or are suffering from the effects of a blow." As the prairie population multiplied after the turn of the century, the demands for inspection put an immense strain on the police capacity to prevent immigration of diseased stock or to deal with all outbreaks as quickly and effectively as formerly. In the circumstances, actual veterinary inspection continued to fall behind while regular police attention became even more vital.[44]

The veterinary experts would be brought in to make final diagnoses and prescriptions, accompanied on their journeys by the ever-present detachment policemen. Only the veterinarian could sometimes quell opposition to destruction of valuable animals. Destruction was always the ultimate answer in cases of anthrax (or "black leg"), and sometimes of glanders, mange, "lumpy jaw," and tuberculosis. Anthrax was so dreaded that settlers themselves could be entrusted with the recommended shooting and cremating procedure even though there was no government compensation forthcoming, but the others required judgements about the stage of disease advancement. It was police business to enforce the orders. Any attempt to treat rather than destroy animals with contagious diseases still involved the order (and sometimes the supervision) for quarantine. After 1894 the designation of quarantine districts of several square miles gradually became a standard practice for dealing with widespread outbreaks. In 1904 and again in 1905, the government found yet another onerous task for the police: the compulsory chemical "dipping" of all North-West Territories cattle each fall. This was a major undertaking, necessitating separation of the untested from the tested by fencing and close quarantining.[45]

In 1899 Commissioner Herchmer expressed pleasure about the general lack of friction between the police and owners of diseased animals. Some early complaints in the Maple Creek area suggested very great interest indeed in this aspect of police assistance: these referred to alleged negligence by detachment policemen not responding quickly enough to requests for veterinary investigations, apparently with the result that disease spread. Obviously, the majority found the veterinary service of the police most valuable; even the occasional reluctance to co-operate was actually a sign that the system worked, for without the police presence it was those very people who would have constituted a danger to their neighbours. Contagious disease, in animals as well as in humans, was one of those conditions which could not but emphasize the co-operative element in the agrarian lifestyle. The mounted police were the available agents to foster that co-operation. But by 1906 the number of stock being imported or drifting into the country annually and the heavy demand for investigation of suspect maladies overstrained the manpower of the Royal North-West Mounted Police, so that the next year the police relinquished those and border quarantine duties to the relevant provincial and federal departments of agriculture.[46]

Before World War I, a fair number of contagious diseases constituted an ever present menace in western Canada to the settlers themselves, but escalation to epidemic proportions was unpredictable. When these emergencies arose, the police were valuable for establishing initial quarantine procedures until the proper authorities could take over (in early years, local boards of health; in later years, medical health officers). Even when others directed the operations, policemen were best able to enforce quarantines and to transport doctors or provisions.[47]

The year 1897 was epidemic for diphtheria and German measles (a deadly disease at the time); police assistance warranted special files on the subject. A good example of the standard procedure concerned an outbreak of diphtheria in and near Saskatoon, at that time a tiny village. Sergeant George Will first reported the odd case being watched, then found himself in a dilemma, for according to custom he was expected to provide both quarantine control at Saskatoon and transportation for the police physician to the neighbouring settlement of Dundurn to check reports of diphtheria there. Reinforcements were both sent and recruited for special constable duty. At infected houses Sergeant Will posted yellow flags and placards on the doors announcing "Diphtheria." Notices at "conspicuous places" warned people to stay away from specified houses. No "ingress or egress" was allowed in an area defined by an eight-mile radius around Saskatoon. A less extensive quarantine procedure involving the service of a special constable was put in place at Dundurn. Sergeant Will drove the doctor around on visits to the sick; when the doctor was absent, Will himself conducted the visits to check the condition of the afflicted, to take them supplies, and to ensure that the quarantine was being observed. At the end, release from quarantine was accomplished with a final sulphur fumigation of the infected residences. Whether or not medical experts were present, then, the police were important to epidemic control procedures and, in this case again, the force was absolutely essential to cover the period before a board of health was properly constituted.[48]

The spread of any contagious disease was in itself serious enough to deserve reprimands for sloppy enforcement of control procedures, but in some circumstances the importance of the police must have escalated considerably in the perceptions of those receiving their assistance. As Inspector A. Ross Cuthbert reported from Prince Albert in 1902:

> As you are aware a very large portion of the inhabitants of this District are very poor and to many of them enforced quarantine is tantamount to starvation unless assisted. There are at present upwards of thirty cases of smallpox, this has entailed in addition many persons being quarantined as suspects from contact with affected persons in the same house or camp, and the issue of necessary relief is becoming a very considerable item of expense.

That Cuthbert would have liked to saddle federal Agriculture Department agents (then responsible for health regulations) with the task of relief provision did not alter the fact that, in such emergencies, it was the police who were seen to act with kindness. In another similar case of smallpox, a police report indicated that of "26 persons . . . quarantined for smallpox, 6 are sick, 25 [are] drawing relief."[49]

Clashes of jurisdiction serve to illustrate the continuing mounted police prominence in actual operations. In July of 1903, Commissioner Perry was still trying to obtain repayment of expenses incurred in May of 1902, when two special constables were placed at the disposal of a quarantine officer of the Dominion Immigration Branch to control diphtheria outbreak among newly arrived Roumanian Jews at South Qu'Appelle. The Territorial government refused to pay the bill, naturally, since the service was performed for immigrants. Yet the Department of the Interior also hesitated to accept responsibility. Before it was resolved, the issue finally involved Territorial MP Walter Scott, to whom Comptroller Fred White remarked in October 1903:

> It is only one of many instances where an emergency arises, the Police have to step in and do what is necessary, and then the other Departments squabble about paying little bills amounting to but a percentage of what the same service would have cost if performed through the proper Department.

White went on to cite the case of about a dozen "foreign immigrants" who were dropped off by the CPR at a wayside station with measles or some other contagious disease, which had already killed a child among them. A mounted policeman who happened to be present "acted the friend in need" and rented shelter. No other government department would reimburse the cost of the police, even though a failure of the policeman to act might easily have resulted in "several other deaths, and a lot of correspondence adverse to our Canadian Immigration system"[50]

The police response fulfilled an expectation among other officials which exasperated at least one commissioned officer, whose very objection betrayed the extent to which police assistance had become common practice. "I think I understand your views," wrote Superintendent P.C.H. Primrose to Commissioner Perry in 1907. "We are cheerfully to assist any branch of the Government if requested to do so, with a view to furthering the best interests of the country." But Primrose rebelled against what he perceived as the growing attitude that any officials could

> say to the nearest Policeman "Here you go and do this" and that it then becomes that policeman's *duty* to go and obey these orders. . . . Fancy asking us to go out and fumigate or assist in fumigating houses; that surely is no part of our duty, nor considering our duties to the general public is it fair to ask our assistance.

He resented that policemen might "be ordered around at will by any rural practitioner who may happen to be in charge of a case," and he thought Alberta communications sufficiently advanced to eliminate any necessity for temporary emergency police help in the absence of medical authorities.[51] At least until the war, however, police assistance of that sort proved unavoidable. Although they were described primarily as duties on behalf of the provincial health departments,[52] they must have confirmed an impression of the mounted police as first on the scene to prevent potentially catastrophic epidemics.

The most lasting impact of the police on the average settler's consciousness might have been made by the police response to the desperation caused for otherwise healthy and thriving immigrants by the sudden deprivations so characteristic of the pioneer experience. One major crop failure in the early stages of his business could cripple a farmer's capacity to recover in the next crop year. The main answer to this form of destitution was "seed grain relief" — that is, advances of seed grain to stimulate a revival of independent agricultural production — and in the early years, especially, the mounted police provided much of the identification and distribution. Failure to recover from economic setbacks or separate climatic disasters led to countless cases of the next level of want: the actual inability to secure sufficient food, fuel, or clothing. Here the requirement for relief was immediate, personal, and dramatic. Repeated hundreds of times, generous assistance through the agency of the mounted police could not help but enhance their reputation among the population at large. The effect was strengthened by two extreme winter-time episodes which brought epic proportions to the story of the mounted police battle against the elements on behalf of the new settlers.

For their relief service to agrarian immigrants, the police had been prepared by the extreme suffering and need of Indian people prior to the North-West Rebellion. After the Rebellion, moreover, the police frequently reported and responded to the needs of "half-breeds" right up to the First World War. But the police did not take up this work simply out of the goodness of their own hearts. One of the prevalent attitudes about relief for any destitute people was expressed already in 1888 in a reference to "half-breed relief" by Superintendent (later to be Commissioner) Perry.

> Free issue of rations must, of course, be made, to prevent actual starvation, but where the Government thus act in a paternal manner great care must be exercised to prevent the recipient from deeming as a right what is given in pity. . . .
> A free issue of rations does not promote industry nor encourage independence in any community. Its demoralizing effects spread rapidly, and too quickly taint those attempting to preserve their independence and self-respect.[53]

He went on to recommend that the work be required in exchange for aid. Nor were the indigent welcomed into Canada by the police. In 1904 a Minnesota woman whose husband was a cripple appeared at North Portal without money and seeking police assistance. She was informed that the mounted police had not authority to relieve destitute immigrants and that, if she did not return to the United States she would be arrested as a vagrant.[54] Again, in the Medicine Hat region early in 1912, a corporal patrolling during extremely harsh and dangerous winter conditions avoided visiting a reportedly needy family because "it was also the unanimous opinion of every one that their improvidence was caused by utter laziness and that their dwelling was in a lousy condition." His superintendent noted in the margin that these were subjects the Immigration officials would on investigation likely deport.[55]

Charity was to be extended to the deserving; the police demonstrated no special talent for sympathy beyond the norm of the day, but frontier circumstances nevertheless ensured that this part of their work would be large. For one thing, as the commissioner noted about one case near Yorkton in 1892, unrelieved distress as a result of crop failures among American immigrants would be very poor advertising to the delegations from various states coming to estimate prospects. On this occasion, he recommended provision of temporary railway construction grading work, even if completion of a line was not projected for the area immediately.[56] Public works were recommended in other situations as well, but the more common practice was to assist those in dire circumstances by supplying essential food and fuel. One example involving a French immigrant family was designated "extreme destitution," warranting emergency relief on the grounds that the children were dying of starvation.[57] When, as in 1895, the Department of the Interior decided a more general policy of seed grain distribution was in order, the NWMP got the extra work, sometimes having to set up temporarily at points where no detachment existed. The police were reported to be far more efficient than those who previously had administered such programs.[58] During the winter of 1895-96, the general policy of relief was extended beyond seed grain to such basic provisions as flour. In the two districts most affected, in the vicinities of Edmonton and Prince Albert, the amount of police time spent receiving, investigating, and satisfying immigrant claims scattered over wide regions left Commissioner Herchmer a trifle grumpy, for relief work superseded what he regarded as proper police work.[59]

The necessity for such a widespread relief policy dissipated after 1896, when some settlers at least were already actually able to pay back their advances,[60] Relief measures returned to the standard form of individual cases treated on their merits. After creation of the new provinces of Alberta and Saskatchewan in 1905, applications for relief provisions were directed to the federal Immigration Branch, to local rural municipalities where they existed, or to the provincial boards of health, according to each applicant's status as immigrant or resident of more than three years.[61] While those were the authorities and the sources of funds, the mounted police continued to do the work, filling in the appropriate application forms, then distributing the relevant items upon authorization. In emergencies, the police would often supply fuel (coal) or work until empowered by the proper agency to do more. With the elimination of great distances between farms during the immigration boom, and especially with the introduction of telephone communication, the traditional mounted police role showed signs of erosion just before the Great War. Settlers began to apply on their own, without waiting to be discovered; while the police detachments were still the points of contact, their patrols were no longer essential or possible in the same way as they had once been.[62] Nevertheless, Immigration authorities, at least, were still happy to receive general reports by district on the likelihood of destitution during impending winters.[63]

A pair of emergency actions in those later years, however, reinforced the impression of mounted police omnipresence to relieve suffering. The winter of 1906-7 was known for its "fuel famine," an extreme shortage of coal. In those places, mainly in Saskatchewan, where coal could not be obtained, settlers were forced to find and haul wood, not always an easy task for novices having to travel long distances in very cold weather and deep snow. Rumours of distress spread, often in newspapers. "A farmer named Radcliffe with his wife and three children have been found frozen to death," reported the Estevan

Evening Journal in February. "Radcliffe was a homesteader, who came here for coal about a fortnight ago. A neighbour called at Radcliffe's during his absence and found his wife and children frozen solid and no fuel or wood in the house." But the police found this to be irresponsible conjecture: though isolated by a snowstorm, the family survived very well.[64] Although Commissioner Perry continued to be convinced that "the casualties resulted from want of knowledge of the country, drunkenness, or other preventable causes,"[65] now and then frozen bodies were indeed found, and some settlers did experience considerable anxiety over the fuel problem. Many worried about their families should they lose their way in search of wood. In at least two cases, south of Battleford and near Moosomin, patrolling policemen reported available bush nearly exhausted for farmers coming for the green wood from some distance.[66]

The severity of the rumours was enough to stimulate action directed by the new Minister of the Interior, Frank Oliver, "not only from the humane point of view," as Comptroller White put it, "but also to prevent reports being circulated injurious to Canadian Immigration interests."[67] At first Immigration officials concentrated on the region south of Battleford, where heavy snowfalls made trail breaking difficult. Fuel, seed grain (later), and other provisions were hauled to Tramping Lake some sixty miles south of Battleford. Mounted policemen patrolled the vicinity to record the extent of suffering and to advise settlers of the provisioning opportunity, then were authorized to carry out the actual distribution as well. On occasion, police constables themselves hauled provisions to families isolated and in distress.[68] As a precaution, the police were soon instructed to patrol every newly settled district in Alberta and Saskatchewan in search of any who might urgently require relief. Prime Minister Laurier himself was kept informed of the results. As it turned out, there was little exceptional suffering to be alleviated anywhere else, except at another new settlement region north of Swift Current.[69]

Though the extent of the problem proved not to be dismayingly widespread, the publicity was enormous, the reports came from mounted policemen, and the burden of work fell on their shoulders. A similar flurry of attention occurred in 1910–11, when exceptionally deep snowfalls in southern Alberta and Saskatchewan created difficulties for feeding stock and prevented many settlers from travelling at appropriate times to obtain food and fuel. By this time the federal immigration policy was to treat aid as an advance, repayable with 5 percent interest per annum but, when urgency dictated immediate action, the police were to issue relief and work out financial responsibilities later. Patrols were made in terrible conditions, through snow drifted six or seven feet deep, constables frequently persevering despite dangerous exposure. One froze the skin of his legs to his pants during an errand of mercy, but most were more sensibly prepared.[70] "Settlers are great in praise of a Government that will send patrols through the District in such weather in order to prevent loss of life," reported Lethbridge police, "and freely state that they would be permitted to freeze to death in any other country before anyone would visit them. . . ." Settlers from the United States in particular were most appreciative. This comment was forwarded to senior Immigration officials by

Comptroller White, again "not as showing what the Mounted Police are doing, but as furnishing another link in your chain of evidence of the satisfactory manner in which immigrants are treated in our Canadian North West."[71] White here indicated not only the standard business-like motivation for government compassion, but also the perception of settlers as to the agency which was most responsible for it.

The summertime problem of prairie fires proved that there were limits to the assistance which could be expected even from the mounted police. Prairie fires were of course less controllable hazards before the major settlement influx; hence the Territorial government was eager already in the 1880s to "secure more fully the services of the North West Mounted Police Force" to prevent and extinguish them. Police officers followed up with "the most stringent orders" both to assist in the suppression of prairie fires and to arrest their perpetrators.[72] The insistent demands made on the police to be the main force responsible for actually putting out the fires were aggravating because they were so impossible of fulfilment, though perhaps understandable among so widely scattered a populace. The investiture of police in charge of detachments as "fire guardians" as of 1889 gave them the added power and responsibility for turning out "all male persons within ten miles of a prairie fire" to proceed immediately to help extinguish it, but the spotlight was not removed from the mounted police when action was required, nor were dangerous practices among settlers effectively curtailed.[73] It would be years before settlers were sufficiently packed together on prairie land that the self-interest of many would stimulate their own response to each fire which threatened their homesteads.

In the meantime, the mounted police were subjected to criticism on this account at a rate to which they were not otherwise accustomed. The terrific extent of damage a prairie fire could do flared tempers. The Calgary *Herald* in 1890 claimed that in one situation the police did "not appear to have stirred a finger until the fire had burnt itself out," even though the editor was persuaded that there were many mounted policemen "in barracks in Calgary not overburdened with serious duties, and on the whole, passing life easily." A settler at Turnip Lake near Edmonton wondered in 1897 what these "paid servants of the government" were supported for if not to prevent destruction of his homestead by prompt attention to raging fires. The Battleford *Star* in 1899 excoriated a police force that waited on civilians to show the first initiative in stopping fires. These protests were of course uttered in the heat of the moment, sometimes without much foundation, and there were also balancing commendations, but they show that public expectations from this particular police force were very great.[74]

The police thought such expectations unrealistic if not grossly irresponsible. Commissioner Herchmer in 1893 outlined the differences between the police and the public understanding of the duties of fire guardians. For him they meant "to turn out all settlers in the locality when a fire is running, to put it out, and to investigate the cause of the fire, and lay information against the parties guilty of setting it, after first submitting the evidence to their Commanding Officers for consideration." The public in most areas (except in ranching regions) seemed to feel that "police should be scattered in small parties throughout the country, and that they should be employed in putting out the fires, and that the settlers should not be called upon, at any rate until the efforts of the police have failed." He cited examples of cases in which extensive police efforts to apprehend those responsible for setting them either failed (as neighbours were reluctant to testify unless they had suffered damage and were angry), or were nullified by fines of less than three dollars, often when serious damage had been done. An example of the result, complained Herchmer, was that settlers would carelessly burn stubble and, if the fires got out of control, "callously let them go believing that if found out it will be cheaper to be fined than to devote their time to putting them out." He saw no alternative to fixing fines at "deterrent sums," despite possible occasional injustices, with a view to enforcing greater settler vigilance and self-help.[75]

Eventually the police were relieved of a good deal of the pressure of coping with prairie fires, which had always been exaggerated by the necessity to handle concurrently a great deal of other business and by civilian fire guardians' unwillingness to discharge their duties because they were "either too lazy or too afraid of making enemies to do anything."[76] Under the jurisdiction of the provincial attorneys general, "Fire Commissioners" and an associated officialdom were established in 1912, and in the matter of investigation of "the cause, origin and circumstances of every fire . . . by which property has been destroyed or damaged," the Mounted Police were not designated.[77] Simultaneously, a long-term aggravation, the exemption of the Canadian Pacific Railway from Territorial and provincial prairie fire ordinances, was eliminated by a 1912 order of the federal Board of Railway Commissioners that railways were required to plough fireguard strips at least sixteen feet wide on both sides of the railway track, except where utterly impracticable. No longer did the police have to beg railway officials to do something to prevent engine sparks from igniting the surrounding countryside.[78]

Even in the sporadic criticism endured by the police about their inability to crush the fearful threat of prairie fires, a basic pioneer attitude to the mounted police stands out, though it was usually expressed more positively. They were there to provide settlement (one might even say colonization) services. Prairie fires were aspects of the environment, like climatic extremes, which were not susceptible to individual conquest. Collective responses co-ordinated by a government agency were hardly avoidable. The same approach was essential for combatting animal and human contagious diseases. Though they had not originally been placed in the prairie west to ensure anything more than legal security, in the absence of any other government initiative the mounted police temporarily filled the need for external aid beyond the settlers' own resources precisely when the settlers were most vulnerable: when they were first establishing themselves. The police therefore inadvertently provided an early example in a particular region of Canada of public responsibility for individual welfare, not to be confused with the judgemental condescension implicit in the old tradition of private charity. Though prime ministers and western parliamentary representatives frequently referred to these services in justification of the force's existence, the way this role was given legitimacy over several decades of pioneer experience undoubtedly made its greatest impact in the west. It is difficult to imagine how the mounted police could fail to earn the gratitude of those they served.

But if Department of the Interior officials left the basic welfare of the settlers to the police, they stubbornly maintained the criterion of agricultural progress as the foundation for estimations of immigrant suitability. Early mounted police scepticism about some foreigners was frequently overcome by this Interior Department preoccupation; later evidence of success stimulated natural admiration. The result was to place the policemen at the side of the alien sometimes against great economic and cultural odds. And for all settlers of whatever origin, the presence of a patrolling police force was the most obvious (sometimes the only) sign of that limited degree of government care which did exist for pioneers thrust into the imposing prairie frontier. It does seem appropriate to conclude that a significant factor contributing to the mounted police popularity in prairie Canada was the force's role in the first faint stirrings of the Canadian welfare state.

Notes

1. R.C. Macleod, *The North-West Mounted Police and Law Enforcement 1873–1905* (Toronto: University of Toronto Press, 1976), ix.

2. Ibid., 46

3. Ibid., 44–45; D.H. Breen, "The Mounted Police and the Ranching Frontier," in *Men in Scarlet*, edited by H.A. Dempsey (Calgary: Historical Society of Alberta/McClelland and Stewart, 1974), 122–24.

4. Superintendent P.R. Neale to Commissioner Herchmer, 30 Aug. 1887: Public Archives of Canada (hereinafter PAC), RG 18-B1, Records of the Royal Canadian Mounted Police.

5. See PAC, file 511 for 1903, n.d., RG 18-A1; Macleod, *The North-West Mounted Police*, 45–49.

6. Canada, *Sessional Papers*, NWMP, *Report*, 1890, 2; NWMP, *Report*, 1898, 13–14.

7. Steele to non-commissioned officer in charge of Porcupine Hills detachment, 14 Oct. 1889, PAC, RG 18-C2.

8. Circular memorandum from NWMP Headquarters to Officers Commanding Division, 12 Apr. 1890, PAC, RG 18-A1.

9. NWMP Comptroller Fred White to Herchmer, 13 Oct. 1892 and 9 Aug. 1897; and correspondence with Interior Department officials, 1894, PAC, RG 18-B1; Canada, *Sessional Papers*, Department of the Interior, *Report*, 1891, part 1, xxiv; Circular memorandum dated 1 June 1895, RG 18-C3; Superintendent A.R. Cuthbert, Battleford, to Sergeant Bird, Duck Lake, 1 June 1901, RG 18-C1.

10. See for example, Inspector V. Williams to Officer Commanding at Calgary, 29 July 1887; and diary report of Sergeant Dee, High River, for week ending 28 Jan. 1893, PAC, RG 18-B1; Diary of Constable William Murray, North Fork of Sheep Creek (Calgary Division), for week ending 4 June 1891, RG 18-A1; Sergeant Saul Martin to Officer Commanding Prince Albert Division, 5 May 1892, RG 18-C1; Milk River Detachment Diary, 17 Aug. 1895; and daily journal, St. Mary's Detachment, 14 Sept. 1896, RG 18-C2; Diary of Medicine Lodge Detachment, 13 Feb. 1900, RG 18-C1.

11. Constable A.W. Oaks, North Fork/Fish Creek Detachment, to Superintendent J.N. McIlree, Calgary, 27 Aug. 1891, PAC, RG 18-A1; Patrol report of Constable J. Thornton, Ft. Qu'Appelle, 7 Feb. 1895, RG 18-C3; Weekly report of Constable D.L. McClean, Willoughby, Prince Albert Division, 2 Nov. 1895, RG 18-C1.

12. Transcripts of interviews by S.W. Horrall with G.J. Duncan, 17 Jan. 1969, 36; and with G.H. Blake, 13 Jan. 1969, 53, RCMP Historical Section, Ottawa; G.J. Duncan, "Retrospect," *Scarlet and Gold*, 1964; Macleod, *The North-West Mounted Police*, 46–47.

13. S.B. Steele, *Forty Years in Canada* (Toronto: McClelland, Goodchild, Stewart, 1918), 256–57; NWMP, *Report*, 1888, 11; NWMP, *Report*, 1901, 3 and 85.

14. Assistant Commissioner, NWMP, to Officer Commanding Battleford Division, 21 Feb. 1900; Begin to Commissioner Perry, n.d. (1903), PAC, RG 18-B1.

15. Steele to Constable P_____ , 10 Aug. 1889; and Deane to the sergeant in charge at Porcupine Detachment, 16 May 1898, PAC, RG 18-C2; Herchmer to Officer Commanding "B" Division, 13 Feb. 1894, RG 18-B1; Circular memorandum to Officers Commanding Divisions, 9 Nov. 1895, RG 18-C3.

16. RNWMP, Standing General Orders, Mar. 1901, 42, RCMP Headquarters, Ottawa; NWMP, *Report*, 1902, part 1, 67; Circular memorandum no. 560, 18 Feb. 1908, PAC, RG 18-B4; McIlree to Perry, 13 June 1910, RG 18-C1.

17. See, for example, patrol reports from "N" Division, 1911, PAC, RG 18-B1.

18. R.C. Macleod, "Canadianizing the West: The North-West Mounted Police as Agents of the National Policy, 1873–1905," in *Essays on Western History*, edited by L.H. Thomas (Edmonton: University of Alberta Press, 1976), 99–110.

19. Department of the Interior, *Reports*, 1894, part 1, xxxiv; part 3, 13; and 1896, part 1, xxx.

20. Canada, *Journals of the House of Commons*, 1900, Appendix No. 1, "Report of the Select Standing Committee on Agriculture and Colonization," 308; Department of the Interior, *Reports*, 1899, part 1, ix; and 1901, ii, xv; and for a clear presentation of Sifton's attitudes, see D.J. Hall, "Clifford Sifton: Immigration and Settlement Policy 1896–1905," in *The Settlement of the West*, edited by Howard Palmer (Calgary: University of Calgary/Comprint, 1977), 60–85.

21. This is not the point made in, but seems a logical conclusion from, Macleod, *The North-West Mounted Police*, 153–55; and Macleod, "Canadianizing the West," 108.

22. Department of the Interior, *Report*, 1893, part 1, 9; NWMP, *Report*, 1890; Sergeant H.E. Bierd and Inspector Albert Hirot, Duck Lake, to Officer Commanding at Prince Albert, 22 June 1892, PAC, RG 18-C1; Superintendent S.V. Gagnon, Prince Albert, to Herchmer, 15 May 1899, RG 18-A1.

23. Department of the Interior, *Report*, 1888, xxi-xxii.

24. NWMP, *Report*, 1888, 22, 58; Steele to Herchmer, 25 Aug. 1889, PAC, RG 18-C2; Steele to Herchmer, confidential, 4 Dec. 1889, RG 18-A1.

25. Correspondence on southern Alberta Mormons in RG 18-A1 for 1890, including copy of a confidential letter from Burgess to Dewdney, 16 Dec. 1889; and another from Card to Burgess, 22 Feb. 1890. See also Macleod, *The North-West Mounted Police*, 155–56.

26. Herchmer to White, 19 Mar. 1890; White to Dewdney, 25 Mar. 1890; and Steele to Herchmer, 1891, PAC, RG 18-A1; Excerpts about the Mormons in NWMP, *Reports*, 1890–97 and 1901.

27. February and March correspondence, 1899, PAC, RG 18-A1; Deane to Herchmer, 17 Mar. 1899, RG 18-C2.

28. See George Woodcock and Ivan Avakumovic, *The Doukhobors* (Toronto: Oxford University Press, 1968); Carl Betke, "The Mounted Police and the Doukhobors in Saskatchewan, 1899–1909," *Saskatchewan History* 27 (Winter 1974): 3–5.

29. Betke, "The Mounted Police and the Doukhobors," 4–12.

30. Department of the Interior, *Report*, 1895–96, part 4, 120; NWMP, *Report*, 1896, 12. For fuller treatments of the exploitive expectations of Canadian immigration policy, see Hall, "Clifford Sifton"; and Donald Avery, *"Dangerous Foreigners"* (Toronto: McClelland and Stewart, 1979).

31. Superintendent A.H. Griesbach to Herchmer, 2 Nov. 1896; and A.M. Burgess to White, 12 Nov. 1896, PAC, RG 18-A1; Assistant Commissioner, NWMP, to Griesbach, 10 Dec. 1897, RG 18-B1. See also the account in Macleod, *The North-West Mounted Police*, 151–52.

32. Correspondence, Aug. 1897 to Feb. 1898, PAC, RG 18-A1; telegrams between Superintendent S. Gagnon, Prince Albert, and Herchmer, 1 May 1899, RG 18-B1; Gagnon to Corporal St. Denis, Rosthern, 12 Sept. 1899, RG 18-C1; RNWMP, *Report*, 1911, 151.

33. Department of the Interior, *Report*, 1902, part 2, 119; Inspector S. Crosthwait to Officer Commanding at Fort Saskatchewan, 12 Feb. 1902, PAC, RG 18-B1; Oliver to Fred White, 1 June 1899; and report of Inspector J.O. Wilson, 21 June 1899, RG 18-A1. See also the account in Macleod, *The North-West Mounted Police*, 151.

34. RNWMP, *Reports*, 1907, 87; 1908, 38, 103; 1909, 67, 83, 87; 1910, 75; 1912, 74–75, 157; 1913, 9.

35. RNWMP, *Report*, 1912, 83.

36. Reports of Inspector D'A.E. Strickland, Duck Lake, 19 Dec. 1893, 8 May and 2 June 1894; of Sergeant H. Keenan, Duck Lake, 22 June 1895; and of Sergeant I.W. Weeks patrolling to Fishing Lakes and Boucher, 28 Sept. 1895, PAC, RG 18-C1; NWMP, *Report*, 1895, 115.

37. NWMP, *Report*, 1892, 49; Report of Constable G.T. Howdey, South Qu'Appelle, 17 May 1902, PAC, RG 18-A1; H. Bolocan to Laurier, June 1904, PAC, Sir Wilfred Laurier Papers, microfilm C813, 87430–38.

38. White to Perry, 15 Apr. 1903; to Interior Deputy Minister Smart, 25 Aug. 1903; and to Perry, 6 and 20 Nov. 1903, PAC, RG 18-A2.

39. Hall, "Clifford Sifton," 74–75; and see Donald Avery, "*Dangerous Foreigners.*"

40. Franklin M. Loew and E.H. Wood, *Vet in the Saddle* (Saskatoon: Western Producer Prairie Books, 1978), 26–28, 49–51, 88–93; Canada, *Sessional Papers*, Department of Agriculture, *Report*, 1893, xii-xiii; "A Précis of Orders in Council Relating to Cattle Quarantine Regulations" (Department of Agriculture, 30 Jan. 1894) in PAC, John Lowe Papers.

41. John Lowe, "Report on Cattle Quarantine . . . Nov. 27, 1895," in John Lowe Papers; Department of Agriculture, *Report*, 1896, viii, 91.

42. Loew and Wood, *Vet in the Saddle*, 50–51; NWMP, General Order no. 11602, referring to Privy Council Order of 22 Oct. 1896, RCMP Headquarters, Ottawa; Circular Memorandum no. 237, 5 Apr. 1897, RG 18-B4; Commissioner Herchmer's press release, 9 July 1897, RG 18-B2.

43. Department of Agriculture, *Report*, 1904, 71.

44. Herchmer to Commissioner of Dominion Lands H.H. Smith, 25 Oct. 1893; and report of Sergeant Blake, Graburn Detachment, 28 June 1895, PAC, RG 18-A1; Circular Memorandum by Inspector J.D. Moodie, Macleod, 20 Mar. 1901, RG 18-C3; Constable H. Thompson to Officer Commanding at Prince Albert, 21 Dec. 1897, RG 18-C1; Department of Agriculture, *Reports*, 1901, 114–17; and 1906, 130–33, 196.

45. Loew and Wood, *Vet in the Saddle*, 106–7; Department of Agriculture, *Reports*, 1892, part 2, 49; 1905, 136; and 1906, 130; telegram, Superintendent J. Cotton, Prince Albert, to Herchmer, 20 June 1892; Lowe to White, 21 July 1892; Robert Evans to Herchmer, 12 Feb. 1894; and Perry to Herchmer, 15 Feb. 1894, PAC, RG 18-B1; Lowe to White, 20 Apr. 1894; and White to Herchmer, 24 Apr. 1894, RG 18-A1; Circular memorandum no. 458, 16 Mar. 1904, RG 18-B4.

46. See, for example, J.M. Cosgrave to Herchmer, 4 Aug. 1893, PAC, RG 18-B1; Department of Agriculture, *Reports*, 1906, 132–33, 196; 1908.

47. See examples of smallpox, diptheria, and scarlet fever reports near Macleod, the Beaver Hills, and Battleford in RG 18-B1 for 1892 and 1897; NWMP, *Report*, 1894, 109.

48. Correspondence among Sergeant G. Will, Superintendent S. Gagnon at Prince Albert, and Herchmer, Oct. 1897, PAC, RG 18-B1.

49. Cuthbert to Sergeant Bird, Duck Lake, 26 Aug. 1902; and to Perry, 15 Apr. and 31 Aug. 1902; Superintendent W.S. Morris, Prince Albert, to Perry, 30 Jan. 1903, PAC, RG 18-A1.

50. Perry to White, 3 July 1903; and White to Walter Scott, 13 Oct. 1903, PAC, RG 18-A1.

51. Alberta Provincial Health Officer L.E.W. Irving to Superintendent P.C.H.Primrose, Macleod, 8 July 1907; and Primrose to Perry, 12 July 1907, PAC, RG 18-B2.

52. Ibid., vol. 50; RNWMP, *Reports*, 1910, 80; and 1911, 87.

53. NWMP, *Report*, 1888, 96.

54. Corporal H. Lett, Estevan, to Officer Commanding at Regina, 17 Aug. 1904, PAC, RG 18-A1.

55. Corporal Wiedeman, Irvine Detachment, to Officer Commanding at Medicine Hat, 18 Jan. 1912, PAC, RG 18-A1.

56. Herchmer to White, forwarded to Department of the Interior, n.d. (1892), PAC, RG 18-A1.

57. Strickland to Herchmer, 26 Feb., 2 and 16 Mar. 1895, PAC, RG 18-C1.

58. A.M. Burgess to White, 27 Mar. 1895; and telegram, Herchmer to White, 31 Mar. 1895; and Herchmer to White, 16 May 1895, PAC, RG 18-A1.

59. See 1896 correspondence in RG 18-A1, files 70 and 151.

60. Will to Officer Commanding at Prince Albert, 22 Dec. 1896, PAC, RG 18-C1; Department of the Interior, *Report*, 1899, xxi.

61. See examples in the thick file 132 of 1912, PAC, RG 18-B1. In the same file, see Perry to Commissioner of Public Health for Saskatchewan, 31 Jan. 1912; and a circular memorandum by Perry, 28 Feb. 1912.

62. A case of this sort appears in correspondence following an initial report by Constable H. Moorhead, Stirling Detachment, 27 Mar. 1913, PAC, RG 18-B1.

63. Perry to Commissioner of Immigration, Winnipeg, 17 Nov. 1913, PAC, RG 18-B1.

64. Estevan *Evening Journal*, 22 Feb. 1907; and report of Sergent H. Lett, Estevan, 24 Feb. 1907, PAC, RG 18-A1.

65. Perry to White, 6 Mar. 1907, PAC, RG 18-B10.

66. Inspector Generaux to Officer Commanding at Battleford, 24 Dec. 1906; Inspector A.M. Jarvis to Officer Commanding at Regina, 11 Feb. 1907; and a report of Saskatoon detachment on a found frozen body beginning to be eaten by wolves, 19 Mar. 1907, PAC, RG 18-A1; W.D. Scott, Superintendent of Immigration, to Frank Oliver, 1 Feb. 1907, RG 18-B10.

67. White to Perry, 5 Feb. 1907, PAC, RG 18-A1.

68. Constable R.C. Bright reporting a Tramping Lake patrol, 19 Dec. 1906; memorandum to Sergeant Adams, Regina, 1 Feb. 1907; W.D. Scott to Oliver, 1 Feb. 1907; and General Colonization Agent C.W. Speers, Battleford, to Assistant Commissioner McIlree, 17 Feb. 1907, PAC, RG 18-B10; Constable W.H. Burke to Officer Commanding at Battleford, 8 Jan. 1907, RG 18-A1.

69. White to Laurier, 8 Feb. 1907; and telegram, Perry to White, 11 Feb. 1907, Laurier Papers, microfilm C843, 119475-76 and 119599.

70. See file on winter destitution in the vicinities of Lethbridge and Maple Creek, PAC, RG 18-B1. See another on relief issued during 1910–11, RG 18-A1, including Circular Memorandum no. 600 of Commissioner Perry, 27 Jan. 1911; and a patrol report by Constable A.P. White, Pendant d'Oreille detachment, 4 Feb. 1911.

71. Extract from monthly RNWMP report from Lethbridge for Jan. 1911, enclosed with a letter from White to W.D. Scott, 2 Mar. 1911, PAC, RG 18-A1.

72. Copy of resolution of NWT Council, signed by A.E. Forget, Clerk of Council, 24 Oct. 1887; Herchmer to Commanding Officers, 25 Oct. 1887; and Lt. Gov. J. Royal to Herchmer, 17 Aug. 1889, PAC, RG 18-B1; NWMP, General Order no. 1863 in 1887, RG 18-B4; Perry to detachment commanders, "F" Division, 27 Oct. 1887, RG 18-C1; Superintendent A.H. Griesbach to Corporal McLellan, Peace Hills, 27 Aug. 1889, RG 18-C7.

73. See, for example, J.G. Gordon to Herchmer, 18 Sept. 1888; and Inspector C. Constantine to Herchmer, 22 Sept. 1888, PAC, RG 18-B1; North-West Territories, *Revised Ordinances*, 1888, chap. 20.

74. Clipping from *Calgary Herald*, 14 Nov. 1890; Inspector A.E. Snyder, Edmonton, to Officer Commanding at Fort Saskatchewan, 29 May 1897, enclosing clipping from *Edmonton Bulletin* of 17 May; Clipping from *Battleford Star*, 12 May 1899; J.W. Ings of Rio Alto Ranche, Lineham, to Superintendent R.B. Deane, Calgary, ca. Aug. 1910, PAC, RG 18-A1.

75. Herchmer to White, 13 Jan. 1893, PAC, RG 18-A1.

76. Constable T.G. Coventry, Castor Detachment, to Superintendent A.R. Cuthbert, Edmonton, 25 Apr. 1910 and Cuthbert's appended note, PAC, RG 18-B1; Constable W.C. Jackson, Kinistino, to Officer Commanding at Prince Albert, 24 Sept. 1894; and Constable R. Beatty to Officer Commanding at Prince Albert, 3 Apr. 1895, RG 18-C1.

77. Fire Prevention Act, *Statutes of Saskatchewan*, 2 Geo. 5 (1912), c. 23.

78. Correspondence involving one Walter Simpson of Greendyke, the Superintendent at Regina, and the Assistant Commissioner of the NWMP, and C.W. Milestone, CPR, Moose Jaw, 16–23 Oct. 1901; and correspondence about railway matters, 1909–12, PAC, RG 18-B1; Inspector Baker, Maple Creek, to White, 21 Nov. 1901, RG 18-A1.

THE PRESERVATION OF THE PEACE IN VANCOUVER: THE AFTERMATH OF THE ANTI-CHINESE RIOT OF 1887†

PATRICIA E. ROY

> Half a League! Half a League!
>   Half a League onward!
> All in the peaceful city
>   Walked the VICTORIA specials.
> Forward, Roycraft cried!
>   March to the City Hall he said.
> In the Terminal City
>   Walked the brave specials.
>
> Forward the blue coat brigade
>   Was there a man dismay'd?
> Not, though the specials knew
>   The Government had blundered;
> Theirs not to make reply
>   Theirs not to reason why;
> Theirs but to loaf and cry;
>   Give us more Vancouver pie,
> The noble specials.
>
> The pig-tailed camp to the right of them!
>   The CPR to the left of them!
> Vancouver to the front of them!
>   All peaceful and calm!
> Stormed at by hiss and yell!
>   Boldly they walked and well,
> Into Water Street pell-mell
>   Walked the gallant specials!
>
> Flashed all their brass buttons bare!
>   Flashed as they turned in air!
> Withering the small boy there!
>   Charging on the frosty air!
> While all VICTORIA wondered!
>   Smelling of tobacco smoke!
> Right through the line they broke
>   News-boy and boot-black shout!
> In a wild hurrah!
> See the whiskey soaks! The red nose galoots!
>   The VICTORIA specials![1]

† *BC Studies* 31 (Autumn 1976): 44–59.

The literary antecedents of this parody are clear to all who are familiar with Tennyson's poetry; its historical origins are not. Historians have described Vancouver's anti-Chinese riot of 1887 without adequately documenting it, correctly recording its consequences or fully exploring its significance.[2] The riot deserves study. It was the most violent manifestation of anti-Chinese sentiment in British Columbia to that time; it illustrates the virulent inter-city rivalry promoted by the press of Vancouver and Victoria; it demonstrates the ease with which lawlessness could occur in an infant city; and it shows the determination of the provincial government to maintain an image of peace and order.

Within a few days of the riot, the provincial legislature temporarily usurped the police powers of the city. Why did the legislature, with its well-established propensity to pass anti-Chinese laws, suddenly pass an act to protect the Chinese of Vancouver from such outrages as assault on their persons, arson of their property, and intimidation designed to prevent them from dwelling in the city or following their lawful occupations there? Was the Vancouver *News* correct in charging that the "Act for the Preservation of Peace within the Municipal Limits of the City of Vancouver"[3] was a Victoria plot, a "sort of sensational way of bringing the 'upstart of a city, Vancouver to book,' "[4] or was the provincial government legitimately concerned about maintaining the law?

Hostility to the Chinese, to their alleged "unfair competition" on the labour market and to their "different" customs and habits was not confined to Vancouver. No matter where they went, the Chinese were unwelcome.[5] In the United States, despite the suspension of legal Chinese immigration for a minimum of ten years beginning in 1882, anti-Chinese agitation persisted. In the Puget Sound cities of Tacoma and Seattle, broadly based groups of white citizens temporarily forced the Chinese out during the fall and winter of 1885–86. In both communities, federal troops restored the peace.[6]

British Columbia had known anti-Chinese sentiment since 1858 but politicians and journalists, not mobs, had expressed it. During the 1870s the provincial legislature disfranchised the Chinese but failed to discourage their immigration or to restrict their employment. The importation of thousands of Chinese coolies to help build the Canadian Pacific Railway in the early 1880s spurred the legislature to pass anti-Chinese laws. After a select committee reported in January 1884 that 16 000 to 18 000 Chinese lived in the province, the legislature passed acts to stop Chinese immigration and to place severe restrictions on the Chinese already in the province. These laws prevented Chinese from acquiring Crown land and regulated their activities by requiring them, among other things, to purchase an annual ten dollar licence which had to be shown to provincial authorities on request. The federal government disallowed the immigration law and the courts ruled the other two laws ultra vires. The aborted laws had one positive result for the legislature: they commanded Ottawa's attention. Sir John A. Macdonald, responding in a now traditional way, appointed a royal commission to investigate Chinese immigration. Subsequently, the federal government passed the Chinese Immigration Act of 1885, imposing a fifty dollar head tax on every Chinese entering Canada and limiting the number of immigrant Chinese each ship could carry. The tax increased government revenues (the provincial government received a quarter of the proceeds) but it did not halt Chinese immigration.[7] Moreover, as construction work on the CPR ended, Chinese labourers were laid off. Many of them went to Victoria, where they formed such a large pool of unemployed labour that the Vancouver *Herald* claimed there were more adult Chinese males than adult white males in the capital city.[8]

Vancouver residents did not want Chinese in their new city. This was clear in the local press. As early as January 1886, the *Herald* warned the presence of Chinese in the business section would lower property values. The *Vancouver World* echoed similar views by describing the reported sale of two city lots to Chinese as "a violent wrench to public sentiment." When a small group of unemployed Chinese tried to establish themselves in business in the city, the *Vancouver Daily Advertiser* protested this "thin edge of the wedge." The *Morning News* well summarized local opinion when it urged that the Chinese be kept out to spare Vancouver "the evil which has cursed all Pacific coast towns." To the many citizens who did not want the Chinese to settle in Vancouver, the virtual destruction of the city by fire on 13 June 1886 offered a second chance to keep them out. During the week after the fire, three street meetings passed resolutions against allowing the Chinese to re-establish themselves. Nothing came of these motions, although Mayor M.A. MacLean, a real estate man, and Alderman L.A. Hamilton, the CPR's chief surveyor, supported their principles. In November, the Knights of Labor stirred up agitation against the employment of Chinese. Mysterious caution signs appeared on the windows of houses employing Chinese and on the sidewalks in front of stores and offices whose proprietors dealt with the Chinese in any way. Responding to manifestos issued by the Knights and by the Wintners' Association during the civic election campaign in December, both Mayor MacLean and his rival, Alderman Thomas Dunn, a hardware merchant, opposed the presence of Chinese in the city and agreed on the difficulty of keeping them out.[9]

Some Vancouverites believed it was possible to keep the Chinese out. During the first stage of the Chinese outrages in January 1887 they used intimidation, inviting new Chinese arrivals to return to Victoria and promoting a boycott of Chinese labour. Intimidation had no permanent results. The arrival of more Chinese in late February marked the beginning of the second and violent stage of the outrages. A mob marched on the Chinese camp, demolished it, and ordered the Chinese to go. This violence led to direct provincial intervention — the "Act for the Preservation of Peace within the Municipal Limits of the City of Vancouver."

The immediate impetus to the Chinese outrages was the arrival from Victoria early on 7 January 1887 of a "batch of Mongolians." They were the first of an expected 250 Chinese hired by John McDougall, a contractor, to clear the Brighouse estate, a 350-acre plot of land covered with stumps and inflammable materials. McDougall explained that Chinese labour saved him 50 percent or

$1.25 to $1.50 per man per day. This did not satisfy the several hundred unemployed white men then in Vancouver.

The intimidation stage of the Chinese outrages began on 8 January 1887. A group of self-proclaimed "representative and business men" [sic] under the chairmanship of R.D. Pitt, a real estate agent and member of the Knights of Labor, met at City Hall. The anti-Chinese meeting decided to have a committee induce the Chinese "to return to the place from whence they came" and to offer them "fair and just compensation" for their expenses. The money would be raised by public collection. Another committee would urge employers to replace Chinese workers with white ones in order to make Vancouver "for all time to come . . . the first and only city of the Pacific Coast in which Chinese did not form a large and very unwelcome population." The meeting named a ten-member committee which included prominent citizens such as Mayor MacLean, Alderman Joseph Humphries, Thomas Dunn and A.G. Ferguson, "a capitalist," to carry out its intentions. A second committee composed of the mayor, W. Brown and J.J. Blake, a stipendiary magistrate, would call on employers. The committees were clearly designed to represent a cross-section of the community but not all of those named agreed to serve.[10]

The day after the meeting, a Sunday, a crowd composed of seventy-five members of the committee (the press did not explain its growth) and 250 others descended on the Brighouse estate at Coal Harbour and persuaded nineteen Chinese to accept a free one-way trip to Victoria. A collection was taken up to pay their fares, and 600 residents — a "quiet, unanimous and orderly" assemblage — watched their departure. Police Chief J.M. Stewart reported no violence but the Victoria *Times* noted the Chinese lost several hundred dollars worth of property. The departure of these nineteen Chinese and of others who left on their own for New Westminster or who joined the exodus to Victoria on succeeding days came to be known as the "expulsion of the Chinese." Each time a group of Chinese sailed for Victoria, a crowd cheered their departure. On the sixteenth, provincial police superintendent H.B. Roycraft, who came to Vancouver to investigate the situation, informed the attorney-general that the city was "remarkably quiet," that there had been no evidence of violence and that the crowd had been good-humoured.[11]

The departure of the Chinese did not end the anti-Chinese movement. Within ten days of the initial "expulsion" there were four well-attended anti-Chinese public meetings at city hall. These meetings echoed the popular feeling that the Chinese must not be allowed to establish themselves in Vancouver, but speakers and the Vancouver newspapers repeatedly emphasized the importance of avoiding violence. Such admonitions were especially timely since an anonymous part of the movement, "The Vigilance Committee," began posting notices warning that:

> all Chinamen must leave the city limits on or before the 16th January instant, and all Chinamen found within the city on or after that date will be forcibly ejected and their goods and chattels moved to False Creek or such other place as convenience may dictate. And we warn the authorities not to interfere with us if they value their lives, as we mean business and are determined in our action.[12]

The same committee also circulated letters advising city residents "to extend your patronage no longer to Chinamen." Public meetings fully endorsed this idea. At a meeting on the fourteenth, the 200 "businessmen and citizens" present signed a pledge not to employ Chinese for any purpose or to deal with them directly or indirectly, effective 1 February 1887. Emphasizing the non-violent aspect of the intimidation, the pledge suggested the imposition of the boycott might be delayed until a joint stock company (then being organized by white men) had purchased all Chinese property in the city. A few days later, however, white crosses appeared on buildings where Chinese were employed. The persistent popularity of the anti-Chinese movement was also demonstrated on 20 January when rumours circulated that the Chinese would be returning on the morning steamer. Three hundred men sped to the wharf to prevent their landing, but no Chinese were on board.[13]

During the uneasy calm that followed the expulsion of the Chinese, small businessmen and transients replaced the more prominent members of the community as members of the anti-Chinese committees. Only R.D. Pitt provided some continuity between the first and second phases of the anti-Chinese agitation. Although he specifically denied leading the movement which he described as spontaneous growth, Pitt presided at several public meetings at city hall. At one of these gatherings, held on 2 February 1887, the decision was made to form an Anti-Chinese League. Developing the earlier idea of a boycott, this league distributed to business houses a card bearing a pledge not to deal directly or indirectly with Chinese labour. The league also appointed a committee consisting of: Pitt; T.D. Cyrs, a hotel keeper; John Mateer, a contractor; and two others, including the secretary, George Pollay, whose names do not appear in the city directory. Several speakers underscored the absence of "leading" citizens by complaining that the prominent citizens who claimed to sympathize with the anti-Chinese movement were not present. Two weeks later, Pollay told another meeting that the majority of businessmen had signed the anti-Chinese pledge but some thought the wording, "not to deal directly or indirectly," too strict. This meeting also heard that at least one hundred Chinese had entered the city during the previous three weeks. The Chinese had not been permanently expelled.[14]

On Thursday, 24 February, Vancouver residents learned that Chinese had again come from Victoria to clear the Brighouse estate. That afternoon, a placard reading "The Chinese have came [sic] Mass meeting in the City Hall to-night" was carried along the streets. An overflow crowd heard unidentified speakers claim that city businessmen had agreed to assist workingmen in keeping the "city clear of celestials." At the meeting's end a voice in the audience called for "those in favour of turning out the Chinese tonight." The crowd responded unanimously, left the hall, and, singing "John's Brown Body," "trudged its way through the snow with remarkable rapidity" to the Chinese camp at Coal Harbour. There the 300 to 400 members of the mob kicked some Chinese and ordered all of them to leave. As the Chinese prepared to go, the mob began demolishing the camp, pulling down shanties, smashing outfits and throwing bedding and provisions in the fire.

When the mob was about to leave, Police Chief Stewart and Superintendent

Roycraft arrived. Roycraft had had an agent at the meeting but had not expected trouble for several days. Roycraft and Stewart immediately took charge and instructed the Chinese to remain in a roofless shed. Stewart then ordered the mob to go home but it paid no attention. The mob met briefly and, in unison, answered "Aye" to two questions: "Who says the Chinese must go?" and "Who says the police must go home?" When a call went out, "Come and drive them out," the mob moved towards the Chinese but stopped short of attacking the law, whose forces had been strengthened by the arrival of the other three members of the city police force. The mob then began to drift home although, en route, some of them raided Chinatown, where they looted houses and set fire to some buildings.[15] Many Chinese escaped to the bush; a few went into the water where they almost died of exposure. About eighty-six, including some from a camp at False Creek, left for New Westminster. According to the *News*, few Chinese remained in the city, but by the twenty-sixth another twenty-four had arrived from Victoria. They escaped molestation only by delaying their debarkation until after the 200 members of the Anti-Chinese League had left the CPR wharf.[16]

The darkness of the night impeded the work of the police in identifying the culprits. Not until the second day after the "outrage" did they lay any charges, and then they arrested only three men: John Frauley, a logger; Thomas Greer, a milkman; and O. Lee Charlton, a clerk. The city's police magistrate, T.T. Black denied them bail but stipendiary magistrate J.J. Blake freed them on $3,000 bail. A few days later they appeared in court before Mayor MacLean, Alderman R.H. Alexander and Black. Their cases were dismissed because eyewitnesses could not state that any of them actually took part in the assault. Indeed, Charlton reminisced, "they just arrested us to save their face."[17]

In the meantime, the provincial government had taken control. Asserting that a "reign of terrorism" that might easily spread to other cities must be put down, that local justices and magistrates could not be trusted, and that "the parties charged with the police protection of the city were not only afraid to enforce the law but were in sympathy with the agitation," Attorney-General Davie introduced legislation to preserve the peace in Vancouver. Specifically, the bill authorized the cabinet to appoint special constables in Vancouver, to turn the city gaol over to the provincial superintendent of police and to suspend the judicial powers of the local magistrates and justices of the peace, including the mayor, as long as a provincial stipendiary magistrate might be within the city. So little did Davie trust the Vancouver magistrates that he admitted one of his reasons for not following the extreme course of calling out the militia was that such an action would require a magistrate's signature. Although some members of the opposition criticized details of the measure, especially the obligation imposed on the city of having to pay the costs of the special constables, the legislature unanimously and quickly passed the bill.[18] Vancouver did not lose its charter, but it did lose its police powers temporarily.[19]

Most Vancouver citizens believed the mob's action was unwarranted and that the lawlessness must be put down.[20] Nevertheless, the government's action incensed them. According to a special correspondent of the Victoria *Times*, groups of excited Vancouver residents could "be seen congregated at every street corner discussing the all absorbing question." These citizens "were paralysed with astonishment at the audacious conduct" of the provincial government in making "a direct insult to the city and its citizens," and "an open menace to civil rights." Vancouverites complained the government seemed to think that "everything and everybody in the province should be governed by Victoria City and Victorians." A special meeting of the Vancouver city council passed a resolution complaining of the practical annulment of its powers over law and order and of the "enormous expenses" of placing the city under control of persons not responsible to the city. City council declared that no special legislation "for the protection of life or property in the city is necessary," that the council was prepared "to take all steps for the protection of persons of all nationalities," and that the cabinet should not enforce that act until the mayor and council showed themselves "unable and unwilling" to enforce the law.[21] In response to a message from John Boultbee, a lawyer who interviewed the attorney-general on the city's behalf, the council made plans to appoint twenty specials of its own and announced that in future a special posse of police would attend every public meeting not sanctioned by the mayor, aldermen, or justices of the peace and would arrest anyone who would incite illegal or unpeaceful action. But the province was already recruiting the thirty-six special provincial police whom it despatched to Vancouver on 2 March in company with Superintendent Roycraft and A.W. Vowell, a stipendiary magistrate.[22] At the wharf in Vancouver, a crowd met the specials and followed them to city hall but attempted nothing unlawful. The mayor gave Vowell the key to the gaol and other city officials were co-operative.[23]

Once the "Victoria specials" arrived the city dismissed the twenty constables it had sworn in. Council decided each alderman should supply the names of four individuals who could serve in case of emergency. Although this would have provided a maximum force of forty, nearly one hundred "leading businessmen" were sworn in as specials a few days later. The realization of property owners that they could not afford to tolerate lawlessness, the appointment of ten extra regular city policemen and the prevalence of peace convinced Vowell that Vancouver could maintain the law itself. On 10 March, fourteen of the specials returned to Victoria. On the eighteenth, Vowell returned the gaol keys to the police chief and joined the last of the specials as they departed for Victoria. Yet despite the attempts of James Orr, one of the MLAs for New Westminster District, the government refused to repeal the law relating to the preservation of peace in Vancouver until the legislative session of 1888.[24]

The presence of the specials permitted the return of the Chinese. About a hundred arrived on 8 March to join the thirty who were already in the city. During succeeding days, additional Chinese entered Vancouver. By 15 March, eighty Chinese were working on the Brighouse Estate and ninety were at other locations in the city. The Chinese were apparently able to work without overt molestation. The only reported incident was a brief strike by the Chinese themselves against a shortage of camp cooks and the high prices charged by the contractors for provisions and other supplies. By mid-July the Chinese work force at Brighouse estate, which had numbered 300, had declined to three. An injunction, not against the Chinese as such but against the danger of clearing land in hot dry weather (a hazard of which Vancouver was acutely conscious), forced them off.[25] The Chinese did not leave Vancouver. Chinatown became a distinct feature of the city's cultural landscape but for many years remained a target of racial hostility. In the short run, however Vancouver was as much concerned about the apparent revenge of Victoria as it was about its own ethnic composition.

The arrival of the "Victoria specials" in Vancouver had provoked a new outburst of popular resentment against the capital city.[26] Many Vancouverites believed their city was subject to the whims of a legislature controlled by a jealous city of Victoria and they resented the fact that many Victorians were absentee landowners in their city. Sentiments similar to those expressed in the opening parody appeared in the satirical journal *The Vancouver Chestnut* which, during its brief life, devoted itself to attacking Victoria and especially John Robson for sending the specials to Vancouver. The daily *Vancouver News* challenged the accuracy of Victoria newspaper accounts of the attacks. It blamed "the influence of Victorians, which has always been exercised against Vancouver" for the reprehensible, rash, and ill-advised conduct of the legislature in passing the preservation-of-the-peace act.[27]

The rivalry of the two cities grew out of the island-versus-mainland conflict which dated back to colonial times and which had been rekindled with the debate over the location of the CPR route through the province. Victoria was naturally jealous of the new city of Vancouver which, as the future terminus of the transcontinental railway, seemed destined to supplant the capital as the commercial metropolis of the province. Victoria, as the *News* indicated, still dominated the politics of the province with eight of the province's twenty-seven MLAs elected for the city or adjacent areas while Vancouver lacked a single MLA to call her own. Since the preservation-of-the-peace legislation was a political act, the Vancouver press could easily perceive it as a Victoria plot. It was easy for Vancouverites to confuse Victoria the city with Victoria the seat of government.

The first Victoria reports of the expulsion of the Chinese in January had sympathetically remarked on the absence of violence. Then, the Vancouver *News* blamed the "mossbacks" of Victoria for launching a suit against the mayor and other citizens implicated in the expulsion and for appealing to the supreme court for an injunction restraining Vancouver citizens from similar acts in the future. The suit, in fact, was launched by a Chinese labour contractor, Lee Shaw, whose men were working for McDougall. The only apparent Victoria connection was a Victoria lawyer, Thornton Fell, whom Lee Shaw engaged to act on his behalf. After contractor McDougall went to Victoria to seek the support of the attorney-general for criminal action against the members of the committee responsible for expelling the Chinese, the newspaper battle intensified. The *News* accused the Victoria press of "gross exaggeration" and "enormous lying" while the Victoria journals complained of the Vancouver papers "pouring out the vials of their wrath" and of making "libellous and absurd" statements about the veracity of the Victoria press.

According to Victoria reporters who interviewed McDougall, the Vancouver police had been unable or unwilling to cope with the mob, there had been violence, and Mayor MacLean and Alderman David Oppenheimer had looked on with open approval as a large portion of the city's "floating population" had "hustled the Chinese in every conceivable way." In an editorial, "Rule of the Mob," the *Times* complained that the majority of the respectable portion of the population unfortunately "hold themselves aloof, and thereby tacitly acquiesce in the actions of the mob, which is directed chiefly by demogogues and hoodlums." McDougall denied having implicated Alderman David Oppenheimer[28] and the *Colonist* later reported that the mayor and other prominent citizens had taken no part in the proceedings. Getting in a final word against the *News*, the *Colonist* blamed it for giving "unnecessary and undue prominence to the whole affair."[29] Whoever's fault it was, the damage had been done. Despite subsequent press denials and private reports of Superintendent Roycraft to the attorney-general that there had been no violence, there was a popular impression abroad in Victoria that violence had been used and that the Vancouver authorities were unwilling or unable to cope with the mob or protect the Chinese.

Thus when Attorney-General Davie introduced the bill to preserve peace in Vancouver he referred to his uncertainty about the unwillingness of civic authorities to enforce the law. Later, in responding to the city council's formal complaint against the measure, the government repeated its belief that civic authorities had "strangely and persistently" refrained from enforcing the law.[30] Even discounting journalistic rhetoric, the government's conclusions were reasonable. The Vancouver city council took no steps to halt the agitation; indeed, many of the anti-Chinese rallies were held in city hall with the council's permission. Mayor MacLean looked on the expulsion without acting against it, though he later denied being a member of the original anti-Chinese committee. At its first meeting after the expulsion, the Vancouver city council did not consider the expellers but passed resolutions to enforce the cubic air bylaw (designed to prevent overcrowding in Chinese quarters), to put down Chinese houses of prostitution and to impose a poll tax on "every Mongolian." Later the council asked the province to appoint a commission of inquiry into the "alleged Chinese riots or outrages" but nothing came of this.[31]

The province was also justifiably uncertain about the city's law enforcement agencies. When contractor McDougall appealed to the police chief at the time of the expulsion, the chief merely ascertained that all but a few of the Chinese were anxious to go to Victoria. Claiming he could prove no intimidation, he did nothing. Even if the police had wanted to halt the agitation, they lacked any real power. The city's entire police force consisted of four men. Only after the province announced the despatch of special police to the city did Vancouver arrange to swear in special constables of its own. City police charged three men with participating in the 25 February attack on the Chinese, and though one other magistrate denied them bail, Blake — a stipendiary magistrate, member of the original anti-Chinese committee and partner of the lawyer of one of the accused — granted it.

In proposing the bill, Davie expressed his hope "for the credit of British

Columbia" that the mob were not citizens of the province but transients from such Puget Sound centres as Seattle and Tacoma.[32] Supporting this "alien" theory, D.W. Higgins, the member for Esquimalt, said he had heard on "good authority"[33] that R.D. Pitt, the leader of the agitation, was a Fenian who had headed a group in Portland, Oregon, which sought to blow up the Esquimalt dockyard. Such an allegation is virtually impossible to substantiate. What is surprising is that none of the legislators tried to link the outrages with the Knights of Labor, despite their well-known antipathy to Chinese competition.[34] Pitt, who denied the leadership of the anti-Chinese movement in Vancouver, took pride in being one of the Knights of Labor whose members, he boasted, included two-thirds of Vancouver's people. Undoubtedly Pitt was not the only Knight to be involved in the Vancouver agitation, but the legislators' ignoring of the Knights, who would be ideal alien villains, suggest that the Knights, as an organization, played little or no part in the outrages.[35]

Although some prominent citizens were linked with the early stages of the agitation, they do not appear to have played an active part in its violent stage. They passively looked on as the anti-Chinese agitation developed. Many were sympathetic to the idea of keeping the Chinese out of the city; some of them pledged not to deal with Chinese. Those who might have been concerned about peace and order lacked an effective means of doing so. The business community itself was still transient. Many of its members were preoccupied with getting their own businesses underway and they lacked any form of organization. The Board of Trade, for example, was not established until September 1887.

Except for two of the men arrested, the mob which carried out the expulsion was a faceless one. Indeed, Charlton and Greer may have been chosen for arrest simply because the police recognized them by name.[36] Negative evidence suggests the mob was largely made up of transients. They were, no doubt, typical young men of the frontier cut "adrift from the order imposed by kinship and association" who had already given Vancouver a reputation for having a rough element.[37] Whether the mob came from Puget Sound, from Victoria (as the Vancouver press suggested) or from elsewhere is not as important as the fact that the mob committed outrages.

Speaking on behalf of the legislation, John Robson, who subscribed to the alien theory, declared that the Vancouver bill gave British Columbians an opportunity "to show to the nations of the earth that we were Britons and not in name alone." The government was determined to maintain British standards of justice.[38] In the context of British Columbia's past attitudes towards the Chinese, it seems at first sight rather odd that the Chinese should benefit from such concern.[39] Other factors must be considered. Robson, no lover of the Chinese,[40] had a personal interest in halting the intimidation. He was, along with the CPR, one of the several owners of lots in the Brighouse estate. It was to his personal advantage to have the land cleared as quickly and as cheaply as possible.[41]

While such a personal consideration may have been in Robson's mind, the government's main reason for passing the law was the preservation of peace in a new city whose law enforcement was uncertain and whose population was unknown. Six weeks later, the legislature amended Vancouver's charter by raising the property qualifications for mayor, alderman and municipal voters. Protecting the Chinese was an incidental consequence of the government's determination to avoid any appearance of a "wild west" or of "frontier democracy" in British Columbia. As Robson implied, the province needed a good image. The Canadian Pacific Railway had just been completed; the province was anxious to attract settlers and capital. British Columbia could not afford such publicity as a report in the *New York World* that if the Chinese had not left in January, the agitators "had everything in readiness to blow up portions of the town" or cables from England asking Vancouver residents, "Are you safe?"[42] The goal of showing that government advertising was correct[43] — that British Colubmia was not a lawless frontier — was accomplished. In eastern Canada, at least, newspapers and periodicals commented on the effectiveness of the legislature in dealing with the emergency.[44] The outrages had shown that the Canadian frontier was not a uniformly peaceful one; the provincial government, however, demonstrated that violent acts would not be tolerated. The provincial government, if not the city, was capable of acting decisively to preserve the peace.[45] The "Act to Preserve the Peace in Vancouver" was not, as newspaper rhetoric claimed, merely a Victoria plot. It reflected a legitimate concern for justice and for the reputation of the province as a whole.

Notes

1. "A Local Tennyson." Ironically, the poem was published in the *Victoria Daily Times*, 7 Mar. 1887.

2. The fullest description may be found in James Morton, *In the Sea of Sterile Mountains* (Vancouver: J.J. Douglas, 1973).

3. British Columbia, *Statutes*, 50 Vict., c. 33.

4. *Vancouver News*, 13 Mar. 1887.

5. See, for example, a recent study, Charles A. Price, *The Great White Walls Are Built* (Canberra: Australian National University Press, 1974). This book endeavours to compare reaction to the Chinese in Australia, New Zealand, the United States, and Canada. Its Canadian section is weak and misinformed.

6. See Jules A. Karlin, "The Anti-Chinese Outbreak in Tacoma, 1885," *Pacific Historical Review* 23 (1954): 271–83, and "The Anti-Chinese Outbreaks in Seattle, 1885–1886," *Pacific Northwest Quarterly* 39 (Apr. 1948): 103–30. Although there are many parallels between these riots and the riot in Vancouver, I have not been able to trace any direct links.

7. This abbreviated account of British Columbia's attitude to Chinese immigration before 1885 can be supplemented through several secondary sources. The most recent and most comprehensive is W.P. Ward, "White Canada Forever: British Columbia's Response to Orientals, 1858–1914" (Ph.D. dissertation, Queen's University, 1972).

8. *Vancouver Herald*, 21 May 1886.

9. *Vancouver News*, 7 Dec. 1886, 8 Jan. 1887; *Vancouver Herald*, 15 Jan. 1886; *Vancouver World*, 2 Apr. 1886; *Vancouver Daily Advertiser*, 2 June 1886; *Vancouver Daily News-Advertiser*, 26 Nov. 1886; *Vancouver Weekly Herald*, 22 June 1886; *Vancouver Morning News*, 2 June 1886. The most outspoken anti-Chinese candidate for municipal office, R.D. Pitt, was badly defeated when he ran for an aldermanic seat in Ward 3.

10. Other members of the committee were: Hugh Keefer, a contractor; T.D. Cyrs, the proprietor of the Granville Hotel; Captain J.M. Ayers, who, if not a member of the Knights of Labor, was sympathetic to its cause; Thomas Stephenson; G. Goodmurphy; and J.C. Huntley. Mayor MacLean later denied acting

with the committee. Keefer and Ferguson were not present at the meeting and Ferguson inserted an advertisement in the *News* (15 Jan. 1887) stating that he had been named to the committee without his knowledge or consent. Huntley later declined to serve.

11. *News*, 11 Jan. 1887. J.M. Stewart, Chief of Police, and Sgt. John McLaren to H.B. Roycraft, 16 Jan. 1887, Provincial Archives of British Columbia (hereafter PABC), Attorney-General's Papers (hereafter AGP), Letters Inward, 1884–87; *Victoria Daily Times*, 10 Jan. 1887.

12. New Westminster *British Columbian*, 11 Jan. 1887. The Victoria *Daily Colonist*, 15 Jan. 1887, quoted a similar but slightly more emphatic notice.

13. *Times*, 14 Jan. 1887; *Colonist*, 21 Jan. 1887; *News*, 15 and 21 Jan. 1887.

14. *News*, 3 and 16 Feb. 1887.

15. This account is based on the following reports: *News*, 25 Feb. 1887; Roycraft to A.E.B. Davie, 25 Feb. 1887, PABC, AGP, Letters Inward, 1884–87; and J.S. Matthews, comp., "Early Vancouver," Vancouver City Archives, typescript vol. 1: 298. Roycraft enclosed a clipping of the *News*' account with his report. He described it as "most truthful" and explained that *News* reporters had had a better chance to observe the incident than he had.

16. *News*, 25 and 26 Feb. 1887.

17. *News*, 27 Feb. and 4 Mar. 1887. See also the conversation of Charlton with J.S. Matthews, 11 Feb. 1941, in Matthews, "Early Vancouver," 6: 73.

18. *Times*, 28 Feb. 1887; *Colonist*, 1 Mar. 1887.

19. For recent examples of this misinterpretation see Paul Phillips, *No Power Greater: A Century of Labour in British Columbia* (Vancouver: B.C. Federation of Labour, 1967), 14; Ward, "White Canada Forever," 104.

20. *News*, 26 Feb. 1887; *Colonist*, 27 Feb. 1887; *Times*, 28 Feb. 1887.

21. *Times*, 1 Mar. 1887; Vancouver City Council, Minute Book, 1 Mar. 1887, Vancouver City Archives (hereafter VCA).

22. *News*, 2 Mar. 1887. Original correspondence in City Clerk's Correspondence, VCA, RG2 A1, vol. 2.

23. A.W. Vowell to Attorney-General, 3 Mar. 1887, PABC, AGP, Letters Inward, 1884–87.

24. *News*, 3 and 5 Mar. 1887; Vowell to A.E.B. Davie, 15 Mar. 1887; PABC, AGP, Letters Inward, 1884–87. The law was repealed at the 1888 legislative session: British Columbia, *Statutes*, 51 Vict., c. 38.

25. Vowell to Davie, 8 and 15 Mar. 1887, PABC, AGP, Letters Inward, 1884–87; *News*, 25 and 27 Mar. 1887; *Vancouver Daily News-Advertiser*, 10 June 1887, 21 July 1887.

26. The *Colonist* (8 Mar. 1887) reported that merchants had introduced a form of boycotting against the specials by charging them especially high prices for provisions.

27. *News*, 2 Mar. 1887.

28. Illness had confined Oppenheimer to his bed on the night of the expulsion.

29. *News*, 16 Jan. 1887; *Times*, 14 Jan. 1887; *Colonist*, 14 and 20 Jan. 1887. The *Columbian* also criticized the *News*' claim that no compulsion was imposed on the Chinese (22 Jan. 1887). The *News* (25 Jan. 1887) merely commented that it had always thought the *Columbian* was anxious to get rid of the Chinese.

30. John Robson to T.F. McGuigan, 5 Mar. 1887, VCA, RG2 A1, vol. 2; *News*, 15 Mar. 1887. Robson also mentioned an incident the previous September when civic officials made no attempt to punish those who had been responsible for the tarring and feathering of a Vancouver resident. I have not found any other references to this incident.

31. *News*, 11 Jan. 1887; Vancouver City Council, Minute Book, 14 Mar. 1887.

32. The *Colonist* (27 Feb. 1887) and the *Times* (28 Feb. 1887) shared this view.

33. The "good authority" may have been a letter from "Commercial Traveller" to the editor of the *Colonist*, 20 Jan. 1887.

34. During most of 1886, the Knights published a weekly newspaper, the *Industrial News*, in Victoria. "Being a labour paper," it was "of necessity . . . a strong anti-Chinese journal" (*Industrial News*, 26 Dec. 1885). The Knights' manifesto in the Vancouver municipal elections of December 1886 included a strong anti-Chinese statement.

35. Pitt to editor, *News*, 21 Nov. 1886. Some writers on B.C. labour history have assigned a significant role to the Knights in developing agitation in Vancouver. For examples, see George Bartley,

"Twenty-Five Years of Labor Movement in Vancouver," *British Columbia Federationist*, 27 Dec. 1912, and William Bennett, *Builders of British Columbia* [Vancouver, 1937], 32.

36. Charlton was born in New Brunswick in 1865. He arrived in Vancouver on 13 September 1886 and remained there until 1926, when he moved to Celista, B.C. He was a member of the CCF from its inception. When he died in 1962, Grace MacInnis spoke at his funeral. (*Salmon Arm Observer*, 23 Aug. 1955 and 5 Apr. 1962.) Greer arrived at Burrard Inlet in May 1882. He remained in Vancouver until his death in 1943 (VCA, J.S. Matthews Collection, "Thomas Greer").

37. A.R.M. Lower, *Canadians in the Making* (Toronto: Longmans, Green, 1958), 360; *Times*, 6 May 1886.

38. *News*, 3 Mar. 1887; *Colonist*, 1 Mar. 1887.

39. For several years, beginning in 1887, the legislature was less active in passing anti-Chinese legislation. See Ward, "White Canada Forever," chap. 5.

40. In 1872 Robson was one of the first MLAs to suggest the imposition of special taxation on the Chinese and a ban on their employment on public works. Nevertheless, on another occasion he argued that Chinese would not be mistreated, that regardless of creed, colour, or nationality, "a man's a man for a' that" (*Dominion Pacific Herald*, 12 Mar. 1881, quoted in Ivan E.M. Antak, "John Robson: British Columbian" (M.A. thesis, University of Victoria, 1972), 138).

41. According to the Vancouver *Herald*, the owners of the Brighouse property were: E.G. Major and Ben Douglas of New Westminster; Messrs. Oppenheimer and Sam Brighouse of Vancouver; John Robson, G. Byrnes, C.T. Dupont, I.W. Powell and Mr. Devlin of Victoria; William Hailstone of England; Mr. Bullen of Montreal; N. R. Reid of Cariboo; J. Morton of Chilliwack; and the Canadian Pacific Railway Company. Quoted in the *Victoria Weekly Times*, 18 Mar. 1887.

42. *New York World*, quoted in *Vancouver News*, 10 Mar. 1887; *News*, 3 Mar. 1887.

43. See for example, *Illustrated British Columbia* (Victoria: J.B. Ferguson, [1884]), 274.

44. *Montreal Witness*, quoted in *Colonist*, 29 Mar. 1887; *Monetary Times*, quoted in *Columbian*, 31 Mar. 1887.

45. The city later accepted some responsibility for damage to Chinese property.

THE ROYAL NORTH-WEST MOUNTED POLICE AND LABOUR UNREST IN WESTERN CANADA, 1919†

S.W. HORRALL

During the early morning hours of 17 June 1919 eight leaders[1] of the Winnipeg General Strike were arrested by members of the RNWMP and charged that as officials of the One Big Union they had conspired together to replace constituted authority with a soviet form of government.[2] Although a royal commission which investigated the causes of the strike[3] found no evidence of any seditious conspiracy, nor any connection between the strike and the OBU,[4] seven of the eight accused were eventually convicted by the courts of trying to "overthrow" the state.[5]

The verdict touched off a controversy which still continues. "Strike or Revolution?" asked Masters in his pioneering study of the labour dispute. Most historians now accept his conclusion, with varying refinements, that it was not an incipient revolution but "an effort to secure the principle of collective bargaining."[6] Nonetheless, it was widely believed at the time that the OBU represented a revolutionary challenge to established authority. Borden, in his memoirs, described the strike as an attempt to supersede the existing government with one based upon "absurd conceptions of what had been accomplished in Russia."[7]

What evidence did the prime minister have for such a view? Although a final study of the role of the federal security agencies has yet to appear, it is generally accepted that the government's action was influenced by information it obtained from a number of intelligence sources. Rodney has emphasized the reports of "Moscow Money" being diverted to Canada for revolutionary purposes as reason for the position of the authorities.[8] Others have turned to the intelligence reports of the Dominion Police, RNWMP, and the Department of Militia to explain its response, although McCormack has shown that there was very little co-ordination in their investigations and their findings were often contradictory.[9]

As the responsible federal police force in western Canada in 1919 the Royal North-West Mounted Police was perhaps the most important of these security agencies. McNaught and Bercuson have suggested that the intelligence reports of the RNWMP supported the official view that the strike was revolutionary in nature.[10] This seems a reasonable conclusion considering that it was the members and secret agents of the Mounted Police who provided the backbone of the evidence that led to the conviction of the strike leaders.

It is a view that has been perpetuated by the writers of quasi-official histories of the force which, although too often preoccupied with justifying its ways

† *Canadian Historical Review* 61, no. 2 (1980): 169–90.

to man, have been widely read in their time. Longstreth wrote colourfully of "Red wisdom" journeying from "sweat shop to sweat shop" and the spread of "Russian venom" by "Muscovite emissaries."[11] Fetherstonhaugh was more explicit, describing the strike as "No ordinary fight for higher wages or improved working conditions . . . but a campaign to impose upon the people a dictatorship by the One Big Union."[12] More recently the Kellys, ignoring the historical scholarship of the last quarter century, have claimed that the strike leaders "were plotting to overthrow the government, by force if necessary."[13]

How true is this interpretation of the intelligence role of the RNWMP during those critical months that led up to the breaking of the strike? What steps did that force take to organize a secret service and how did it operate? Did the Mounties see Bolsheviks and caches of arms behind every tree? Did they advise the government that the One Big Union and the Winnipeg strike were all a part of a plot to kick it off Parliament Hill? For so convinced was Borden of the revolutionary nature of the labour unrest that following the strike he quickly took steps to use the legendary frontier force as the nucleus for a new nation-wide, centrally controlled, federal security organization — the Royal Canadian Mounted Police.

The Mounted Police was initiated into the world of secret agents and espionage in 1914 when it became a part of the intelligence network organized under the Dominion Police to protect national security. As the provincial police force in Alberta and Saskatchewan it spent the early years of the war investigating the rumoured plots of German spies and enforcing the various regulations under the War Measures Act which were aimed at restricting the activities of the large enemy alien population on the prairies.

As the war drew to a close the RNWMP began to direct its attention to radical labour organizations like the Industrial Workers of the World. These security investigations were gradually curtailed, however, following the termination of the contracts for provincial policing in 1917 and the government's decision to allow members of the force to volunteer for overseas military service.[14] By the fall of 1918 over eighty police posts had been closed in Alberta and Saskatchewan, and the transfer of men to the Canadian army had reduced the Mounted Police to little more than a border patrol.

Just when it looked as if the Mounted Police was about to disappear into the pages of history, an important intelligence-gathering role was suddenly thrust upon it. Behind the change was the federal government's dogged belief that a sinister conspiracy lay at the root of the growing number of strikes and industrial disputes that occurred in 1918. Reports from the Dominion Police and the Department of Militia on the labour situation were contradictory.[15] As a result Borden asked an old political colleague, C.H. Cahan, later director of public safety, to investigate the revolutionary propaganda prevalent in the country.[16] Cahan submitted the results of the enquiry to the minister of justice in September. It was not the Germans or the IWW, he reported, that were behind the unrest, but the Bolsheviks. If there was any doubt about these findings they must have been dispelled when Borden learned from British intelligence sources in December 1918 that the Soviet government intended to launch a propaganda campaign in North America.[17]

Among the measures taken to meet this perceived threat was a reorganization of the federal security and intelligence system in western Canada. Hitherto the Dominion Police had had nation-wide responsibility for the enforcement of federal laws and the security provisions of the War Measures Act. On 12 December 1918 this responsibility was geographically cut in half.[18] The RNWMP took over from the Dominion Police from the Lakehead to the Pacific, leaving the operations of the latter force confined to eastern Canada. In addition, the strength of the Mounted Police was increased to twelve hundred men.

One of the principal thrusts of this reorganization was the desire to ensure that there was an adequate mobile force in the west to meet any civil disturbance. N.W. Rowell, the minister in charge of the Mounted Police, was at pains to inform the provincial governments later in the new year that the force was available to assist them should any disorders occur.[19] With many of the municipal police forces already unionized, the government had already taken steps to ensure that the Mounties themselves could not be affected by the unrest by passing an order-in-council which prevented them from joining or associating in any way with any union or association of employees.[20]

Another result of this change was that it created two secret services where formerly there had been only one. The RNWMP reported to the president of the Privy Council, the Dominion Police to the minister of justice. No provision was made for any overall direction of their operations or analysis of their intelligence. Cahan, the director of public safety, was supposed to advise the government on security matters but he resigned early in 1919. Lacking centralized control, each departmental intelligence service more or less went its own way, each carrying out its own investigations, sometimes tripping over each others' toes in the process, and each drawing up its own assessment of conditions. They tried to keep each other informed of the results of their work by circulating the reports of their agents among the five or six key ministers and their senior advisers in Ottawa. It was not the best of security systems at a time when the country needed reliable intelligence and analysis of what was happening and was likely to happen. Added to this, the effective leader of the government, Sir Robert Borden, was in Europe from November 1918 to May 1919 attending the Peace Conference.

Since October 1917 the minister responsible for the RNWMP had been Newton Wesley Rowell. A one-time leader of the Liberal party in Ontario, he had broken with his party over the conscription issue and joined Borden's Union Government. Rowell quickly set about organizing an effective secret service and laying down guidelines for its operation. Following the transfer of responsibility to the Mounted Police in December 1918 he had taken steps to secure the return of the Mounted Police cavalry squadrons serving overseas.[21] Early in the new year he informed his deputy minister, A.A. Maclean, the comptroller or administrative head of the force, of the priorities he wished given to secret service duties: "It is most important that this branch of the service should receive most careful consideration and that an efficient service should be maintained so that the government would be kept thoroughly advised of what is going on in the principal centres where I.W.W. or other revolutionary agitators might be at work."[22]

Rowell did not share the opinion of the hardliners among officials in Ottawa on the extent of the Bolshevik conspiracy and the measures needed to confront it.[23] He was conciliatory in his attitude towards labour and opposed to a repressive policy.[24] This was apparent in his assessment of the labour unrest, and the operational guidelines he brought to the attention of A.A. Maclean. Most of the leaders of organized labour, he informed Maclean, were opposed to Bolshevik propaganda. The ordinary workers who appear to express approval of revolutionary doctrine do so, he continued, without clearly understanding its real nature or what is actually happening in Russia. In Rowell's view, their ignorance had to be met with education. Finally, he identified a "small minority," largely of "foreign birth," who had imbibed the doctrines of class war and believed in revolutions to achieve their ends. "Take care," he warned the comptroller, that where prosecutions are begun they are only taken up against this final group.[25]

As soon as he was informed of the minister's policy, Commissioner Perry of the RNWMP took steps to draft operational directives for the guidance of his divisional commanders. In the first of these he outlined the main threat to security and the legal action which was to be taken against those behind it. The objects of security investigations, he informed his field officers, were to be those individuals and organizations that espoused the pernicious doctrines of Bolshevism. He identified the main centres of radical activity as Winnipeg, Edmonton, and Vancouver. All those suspected of revolutionary activities, he ordered, were to be watched and a careful record kept of all their public utterances. In addition, the divisions were to keep themselves informed on all radical publications in their area. Legal proceedings, he instructed, were to be taken up where possible under the various wartime regulations and the sections of the Criminal Code dealing with sedition. Perry also requested that each commanding officer forward a summary of the secret service activities in his district to headquarters every month.[26]

In his second memorandum the commissioner drew the attention of his immediate subordinates to the need to create an efficient detective service of carefully selected men who could operate without drawing suspicion on themselves. Their primary task was to penetrate all labour organizations in their district, identifying which groups and which leaders favoured revolutionary action. Finally Perry demonstrated that he had well and truly grasped the fundamental objectives of any intelligence service. "It must be borne in mind," he stated, "that the only information which is of any value in connection with Bolshevism is the valuable and first-hand information of what is going to happen before it occurs in sufficient time to permit arrangements being made to offset any intended disturbance."[27]

The new duties required a considerable amount of reorganization. Men had to be transferred to Manitoba and British Columbia, and accommodation found there for new divisional headquarters and detachments. Funds had to be found to support the new operations. During the war Perry had employed individuals from time to time to assist him with the administration of secret service investigations. With the expansion of responsibilities some of this work was now taken over by a new department at headquarters in Regina known as the Criminal Investigation Branch.[28] Its first head was Assistant Commissioner W.H. Routledge. CIB became responsible for all correspondence and instructions regarding criminal and security matters between headquarters and the field divisions. The change resulted in a significant delegation of the commissioner's authority, although during 1919 Perry continued to exercise close personal control over all secret service duties.

One of the commissioner's immediate problems was lack of personnel. In December 1918 he had only eight secret agents and a half dozen detectives in his entire command.[29] Most of the agents employed during the war to investigate enemy aliens had been discharged. Several of his most experienced detectives were overseas with the cavalry squadrons. While he awaited their return he requested immediate authority to hire twenty additional agents. Perry estimated the cost of the new secret service operations during the coming fiscal year at $87 500. This sum included salaries for the agents at $125 per month, their expenses, and the pay of informants. The government readily agreed to his request and the funds were made available in February 1919 from the War Appropriation.[30]

Procuring suitable men to operate undercover at such short notice was not easy. As the officer in charge of the Crow's Nest Pass District wrote after turning down a clean-cut Anglo-Saxon applicant: "What we need is men who can speak several Slavic languages, and do the work of a coal miner."[31] At the end of February the commanding officer in Winnipeg was still without suitable men who had the language requirements to investigate the unions in the Fort William area.[32] Not surprisingly, many of the agents and many of the regular members who were recruited to work undercover were of central eastern European origin.

One of the most successful of these was Detective Constable F.W. Zaneth. Born in Italy, Zaneth (Zanetti) emigrated as a boy with his family to Moose Jaw where they eventually became naturalized British subjects. Later the family moved to the United States, but the young Zaneth returned and joined the RNWMP in 1917. In the spring of the following year he was sent to Drumheller to investigate the radicals believed to be behind the coal strike there. His success depended largely upon his own initiative. A factor in his favour was his ability to speak several languages. If he succeeded in infiltrating the union and providing useful intelligence, he would be kept on. If not, he would be withdrawn and transferred back to regular police work.

Zaneth did so well that Perry sent him back to Drumheller in September 1918, posing as Harry Blask, a member of the IWW from the United States. He soon gained the confidence of the union leaders and was initiated into the "secret grip" and other clandestine practices. In December he moved to Calgary where he became an organizer for the Socialist Party of Canada, and an acquaintance of most of the leading radicals in Alberta. A month later he attended the conference of the Alberta Federation of Labour in Medicine Hat.

In March 1919 he was a delegate at the all-important Western Labour Conference in Calgary that spawned the One Big Union. Zaneth was one of Perry's prime sources of intelligence during the critical months that led up to the strike in Winnipeg. He was also to be the star witness for the prosecution in the trial of the strike leaders.[33]

To many of the labour organizations the secret agents and detectives of the RNWMP were police spies or agent provocateurs, a despicable group of men who carried out what they believed were dishonest and unlawful assignments simply for money. Elaborate precautions were often taken to prevent them from penetrating unions and political parties. In Winnipeg Superintendent Starnes reported that his agents had to operate with great care, as members of the Socialist Party of Canada suspected every stranger of being a police spy.[34] The commanding officer in Vancouver, meanwhile, reported that the radicals had formed their own counter-intelligence service called the "Holy of Holies," which had his offices under constant surveillance and attempted to follow his men whenever they left the building.[35]

By one means or another the Mounted Police were able to evade these precautions skillfully. In Calgary, for example, some IWW sympathizers suspected that there was a "stool pigeon" in their midst. It was decided that he had to be unmasked, The object of their anger, Deputy Constable Zaneth (Harry Blask), who was present, heartily endorsed their resolve to do away with the "son of a bitch." To allay any suspicion from falling upon himself Zaneth made an excuse to travel to Regina. Once there, Perry arranged for him to be arrested under the Wartime Regulations as an alien travelling without a permit. He was subsequently brought to court, fined, and released. The local press gave considerable prominence to the case, which didn't go unnoticed in Calgary. As a result Zaneth was able to return to that city without any doubt in the minds of his fellow radicals that he was anything other than a union organizer.[36]

A more serious threat to the intelligence network occurred in Vancouver. Two secret agents of the Mounted Police had infiltrated the Russian Workers Union, one of the organizations declared illegal on Cahan's recommendation in September 1918. In June of the following year fourteen of its members were arrested and deportation proceedings were started against them based upon the evidence supplied by the two agents. Shortly after their arrest friends of the Russians brought charges of perjury against the Mounted Police agents, contending that the testimony they gave at the deportation hearings was completely false. The case dragged on through the courts, attracting a great deal of publicity as the identity of the two men was revealed. Perry anxiously awaited the outcome. If they were convicted, the whole secret agent system would be endangered. The credibility of the force's agents was as stake. In addition, no intelligence organization was likely to succeed unless the agents it employed could be sure that their anonymity would be protected, even after they had left its service. Fortunately for the commissioner they were finally acquitted.[37]

The decision to reorganize the secret service in Western Canada was not without its critics. Opposition centred on the transfer of duties in British

Columbia, where M.J. Reid, an official of the Immigration Department, had acted for several years as agent for both the Dominion Police and British Intelligence. Reid had built up an organization of secret agents and informers who were investigating radical labour unions as well as Chinese and Hindu nationalist groups. Cahan objected strongly to the reorganization. He felt that it was ridiculous to replace Reid, who had years of experience in security on the west coast, with the Mounted Police who had none.[38] Cahan was supported in his view by two influential Conservative members of parliament, H.H. Stevens and J.A. Calder.[39]

Pressure was brought to bear upon Perry to retain Reid's services in the same manner that he had been employed by the Dominion Police. With the apparent support of Rowell, the commissioner dug in his heels and refused to agree to any modification of the policy to place federal security matters in the west under the direct control of the RNWMP. For one thing Perry's staff in Vancouver had already gathered intelligence on Reid which led Perry to believe that he could not be trusted.[40] While Ottawa considered the subject, Reid dragged his feet, finding one excuse after another for not turning over his files to the officer commanding the Mounted Police in Vancouver. Perry, meanwhile, took steps to reinforce his position. Upon his prompting the comptroller wrote to the heads of the other security agencies in Ottawa, informing them that henceforth any enquiries on security matters in British Columbia should be directed to the RNWMP. Perry also moved to have British intelligence authorities informed that the Mounted Police had taken over from Reid, and that in future they should communicate with his office, if they required any investigation carried out.[41] The commissioner was determined to put an end, in western Canada at least, to the disjointed kind of security system that had existed. In the end Cahan and Stevens failed to get their way, which was perhaps one reason why the former eventually resigned as director of public safety.

In spite of the difficulties, by April 1919 the RNWMP had organized a highly successful covert intelligence operation in western Canada. Secret agents or detectives had managed to penetrate every important radical organization, some of them occupying executive positions in which they had the confidence of the leadership. Their reports gave a detailed account of the activities of the radicals, as well as a verbatim record of their public speeches. It is in these that one finds the problem of language which Bercuson and McNaught have noted.[42] Union agitators are frequently described as "Reds" or "Bolsheviks," their speeches as "Revolutionary." One suspects that these descriptions reflect not only the prejudices of the agents and informers, but also the universal difficulty encountered with the rhetoric of the radicals. Baxter has shown the diversity of opinion at the time as to the meaning of phrases like "Russian Revolution" and "Bolshevism."[43]

It was this kind of undigested intelligence that the Crown used to prosecute its case against the strike leaders. Although some of this raw material found its way to Ottawa, it did not form the primary means by which the Mounted Police informed its minister on conditions in the west. In each division the agents' reports were analyzed by the commanding officer who used them to draw up his own monthly assessment of the situation in his area. These, as Perry had ordered, were forwarded to the CIB at headquarters in Regina. From there copies were sent, often with additional assessments by the commissioner, to the comptroller in Ottawa who circulated them among the departments concerned. In this manner the government was being kept fully informed, as Rowell had requested.

The first of these monthly reports, which were for February, began to reach Regina early in March. It was clear from the beginning that the industrial areas were the ones which would give cause for concern. The commanding officer in Prince Albert, for example, in his report for March informed the commissioner that there was little in the way of radical activity among the unions, and no evidence of any sinister agency at work. A month later he expressed the view that the OBU would get little support in his area.[44] From the Maple Creek district, meanwhile, it was repeatedly reported that investigations had revealed nothing in the way of labour unrest, nor were they expected to as the area was largely rural and there were no organized unions.[45]

Of more concern were the Lethbridge and Fort Macleod Divisions which had large mining industries in their areas. By March agents from Fort Macleod had already established themselves among the mining unions of the Crow's Nest Pass. They reported that a number of revolutionary speeches had been made, and that most of the agitators were Russians connected with the Russian Social Democratic party in Winnipeg. The commanding officer estimated that 90 percent of the miners supported the radicals, and that a serious strike could result if they did not get their demands.[46]

In Lethbridge the February report indicated that the miners in the district were not as radical as those in the Crow's Nest Pass, and that there appeared no organized attempt to make trouble. These conditions changed after the March meeting of the Western Labour Conference in Calgary, and its decision to organize the One Big Union. The reports for April, May, and June highlight the effect of this event. The influx of OBU propaganda was noted as well as the presence of OBU spokesmen who were holding meetings at the various mines. The commanding officer believed that the OBU was gaining considerable support, especially amongst the "foreign element," and that a strike was possible, but nothing more sinister than this.[47]

From Edmonton the reports followed much the same pattern. There, however, considerable attention was paid to the activities of Joe Knight, the organizer for the Socialist Party of Canada. In June the sympathetic strike was reported as "orderly." A month later, at the behest of the crown prosecutor in Winnipeg, Knight's home, as well as the Trades and Labour Council office, was raided and material seized and forwarded to the city to be used in the trial of the strike leaders.[48]

One of the earliest areas of concern was British Columbia, where the Mounted Police had to start its security organization from scratch. What with the size of the province, the lack of staff, and Reid's obstruction, the commanding officer encountered some delay in establishing agents in all the industrial areas, especially outside the Lower Mainland.[49] By the end of March this situation appears to have been rectified and agents had penetrated most of the radical labour groups. As elsewhere, discontent appears to have quickly polarized in support of the OBU following the Calgary conference. In the March report the British Columbia Federation of Labour was stated to be all in favour of the new organization and the use of a general strike as a means of securing economic change. As a result, particular attention was paid to the activities of Kavanagh and Naylor, two OBU organizers. Superintendent Horrigan, the commanding officer, predicted the possibility of a general strike occurring, probably in June. His reports, however, were more concerned with the likelihood of trouble from the returned soldiers and the small "anarchial" organizations like the Russian Workers Union than they were in the OBU.[50]

As the OBU emerged as the catalyst of western discontent, attention naturally focused on the reports of the Western Labour Conference in Calgary's Paget Hall, from 13 to 15 March. This gathering was attended by two Mounted Police agents, Deputy Constable Zaneth and Agent No. 10, who Perry described as having "for many years taken an active part in the Industrial Workers of the World and kindred associations, and is therefore peculiarly competent to discuss the leaders in such movements and their aims and objectives."[51] No. 10 was alarmed by the events which took place at the conference. The radicals, he reported, largely members of the Socialist Party of Canada, had gained control and their resolutions had all been accepted. The ultimate aim of this leadership, he continued, was the overthrow of the existing "social order." To achieve this, they intended to unite organized labour in the west into One Big Union, and under the rallying cry of the "Six Hour Day" pull off a general strike about 1 June. Publicly, he stated, these leaders, who he identified as Knight, Kavanagh, Midgely, Pritchard, Naylor, and Johns, declare that they intend to reach their objective within legal bounds, but privately, he continued, their hope is that the strike will precipitate such drastic action by extreme individuals or groups as to lead to a breakdown of civil order which they can then exploit.

No. 10 had some recommendations which he believed would prevent this from happening. First of all, he suggested that the leadership of the present labour organizations should be strengthened as they were by no means unanimous in their support for the OBU. Following this, some progressive reforms in the area of wages, unemployment, and minimum working hours should be undertaken by the government. His most startling suggestion, however, was that the leaders should be illegally detained and held in secret custody until the danger period had passed. This he considered necessary if the government was to avoid going "down to defeat."[52]

None of the other intelligence reports of the Mounted Police had suggested anything quite like this. It was just the kind of evidence the hardliners in Ottawa would seize on to support their position. The officer in charge of the CIB in Regina recognized that it needed careful analysis before being forwarded east. He believed that No. 10's assessment of the situation was "considerably 'over drawn,'" based upon the mistaken view that the radical leaders "had actually accomplished something, and the masses were ready to do their will." The aims of these individuals for a change in the social order are only "far fetched dreams," he wrote in his forwarding note to Perry, and unlikely to be accepted by the general public once they are shown in their true light. After all, he continued, the labour organizations seem to be "split" over the question of support for the One Big Union. "I have refrained from forwarding No. 10's report to Ottawa," he informed the commissioner, "as I concluded that you would wish to express your personal opinion with regard to the situation."[53]

Perry's subsequent comments on the proposed OBU were probably the most judicious and accurate assessment of conditions in the west that one can find among the plethora of intelligence reports to reach Ottawa. Avoiding inflammatory references to revolutionaries and Bolsheviks, he clearly identified that what he meant by "reds" were socialist "agitators." The commissioner agreed that the ultimate aim of the OBU was a fundamental change in the social and economic order of the country, but nothing would be done to achieve this, he informed the comptroller, until the five-man organization committee appointed at the conference had had an opportunity to gain the support of a majority of the union members in the western provinces.

Perry's analysis was largely based upon an extraordinary meeting that he had with three members of that committee — Midgely, Pritchard, and Kavanagh — shortly after the Calgary conference. At this face-to-face encounter there appears to have been a frank discussion between the head of security in the west and the union leaders concerning their aims and objectives. Perry described them afterwards as "Revolutionary Socialists," able and determined men who sought to bring about a change in social and economic conditions, but were "opposed to force or violence." Their immediate objective, they informed him, was to perfect the organization of the OBU, following which they would call a general strike to demand a six-hour working day. This, they believed, would occur sometime in June.

"I am not prepared to say that they are aiming at a revolution," wrote Perry, but they are "influencing a section of labour in the west, and unchaining forces which, even if they so desire, some day they would be unable to control." There was a "possibility" of a revolution, the commissioner believed, if the strike was to lead to a breakdown of civil order which could be exploited by extremists. He identified Vancouver and Victoria as the most dangerous points, and suggested that the naval forces there be strengthened as a precaution. Perry concluded his analysis with a number of recommendations which were to go largely unheeded by government leaders in the weeks ahead. Above all, he warned against interfering with the organization of the OBU, prosecuting its leaders, or preventing them from publicly expressing their opinions. Such action, he continued, would only antagonize the larger and more moderate element of the labour movement who were sensitive about their civil liberties. Finally, he urged, measures must be adopted to provide employment for the returned soldiers.[54] He did not identify the existence of any sinister plot to overthrow the government by force, either by the western radicals or foreign agents.

Perry's report reached the comptroller's office in Ottawa by 12 April, on which day a copy was forwarded to White, the acting prime minister.[55] Government leaders, it appears, were already in a near state of panic over the situation in British Columbia. On 16 April White cabled Borden in Paris expressing the cabinet's alarm over plans "being laid for a revolutionary movement" among the "workers and soldiers there." Fearing serious disturbances, White asked Borden to arrange for a British cruiser to be sent to Vancouver or Victoria.[56]

Understandably, Borden, who was in the throes of asserting Canada's sovereign status at the Peace Conference, balked at the suggestion. Assistance from the British government, he replied, should only be solicited "as a last resort." Why not, he suggested, use the RNWMP with its strength increased if necessary?[57] Plans began to increase the strength of the Mounted Police to 2500 men, but White was still not satisfied. He cabled Borden again a few days later on account of the "serious conditions in British Columbia and projected revolution movement about June first," again urging the despatch of a British warship.[58] The source of this intelligence, he informed Borden, was the comptroller of the RNWMP and the Militia Department.

The RNWMP source that White referred to was most likely a "Memorandum on Revolutionary Tendencies in Western Canada" drawn up by the assistant comptroller of the force, C.F. Hamilton, early in April. Hamilton had only recently returned to his position with the Mounted Police after serving during the war as deputy chief censor for Canada. His assessment reflected the views of the hardliners in Ottawa like Cahan, and it differed both in tone and substance from those of Perry and his officers.

Hamilton identified the existence of a sinister organization which was under the control of a "central directing body somewhere in Canada." Its influence could be seen not only in the OBU but in many other radical groups. The ultimate aim, he reported, of those behind it was the subversion of the existing social and political institutions and the establishment of a "Soviet Government" based upon the "Dictatorship of the proletariat." Although the "weapons and explosives" they had were insufficient for serious fighting, a "revolution by force of arms," he advised, "was conceivable under existing conditions."[59]

Within a few days of White's last cable to Borden regarding the situation in British Columbia, government leaders in Ottawa began to turn their attention more and more to events which were taking place in Winnipeg. On 1 May in that city workers in the building and metal trades walked off their jobs over demands for wage increases and the refusal of employers to bargain collectively. Two weeks later they were joined by some 30 000 other workers and the Winnipeg General Strike had begun.

The commanding officer of the RNWMP in Manitoba was Superintendent Cortlandt Starnes, who was later to succeed Perry as commissioner. Throughout the months that led up to the breaking of the strike, Starnes never identified it as anything other than a labour dispute.[60] He did not connect it to the OBU, although many of his agents' reports, which were also forwarded to Ottawa, did contain alarming rumours of events in Winnipeg and accounts of the inflammatory statements of the strike leaders.

As in the case of British Columbia, the Mounted Police had no existing organization in Winnipeg. This resulted in some delay, but by the end of

March Starnes was able to report that his agents had penetrated the three main areas of radical activity, the Socialist Party of Canada, the Ukrainian Social Democratic party, and the socialist organizations among the Finns at Lakehead.[61] Early in April Starnes was optimistic about the labour scene in the city, and his assessment gave no hint of the bitter conflict that was to occur a month later. The Socialist Party of Canada, he reported, had been working hard to win the support of the returned soldiers, but was having little success. As to the possibility of a strike, he expressed the view that many of the unions had just received wage increases "and danger of a large scale strike has been averted."[62] A month later conditions had changed. The effect of the Calgary conference was once again evident. There has been much discussion, he reported, in union circles over the OBU and all appear to be in favour of it. He also warned that the dispute between the workers in the building and metal trades would likely to lead to a "sympathetic strike involving all the unions in the city."[63]

In spite of Starnes' reports, officials in Ottawa continued to see the strike as a seditious conspiracy. On 21 May 1919 two federal cabinet ministers, Meighen and Robertson, arrived in Winnipeg to try to bring an end to the general strike. Like the Citizens Committee and others, they already regarded the strike as an attempt at revolution.[64] As the crisis heightened, in the weeks which followed, this conviction among government leaders would grow until steps were finally taken to break the strike. Incredible as it may seem, however, Starnes was still reporting on 10 June that "indications are that the backbone of the strike is broken, and it should only be a matter of a few days before the majority of the strikers are back at work."[65] He also informed his superiors that his agents had found no trace of any outside support for the strike. Seven days later, with the cabinet's approval, the strike leaders were arrested and charged with trying to overthrow the state.[66]

In the months that had preceded the arrests the Mounted Police had developed an effective intelligence service. All suspected organizations were successfully penetrated and enough information obtained to give a reliable indication of their aims and the plans of their leaders. To obtain this intelligence the RNWMP had established a body of paid informers and undercover agents who had covertly infiltrated the various groups posing as fellow radicals. In selecting these agents the police had shown a willingness to recruit individuals of a suitable cultural or linguistic background, and to maintain them, if necessary, in their double role for months or even years at a time. These were professional developments which were to be important for the future.

A systematic means of reporting and analyzing the results of undercover operations had also been established. The agents submitted regular lengthy accounts of their investigations and the information supplied by their informers. These were evaluated by local area commanders, who used them to draw up monthly reports on the conditions in their districts. These in turn were forwarded to CIB at Headquarters in Regina for yet further analysis and comment.

Where this system seems to have fallen down was in Ottawa. It appears to have been the practice to forward to the comptroller's office not only the monthly reports and the additional assessments of Commissioner Perry, but also the grass roots material provided by the undercover agents. These were often heavily laden with the alarming and inflammatory statements of the radical leaders. They were recorded verbatim with the intention that they could be used later, if criminal charges were laid. What the agents reported could differ markedly from the conclusions and assessments of their commanding officers. These would be based upon the information provided by several agents working independently of each other.

In Ottawa there was no central body responsible for evaluating the material forwarded by the various security forces, resolving any contradictions in it, and advising the cabinet on conditions. All the comptroller could do was circulate copies of such reports as he felt necessary, or important, to other department heads and ministers. They in turn reciprocated in a similar manner. No overall analysis of the information received on the situation in the west seems to have been attempted. Instead, government leaders were faced with a miscellaneous collection of material that at times must have been understandably alarming and confusing.

Apart from Hamilton's unsubstantiated claims, there had been nothing in the reports of the RNWMP during the months prior to the breaking-up of the strike which revealed a revolutionary plot. Perry had expressed his concern over the possibility of disorder, if strikes and demonstrations should get out of hand, but he had not identified caches of arms, secret armies drilling, or foreign agents hatching a conspiracy.

Government leaders, nevertheless, stuck to the sinister-plot theory expounded by Cahan in the fall of 1918. One cannot be precise about why Borden and some of his colleagues continued to take the position they did. It is possible that they were affected to some degree by the widespread fear of red revolution that gripped the country. The strikes in the United States, revolution in Europe, the rhetoric of the radicals, and the conduct of the strikers may have helped to reinforce their convictions. There were also intelligence reports from other sources which usually conflicted markedly with those of the Mounted Police. It was reported by Chambers, the chief censor, for example, that a prominent Ukrainian socialist in Winnipeg was actually an ambassador of the Soviet government.[67] Meighen, the acting minister of justice, learned from a member of the Manitoba legislature that the Ukrainians in his province had guns and ammunition ready for a revolution.[68]

There was also Cahan's dogged belief in a Bolshevik conspiracy. The former director of public safety told Borden, on the latter's return from Europe, that the OBU intended to "kick the Government off Parliament Hill."[69] This conclusion was supported by reports received by the Directorate of Military Intelligence in Ottawa. The commander of the military forces in Winnipeg stated the "Evidence so far searched proves conclusively Bolshevik money from United States has been received; also Strike Committee working closely with supporters 'One Big Union.' No doubt seriousness of conspiracy throughout West."[70]

It is strange that the largest and best organized security force in western Canada, whose agents had penetrated the senior levels of the most radical organizations, should have had such little impact in Ottawa. Perhaps it fits the familiar pattern of miscalculation and ignorance on the part of Ottawa with regard to western conditions. How far did officials in Ottawa select those intelligence reports which suited their own preconceptions of the situation there? How far did they still see the prairies as a violent uncivilized frontier, albeit populated with radical foreigners rather than savage Indians, which had to be firmly dealt with?

Borden's obscure role is yet another factor in the whole affair. We know from the warning he cabled in December 1918 of Soviet plans to launch a propaganda campaign in North America that he had access to British intelligence sources. It appears that during his months in Paris these same sources continued to inform him on matters relating to Canada, and that after his return he regularly received a digest of a special weekly intelligence report prepared by the British Intelligence Service for the British cabinet.[71] What these reports told him, and how they affected his decisions regarding events in Winnpeg, remains a mystery. It is possible however, that the British may have been deliberately selective in the nature of the information they made available to Borden in the hope of promoting anti-Soviet feelings in Ottawa which would strengthen Canadian support for measures like the allied intervention in Siberia.

The Winnipeg General Strike does seem to have brought one thing home to Borden — that the country's secret service system was inadequate. When the responsibility for security had been geographically divided in December 1918 between the RNWMP and the Dominion Police, Sir Percy Sherwood, the chief commissioner of police, had retired. During the war years Sherwood had established a high profile as the head of the nation's security forces. His departure left a vacuum that his interim replacement, A.J. Cawdron, could not fill, and it also appears to have disrupted the close intelligence liaison between the Dominion Police and Scotland Yard's Special Branch.[72]

The lack of leadership was brought to Borden's attention by the premier of Ontario who informed him that the chief of the Toronto Police Department had complained that "at this very difficult and crucial time there is really no head to the organization of the Secret Service of the Dominion."[73] Borden readily agreed that a successor had to be found for Sherwood, and his comment in reply that "until my return I supposed that this had received attention" indicated a lack of direction on security matters within the cabinet itself during his prolonged absence.[74]

Obviously concerned about any recurrence of industrial unrest or general strikes, the prime minister proceeded to bring about a radical change in the federal system of security and policing. On 5 August 1919 he held discussions on the subject with Perry in Ottawa. As a consequence the commissioner, who had already decided views on the deficiencies of the existing security system, drew up recommendations for a new federal police force.[75]

Perry's primary criticism was the division in ministerial responsibility; the Mounted Police reported to the president of the Privy Council, the Dominion Police to the minister of justice. His first recommendation, therefore, called for the two forces to be brought under one department without delay. This he suggested could be accomplished in two ways: (a) by bringing them under one minister, leaving each with its existing area of jurisdiction, and its own executive head; (b) by amalgamating the two forces into one, which might take the form of absorption of one by another.

In considering the merits of these two choices, he drew Borden's attention to the differences between the RNWMP and the Dominion Police. The first, he pointed out, was subject to military-type training, strict discipline, and was also armed. As well as being peace officers, he continued, its members were prohibited by law from becoming unionized. Perry was also careful to note that it had experienced detectives, commissioned officers who had a recognized social status and a reputation that was respected throughout the country.

The Dominion Police, in contrast, was organized like a municipal force. It was not armed, had no military training, and its discipline could only be enforced by a civil court. Because of its size, about 140 men as compared to the Mounted Police strength of 2500, it had to rely on other agencies to assist it in carrying out its duties. Here, thought Perry, was the basic weakness of any federal police service established under the Dominion Police. The latter agency depended upon the public, the assistance of the municipal police forces, and the employment of agents from private detective firms, about half of whom were American, to operate its secret service. It could not provide the basis for a federal police and security institution which was truly national in organization, sentiment, and direction.

Perry also believed that it was no longer possible to depend upon the ordinary citizen as a source of intelligence. During the war Canadians had been patriotically united in the cause to defeat Germany. But the war was over and the public was divided over the issues facing the country. As for the municipal police forces, they were no longer reliable either. Many of them had become unionized. In Winnipeg and Vancouver they had participated in the recent strikes. In the United States there had also been some serious labour disputes involving city forces. In London, England, even the Bobbies had gone on strike. Municipal forces, argued the commissioner, could not be depended on where industrial disputes were concerned. The government must have a force which would stand by the civil authorities when a breakdown in public order occurred.

Perry reserved his final criticism for the Dominion Police practice of hiring private investigators. The federal force had not developed its own body of experienced detectives. Some believe, he stated, that the detectives provided by such companies as the Pinkertons were the best in the world. This, he continued, had not been his experience. The country's secret service investigation should not be conducted by Americans, but by detectives who were "Canadian in nationality and sentiment." In concluding his memorandum Perry recommended that the best interests of the nation would be served by extending the jurisdiction of the RNWMP to all of Canada.[76]

The commissioner's recommendations became the blueprint for a new federal police force. After some discussion with Rowell, the president of the Privy Council, Borden took steps to implement the proposals. On 10 November 1919 the RNWMP Act was amended.[77] The legislation provided for the absorption of the Dominion Police and its duties by the western force. The headquarters of the new body was to be located in Ottawa, and it would be answerable to one cabinet minister for its "control and management." It was to be responsible for federal law enforcement and national security throughout Canada. In keeping with its new role the RNWMP was to be renamed the Royal Canadian Mounted Police. To head the force the government named Perry. As a young man he had been one of the first graduates from the Royal Military College of Canada. Later he served as an officer with the NWMP during the North-West Rebellion. Laurier had promoted him to the office of commissioner in 1900 when the Boer War gave the government an opportunity to rid itself of his troublesome predecessor. Now, at the age of sixty, he prepared to take on the task of organizing the new body when the legislation came into effect on 1 February 1920.

Canada's secret service dated back to the days of Confederation when John A. Macdonald employed a number of agents under the umbrella of the Dominion Police to ferret out the plots of the Fenians. Thereafter, the Secret Service Section, as it came to be called, saw only flurries of activity prior to 1914. With the outbreak of war the dominion was faced with the biggest security problem in its history. At issue was the possibility of espionage and sabotage by the large population, mainly in western Canada, of enemy aliens. To meet this threat the government secured passage of the War Measures Act and organized a highly decentralized intelligence network which, although co-ordinated to a degree by the Dominion Police, relied upon municipal forces, officials in a number of federal government departments, and private detective agencies to carry out its investigations. The threat from the German and Austrian settlers, however, proved to be a hollow one, and the wartime security system was never severely tested.

In the industrial dislocation of the postwar period in Ottawa thought it saw a far more serious threat to its authority. Its reponse was the establishment of a non-civilian centralized federal police and security force. The change contrasted with developments in the same area among its closest allies, Great Britain and the United States. In Washington and London responsibility for security and intelligence was to remain divided among a variety of government departments. It also reflected the growing influence of the federal government in the life and affairs of the nation. With the War Measures Act Ottawa showed that it was prepared to assume powers unto itself when questions involving the security of the country arose. With the creation of the RCMP it gave itself a capability of enforcing that authority. These developments were to provide the means for future action in times of national emergency. As a model for the new organization, the government turned back to the country's frontier experience, selecting a semi-military police force which had been founded half a century before to bring to order to the western plains, an institution whose origins lay in the traditions of British colonial rule.

The change made the federal government the number one police power in the nation. It was not without its critics. There was concern that the RCMP would infringe upon the rights of the provinces under the BNA Act to administer justice. Prior to 1920 the enforcement of federal statutes was largely left to local police forces. As a result, Ottawa proceeded to tread softly throughout the 1920s, maintaining little more than a token federal police presence in provinces like British Columbia and Quebec. In Parliament, meanwhile, J.S. Woodsworth, who saw the RCMP as an authoritarian threat to civil liberties, would persist for years without success in trying to reverse Borden's decision. One of the most important developments, however, of the reorganization of 1920 was that it paved the way later for federal-provincial contracts for the RCMP as a provincial and municipal police force, eventually giving Canada a unique system of law enforcement in all but two of its provinces. Finally, of course, it is no exaggeration to say that the Royal Canadian Mounted Police is but one more offspring of the Winnipeg General Strike.

Notes

1. R.B. Russell, W. Pritchard, J. Queen, A.A. Heaps, G. Armstrong, R.E. Bray, W. Ivens, and R.J. Jones.

2. D.C. Masters, *The Winnipeg General Strike* (Toronto, 1950), 115.

3. "Report of the Royal Commission . . . upon the causes and effects of the General Strike, H.A. Robson, KC, Commissioner," 1919, 3.

4. Ibid., 13.

5. W.J. Tremeear, ed., *Canadian Criminal Cases* (Toronto), 33: 12.

6. Masters, *Winnipeg General Strike*, 134.

7. H. Borden, ed., *R.L. Borden: His Memoirs* (Toronto, 1938), 972.

8. W. Rodney, *Soldiers of the International* (Toronto, 1968), 26.

9. R. McCormack, *Reformers, Rebels, and Revolutionaries* (Toronto, 1977), 178.

10. K. McNaught and D.J. Bercuson, *The Winnipeg Strike: 1919* (Toronto, 1974), 91.

11. T.M. Longstreth, *The Silent Force* (New York, 1927), 290.

12. R.C. Fetherstonhaugh, *The Royal Canadian Mounted Police* (New York, 1938), 179.

13. N. and W. Kelly, *The Royal Canadian Mounted Police: A Century of History* (Edmonton, 1973), 151.

14. Canada, *Sessional Papers*, "Report of the Commissioner of the RNWMP for 1918," 7–8.

15. R. McCormack, *Reformers, Rebels and Revolutionaries* (Toronto, 1977), 441–42.

16. Public Archives of Canada (hereafter PAC), Borden Papers, 56642, Borden to Cahan, 19 May 1918.

17. PAC, Borden Papers, 60920, Borden to White, 2 Dec. 1918, telegram.

18. PC Order 3087, 2 Dec. 1918.

19. RCMP Headquarters, Ottawa, RCMP Records, G–2–6, Rowell to the attorneys-general of BC, Alberta, Saskatchewan, and Manitoba, 16 May 1919.

20. PC Order 2213, 7 Oct. 1918.

21. PAC, Borden Papers, 49413, White to Borden, 16 Dec. 1918, telegram.

22. RCMP Records, G–2–6, Rowell to Maclean, 4 Jan. 1919.

23. McCormack, *Reformers, Rebels and Revolutionaries*, 445.

24. M. Prang, *N.W. Rowell: Ontario Nationalist* (Toronto, 1975), 267.

25. RCMP Records, G–2–6, Rowell to Maclean, 20 Jan. 1919.

26. Ibid., B–1, 958, Circular Memorandum 807, 6 Jan. 1919.

27. Ibid., Circular Memorandum 807A, 6 Jan. 1919.

28. Ibid., General Order No. 13176, 2 Feb. 1919.

29. RCMP Records, G–2–6, Perry to Maclean, 14 Jan. 1919.

30. PC Order 363, 20 Feb. 1919.

31. RCMP Records, B–1, 955, Junget to Spalding, 21 Jan. 1919.

32. Ibid., Starnes to Perry, 27 Feb. 1919.

33. RCMP Records, SF, 0–284.

34. Ibid., B–2, 20, Starnes to Perry, 15 Apr. 1919.

35. Ibid., B–1, 930, Horrigan to Perry, Feb. 1919.

36. Ibid., SF, 0–284, Pennefather to Perry, 26 July 1919.

37. Ibid., A–1, 589.

38. Ibid., A–1, 1919, Cahan to deputy minister of justice, 9 Jan. 1919.

39. Ibid., G–2–6, Stevens to Rowell, 20 Feb. 1919.

40. Ibid., Horrigan to Perry, 24 Jan. 1919.

41. Ibid., Maclean to Rowell, 24 Feb. 1919.

42. McNaught and Bercuson, *Winnipeg Strike: 1919*, 43.

43. T.C. Baxter, "Selected Aspects of Canada Public Opinion on the Russian Revolution and its Impact in Canada, 1917–19" (M.A. thesis, University of Western Ontario, 1973).

44. RCMP Records, B-1, West to Perry, 5 May 1919.

45. Ibid., Demers to Perry, 12 Apr. 1919.

46. Ibid., Tucker to Perry, 28 Feb. 1919.

47. Ibid., Pennefather to Perry, 8 May 1919.

48. Ibid., Wroughton to Perry, 6 Aug. 1919.

49. RCMP Records, B-2, 70, Horrigan to Perry, 24 Feb. 1919.

50. Ibid., B–1, 930, Horrigan to Perry, 4 Apr. 1919.

51. PAC, Borden Papers, 56825, Perry to Maclean, 2 Apr. 1919.

52. Ibid., 56831–35, Report of Agent No. 10 re Inter-provincial Labour Convention, Calgary, Mar. 1919.

53. Ibid., 56830, Notes for Commissioner's Perusal re Report of Agent No. 10 (n.d.).

54. Ibid., 56825–28, Perry to Maclean, 2 Apr. 1919.

55. Ibid., 56824, Maclean to White, 12 Apr. 1919.

56. Ibid., 60923, White to Borden, 16 Apr. 1919, telegram.

57. Ibid., 60924, Borden to White, 18 Apr. 1919, telegram.

58. Ibid., 60926, White to Borden, 28 Apr. 1919, telegram.

59. PAC, RG 24, vol. 3985, file NSC 1055-2-21, Memorandum on Revolutionary Tendencies in Western Canada, contained in Gwatkin to Stephens, 12 Apr. 1919.

60. See, for example, Canada, *Sessional Papers*, Report of Commissioner of RNWMP, 1919, 11–12.

61. RCMP Records, B–1, 929, Starnes to Perry, 22 Mar. 1919.

62. Ibid., Starnes to Perry, 9 Apr. 1919.

63. Ibid., Starnes to Perry, 9 May 1919.

64. McNaught and Bercuson, *Winnipeg Strike: 1919*, 57.

65. RCMP Records, H-V–1, vol. 2, Starnes to Perry, 10 June 1919.

66. McNaught and Bercuson, *Winnipeg Strike: 1919*, 79.

67. D. Avery, "The Radical Alien and the Winnipeg General Strike," in *The West and the Nation*, edited by C. Berger and R. Cook (Toronto, 1976), 218.

68. Ibid., 219.

69. PAC, Borden Papers, 61631, Cahan to Borden, 28 May 1919.

70. Ibid., 62009, general officer commanding Military District No. 10 to adjutant-general of militia, 18 June 1919.

71. Ibid., 60930, colonial secretary to governor general, 27 May 1919, telegram.

72. Ibid., 60940, colonial secretary to governor general, 4 June 1919.

73. Ibid., 60947, Sir William Hearst, premier of Ontario, to Borden, 5 June 1919.

74. Ibid., 60954, Borden to Hearst, 6 June 1919.

75. Ibid., 50763, Perry to Borden, 7 Aug. 1919.

76. Ibid.

77. *Statutes of Canada*, 1919 (2nd Session), 10 Geo. 5, c. 28.

SECTION 3

COURTS AND THE CRIMINAL LAW

Canadian criminal law derives from that of Britain, although the question of exactly what the starting point is in the case of each British colony is extremely complex. The general rule is that when a territory became part of the British Empire, it acquired the law of Britain in its entirety. This included not just statutes passed by Parliament but the great body of legal rules and principles accumulated through centuries of judicial decisions known as the common law. British laws passed after the colony became part of the Empire no longer applied; the colony began creating its own body of law, which was added to the foundation inherited from Britain. In Canada's case this meant that until 1867 each of the British North American colonies had its own criminal law. Not only did the criminal law of Upper and Lower Canada, Nova Scotia, New Brunswick, Prince Edward Island, Newfoundland and British Columbia diverge from that of Britain at different points, each developed on its own thereafter. There was, of course, much copying of British statutes and to a lesser degree of those of other colonies, but substantial differences remained.

When the time came to plan the Canadian confederation in the 1860s it was widely accepted that the criminal law should be uniform throughout the country. There was much concern at the time about strengthening the powers of the central government as much as possible to avoid the kind of breakdown that had led to the American civil war. All the provinces could agree that a single system of criminal law under federal control was desirable. Unlike language and education, the criminal law was not seen as essential to the preservation of French-Canadian culture, hence there was no pressure to make it an area of provincial responsibility. London had imposed English criminal law on the French-Canadian population immediately after the decision to keep the country in 1763. After some initial reluctance the population of Quebec adapted to the English system without any lingering regrets.

The decision to have a single criminal law implied change for at least some parts of the country. Since changes had to be made in any case, why not seize the opportunity to improve and reform the law? This was the opinion of the man who was given the task of consolidating the laws of the various colonies into a single body of statutes in 1869, Judge James Robert Gowan. Gowan pleaded with Prime Minister John A. Macdonald to be allowed to take the next logical step and codify the criminal law. This would have involved putting all of the criminal law into a single comprehensive statute, thus eliminating much overlapping and confusion. Opponents of codification argued that the common law represented the accumulated wisdom of generations and should not lightly be discarded. So far, in Britain itself, the opponents had prevailed and John A. Macdonald was not prepared to experiment.

The project was revived two decades later and reached fruition under John S.D. Thompson, first as Minister of Justice and later as Prime Minister. In 1892 Canada became the first jurisdiction in the British Empire to codify its criminal law. Alan Mewett's article, written in 1967 before any substantial historical research had been done on the subject, tends to underplay the significance of this achievement. The 1892 Criminal Code was certainly far from perfect but it provided a rational framework for further reform. The code was amended frequently after 1892 but its internal logic discouraged the indiscriminate creation of new crimes. It survived sixty years without major changes and even the complete review undertaken in the 1950s left the basic structure intact.

The Criminal Code has frequently been criticized on the grounds that it lacks the philosophical coherence of, for example, the French code. The Canadian code, however, was no mere jumble of individual crimes and punishments. It had a good deal of internal consistency from the time of its introduction in 1892. Probably the clearest illustration of this fact came with the introduction of narcotics legislation in the first decade of the twentieth century. The attachment of criminal penalties to what had previously been lawful activities amounted to the creation of new crimes. Yet the government quite deliberately chose not to include its anti-drug measures in the Criminal Code. The reason was quite straightforward: the narcotics legislation violated one of the basic principles of the code by placing the burden of proof on the accused. The civil servants in the Department of Justice jealously guarded the integrity of the code and it was simpler to avoid the issue altogether.

Because Canadian narcotics legislation stood by itself and represented an entirely new departure in criminal law, it has attracted a good deal of attention from scholars concerned with the origins of law. Conflict theorists, labelling theorists, and Marxists have all endeavoured to use the passage of the narcotics laws as a case study. The success of their arguments must be left to the individual reader's judgement. What is readily apparent in a review of the literature is how each successive study has revealed new complexities. Economic and racial motivations are anything but straightforward. International pressures may have been more important than internal forces in causing the government to act. Neil Boyd's article provides a good review of the literature in the context of a neo-Marxist reinterpretation of the events. Boyd has also made perhaps the most thorough examination so far of the primary sources and his article continues the process of revealing new layers of complexity. It seems highly unlikely that we have heard the last word on this subject.

It is relatively easy to find out how very serious crimes were handled in the past. Murders frequently attracted a great deal of public attention and murder trials in the nineteenth century certainly served as public entertainment to a greater degree than at present. The trial process in such cases, as Martin Friedland points out, has changed less over the last century than any other component of the criminal justice system. The interest in nineteenth-century murder trials comes mainly from what they reveal about public and official attitudes to crime and punishment.

At the other end of the judicial scale lay the police court with its thousands of petty offences to process every month. George T. Denison, Toronto police magistrate for the extraordinary period of forty-four years before 1921, was a noted eccentric but his approach to dispensing justice at this level was probably more typical than his idiosyncracies would indicate. As Gene Howard Homel demonstrates, Denison's court had numerous flaws but remained a functional and even popular institution among those who were subject to its authority. Denison's common sense approach seemed embarrassingly outdated by the 1920s and disappeared in the rising tide of professionalization at that time. It is still possible to doubt that the new approach produced significantly better results.

THE CRIMINAL LAW, 1867–1967†

ALAN W. MEWETT

The federal Parliament of Canada was quick to act on the criminal law powers ascribed to it under the British North America Act[1] and to begin the task of consolidating the overwhelming mass of previously existing colonial laws. These were made up basically of common law importations as applicable to colonial conditions, but there was also a substantial amount of legislation from colonial assemblies. In Upper Canada, for example, an act of 1836 provided the right to have defence counsel for persons accused of a felony;[2] in the Province of Canada, an act of 1851 set out various appeal procedures and other reforms.[3] There were also enactments relating to speedy trials,[4] coinage offences,[5] accessories and abettors of indictable offences,[6] kidnapping[7] and the like. Furthermore, most of this legislation was paralleled in similar, but by no means identical enactments in the other provinces of British North America.[8]

The year 1869 saw the real beginning of the campaign to consolidate the criminal law of Canada and one session produced Dominion legislation on a variety of substantive and procedural matters. These included acts on forgery, larceny, malicious injury to property, offences against the person and coinage offences and, in the procedural field, on juvenile offenders, summary convictions, indictable offences and the significant Criminal Procedure Act which remains the basis of much of our present procedure.[9]

Between 1869 and 1892 a series of enactments continued this process[10] and by the latter date much of the bulk of the work of consolidation had been done. However, there still existed a large amount of pre-Confederation provincial criminal legislaton which resulted in the Canadian criminal law presenting a more or less confused picture (depending upon whether the date was closer to 1869 or 1892) of such common law offences as were introduced into the provinces[11] and remained unaltered, provincial legislation which had not been repealed by its assumption under Dominion authority[12] and the ever increasing body of Dominion statute law.

For a large part of the nineteenth century, the idea of codification of the criminal law had been mooted in England and elsewhere in the English-speaking world. In 1838 in England the first criminal law commissioners were appointed to report on and draft such a code and in 1878, largely as a result of the work of Sir James Stephen, the English Draft Code, dealing with indictable offences, was formulated. Although this formed the basis of two bills presented to the English Parliament, both attempts to introduce a comprehensive criminal code were abortive.

In Canada, the Bill Respecting Criminal Law of 1892 was expressed by Sir John Thompson to be founded on the Draft Code prepared by the royal

† *The Canadian Bar Review* 45 (1967): 726–40.

commission in Great Britain in 1880, on Stephen's *Digest of the Criminal Law*, the edition of 1887, Burbidge's *Digest of the Canadian Criminal Law* of 1889, and the Canadian statutory law.[13] He quoted from the Commission Report to define the codification as follows:[14]

> It is a reduction of the existing law to an orderly written system, freed from needless technicalities, obscurities and other defects which the experience of its administration has disclosed. It aims at the reduction to a system of that kind of substantive law relating to crimes and the law of procedure, both as to indictable offences and as to summary convictions.

The proposed code contained little in the way of change. In introducing the bill on its second reading, the attorney general stated:[15]

> Substantially it follows the existing law. It proposes, however, to abolish the distinction between principals and accessories. It aims at making punishments . . . more uniform. It discontinues the use of the word "malice" and the word "maliciously". . . . It defines murder and in cases of doubt settles what murder is. With that view it defines provocation. . . . It deals with the offence of bigamy. . . . It proposes to abolish the term "larceny" and to adopt the term "theft" instead. . . .With regard to the law of procedure, I propose to abolish the distinction between felonies and misdemeanours. . . . It is proposed likewise to abolish the provision of the existing law with regard to venue. . . . It abolishes writs of error and provides an appeal court.

The debate on the bill did not prove particularly edifying. The grand jury, though threatened, was saved from abolition. There was some discussion on territorial jurisdiction, and an argument, which had surprisingly modern overtones, on the wisdom and applicability of the McNaughton Rules. The House was unhappy about some of the powers of arrest which were to be given to peace officers and to private persons, and several of the proposed maximum penalties were changed without very much discussion. On 28 June 1892, after the third reading, the bill finally passed the House, received royal assent on 9 July 1892, and came into force on 1 July 1893.[16]

A series of amendments resulted in the consolidations of 1906 and 1927, but neither of these could be called revisions. In 1947, a Royal Commission to Revise the Criminal Code was appointed, reported in 1952 and in 1953 the Revised Code was enacted.[17] This revision did not greatly alter the structure or substance of the original code, no attempt being made to consider or redefine fundamental criminal law concepts. The system of punishments was rationalized, certain procedural reforms were introduced and a relatively small number of specific offences were either redefined or introduced.

One significant change was that enacted by section 8, stating:

> Notwithstanding anything in this Act or any other Act no person shall be convicted
> a) of an offence at common law,
> b) of an offence under an Act of the Parliament of England, or of Great Britain, or of the United Kingdom of Great Britain and Ireland, or

    c) of an offence under an Act or ordinance in force in any province, territory or place before that province, territory or place became a province of Canada . . . .

The original code, while comprehensive, did not purport to reduce all the Dominion criminal law into one statute. It preserved a number of previously enacted provisions, listed in the schedule, and while section 5 provided that no person shall be proceeded against for any offence against any act of the Parliament of England, Great Britain or the United Kingdom unless made expressly applicable to Canada, it was silent as to the applicability of common law offences. The British North America Act had preserved the existing common law (insofar as received and not altered by statute) for the original provinces[18] and a series of acts[19] provides the same for the other provinces and territories. It is thus not surprising to find that in the 1906 consolidation various sections appeared expressly preserving the criminal law of England in various provinces. Those not listed in the code, had the criminal law preserved in other statutes.[20] Prior to the enactment of section 8 of the 1953 revision, prosecutions were successful for such common law offences as abuse of office in taking fees wrongfully,[21] public mischief,[22] champerty and maintenance[23] and perhaps barratry.[24]

    It was thus not until 1953 that all common law offences were abolished throughout Canada. It is interesting to note that, in contrast, the first English Draft Code proposed the abolition of all common law offences not specifically enacted in the code. It could not, however, be maintained that prosecution for common law offences was a very frequent occurrence in Canada after 1892, and the revision commissioners decided that there was no point in preserving them after 1953. Instead, all those thought applicable to Canada were specifically enacted, such as compounding indictable offences,[25] indemnification of bail,[26] public mischief[27] and common law conspiracy.[28] On the other hand, faced with the difficulty, if not impossibility of attempting to codify common law defences, the commissioners merely recommended, and Parliament enacted, section 7(2) providing:

> Every rule and principle of the common law that renders any circumstance a justification or excuse for an act or a defence to a charge continues in force and applies in respect of proceedings for an offence under this Act or any other Act of the Parliament of Canada, except insofar as they are altered by or are inconsistent with this Act or any other Act of the Parliament of Canada.

The Criminal Code does not purport, of course, to contain all the criminal law of Canada. A surpisingly large number of federal statutes, such as the Extradition Act,[29] Official Secrets Act,[30] Penitentiary Act,[31] Customs Act,[32] Post Office Act[33] and the like contain important criminal provisions respecting various acts, but two in particular, the Juvenile Delinquents Act[34] and the Narcotic Control Act,[35] should be noted.

    After some seventy-five years, it is possible to evaluate the impact of the code on the criminal jurisprudence of Canada and to make some estimate of the trends which appear to be emerging. The code, being a codification to a large extent of the existing common law is not a code in the civil law sense of being the *fons et origo* of the law. Most of its substantive provisions have their counterpart in English and Commonwealth law, both statutory and common law. It is not surprising, therefore, that Canadian courts have, in the past, relied heavily upon precedents from England. Nevertheless, the codification entailed the development of a substantive amount of Canadian criminal jurisprudence. While it is true that the original code of 1892 followed very closely the English Draft Code which, in turn, followed closely the existing common law, the considerable number of alterations, developments and amendments has led to an ever-increasing gap between Canadian and English criminal law. Indeed, in all the major areas, it is difficult to think of many sections of the code in which interpretations by English courts would be, in themselves, of immediate relevance.

Offences against the person, particularly homicide, many sexual offences, most property offences, offences relating to the administration of justice, the law relating to parties to offences, the provision respecting habitual criminals and dangerous sexual offenders as well as practically the whole of the law of procedure bear no relation to existing criminal law of England.

The introduction of codal legislation necessarily reduces the scope of judicial law-making, but no code of this character can be so precise as to reduce the judiciary's function to that of a mere administrator and the Criminal Code is less precise than many others. Furthermore, while section 7(2) preserves the common law defences, a number have been altered by the code to the extent of requiring specifically Canadian interpretations, such as, for example insanity or compulsion. In addition, the peculiar provisions relating to homicide necessitate that even where English decisions are adopted or considered (such as *Bratty v. A.-G. Northern Ireland*[36] or *A.-G. Northern Ireland v. Gallacher*[37]) their application is by no means automatic.

The law relating to homicide, for example, illustrates the development of Canadian law by the judges even within the confines of fairly precise legislation. In the 1892 code murder was defined along the lines set out in the English Draft Code presenting a more specific definition than "unlawful killing with malice aforethought" but not, probably, altering the existing common law. Murder in the commission of a felony was reduced in scope to those deaths caused to facilitate the commission of or flight from certain defined offences or doing certain other acts for the same purpose. Those offences were treason, piracy, escape from prison, resisting arrest, murder (of someone other than the victim), rape, forcible abduction, robbery, burglary and arson. To this list, the Canadian Criminal Code added, in 1947, indecent assault.[38] Also in 1947, paragraph (d) was added to section 202 as follows:

> or he uses a weapon or has it upon his person
>
> (i) during or at the time he commits or attempts to commit the offence, or;
>
> (ii) during or at the time of his flight after committing or attempting to commit the offence, and the death ensues as a consequence.

Interestingly, while the House of Commons wished to preserve some element of *mens rea*, following the Supreme Court decision in *R. v. Hughes*[39] by requiring the accused to *use* the weapon for a purpose, the Senate insisted that having a weapon upon his person should be sufficient, so long as there was a causal connection between possessing the weapon and the death. This view prevailed and in *Rowe v. The Queen*[40], the Supreme Court agreed that this was the effect of the amendment.

In 1961,[41] the legislature adopted the distinction between capital and non-capital murder by retaining murder as a capital offence only where the death is planned and deliberate or where, in the circumstances, of the "constructive murder" situations the offender causes death by his own act, or where the deceased is a law enforcement officer. The phrase "planned and deliberate" is not a happy choice. Apart from the fact that the meaning is not clear, it is the sort of phrase upon which it is difficult adequately to instruct a jury.[42] But over the past six years the courts have succeeded in equating planning and deliberation with a rational choice to kill. In *More v. The Queen*,[43] the Supreme Court excluded an act committed on a sudden impulse and acts committed under the influence of alcohol or provocation have also been held not to be within the definition of capital murder.[44] From *Bleta v. The Queen*[45] it is also clear that a mental condition falling short of insanity within section 16 may nevertheless prevent a killing from being planned and deliberate. Although these interpretations have been criticized as introducing a concept of diminished responsibility, in fact they merely define more specifically the phrase "planned and deliberate." It is true that some difficulty is presented in instructing juries since on a charge of capital murder, drunkenness or provocation may operate as a defence to murder, thus reducing the offence to manslaughter or only as a defence to capital murder, thus reducing it to non-capital murder. With insanity defences, there may be the four verdicts of not guilty, not guilty by reason of insanity, guilty of capital murder, or guilty of non-capital murder. Furthermore, the jury must be instructed[46] both on the code definition of provocation or insanity and also on that type of provocation or insanity which may not be a defence but which would prevent a murder from being planned and deliberate.

The problem of driving offences also gives some clue to the trends in Canadian jurisprudence. Although the cases cause difficulty because of the constitutional questions, the solution has involved a thorough analysis of negligence and the concept of *mens rea*. Under the code, section 221(1) provides for the offence of criminally negligent driving (criminal negligence being defined in section 191 as a wanton or reckless disregard for the lives or safety of other persons) and section 221(4) provides for the offence of driving in a manner that is dangerous to the public. In addition, all provinces have an offence of careless driving, driving without due care and attention, or some such similar offence. The Supreme Court in *O'Grady v. Sparling*[47] was able to uphold the constitutional validity of the provincial legislation on the grounds that section 221 was concerned with criminal law and the provincial statute with the regulation and control of highway traffic. However, at that time section 221(4) had not been enacted and the court was solely concerned with differentiating between negligent driving and careless driving, being able to hold that the former, being criminal, required advertent negligence, while the latter did not.

In *Mann v. The Queen*,[48] the court was again required to rule on the validity of the provincial legislation, but with the added complication of section 221(4), dealing with dangerous driving. Although the court upheld the validity of the impugned legislation, the *ratio decidendi* was far from clear. Certainly, *O'Grady v. Sparling* authoritatively decided that the provincial legislation was constitutionally *intra vires*, but if Parliament had occupied the field of "inadvertent negligent driving" then, it was argued, that area had been pre-empted by the federal legislation in section 221(4). The court rejected this argument, holding that section 221(4) legislated against driving in a manner that was dangerous and did not affect provincial legislation dealing with careless driving. As might be expected, the courts were finally asked in *R. v. Binus*,[49] in effect, to explain the difference between the two provisions. it was held that *mens rea* was not required either under section 221(4) or under the provincial legislation, but that if careless driving contained the added element of dangerousness to the public, then it moved out of the provincial offence into the federal offence. Since this means that they are merely different degrees of the same act, one might ask whether the original ruling that the provincial legislation is *intra vires* (decided by *O'Grady v. Sparling* and accepted in *Mann v. The Queen*) should not have been queried, after the re-enactment of section 221(4).

However, whatever the constitutional difficulties, the Canadian courts have clearly accepted that *mens rea* can consist in "advertent negligence" and, although in other areas have reiterated the necessity of the requirement of *mens rea*,[50] have been forced to conclude that neither dangerous nor careless driving requires any subjective intent.

It is not, I think, unfair to characterize the basic approach of the Supreme Court to criminal matters as traditional. Looking at recent decisions, one has difficulty in seeing any outstanding landmarks in criminal jurisprudence, though this is not to say that there have not been a number of welcome judgements. The development of the decisions on capital murder has been encouraging, and the cases involving obscenity,[51] drunkenness,[52] *mens rea*,[53] automatism,[54] and conspiracy[55] have been helpful. Less encouraging have been the court's decisions on the restricted nature of the defence of coercion[56] or the circumstances of the admissibility of confessions.[57]

The law of evidence and law of procedure have remained remarkably static over the past century, but this is due less to the courts than to the legislature. Within the relatively detailed federal and provincial evidence acts, the courts have had little chance to develop the law, though the Supreme Court has, as far as possible, preserved the right of the accused to choose not to testify, however much this right has been whittled away by provincial legislation.[58] Similarly, the procedural rules still stem very largely from the Criminal Procedure Act of 1869[59] with little judicial development.

In the penological area, some considerable progress has been made, though the situation is by no means one to induce complacency. The *Fauteux Com-*

mittee Report of 1956[60] is a significant document. Although much of it remains unimplemented, it is a statement of the essential interrelation between substantive criminal law, the administration of justice and the effective use of criminal sanctions. Many provincial departments of reform institutions have embarked upon programmes of building and development to conform to more enlightened concepts of rehabilitation. The establishment of a system of parole under the National Parole Board has similarly constituted a step in the right direction.

This brief survey of the development of criminal law in Canada over the past one hundred years pinpoints several defects and it would be beneficial to see what lessons can be drawn.

Even the original code of 1892 was not subject to the intense and sophisticated enquiry which one would have expected of such a major piece of legislation. Most of the preliminary work had been done by the English Commissioners and it is clear, from a reading of *Hansard*, that the movers of the Bill Respecting Criminal Law were content to present a combination of the English Draft Code and the Canadian statutory law, as explained by Burbidge's *Digest*. This is not to say that they were not aware that some of the English Draft Code was not applicable, nor that conditions in England were not necessarily duplicated in this country. It does mean, however, that there was no distinctly Canadian examination of any of the fundamental premises upon which the bill was based. It was, essentially, a codification of existing law.

The numerous amendments present a shocking indictment of the process of criminal legislation. Maximum penalties have been fixed without the slightest regard for the objectives in mind;[61] major alterations have been based upon the panic induced by isolated criminal activities;[62] compromises between the Senate and the House have resulted in legislation supportable on no grounds;[63] and absurd formulas adopted which disguise real aims.[64] The only revision, that of 1953, should not be underestimated for the Commissioners did, indeed, remove anomalies, rationalize punishments and make procedural reforms. But their terms of reference were limited in the extreme and did not change the fundamental reflection of the code. Thus, tampered with and tinkered with, it remains the monument of the eminent Victorian, Sir James Stephen.

Two striking object lessons emerge. The first is that the process of criminal legislation must be removed from the petty political arena as quickly as possible, and the second is that criminal law can no longer be regarded in isolation from the other aspects of the criminal process, the investigation, the trial and the disposition of the offender.

To take the second lesson first, it may not, at first sight, make very much difference whether one has a criminal code or a penal code, but a criminal code starts from a fundamental premise that substantive and procedural "criminal law" can be neatly tied up in a package and presented as a comprehensive unit. It presupposes that one can talk in the abstract about "a crime," about, for example, the offence of abortion, or of selling obscene literature, or of murder, It presupposes, also, that the legislative problems can be solved as a literary exercise — the problem of adequately defining, for example, obscene literature, of delimiting the scope of capital murder or of establishing the criteria for finding a person an habitual criminal. In fact, what has become apparent in the last century is that the whole criminal process is not a series of compartmentalized topics. The substantive criminal law cannot be divorced from its social context, and criminal legislation is at least as much a matter of analysing the social problem, discussing alternatives, thinking of the investigative problems, deciding upon the sanction and weighing the consequences as it is of proper drafting. In my opinion, any code has to reflect all of these issues and this is better done in the framework of a comprehensive penal code than in the framework of an isolated criminal code, for the former would, insofar as it is possible within the federal jurisdiction, provide for the conduct of investigation, the process of trial, the technique of sentencing and the disposition of the offender, as well as for "criminal law and procedure."

The difficulty in this country has been the lack of adequate machinery for reform. There have been commissions and committees that have had significance. The Fauteux Committee has already been mentioned, and the Archambault Commission[65] of 1938 presented a report that was forward-looking and useful. One must not overlook the worth of the reports of more recent departmental committees on capital punishment,[66] juvenile delinquency[67] and hate propaganda.[68] But such ad hoc enquiries are not at all the answer to the difficulty. There has never been any enquiry into the fundamental basis of the code, as such, nor can ad hoc recommendations ever take the place of such an enquiry. There is no machinery for putting even those recommendations in their proper social and legislative context.

This leads to the second object lesson. All legislation in the Canadian system must be political in the sense of being an enactment of the sovereign in Parliament. No one, presumably, would wish it otherwise. But both the House and Senate need, and are entitled to receive advice, and the more aware one becomes of the real significance of criminal legislation, the more urgent becomes the need for advice. No one can give advice without the data that only research can bring forth, the statistics upon which assumptions are based, comparative studies, social and moral implications, how isolated proposals will fit into the general scheme and so on.

The most urgent need, it appears, is for some sort of permanent criminal law reform machinery which will undertake these tasks and will tender advice to the appropriate minister. What he does with it, is, of course, a political question which is for him and Parliament to decide. But the present hit-or-miss method of reform which is sparked by a newspaper story, by a private member's interest, by an influential agitator, has highlighted the most outstanding problem of Canadian criminal law, the simple problem of criminal legislation.

In the judicial area there have been problems of a different character. The Criminal Procedure Act of 1869 laid the foundation for the wide jurisdiction now exercised by magistrates and as a result the Canadian trial process is among the most expeditious in the world. Somewhere between 85 percent and 90 percent of all criminal cases are tried by magistrates in the first instance either on summary conviction or on speedy trials of indictable offences. Many involve pleas of guilty and in most of the others the only disputes are factual. Appeals to the Supreme Court are so restricted[69] that in the overwhelmingly large majority of cases, the final court of appeal, even on questions of law, is the provincial court of appeal. Apart, entirely, from the fact that in many instances local authorities have not realized the importance of the magistrate in the administration of criminal justice and still provide him with inadequate facilities and are satisfied with inadequate qualifications, there is no court to which the lower trial court can look for guidance on practice points or sentencing principles.

Allowances being made for the inadequacies and dangers of generalizations, provincial courts of appeal have not assumed the role of *assisting* magistrates, as has the Court of Criminal Appeal in England. They also exercise civil appellate jurisdiction, and do not, with any degree of regularity give reasons for sentence variations or issue generally applicable instruction on procedural and practice matters. One sees, therefore, not only variations from province to province, but also variations from jurisdiction to jurisdiction within the same province. Nor is there any court, apart from the Supreme Court of Canada, which can give an authoritative interpretation of Canadian criminal law, and, in view of its limited appellate jurisdiction, it is not unusual to find the same section being interpreted differently in different provinces.[70]

One may question whether the civil appellate system is necessarily the best method of dealing with criminal appeals. Is it possible that a Supreme Criminal Court of Canada would have the time to accept wider grounds of appeal, issue directions to lower courts, co-ordinate practice and procedure matters and so on? Perhaps some jurisdictions could already usefully adopt a provincial court of criminal appeal. It is not possible, at this stage, to do any more than pose the questions, but rather than accept the present status quo without question, a fruitful line of enquiry and research may well tie into the whole question of the administration of criminal justice in this country. Not only might the appeal system be modernized, but the entire pre-trial process — the preliminary hearing, the grand jury and so on — be reorganized.

At the time of writing, the *Report* of the Canadian Committee on Corrections, established in 1965, has not appeared. The committee was appointed to "study the broad field of corrections from the initial investigation . . . through to the final discharge of a prisoner . . . but excluding consideration of specific offences except where such consideration bears directly upon" other matters within its terms of reference. The committee has stated that it intends to study the investigation of offences, the procuring of the attendance of the suspect in court, representation of the suspect, conviction, sentence, and correctional services. The *Report* may constitute a major step forward in the field of corrections in Canada and criticisms of developments over the past hundred years may be pointless. However, the task of the committee is enormous and it may be doubted whether it is feasible to expect significant concrete proposals in a limited period of time from a committee with relatively limited resources. The entire problem of sentencing is obscured by lack of statistical information and of any definite philosophy or policy.[71] Random attempts to improve the situation such as judicial conferences and seminars should by no means be discouraged but are, at best, only partial answers to the problem.

In the correctional field itself, the divided jurisdiction between federal and provincial responsibilities makes it difficult to generalize without being unfair. By and large, advances in the provincial correctional services have far outstripped those in the federal. British Columbia, Saskatchewan, and Ontario, while far behind other jurisdictions such as California, New York, and Massachusetts in the field of probation, after-care services and rehabilitation techniques, are, nevertheless, many years in advance of other provinces. At the same time, federal training, education and treatment programmes remain inadequate and many of the institutions themselves are archaic and totally unsuited to modern concepts. The parole service lacks the necessary resources to ensure proper selection and meaningful supervision, though this is not to deny the progress it has already made. But behind these generalized criticisms lies the fact that advances have been and are being made, and it perhaps impatience that they are not being made quickly or scientifically enough that generates the criticisms.

Whatever one may consider the function of the criminal law to be, it is apparent that the criminal process is a complex interaction of sociological, psychological and legal phenomena — and doubtless this is true of the whole legal process. Whereas in the year 1867 the criminal law was considered to be virtually the exclusive preserve of the criminal lawyer, today it is recognized that no adequate system can be devised without the help of other specialists. The function of the law is to resolve the problems of society, but the lawyer does not abdicate his responsibility by turning to others for assistance. The plain fact of the matter is that the lawyer can no longer himself answer the questions he must ask. The development of the law and the legal system must be the responsibility of the lawyer and must remain his responsibility, for he, alone, knows what questions to ask. He must also know of whom those questions should be asked.

Nowhere is this more apparent than in every area of the criminal process. It is not so much the techniques which need examining as the fundamental premises upon which the entire structure is based. One talks blandly about the rules of evidence without considering whether the conceptions of inference-finding and assumption of relevance and weight upon which they are based are valid. How can anyone tell what acts ought to be criminal in character without examining the function of the criminal law in society? Could not the sociologist and psychologist usefully analyse the effects and methods of police investigation and the role of the police in the community?

The sad conclusion is that the criminal law has not progressed in one hundred years nor can it progress beyond a slight reshuffling within assumed boundaries so long as those boundaries are accepted as absolutes. There have, of course, been changes that, within the structure, have been beneficial and to that extent advances have been made. But it is not a cause for congratulation that Sir James Stephen would be quite at home with the Criminal Code of 1967.

Notes

1. (1867), 30 & 31 Vict., c. 3, s. 91, para. 27, "the criminal law, including the procedure in criminal matters."
2. (1836), 6 Will. 4, c. 48
3. (1851), 14 & 15 Vict., c. 13.
4. (1857), 20 Vict., c. 27.
5. (1857), 20 Vict., c. 30.
6. (1864), 27–28 Vict., c. 19.
7. (1865), 29 Vict., c. 14.
8. For example: New Brunswick (1860), 23 Vict., c. 34 (false pretences); (1860), 23 Vict., c. 23 (criminal procedure); (1862), 25 Vict., c. 10 (offences against the person); Nova Scotia (1855), 18 Vict., c. 9 (evidence).
9. These were consolidated in the *Revised Statutes* of 1886.
10. For example, Cruelty to Animals, 1880; Penitentiaries, 1883; Procedure, 1887.
11. The dates, of course, vary: Quebec, 1763; Ontario, 1792; British Columbia, 1859; Manitoba, Saskatchewan, Alberta, and the Northwest Territories, and the Yukon, 1870; Nova Scotia, New Brunswick and Prince Edward Island, presumably from the date of their legislative independent existence in 1758.
12. Authority to repeal such provincial legislation passed to the Dominion. *R. v. Halifax Electric Tramway Co.* (1898), 1 C.C.C. 424.
13. *Hansard* (1892), 1: 1312.
14. Ibid.
15. Ibid., 1313.
16. (1892), 55–56 Vict., c. 29.
17. *Statutes of Canada* (hereafter S.C.) 1952–54, c. 51.
18. British North America Act, 1867, 30 & 31 Vict., c. 3, s. 129.
19. E.g., the Alberta Act, 1905, the Saskatchewan Act, 1905, etc.
20. Criminal Code, s. 10 for Ontario; s. 11 for British Columbia; s. 12 for Manitoba.
21. *R. v. Graham* (1910), 17 O.W.R. 660, 2 O.W.N. 326, 17 C.C.C 264.
22. *R. v. Leffler* (1936), 67 C.C.C. 330.
23. *R. v. Bordoff* (1938), 70 C.C.C. 35.
24. *MacKenzie v. Goodfellow* (1908), 13 O.W.R. 30.
25. Criminal Code, s. 121.
26. Criminal Code, s. 119(2)(d).
27. Criminal Code, s. 120.
28. Criminal Code, s. 408(2).
29. *Revised Statutes of Canada* (hereafter R.S.C.) 1952, c. 322, as amended.
30. R.S.C. 1952, c. 198.
31. R.S.C. 1952, c. 206, as amended.
32. R.S.C. 1952, c. 58, as amended.
33. R.S.C. 1952, c. 212, as amended.
34. R.S.C. 1952, c. 160.
35. S.C. 1961, c. 35.
36. *Bratty v. A.-G. Northern Ireland,* [1961] 3 All E.R. 523, 46 Cr. App. Rep 1.
37. *A.-G. Northern Ireland v. Gallacher,* [1961] 3 All E.R. 299.
38. S.C. 1947, c. 55, s. 6.
39. *R. v. Hughes,* [1942] S.C.R. 517.
40. *Rowe v. The Queen* (1951), 100 C.C.C. 97.
41. S.C. 1960–61, c. 44, s. 1.
42. See *R. v. Widdifield* (1962), 6 Crim. L.Q. 152 for a charge to the jury.

43. *More v. The Queen*, [1963] 3 C.C.C. 289, 41 C.R. 98.

44. *R. v. Mitchell*, [1965] 1 C.C.C. 155, 43 C.R. 391.

45. *Bleta v. The Queen*, [1965] 1 C.C.C. 1, 44 C.R. 193.

46. See *R. v. Mitchell*, note 44.

47. *O'Grady v. Sparling* (1960), 128 C.C.C. 1, 33 C.R. 293.

48. *Mann v. The Queen*, [1966] 2 C.C.C. 273, 47 C.R. 400.

49. *R. v. Binus*, [1966] 4 C.C.C. 193, 48 C.R. 279, upheld by the Supreme Court.

50. For example, *R. v. King* (1961), 129 C.C.C. 391, 34 C.R. 264 (driving under the influence of a drug); *Beaver v. R.* (1957), 118 C.C.C. 129, 26 C.R. 193 (possession of drugs).

51. *R. v. Brodie* (1962), 132 C.C.C. 161, 37 C.R. 120; *Dominion News & Gifts (1962) Ltd. v. R.*, [1964] 3 C.C.C. 1, 42 C.R. 209; *R. v. Cameron*, [1966] 4 C.C.C. 273, 44 C.R. 49.

52. *R. v. Mitchell*, note 44; *R. v. Lachance*, [1963] 2 C.C.C. 14, 39 C.R. 127.

53. See cases cited in note 50.

54. *Bleta v. R.*, note 45.

55. *Wright, McDermott and Feeley v. R.*, [1964] 2 C.C.C. 207; *Kour v. R.*, [1964] 2 C.C.C. 97, 42 C.R. 210.

56. *R. v. Carker (No. 2)*, [1967] 2 C.C.C. 190.

57. *O'Connor v. R.*, [1966] 4 C.C.C. 352, 48 C.R. 271.

58. See *Batary v. A.G. Sask.*, [1966] 3 C.C.C. 152, 46 C.R. 35.

59. Criminal Procedure Act (1869), 32–33 Vict., c. 29.

60. Report of a committee to enquire into the principles and procedures followed in the remission service of the Department of Justice of Canada (1956).

61. See *Hansard* debates on the Draft Bill, (1892), 2: 2840, 2846, 2964ff.

62. For example, *Hansard* (1947), 4: 5026–37.

63. For example, Criminal Code, s. 202(d).

64. For example, the definition of obscenity, Criminal Code, s. 150(8); and the capital murder provisions, s. 203A.

65. Royal Commission to Investigate the Penal System of Canada (1938).

66. Department of Justice, "Capital Punishment; material relating to its purpose and value" (1965).

67. Department of Justice, Committee on Juvenile Delinquency (1965), Allen J. Macleod, Q.C., Chairman.

68. Department of Justice Special Committee on Hate Propaganda in Canada (1966), Maxwell Cohen, Q.C., Chairman.

69. Criminal Code, ss. 597–600.

70. Ss. 149, 150, 222, 223 of the Criminal Code are examples of provincial disagreements in interpretation.

71. Currently, two projects, one under Professor Hogarth for the Centre of Criminology and one under W.B. Common, Q.C., for the Canadian Bar Research Foundation, are being conducted into aspects of this problem.

DENISON'S LAW: CRIMINAL JUSTICE AND THE POLICE COURT IN TORONTO, 1877–1921†

GENE HOWARD HOMEL

One critical measure of social progress is the treatment of crime and criminals. Historians have stressed the development of a broad reform outlook in Canada between the 1880s and 1920s, which shifted criminology from punitive to rehabilitative goals, and which resulted in the establishment of special procedures and personnel for female and underage offenders. While the diversification of the court system and the shift from punitive attitudes are considered significant developments in the late nineteenth and early twentieth centuries, the following study of the Toronto police court during this period suggests that such innovations had a relatively minor impact upon the normative methods and assumptions of criminal justice. A whiggish view of history, a tendency to focus only on those targets of reform concern, and a failure to examine critically the disparity between reform pronouncements and actual accomplishments have contributed to what is probably an inflated assessment of reform advance in the court system. Traditional methods and ideas of dispensing criminal justice continued to dominate Toronto's police court in this era.

The police court was the essential first level of the court system, and most cases were taken no further.[1] The focus of this article is not upon the spectacular crimes of the period, nor on crime itself. The charges of drunk and disorderly behaviour usually comprised roughly half the cases in Toronto's police court; other frequent charges were theft and assault.[2] Instead, my primary concern is the court's process of trying and sentencing defendants. This process can best be illustrated by examining the practices of Toronto's chief police-court magistrate between 1877 and 1921, Colonel George T. Denison III (1839–1925). During his forty-four-year tenure as magistrate, Denison handled most of the roughly 650 000 cases before the police court, and tried about 90 percent of indictable offences.[3]

Member of a wealthy and prominent Toronto family, soldier, military historian, and one of Canada's leading supporters of British imperialism, Denison could claim no particular expertise with regard to crime. His task as magistrate of the court occupied only a few hours a week. While intensely involved in national and international affairs, the colonel seemed to have paid little if any attention to crime prevention or to the causes of crime. Indeed, his appointment as magistrate for a salary of $4000 a year derived from his friendship with Oliver Mowat, the premier of Ontario, who offered him the post in 1877.[4] Denison received his salary from the city of Toronto.

† *Ontario History* 72 (1980): 171–86.

If there was a Canadian aristocracy of status, property, or merit during the late nineteenth-century, Denison was a charter member. He had little exposure to the conditions in which most crimes were committed. Harry Wodson, a long-time police-court reporter for the *Toronto Telegram*, summed up Denison accurately by asserting that he was "of the governing class. His mind is more or less remote from the affairs of the rank and file of humanity." He regarded "their street fights, domestic wrangles, and lesser crimes, as incidental to the commoner's life."[5]

Denison's assumption that drunkenness, theft and assault were closely associated with the commoner's life was widely shared. In 1890 the Ontario government's commission of inquiry into the prison and reformatory system of the province questioned scores of witnesses on what they considered the causes of crime. The most frequent response was that intemperance and drink caused crime, while others maintained that idleness, evil associations, or the "hereditary transmission of evil tendencies" were to blame.[6] Rev. W.S. Blackstock, writing in the *Canadian Magazine*, asserted that the primary cause of crime was "organicity" — physical heredity. A high proportion of habitual criminals was born with criminal tendencies.[7]

With his famous energy and crustiness, Denison was the unchallenged monarch of his court.

> A swift thinker, a keen student of human nature, the possessor of an
> incisive tongue, he extinguishes academic lawyers, parries thrusts with the
> skill of a practised swordsman, confounds the deadly-in-earnest barrister
> with a witticism, scatters legal intricacies to the winds, will not tolerate the
> brow-beating of witnesses, cleans off the "slate" before the bewildered
> stranger has finished gaping, shuts the book with a bang, orders
> adjournment of the court, then, stick in hand, strolls off to lunch at the
> National Club.[8]

His flamboyant manner, along with the endless procession of human curiosities, lured a steady steam of visitors to the court for "a morning's entertainment."[9] For tourists, a visit to Queen City without visiting Denison's landmark "would be like going to Rome and not seeing the Pope."[10] A prime Toronto attraction for John Foster Fraser, the British author-tourist, was the police court, the only place in the city where "hustle" was to be found.[11] On one sweltering day in July, a group of fashionably dressed women from the United States arrived in court to view the man they had heard so much about. Denison's "witty sayings" were reportedly "published in the funny columns of a considerable number of State newspapers across the line. . . ."[12]

Not only were court proceedings a popular public attraction, the criminals themselves were objects of the newspapers' attentions. The new "people's journals" of the late nineteenth century reported crime in spectacular fashion. This was obviously true of major crimes such as murder. Startled readers, for example, were told in great detail about how a woman had murdered and cooked her baby. Even the most petty offences, including the names of those arrested, were described by the *Telegram*, *News*, and other evening papers. This reflected more than just the demand for popular entertainment. Toronto was still to a great extent a conglomeration of tightly knit neighbourhoods in which criminals were of immediate and recognizable interest. As late as 1904 the police matron, Mrs. Whiddon, could expect to recognize her female offenders in the streets around the Court St. police station.[13] Crime reporters frequently referred to certain characters in familiar, even intimate terms. Many examples could be cited. One William Murphy was reported to be "a wife-beater of considerable notoriety. His better half recently presented him with a young Murphy, and since that event he is said to have been treating her very badly."[14] Walter Gains, a 6'6" black man, was alleged to be one of the Toronto's best-known characters, and the recognized authority on baseball in the downtown Ward.[15] Another black, Josie Skelton, frequently made her neighbours "fully aware that she is on a tear by the exuberance of her 'joy.' "[16]

Because most of those who came before the police court were sentenced by Denison, and because it was "the magistrate alone who determines the sentence,"[17] it is important to consider his methods of dealing with court cases. He did not attempt to understand most cases in any detail, and was not interested in legal points pertaining to them. His goal was to render justice — and quickly. Usually a moment or two sufficed. It was not uncommon for Denison to deal with 250 cases in 180 minutes.[18] He read the names of those before the court and administered the oaths himself to speed up the process. "There was no red tape," Fraser told his readers. "I was a little breathless at the slapdash manner in which he disposed of forty cases in exactly forty minutes."[19] Fates were decided swiftly. "I have known a man stand up in the dock," declared Wodson, "enter a plea of guilty to a series of crimes, and be on his way to serve a five-year term at the penitentiary, all in six minutes." Despite the magistrate's "common sense and intuitive accuracy,"[20] some people objected to Denison's celebrated pace. The *Telegram*, commenting on a case in which a boy was wrongly sentenced to five years in the penitentiary, argued that Colonel Denison was "not above trifling away a prisoner's liberty and ruining his life in order that he may get through the day's work before eleven a.m."[21] His abbreviated working hours infuriated lawyers as well as civic politicians, who doubted that he gave a fair day's work for a fair day's pay.

Moreover, Denison, though a lawyer, had no use for legal technicalities and niceties, which he felt interfered with the rendering of true justice. "I never allow a point of law to be raised." he warned. "This is a court of justice, not a court of law."[22] Denison was as good as his word. In his opinion, the distinction made by a judge between playing a drum and beating a drum showed that there was a "difference between so-called law, and real justice and common sense." He remained unimpressed with the higher courts throughout his career as magistrate: "I never follow precedents unless they agree with my views."[23] Once, when the Supreme Court upheld one of his decisions, he retorted, "Nevertheless, I feel sure that I was right,"[24]

How, then, did Denison decide on the cases before him? In his *Recollections of a Police Magistrate*, written shortly before his retirement, he explained that he replied upon "an intuitive feeling as to a man's guilt or innocence and not to weighing and balancing the evidence."[25] The logic of a newspaper reporter that a certain prisoner "did not look like a dishonest man" because he "was respectably dressed" was not alien to Denison's own mind.[26] His memoirs record a number of examples in which his "intuitive feeling" determined the guilt or innocence of a prisoner. In one case, a "respectable looking young woman" employed as a maid was accused of theft from her mistress. The woman heartily proclaimed her innocence to Denison, and "I was impressed at once with the feeling that she was innocent." Further investigation determined that this was the case, and "I was glad that I had paid attention to what was only an intuitive feeling." On another occasion, he intervened to force detectives to reconsider their work, which finally proved that a prisoner before him was not in fact guilty.[27]

Still, Denison's intuitive feelings were not neutral; they seemed to be more favourably inclined towards some groups than towards others. His preconceptions about certain defendants were strongly and publicly expressed. Retired soldiers "had an idea, which was well founded, that I had a friendly feeling for them," and when soldiers were brought in for drunkenness, "I generally made any excuse I could for letting them off." His ability to "detect a bogus salute" and his knowledge of military regiments caught charlatans attempting to pose as pensioned soldiers.[28] A cartoon in the *Telegram* showed prisoners standing before him, reading books which he had authored. Denison asked the court how gentlemen reading such fine works could have been charged. The avid readers were discharged.[29]

On the other hand, Denison held a low opinion of certain ethnic groups, which he viewed as unsavoury and inclined to criminality. Toronto's Irish and Negro citizens were discussed by the Colonel with bemused contempt. The blacks provided a "source of amusement in the court because of their many peculiarities." He scoffed at the financial poverty of the Baptist Church literary society and at the class distinctions within the black community.[30] Among those who graced the court were a wood sawyer, who required "a quarter of an hour's speech" to prove he was not a vagrant, and John Randolph, reportedly involved in "shady transactions" and keeping a "whiskey dive." Randolph was arrested "while acting in a disorderly manner with a white girl named Mary Murphy."[31] These and other cases convinced Denison that blacks were an undesirable element in Toronto.

For Denison, as for many other Torontonians, working-class Irish neighbourhoods were synonymous with drunkenness, brawling, and brutality. The Irish, he reminisced, "added very much to the humour of the proceedings in the Court when I first occupied the Bench." "The old wooden shanties" of the Lombart Street area "were inhabited by Irish labourers, carters, woodsawyers, etc." A similar community named Claretown flourished in the vicinity of Ryerson and Carr streets. Denison frequently punished street rioters from these neighbourhoods, where whiskey was "the peculiar system of first aid to the wounded."[32] Irish criminals ranged from Ellen McInerney, charged with tossing carbolic acid on Mary O'Neill, to Michael O'Neill, who was arrested for stealing part of the latest *Irish Canadian* from the public library.[33] An overwhelmingly Anglo-Saxon city during Denison's magistracy, Toronto still had sufficient numbers of European immigrants to rouse Denison's sarcasm. "A policeman is seldom a welcome visitor in a Jew's rag shop," he informed his readers, emphasizing that Jews sometimes made their living by shady means.[34] A member of the Italian "colony" was lectured by Denison that he "did not propose allowing foreigners to draw their knives on the slightest pretence of self-defence."[35]

The Colonel despised those arrested in labour disputes. In his view, the striking workman who discouraged another man from earning his daily bread was guilty of a crime which could not be tolerated. Strikers and their supporters in the 1886 closure of the Toronto Street Railway system were hauled into court for blocking streetcar tracks, hurling missiles at strikebearers, and using abusive language. One of the accused admitted he had shouted "you dirty rascal" at a scab, but a police officer countered that he had used language "which is unfit for publication." One streetcar conductor was fined ten dollars and costs for calling another man a scab.[36] The 1886 streetcar strike was not the only incident bringing labour supporters before Denison; crimes such as "pelting stones at the delivery waggon of Mr. Wilkins, the boycotted baker,"[37] were part of the new wave of labour organization and class consciousness.

After the turn of the century, with intensified industrial conflict and the use of court injunctions against unions, Denison imposed harsh penalties on employees who referred to strikebreakers as "scabs." "I want it distinctly understood that I object to that word," ordered the chief magistrate.[38] Unionists reacted angrily. *The Toiler*, a Toronto labour paper, castigated his courtroom partisanship,[39] and a printer complained, "Between judge and Denison made laws the workingmen of Toronto are beginning to think they are living in the days of the Family Compact — 1837."[40] Phillips Thompson, socialist and journalist, similarly referred to Denison's family background when he wrote, "He is true as hell to the ideals of his Tory U.E. Loyalist ancestors, and holds like them that all popular notions of liberty are rank delusions and that the masses were bound to be exploited for the benefit of the ruling class."[41]

On the other hand, "the respectable and wealthy classes," as Denison called them, rarely appeared in his court, and then invariably for traffic tickets. Such persons were charged in the 1880s with "driving on Spadina Ave. at the rate of from 12 to 16 miles an hour, which is considered an immodest pace."[42] By the early twentieth century, the well-to-do occasionally came before Denison on automobile violations, and left the court with bitter feelings towards judges.[43] Denison did not care for the men of new money who lacked the old virtues. He denied a hearing to those who sought to escape traffic fines by using unfair influences, and he refused to accept gifts from companies, including railways, which were constantly prosecuting thieves and trespassers.[44] "I have been seated at tables with millionaires, particularly motor owners;" he told a police banquet in 1912, "they have said to me, 'Why don't you instruct Mag. Kingsford [another police-court magistrate] to be a little easier on us motorists who happen to commit a small breach of the by-law.' "[45] Such men were a disgrace to their rank and position. But Sir William Howland, a Father of Confederation, was another type entirely. After Denison had to fine him for failing to remove snow from the front of one of his "various vacant properties," the two men met each other in their club and exchanged humourous pleasantries about the fine.[46]

Along with his post as chief magistrate, Colonel Denison sat on the three-man Board of Police Commissioners for Toronto. He thus had a hand in the general administration of the city policy, and quite naturally he used his position to defend and praise Toronto's force. However, his magistrate's job required him to decide upon assault cases between policemen and civilians, and hence he was in a conflict of interest. In fact there seemed to be occasional instances of police officers being assaulted, and charges by wounded citizens that they had been beaten by officers.[47] C.S. Clark's social survey of Toronto reported some allegations of police wrongdoing in which the victims had been unable to rectify the injustice until they had appealed above the police court.[48]

Magistrate Denison stressed that in his court there was but one standard of justice for all. He would have agreed with the sentiment expressed in the 1880s by Mayor W.H. Howland, a moral reformer, that "all offenders whether in purple and fine linen or in rags, shall have the same even-handed justice meted out to them."[49] There were, however, some who doubted that those in linen received the same treatment from the police court as those in rags. Harry Wodson, while an admirer of Denison, wrote after many years of observing the court that there were two standards of justice. "Men with political 'pull,' whose sons, or friends, have committed crime, are able to evade the chastening hand of justice by having the wrongdoers railroaded into an asylum, the brevity of their sojourn suggesting that the 'lunatics' merely go in at the front door and come out at the back!" Nor did the wealthy youth, despite his sins, appear as frequently before the magistrate as the low-income delinquent. He had no reason to frequent street corners and pool rooms, "simply because he has a spacious and attractive home to loaf in, and a private billiard table upstairs." In any case the Toronto policeman "regards it a privilege to turn his back upon the roysterings of moneyed youth." Wodson's argument was put more succinctly by Biddy, "a mammoth type of Irish woman" and a chronic drunk, who told Denison: "The only diff'rence between me and Lady O'Flaherty up in Rosedale, is that I have no powdered flunkeys to carry me up to bed whin I'm drunk."[50]

In view of Denison's character and police-court methods, it might be expected that he was heartily despised by the tens of thousands of those tried before him each year. This did not appear to be the case. Although it is difficult to ascertain directly the feelings of those before the court, many of the accounts of Denison's court assert that the man whom criminals nicknamed "the Beak" was held by them in high regard. His usually "genial" and "informal" manner, as well as what were generally considered lenient sentences, convinced even prisoners who received stiff sentences for serious crimes that the Colonel was decent and humane. He was even popular with many defendants, who elected to go before him when they had the choice. In contrast with other magistrates he refrained from humiliating or lecturing the prisoners.[51] One cartoon in 1913 pictured a tattered husband and wife jostling each other in front of the magistrate, while the woman scolded her husband, "Ain't I got as much right to enjoy the pleasure of bein' tried by Colonel Denison as you have?"[52] A woman who had been beaten by her husband closed her testimony with a plea for understanding: "He's my husband, your worship, an' he's a perfect right to take a swipe at me now an' then, but he went a little too far this time." According to Wodson, the magistrate appreciated her viewpoint and "gallantly regulated the punishment accordingly."[53]

In the Beak's courtroom, prisoners enjoyed a sort of tolerant if paternal Toryism. If crime was incidental to the commoner, he still deserved fair play and the benefits of mercy and good sense. For Denison, Canada's legal system too often stood in the way of these goals. Sometimes in the case of a defendant unrepresented by counsel, Denison quietly informed him that he would "keep an eye upon his interests."[54] This derived at least in part from his criticism of the legal establishment: low-income citizens in particular could not afford decent lawyers and therefore the state should assume the responsibility of providing legal aid for defendants. "I would do away with the legal profession altogether," he once told his court. "All the business now done by lawyers could be done just as well by the state." This remark led *Citizen and Country*, a Christian socialist paper, to chide: "George, my dear boy, don't you know that state ownership is one of our planks?"[55]

The radical readers of *Citizen and Country* may have been pleased by the Colonel's sentiments, but the legal establishment was not amused. Particularly irksome was his criticism of the high cost of justice in civil actions, because of the "enormous charges" made by lawyers against their clients. In many instances "there has been little or nothing left for clients when the charges for lawyers' services have been paid." The *Canadian Law Journal* responded harshly, calling Denison's accusations a "collection of reckless statements and false charges" from a man who boasted that "he does not know or care anything about law — that he is a law unto himself." "What a wide knowledge comes from the sing-song of Police Court practice: 'A dollar and costs or thirty days — Next case!' " As far as money was concerned, the *Law Journal* contended, both police-court costs and Denison's salary were excessive. His remarks about supplanting the legal profession with the state were absurd — perhaps what he really meant was "to transfer all the litigation of the Province to the Toronto Police Court, where prompt justice will be administered at a 'very small' cost and without the intervention of such unnecessary and objectionable characters as lawyers."[56]

Denison calmly replied that he worked very hard, trying more cases than any other judge in Canada, and with little recompense in salary or time off. His criticism, he explained, was aimed not at the legal profession itself, but at the system of civil justice, which was in need of reform. Under the present system, a simple dispute dragged on almost endlessly, reiterating the same worn points of law and adding up costs into the thousands. Neither man really won in the end, and the case "might have been satisfactorily settled without expense, and with just as much certainty if the parties had tossed a copper to decide it at the start." The best solution was a system in which

> judges should decide disputes quickly and simply, without formalities, and without regard to anything except the absolute justice in each case, that there should be only one appeal which should be final, that musty precedents, perhaps the mistakes of men gone by, should not be worshipped or followed to create injustice. If the State did this, did away

with all fees of every kind, and hired the lawyers at fixed salaries to assist the judges in bringing forward evidence, there is no occasion why disputes could not be settled in one tenth of the time and at one twentieth the expense now incurred.

But for the *Canada Law Journal*, such a proposal "reads like a chapter intended for a revised edition of Bellamy's 'Looking Backward.' "[57]

Denison had to continue coping with the established legal system, and on a much larger scale. With the great growth of Toronto between 1877 and 1921, the number of court cases multiplied. While there were about 5000 cases in 1877, 39 654 people appeared before the court in 1913, and the numbers continued to increase thereafter.[58] Total arrests climbed from 17 640 in 1907 to 45 614 in 1922, while Toronto's police force expanded from seven stations and 376 men in the former year to eleven stations and 824 men in the latter.[59] Court personnel were therefore augmented over the years. When Denison was initially appointed, he was the lone magistrate and was aided by only one clerk. R.E. Kingsford was added in the 1890s, followed on the eve of the Great War by Ellis and by Cohen, who "shepherds the chosen people through the Colonel's court in the morning," By 1920 there were four magistrates and seven clerks. The growth of Toronto's immigrant population forced the court to expand its corps of translators from one to four.[60] More important than the additional personnel was the creation of a separate children's court in the 1890s, and separate trials for women which, Denison admitted, kept female wrongdoers "away from the mob," preventing "a young girl from going astray."[61] The new courts removed much of the "romance and pathos" for newspaper reporters.[62]

The effect of these reforms on the Toronto police court should not be exaggerated. Special systems for women and children evolved only gradually.[63] Innovation took place within the shell of traditional methods. Certainly most offenders were not eligible to be sentenced in children's or women's courts. Denison in any case continued to preside over Toronto's police court as senior magistrate until his retirement in the summer of 1921. He appeared never to have changed his accustomed attitudes and methods with regard to criminal justice. And he continued to receive the apparent approval of most citizens for his conduct as magistrate. It would be difficult to find "a shrewder, juster or more sanely sympathetic magistrate," declared *Saturday Night* in July 1921.[64]

Some commentary around the time of his retirement, however, suggests the growing unease felt by those reformers who, concerned with crime and the courts, wished to replace traditional methods embodied by Denison with what they considered efficient, legalized and rationalized standards. The *Toronto Star*, referring to the Colonel's statement in his memoirs that he relied on intuitive feeling rather than evidence to establish guilt or innocence, wondered whether it was "risky" to disregard the evidence. Perhaps Denison had a sixth sense, but did other magistrates possess it?[65] With the end of his magistracy, the *Star* demanded the overhauling of the court system. Although Denison's character had guaranteed protection from gross abuses, "we shall not look upon his like again, and the present system could not command public confidence without him." Among the reforms urgently required was a reorganization of personnel. Never again should a magistrate be allowed to sit on the Board of Police Commissioners as had Denison.[66]

A more thoroughgoing statement of reform imperatives was issued by a writer in the *Canadian Law Times*. Police courts were criticized as inefficient in preventing crime. They practically ran themselves, and little or no instruction was given to magistrates.[67] Each case required more attention than usually given, for speed "must in the end result in injustice." Adequate records were needed on defendants' criminal backgrounds, and co-ordination should be imposed so that sentences were reasonably equalized among various magistrates. The article demanded a degree of centralization and rationalization that transcended mere self-interest on the part of lawyers.

After Denison's death in 1925, Harry Wodson, the veteran crime reporter, issued a volume of reminiscences. Turning from the past to consider the present, a bewildered Wodson saw startling social innovations on all sides. "Barnacles are being scraped from the Ship of State":

> Even the courts of the land, symbolic of the very bulwarks of the
> Constitution, have had their dusty doors flung open by the obnoxious
> house-cleaner. Where, here-to-fore, the court was concerned only with the
> overt act, it is now in order to make a scientific study of the culprit to find
> out the why and wherefore of his conduct, — the cause, not the effect of
> his act, creating the greater concern. The Psychiatrist is at work. Science
> has invaded one of the most jealously guarded sanctuaries of gravity, the
> Court of Law.

But the worst was yet to come, Wodson predicted:

> The day may not be far distant when the burglar, appearing in a police
> court, will find himself facing a solemn-visaged group of specialists, instead
> of a solitary magistrate — the pathologist, the biologist, the mental alienist,
> the behaviourist, the socialogist [sic], and the spiritual mentor. No charge
> will be read, the first question to be decided being the prisoner's mental
> and physical fitness to stand the ordeal of trial. After that, he will be
> passed on from one specialist to another, each man so highly trained, so
> expert in his branch of science, or near science as to be qualified to give
> the court an immediate, authoritative, and conclusive opinion. . . .
> And when the last test has been made, and the prisoner has been
> "o.k.'d" by each of the experts, he will be returned to the dock for trial,
> having earned the highest possible number of marks for General
> Proficiency. Failure, even in one subject, will qualify him for immediate
> discharge, "without stain upon his character." It would surely be an
> outrage to try, and perhaps to commit to prison, a poor fellow, (even
> though he may have shot a policeman or two to death), when the whole
> thing was due to spots upon his liver, or having the misfortune to reside at
> No. 23 Badd Street, instead of No. 1 Virtue Crescent.[68]

Wodson's lament highlights the traditional nature of police-court operations between 1877 and 1921. The origins or causes of conduct were normally of no concern to Denison. The application of social scientific expertise by courtroom specialists, and the notion of discharging prisoners for "failure" to meet certain standards of fitness, were hardly conceivable. Spots on the liver or residency at No. 23 Badd Street were irrelevant.

Instead, Denison's concern was the overt criminal act and its immediate effects. Little or no case information had to be acquired, and little time had to be spent on each case. The magistrate ventured no opinion on the causes of crime, assuming that crime was simply an innate tendency in the character of many commoners. There was no reason why the court as well as the criminals themselves should not be an attraction to the public, or why the magistrate should not enunciate publicly his feelings about certain groups and classes. For Denison, intuitive feeling was more useful and accurate in determining guilt than weighing factual evidence. His intuition was likely to be more favourable towards some defendants than others. All of these characteristics of the police court embody assumptions in conflict with reform demands for scientific investigation, bureaucratic efficiency, uniformity, and above all, establishing the social context in which crime was committed. Notwithstanding the evolution of separate trials for women and children, the addition of court translators, and the like, there was essentially little implementation of these reform goals in the police-court system while Denison presided as chief magistrate.

But Denison's methods cannot be described as tyrannical. His hostility to legalisms and the legal system mirrored his conviction that men and women before the bench were afforded greater protection by the judge's innate capacity for intuitive good sense and mercy. His resistance to the adversarial imperatives of the legal profession reflected his desire for an inexpensive, accessible, and commonsensical justice system. Denison's "genial" Toryism was apparent in his attempts to safeguard the commoner and in his willingness to call upon "the State." In a city of "shall-nots" as Wodson put it, where it was more important for citizens to memorize 6000 by-laws than the Ten Commandments,[69] Denison disliked moral reform campaigns to curb the lower orders. He accused the worthies of the Ministerial Association of trying to force cruel and drastic punishment "upon certain classes of the criminal population who offended their tender susceptibilities."[70]

This study of the Toronto police court's process of trying and sentencing defendants indicates that in an era considered amenable to humanitarian and bureaucratic reform, traditional methods and ideas of treating the criminal retained their hegemony. The police-court system continued, for example, to focus on the overt act and not the social context or the individual's motives. Denison's unpredictability contrasted with the drive for rationalization. On the other hand, he was not impermeable to reform which would enhance British fair play.

Moreover, one might be cautious about assuming that traditional court practices were completely harsh and punitive, at least until the imposition of modern criminology. Sentences such as a sixty-day jail term for attempting to commit suicide, one year for failure to support a family, or six months for begging[71] appear harsh. But only a statistical analysis of sentencing over a lengthy period based on magistrates' records can place them in a proper context. Did lighter sentences go hand in hand with the development of court reform? One index of certain measures of punitiveness (convictions, penitentiary sentences, and executions) shows, not a linear development, but wave-like fluctuations between 1893 and 1923.[72] Recourse to statistics may be able to test the popular supposition of Denison's leniency relative to other magistrates and judges, or whether certain ethnic groups received harsher sentences. An examination of police magistrates' practices in other cities could determine to what extent Toronto's experience was unique. Certainly for Walter Gains, William Murphy, and thousands of other offenders, Colonel George Denison was the living embodiment of the law in Toronto.

Notes

1. On legal aspects of the police-court system see James Crankshaw, *A Practical Guide to Police Magistrates and Justices of the Peace*, 2nd ed. (Montreal, 1905); Stuart Ryan, "The Adult Court," in *Crime and Its Treatment in Canada*, edited by W.T. McGrath (Toronto, 1965).

2. A detailed breakdown of crime statistics can be found in the annual City Council Minutes of Toronto, as an appendix to the Chief Constable's Report.

3. Col. George T. Denison, *Recollections of a Police Magistrate* (Toronto, 1920), vi, 4.

4. Ibid., 1; David Gagan, *The Denison Family of Toronto 1792–1925* (Toronto, 1973), 64; *Canada Law Journal* 36, no. 21, (1 Nov. 1900), 632. For more on Denison see Gagan; Carl Berger, *The Sense of Power: Studies in the Ideas of Canadian Imperialism 1867–1914* (Toronto, 1970); and Norman Shrive, *Charles Mair: Literary Nationalist* (Toronto, 1965).

5. Harry M. Wodson, *The Whirlpool: Scenes from Toronto Police Court* (Toronto, 1917), 27.

6. Ontario, *Report of the Commissioners Appointed to Enquire into the Prison and Reformatory System of Ontario, 1890* (Toronto, 1891).

7. Rev. W.S. Blackstock, "A Study in Criminology," *The Canadian Magazine* 1, no. 7 (Sept. 1893): 523–30.

8. Wodson, *The Whirlpool*, 26–27.

9. Ibid., 39.

10. Public Archives of Canada (hereafter PAC), George T. Denison Papers, vol. 38, scrapbook 1909–25, *Jack Canuck*, 9 Nov. 1912.

11. John Foster Fraser, *Canada As It Is* (London, 1909), 50–51.

12. Toronto *Globe*, 30 July 1912. (The names of Toronto newspapers are hereafter used in shortened form.)

13. *Star*, 30 Jan. 1904.

14. *World*, 1 Dec. 1887.

15. *Mail and Empire*, 9 June 1899.

16. *Telegram*, 15 Feb. 1886.

17. Wodson, *The Whirlpool*, 30.

18. Robson Black, "A Dollar and Costs," *Canada Monthly* 14, no. 4 (Aug. 1913).

19. Fraser, *Canada As It Is*, 50–51.

20. Wodson, *The Whirlpool*, 16, 28–29.

21. C.S. Clark, *Of Toronto The Good* (Montreal, 1898), 19.

22. Fraser, *Canada As It Is*, 50–51.

23. Denison, *Recollections*, 198, 9.

24. *Saturday Night*, 23 July 1921.

25. Denison, *Recollections*, 12.

26. *Telegram*, 12 Feb. 1886.

27. Denison, *Recollections*, 51–53.

28. Ibid., 91–93.

29. PAC, Denison Papers, vol. 38, scrapbook 1909–25, *Telegram*, 10 Apr. 1909.

30. Denison, *Recollections*, 39–50.

31. *Telegram*, 5 and 6 May 1886.

32. Denison, *Recollections*, 178, 182, 217, 231.

33. *Telegram*, 5 Feb. 1886; *Globe*, 14 May 1890.

34. Denison, *Recollections*, 119.

35. *Telegram*, 18 May 1886.

36. *Telegram* and *Globe*, 13 and 14 May 1886; *Telegram*, 20 May 1886. See also Gregory Kealey, *Toronto Workers Respond to Industrial Capitalism 1867–1892* (Toronto, 1980), 205–7.

37. *Telegram*, 14 Oct. 1886.

38. Craig Heron and Bryan D. Palmer, "Through the Prism of the Strike: Industrial Conflict in Southern Ontario, 1901–14," *Canadian Historical Review* 53, no. 4 (Dec. 1977): 451. In a few cases those convicted were fined $75 and costs, an unusually high sum.

39. *The Toiler* 4, no. 10 (12 Feb. 1904).

40. *The Typographical Journal*, Sept. 1903, 259.

41. *The Western Clarion*, 24 July 1903.

42. *Telegram*, 14 Apr. 1886.

43. Denison, *Recollections*, 29.

44. Wodson, *The Whirlpool*, 27–28; Denison, *Recollections*, 3.

45. *Star*, 13 July 1912.

46. Denison, *Recollections*, 88.

47. *Mail and Empire*, 26 Dec. 1898, and 9 June 1899; *Telegram*, 8 Feb. 1886, and 2 Apr. 1886.

48. Clark, *Of Toronto The Good*, 16–22.

49. Globe, 15 May 1886.

50. Wodson, *The Whirlpool*, 80–81, 100, 152.

51. Robson Black, "A Dollar and Costs"; PAC, Denison Papers, vol. 38, scrapbook 1909–25, *Star Weekly*, 25 Apr. 1916.

52. PAC, Denison Papers, vol. 38, scrapbook 1909–25, *Jack Canuck*, 19 Apr. 1913.

53. Wodson, *The Whirlpool*, 28.

54. Ibid., 31.

55. *Citizen and Country*, 5 Oct. 1900.

56. *Canada Law Journal*, 36, no. 19, (Oct. 1900): 517–20.

57. Ibid., no. 21 (1 Nov. 1900): 631–35, 610.

58. Denison, *Recollections*, 7.

59. *City of Toronto Municipal Handbook*, 1908–1923, passim.

60. Ibid.; Denison, *Recollections*, 39; PAC, Denison Papers, vol. 37, scrapbook 1897–1915, *Star*, H.F. Gadsby, "Under Big Ben" series, c. 1914.

61. Denison, *Recollections*, 257.

62. PAC, Denison Papers, vol. 37, scrapbook 1897–1915, *Star*, H.F. Gadsby, "Under Big Ben."

63. On children, see Neil Sutherland, *Children in English-Canadian Society: Framing the Twentieth-Century Consensus* (Toronto, 1976), 119, 127–28, 133–34. Sutherland is rightfully sceptical about the salutary effects of reform campaigns; see especially 148–51.

64. *Saturday Night*, 23 July 1921.

65. PAC, Denison Papers, vol. 38, scrapbook 1909–25, *Star*, 10 July 1919.

66. *Star*, 16 July 1921.

67. A.B. Popple, "Police Court Systems," *The Canadian Law Times* 41, nos. 8 and 9 (Aug. and Sept. 1921).

68. Harry M. Wodson, *The Justice Shop* (Toronto, 1931), 112–14.

69. Wodson, *The Whirlpool*, 194.

70. Denison, *Recollections*, 58.

71. *Globe*, 18 Mar. 1890; *Star*, 2 Nov. 1899 ("Annie Hauge, an unmarried woman who has a delusion that she is encumbered with a husband who persists in pulling her hair, was sent to the Mercer for six months for begging.").

72. Lorne Tepperman, *Crime Control: The Urge Toward Authority* (Toronto, 1977), 62–65. The trend in this period was to tighten up Canada's Criminal Code to increase its punitiveness. R.C. MacLeod, "The Shaping of Canadian Criminal Law, 1892 to 1902," Canadian Historical Association, *Historical Papers*, 1978. For a brief review of some historical problems raised in the literature on urban crime, see John W. Fierheller, "Approaches to the Study of Urban Crime: A Review Article," *Urban History Review* 8, no. 2 (Oct. 1979).

A CENTURY OF CRIMINAL JUSTICE†

MARTIN L. FRIEDLAND

In order to show the changes in Canadian criminal law and procedure over the past century I will analyze a number of murder trials which took place in Ontario exactly one hundred years ago and consider how similar trials would be conducted today.

Introduction

First, let me say how the cases were selected. The Public Archives of Canada contains very full records of capital cases for which the Minister of Justice had to decide whether to recommend to the Governor General that a reprieve be granted.[1] Murder and, of course, treason[2] were the only capital offences at the time. In 1882 there were only eight murder convictions in all of Canada, including the West, which certainly confirms the view of historians that Canada was a more peaceable and law-abiding country than our neighbour to the south. And it still is: the per capita murder rate in the United States is four times the Canadian rate. Out of the eight Canadian cases in 1882, five occurred in Ontario and I have selected three of these for discussion in this paper.[3]

Murder cases may not be typical of other offences, but they do illustrate how major criminal trials were conducted. Moreover, transcripts for non-murder cases are not available for trials that took place a hundred years ago because there were then no appeals in criminal cases and so transcripts were not prepared. They were prepared in capital cases, for the use of the Minister of Justice, and contain a vast reservoir of information for legal historians.

The three trials took place in Napanee, Milton, and Toronto. After studying these cases, and looking at other cases around that time, I am struck by the fact that the trial of serious criminal cases has not changed as much in the past hundred years as almost all other areas of the law and, indeed, of society. There have been changes of course — many of them very significant. Still, the present-day lawyer would feel very much at home in a courtroom one hundred years ago, and the lawyers of that time would be surprised at how little change has occurred over the course of the century.

† Martin L. Friedland, ed., *A Century of Criminal Justice: Perspectives on the Development of Canadian Law* (Toronto: Carswell, 1984), 233-45. This paper was prepared for the Annual Meeting of the Royal Society of Canada held in Ottawa, June 1982, celebrating the one hundredth anniversary of the founding of the Society and was published in *Transactions of the Royal Society of Canada* 20 (1982): 285ff, reprinted in *Law Society of Upper Canada Gazette* 16 (1982): 336ff. The author is indebted to Justices John Arnup and G. Arthur Martin of the Ontario Court of Appeal and to Professors John Beattie, Department of History, and R.C.B. Risk, Faculty of Law, University of Toronto, for reading and commenting on an earlier version of this paper.

The judge then and now would be a Supreme Court of Ontario judge travelling on circuit from Toronto. There are, of course, many more Ontario High Court trial judges today: about forty-five compared to nine a hundred years ago, but this is not much greater than the fourfold growth in the population and far less than in other areas of the criminal justice system, such as the spectacular growth in the number of police officers, from under 1500 in 1882 for all of Canada to over 60 000 in 1982 — a forty-fold increase.[4] Counsel and the judge would be dressed in much the same gowns now as then. In some cases the same courtroom would be used. The Napanee courthouse is still in use (the fluorescent fixtures are new, of course) and the Milton courthouse was used until a few years ago.[5] The Toronto Courthouse of 1882 is now, appropriately, the Adelaide Court Theatre. Counsel from the past would no doubt be surprised at the number of women lawyers today — now about one third of the graduating class. Women were not admitted to the bar until the 1890s in Ontario, the first jurisdiction in the British Empire to admit female lawyers.[6] Counsel from the past would certainly be surprised at the large number of Queen's Counsel practising in Ontario. The present-day lawyer might, perhaps, be surprised at the number of Irishmen practising law one hundred years ago. There were four times as many persons with Irish backgrounds entering the legal profession in Ontario in the middle of the last century than persons with English backgrounds.[7] In general, though, the various participants in the trial, including the accused, would be much the same today as one hundred years ago.

The locales of murders change over time, reflecting changes in society. One of the three murders took place on a farm, and another in a stable. And the weapons have changed: two of the three murders were committed with an axe, a weapon which is rarely used today. The motives, however, have not changed over the years — jealousy, anger, and revenge will be with us for some time.

Before turning to the individual cases, I want to point out that there was no Canadian Criminal Code in 1882. (Indirectly, this lack of codification may, in part, be traced to the influence of the English Royal Society.) Today, the criminal law is contained in the Criminal Code, a statute first passed by Parliament in 1892.[8] In 1882, however, the criminal law of Canada was contained in various statutes and in the judge-made common law. The law of murder was found solely in the common law. England still does not have a Criminal Code. One of the main reasons why there has always been strong resistance to codification in common-law jurisdictions, but widespread acceptance of the concept in continental law, may be because of the close identification of legal and scientific thought in England in the seventeenth century.[9] One of the most famous scientists of the time, Sir Francis Bacon, was also one of the most famous jurists, and lawyers were actively involved in the work of the Royal Society, which was founded in London in 1662. The English Royal Society was, in fact, begun in a lawyer's chamber in the Middle Temple, and some of the earliest presidents of the Society were lawyers. Lawyers were part of the intellectual community and were influenced by and, in turn, influenced scientific ideas. The Chief Justice of England, Sir Matthew Hale, like Lord

Chancellor Bacon, was both a lawyer and a scientist, and believed in the inductive approach to knowledge. In 1677, for example, he published *Observations touching the Principles of Natural Motions, and especially touching Rarefaction and Condensation*. He was also a great jurist and the first major writer on the criminal law in England. I see a close relationship, therefore, between the Baconian method of scientific empiricism and the common law case-by-case method of building general principles from specific instances. Both use the inductive approach. Similarly, one can see a close relationship between the continental Cartesian method of deductive analysis and the concept of codification, which necessarily goes from general principles to special applications. But I am getting out of my depth and, like a good common-law lawyer, I will return to specific cases.

The High Park Case

The first murder case took place in High Park in Toronto during the summer of 1882. Part of High Park had been given to the city by the architect John Howard in 1873 in exchange for a yearly pension.[10] The southern part of what is now High Park, including Grenadier Pond, was kept by Howard as his private property and was only to become city property at his death. Not only did the city give John Howard a pension, but they provided him with a constable, John Albert, to keep trespassers off his property. Albert was kept very busy that summer, at the urging of John Howard, trying to keep the nearby Parkdale children from using Grenadier Pond.

On Sunday, 23 July 1882, just before noon, a seventeen-year old boy, Andrew Young, was boating on the water with some of his friends. Constable Albert went to the pond, fired a warning shot in the air, and when the boat landed on the shore ran after Young. Constable Albert's gun went off and the bullet went through Young's head, causing his almost immediate death. A witness had heard Albert shout "Stop or I'll shoot." The Crown Attorney charged Albert with murder, claiming the shooting was intentional.

The trial took place at the next assizes, on 12 October 1882, within three months of the killing. Aemilius Irving, Q.C., later the treasurer of the Law Society of Upper Canada for a remarkable twenty-year span, prosecuted; Nicholas Murphy defended. The Milton trial also took place at the next assizes, also within three months of the killing. The Napanee case took a little over six months before it was tried, but, as we will see, it was complicated by psychiatric evidence. Today, of course, it takes considerably longer before a case is heard. Not only does it take longer before a case is tried, but the trial lasts much longer today. While preparing this section I called the Crown Attorney's offices in Napanee and Milton to get some comparative figures. The Napanee Crown Attorney was not in; his secretary told me that he was then on the third week of a murder case. I did speak to the assistant Crown Attorney for Milton just before he was to enter court for the fourth week of the murder case he was then prosecuting.

In contrast, the High Park case took one day to try, the Milton case two days, and the Napanee case three days. Some of the reasons for the lengthening of trials over the years will become apparent as we examine each case. One reason for delay before trial today is that some of those accused of murder are released on bail pending their trial, thus decreasing the pressure for an early hearing. None of the three accused in 1882 was released before trial. Four out of the six persons tried for murder in Milton over the past year were released on bail.

The issue in the Albert case was a simple one. Did the gun go off by accident, or did Albert intentionally shoot the lad? Albert was convicted of murder by the jury, with a strong recommendation for mercy, and was sentenced to be hanged. I must say that after reading the file and the transcript I probably would have acquitted Albert of murder. The evidence indicated that Albert was right-handed but was holding the gun, with which he was unfamiliar, in his left hand.

Would Albert be convicted today? Although the law is essentially the same today as it was then, there are two major differences in procedure which might affect the outcome. The first is that one hundred years ago the accused was not permitted to give evidence at his trial. The reason was that he was disqualified because of his interest in the outcome — not a particularly persuasive reason for excluding him. In 1893[11] the rule was changed in Canada, and in 1898[12] in England. Indeed, in 1882[13] some of the judges in England, and in the late 1880s[14] some in Canada, permitted the accused to give unsworn evidence from the dock. But in 1882 this was not yet permitted in Canada and so the jury in the Albert case never heard Albert give his version of the story. Today he would almost certainly go into the witness box.

Another crucial change over the last hundred years in that the presumption of innocence is now more solidly a part of our law than it was then. The change came about because of the House of Lords' case of *Woolmington v. D.P.P.*[15] in 1935. Until 1935 — and in the Albert case the trial judge would have so told the jury — the onus was on the Crown to show that the accused committed the physical act but on the *accused* to satisfy the jury that the shooting was accidental. After *Woolmington* the onus of showing that it was *not* an accident was on the Crown, and the Crown had to show this **beyond a reasonable doubt**. So Constable Albert today probably would not have been convicted of murder, although he may well have been convicted of manslaughter because of his recklessness.

Albert was sentenced to be hanged on 10 November 1882. The focus then shifted to the Minister of Justice in Ottawa. There was then no right of appeal on matters of law or fact in criminal cases. Appeals would delay the desired deterrent effect of a hanging. Appeals in criminal cases were not introduced in Canada until 1892[16] and not until 1907[17] in England. In the Albert case, petitions to commute the sentence were sent to the Minister of Justice by all twelve jurymen, by the mayor and aldermen of Toronto, by the three Toronto MPs, by many of the police officers in Toronto, and by a large number of influential citizens. The chief constable of York pointed out that Albert's "obnoxious . . . vigilant conduct" in the park over the years may have influenced the jury. The Minister (actually the Governor General on the recommendation of the Cabinet) commuted the sentence to twenty years in the penitentiary, which at that time meant Kingston penitentiary. There was then only one class of penitentiary, maximum security, with a harsh regimen.

What would happen in a similar case today? Capital punishment was officially abolished in Canada in 1976[18] and Albert would today have been sentenced to life imprisonment. There are now two classes of murder, first- and second-degree murder. Albert's case would today be classified as second-degree murder because it would not be considered "planned and deliberate," one of the categories of first-degree murder.[19] After the Albert jury had been out about three hours they returned and asked whether the required "intent" or, as it was then called, "malice," had to be present more than two minutes before the shooting. The trial judge told them that "if the malice exists at the time the act is done which caused death, that is sufficient." Fifteen minutes later the jury returned the verdict of guilty. So the result today, assuming the jury found Albert guilty of murder, would be life imprisonment, without eligibility for parole for ten years.[20] Note that the decision to release today is made by the Parole Board acting under the Parole Act.[21] This is a relatively new institution, having been introduced in Canada in its present form only in 1959.[22] Before that, the release was under what was called the Ticket of Leave Act enacted in 1899.[23] In 1882 release was through the Governor General's royal prerogative of mercy on the recommendation of the Minister of Justice.[24]

The parole system and the Ticket of Leave Act were part of the renewed quest for the rehabilitation of offenders in a prison setting. Deterrence and retribution, the principal objectives of the penal system in 1882, were replaced by rehabilitation. The influential Archambault Royal Commission on the Penal System of Canada,[25] for example, reported in 1938 that "it is admitted by all the foremost students of penology that the revengeful or retributive character of punishment should be completely *eliminated*, and that the deterrent effect of punishment alone . . . is practically valueless. . . ." The Commission recommended that "the task of the prison should be . . . the *transformation* of reformable criminals into law abiding citizens."[26] In the 1960s, however, a revolution occurred in penal philosophy and the quest for the "rehabilitative ideal" was jettisoned by many influential writers[27] — in my opinion jettisoned a little too vigorously. A number of American states have now eliminated parole and introduced fixed sentences. Normally change comes slowly and gradually in the law; the abandonment of rehabilitation through the penal system may be one of the very few revolutions in thought (as the concept is used by Thomas Kuhn)[28] in the law. So we have come almost full circle in the last century on the central issue of penal policy.

A great effort was made over the years to have Albert released, but without success. Many of the letters stressed the hardship faced by Albert's wife, who had to raise six children herself. There is a poignant letter in the file to the Minister of Justice from Mrs. Albert in 1890 where she says: "My health is now failing me, and our three younger children are still unable to support themselves." These were the days before public welfare, and the family of the convict suffered greatly. But so did the family of the deceased. There was then no scheme, as there is now, for compensating victims of crime. The deceased boy's sister wrote to the papers stating: "I hope the public will not forget the cruel way in which he deprived my mother of a son and an honest support." Perhaps the main reason why Albert was not released was because the trial judge was against it. Mr. Justice Armour took an extremely harsh position, reporting several years later that "if ever there was a case of murder this was one and deserved the extreme penalty of the law."

The Milton Case

The second murder, in this case a double murder, of eighty-five-year old Edward Maher and his thirty-five-year-old daughter Bridget, occurred in a farmhouse near Hamilton. The trial took place at the Milton assizes. Michael O'Rourke, the accused, had worked on the farm cutting wood. On the evening of the murders in January 1882, he appeared at a neighbour's farmhouse and told of quitting his job that morning, drinking in town, and then returning to the Mahers later that night to pay a visit. The farmer's daughter, O'Rourke said, was sitting on his knee with her arms around his neck when her brother appeared and was so infuriated that he killed her and their father and wounded him, O'Rourke. The next morning the police set out to arrest the brother, but did not do so because that morning O'Rourke made a confession of guilt.

An officer staying with the injured O'Rourke suggested that Bridget Maher had been "violated" by O'Rourke, and O'Rourke is alleged to have said: "I neither ravished her before I killed her or after." When the officer asked whom he killed first, O'Rourke replied: "The old man first; now you have it." O'Rourke later gave a fuller confession which was taken down in writing and acknowledged with O'Rourke's mark.

The crucial issue in the case, as in so many murder cases today, was the admissibility of the confession. In the nineteenth century the judges were more inclined to exclude a confession than they are today.[29] Today, the underlying question is simply: "Is the statement freely and voluntarily made?"[30] One hundred years ago there was a far better chance of having the statement excluded on a technicality. In 1881 Lord Coleridge, the Chief Justice of England, had adopted the view that "a confession, in order to be admissible, must be free and voluntary: that is, must not be extracted by any sort of threats or violence, nor obtained by any direct or implied promises, *however slight*, nor by the exertion of any improper influence"[31] (italics added). I stress the words "however slight." The defence concentrated on trying to show that the police officer had improperly questioned O'Rourke. A witness claimed to have heard the officer say: "You are guilty, Michael, and you had better confess at once; it will be better for you." The officer denied making the statement. The transcript does not contain counsel's argument, but no doubt defence counsel also argued that the liquor the police gave O'Rourke that morning was an improper inducement. The judge, Mr. Justice Cameron, ruled that the confession was admissible. The almost inevitable result was that O'Rourke was found guilty of murder and was sentenced to be hanged.

It came as a surprise to me to note that the evidence respecting the admissibility of the confession was heard in the presence of the jury. Today, the evidence would be heard in what is referred to as a *voir dire*, that is, a trial within a trial, in the absence of the jury.[32] The reason for a *voir dire* is that a jury would not be able to disregard the prejudicial evidence if the trial judge excluded the confession. Today, if the confession is held to be admissible, the evidence is then presented before the jury. The present practice is certainly much fairer to the accused, but it necessarily results in a much lengthier trial because if the confession is admitted much of the evidence is heard twice.

Another factor in causing lengthier trials today is that legal aid is now available, but was not then. The defence counsel, Murphy, the same counsel who had lost the High Park case, took the case as an act of charity and later admitted that the conduct of the accused's defence was not as good as it might have been. Indeed, he used this as a reason why the Minister of Justice should commute the sentence: "The jury would have been justified on the evidence in finding a verdict of manslaughter and perhaps would have done so, had the case for the defence been marked up [i.e., with a fee] as capital cases usually are and not by counsel without funds at his command and who was only imported into the case as an act of charity towards the unfortunate O'Rourke." Crown counsel was B.B. Osler, Q.C.,[33] the brother of the famous doctor, and the person who successfully prosecuted Louis Riel for treason three years later. Osler, who I might add, was the first professor of criminal law at the University of Toronto, was a partner in the seven-man firm of McCarthy, Olser, Hoskin and Creelman. The firm split some years later, one part growing into the well-known firm of McCarthy & McCarthy, and the other half into the equally well-known firm of Osler, Hoskin & Harcourt, each of which now has well over a hundred lawyers. So this aside tells us something about the growth of the legal profession in Ontario. As a further aside, I should note that the Osler, Hoskin firm does not handle murder cases today.

A striking difference between the O'Rourke case and a similar case today is the almost complete absence of scientific evidence then introduced by the Crown. Such evidence is now standard practice in similar cases. Today, scientists at the Centre of Forensic Sciences in Toronto would provide evidence dealing with blood types, fingerprints, possible semen stains, hair fibres, and many other pieces of circumstantial evidence. Much of this type of evidence was not available a century ago. Even when it was available, being circumstantial evidence, it was considered suspect and a special warning, now no longer strictly required,[34] had to be given to the jury. The growth in scientific evidence in criminal trials again causes trials today to be lengthier than in the past.

Murphy, the defence counsel, to his credit, did not abandon the case after the conviction. He obtained the Attorney General's consent to appeal the conviction by way of writ of error, a very limited technical form of appeal. As I mentioned earlier, there was then no general right of appeal in criminal cases. A writ of error was used to attack convictions on formal grounds,[35] and in this case Murphy repeated before the Queen's Bench Division of Ontario[36] the argument that he had made at the commencement of the trial: that the jury were improperly chosen (technically referred to as "challenging the array"). There were two grounds to his argument. The first was that all the members of the jury had been chosen from the same letter of the alphabet—apparently the letter "P"; the second was that the federal Parliament, which was responsible for criminal law and procedure under the British North America Act,[37] had improperly delegated the responsibility for determining the qualifications for jury service to the provinces. In December 1882, the Divisional Court dismissed the appeal on both grounds; the Minister of Justice recommended that "the law be allowed to take its course," and on Friday, 5 January 1883, Michael O'Rourke was hanged in the Milton jail.

Would O'Rourke be convicted of murder today? There is little doubt that the confession would now also be admissible. But I believe that there would be a very good chance for a manslaughter verdict on the basis that drunkenness may have affected O'Rourke's mental state. One hundred years ago, to quote from another case in 1882,[38] "drunkenness in the slayer at the moment of causing death was no answer to the charge either in whole or in part."

The Napanee Case

The final case to be explored here is *The Queen v. Michael Lee* involving a murder in the spring of 1882 in Napanee. The defence was insanity. Lee admitted killing eighteen-year-old Maggie Howie with an axe in the stable attached to the hotel where they both worked. They had been engaged, but the night before the murder she had given him back the engagement ring. Apparently she had discovered that he was keeping a mistress. The next morning when she went to the stable to milk the cow he struck her with the axe which he had hidden under his coat. The only question at the trial was whether he was insane at the time the act was committed. The case is still well known in eastern Ontario because of the folk song "Maggie Howie," which starts with the words

> I am an Irishman by birth, my name is Michael Lee.
> I fell in love with a pretty girl, which proved my destiny.

It ends with the verse:

> So it's now I am a prisoner in the town of Napanee,
> It's there I'll stand my trial and the judge will sentence me.
> For I know that I am guilty and I do deserve to die
> For the murder of my own true love upon the gallows high.

The folk song contains no mention of the insanity defence.

The case has a particularly modern flavour because cases today still result in the same clash of psychiatrists and there continues to be controversy over the proper tests for insanity. There was evidence that Lee had had delusions in the past: he believed persons were trying to poison him and were shooting symbolic arrows at him. Moreover, he saw special signs in ordinary conduct. A number of his cousins had already been committed to mental institutions.

Two highly respected psychiatrists, at the request of the Crown, examined Lee shortly before the trial: Dr. W.G. Metcalfe, the medical head of the 400-bed Kingston Asylum for the Insane, and Dr. Daniel Clark, the medical superintendent of the 700-bed Queen Street Lunatic Asylum in Toronto. Clark was the predecessor at the Asylum of Dr. C.K. Clarke, after whom the Clarke Institute of Psychiatry is named, although they were not related. It is worth noting that the number of beds in Queen Street Mental Health Centre is under 600 today, compared to 700 a century ago, and of the 600, less than 100 persons at any one time are compulsorily confined. One hundred years ago everyone in the institution was held compulsorily. Science has produced drugs to control mental instability, but not criminal activity.

Clark and Metcalfe were not called by the Crown. Their evidence strongly supported insanity, and so they were called by the defence. Clark (Metcalfe's evidence was similar) testified that Lee was suffering from "acute dementia" and should not be considered responsible for his act. Was Lee faking? Clark was sure he was not: Q: "You have no doubt in your mind at all?" A: "No doubt in my own mind at all." A few years later Clark was one of the principal defence witnesses in the treason trial of Louis Riel, but on that occasion he was much more cautious in his testimony, stating, "I assume . . . that not only the evidence given is correct, but that he was not a deceiver." Some writers consider that Clark's weak "assumption" rather than a positive "belief" may have been responsible for the failure of Riel's insanity defence.[39]

Clark disagreed with the legal view of insanity derived from the well-known M'Naghten Rules of 1843,[40] still the basis of the test in Canada.[41] M'Naghten's case had decided that an accused is insane if "at the time of the committing of the act the party accused was labouring under such a defect of reason, from disease of the mind, as not to know the nature and quality of the act he was doing, or, if he did know it, that he did not know he was doing what was wrong." Clark testified: "I say right and wrong is no test of insanity." Moreover, he disagreed with the view that a person could have delusions but be in other respects sane: "I don't believe at all in partial insanity." One interesting question asked by the Crown in cross-examination dates the trial: "What do you say about the general appearance and formation of the person's head?" I like Clark's reply: "There is nothing in that. Most of us would not like to be judged by the shape of our head."

The trial judge's charges to the jury left them little choice other than to reject insanity: Chief Justice Wilson did not agree with Clark's idea about the unity of the mind:

> It does not it seems to me follow that if a mind is deranged on one subject it is deranged altogether. Dr. Clark and the other gentleman both admitted that that was the view entertained by many professional men and I venture to say it is the view entertained by most professional men and by most people who are not professional men and it is the view which the law lays down to be the correct view; that a person may have a delusion upon some particular subject and not upon another at all.

But even if the accused was medically insane, that was not enough. Insanity is a legal test: the accused must not know the difference between right and wrong, that is, according to Chief Justice Wilson's charge to the jury, whether the act was contrary to the law or not. The evidence, the Chief Justice said, showed that Lee knew the act was contrary to law. The issue whether the word "wrong" means "contrary to law" or "wrong in a moral sense" is still a live issue in Canada. A few years ago the Supreme Court of Canada in *Schwartz v. R.*,[42] a five-to-four decision, held that it meant "contrary to law." The decision has been much criticized, however, and many think that the Supreme Court of Canada will reverse the decision at some future time.

The jury in the Lee case retired at 3:30 and returned at 6:00 stating that Lee was guilty and "did know the difference between right and wrong." It is likely that a jury today in the light of the *Schwartz* case, and assuming the Crown did not agree to accept a plea of guilty of manslaughter, would find a similar verdict. Lee was sentenced to be hanged.

Lee did not hang. His mental condition became progressively worse. The Minister of Justice commuted the sentence after further representations by a number of doctors including Dr. Metcalfe, who put it quite bluntly: "I do not see what will be gained by hanging a lunatic." Even the trial judge, who was of the view in his report to the Minister that Lee "did the act by design, knowing well the difference between right and wrong," suggested that "It may . . . be that his excellency the Governor General may not enforce a greater penalty than imprisonment for life." Lee was sent to Kingston Penitentiary where for the rest of his life he was kept in the new ward for the insane.[43]

Conclusion

The analysis of the three cases illustrates, I believe, that in the main the criminal law and the trial process have not changed much in the past hundred years. The same key arguments regarding the accused's mental state in the High Park case, the question of the admissibility of the confession in the O'Rourke case, and the issue of insanity of the accused in the Lee case could all have taken place in a courtroom today.

There have, of course, been changes, but most have taken place outside the formal structure of the trial. Techniques of police and scientific investigation have changed; legal aid is available in all serious cases; bail is more readily granted; plea bargaining is now widespread; capital punishment has been abolished; and a parole system has been brought in. Within the trial process itself perhaps the most significant changes in the past hundred years have been the placing of the onus of proof on the prosecution, giving the accused the right to give evidence on his own behalf, and the lengthening of the trial. But, in general, the criminal process has not been subject to radical change, nor is it likely to undergo such change in the future, as many of the procedures have been now been included in the Charter of Rights and thus entrenched in the Constitution. So a present-day lawyer would also likely feel at home in a major criminal case a century from now.

Notes

1. Public Archives of Canada (hereinafter PAC), RG 13, c-1, vol. 1419. In addition, the Ontario Archives has Assize Records (RG 22) for each county, which contain additional, although sketchy, information on the cases. Further, the *Globe* and, of course, local papers contain very full coverage of all the trials.

2. The only treason case close to 1882 was the trial of Louis Riel in 1885.

3. The non-Ontario cases do not contain trial transcripts and so are less useful. The file of one of the Ontario cases is missing and another case (dealing with insanity) is similar to one of the cases selected.

4. See the Government of Canada policy paper, *The Criminal Law in Canadian Society* (Ottawa, 1982).

5. Early Ontario courthouses are described in M. MacRae and A. Adamson, *Cornerstones of Order: Courthouses and Town Halls of Ontario 1783–1914* (Toronto: Clarke Irwin, 1983).

6. See Wright, "Admission of Women to the Bar: An Historical Note," *Law Society Gazette* 16 (1982): 42ff.

7. See G.B. Baker, "Legal Education in Upper Canada 1785–1889" in *Essays in the History of Canadian Law*, vol. 2, edited by D.H. Flaherty (Toronto: University of Toronto Press, 1983).

8. The Criminal Code, 1892, c. 29.

9. See the fine article, Shapiro, "Law and Science in Seventeenth-Century England," *Stanford Law Review* 21 (1969): 727ff. on which I have relied for much of the factual material in this paragraph.

10. See *Dictionary of Canadian Biography* (Toronto: University of Toronto Press, 1982), 11: 426–28.

11. Canada Evidence Act, 1893, c. 31.

12. Criminal Evidence Act, 1898, 61 & 62 Vict., c. 36.

13. See *R. v. Shimmin* (1882), 15 Cox C.C. 122 per Cave J.

14. See *R. v. Rogers* (1888), 1 B.C.L.R. (part 2) 119 per Crease J.

15. *Woolmington v. D.P.P.*, [1935] A.C. 462.

16. Canadian Criminal Code, *Statutes of Canada* (hereafter S.C.) 1892, c. 29, s. 742.

17. Criminal Appeal Act 1907, 7 Edw. 7, c. 23.

18. Criminal Law Amendment Act (No. 2), 1976, c. 105.

19. S. 214 of the Criminal Code

20. Ibid, s. 669.

21. *Revised Statutes of Canada* 1970, c. P-2.

22. See the *Report of the Canadian Committee on Corrections* (the *Ouimet Report*) (Ottawa, 1969), 333.

23. Ticket of Leave Act, S.C. 1899, c. 49.

24. *Ouimet Report*, 332.

25. *Report of the Royal Commission to Investigate the Penal System of Canada* (Ottawa, 1938), 9.

26. Ibid.

27. Perhaps the most influential legal article was Francis Allen, "Criminal Justice, Legal Values and the Rehabilitative Ideal" (1959), 50 J. Crim. L.C. & P.S. 226. An earlier important article by a non-lawyer was C.S. Lewis, "The Humanitarian Theory of Punishment," *Res Judicatae* 6 (1953), 224.

28. T.A. Kuhn, *The Structure of Scientific Revolutions*, 2nd ed. (Chicago: University of Chicago Press, 1970).

29. See *Wigmore on Evidence*, vol. 3, Chadbourn edition (Boston: Little, Brown, 1970), 297ff.

30. *Boudreau v. R.* (1949), 94 C.C.C. 1 at 8 (S.C.C.) per Rand J.

31. *R. v. Fennell* (1881), 7 Q.B.D. 147 at 151.

32. See, for example, *R. v. Viau* (1898), 7 Que. Q.B. 362 (C.A.), appeal quashed 29 S.C.R. 90; *R. v. Sonyer* (1898), 2 C.C.C. 501 (B.C.C.A); *R. v. De Mesquito* (1915), 24 C.C.C. 407 (B.C.C.A.).

33. See Note, "B.B. Osler," *Law Society Gazette* 2 (1968): 27ff.

34. See *R. v. Cooper* (1977), 34 C.C.C. (2d) 18 (S.C.C.).

35. See generally, M.L. Friedland, *Double Jeopardy* (Oxford: Clarendon Press, 1969), 238ff.

36. *R. v. O'Rourke* (1882), 1 O.R. 464. The trial judge had reserved the case at trial for hearing by the Common Pleas Division, but that court held that it was not a proper case for reserving a point of law: see (1882), 32 C.P. 388.

37. British North America Act, 1867, 30 & 31 Vict., c. 3, s. 91(27).

38. *R. v. Marcel* (1882), RG 13 c–1, vol. 1419, no. 160.

39. See G.F.G. Stanley, *Louis Riel* (Toronto: McGraw-Hill Ryerson, 1963), 353; Verdun-Jones, "The Evolution of the Defences of Insanity and Automatism in Canada from 1843 to 1979: A Saga of Judicial Reluctance to Sever the Umbilical Cord to the Mother Country?" *University of British Columbia Law Review* 14, no. 1 (1979): 9.

40. M'Naghten's Case (1843), 10 Cl. & Fin. 200, 8 E.R. 718.

41. S. 16(2) of the present Criminal Code states that "a person is insane when he . . . has disease of the mind to an extent that renders him incapable of appreciating the nature and quality of an act or omission or of knowing that an act or omission is wrong." The principal difference between the M'Naghten test and s. 16 is the wide meaning given by Canadian courts to the word "appreciate" in contrast to the narrow meaning given in England to the word "know": see *R. v. Cooper* (1979), 51 C.C.C. (2d) 129 (S.C.C.).

42. *Schwartz v. R.* (1976), 29 C.C.C. (2d) 1.

43. Such a ward was kept at Kingston Penitentiary until 1915 when arrangements were made to transfer insane prisoners to provincial mental institutions: see the *Archambault Report* (1938), 150. The ward, constructed in 1881, is described in Calder, "Convict Life in Canadian Federal Penitentiaries, 1867–1900" in *Crime and Criminal Justice in Europe and Canada*, edited by L.A. Knafla (Waterloo: Wilfred Laurier University Press, 1981), 308.

THE ORIGINS OF CANADIAN NARCOTICS LEGISLATION: THE PROCESS OF CRIMINALIZATION IN HISTORICAL CONTEXT†

NEIL BOYD

The year 1972 saw a federal commission investigating the non-medical use of drugs recommend repeal of the offence of possession of marijuana,[1] an indication that state policy with respect to the social control of psychoactive substances was undergoing a thorough reappraisal. It is not surprising, then, that the past decade should also have seen a considerable degree of academic interest in Canada's initial attempt to make criminal the citizen's desire to alter consciousness.

A comprehensive review of this admirable collection of research reveals that Canada ought not to take pride in these initial efforts. The initial statute has been explained with reference to its "racist and moralistic foundation," by the "galloping reformist zeal of Mackenzie King" and by the increasing affront of "cheap Oriental labour."[2] The creation of law is viewed as the product of a process of social conflict; it is not suggested that the law was the reflection of an emerging consensus of opinion within the Canadian people.[3]

What remains unclear, however, is the process of social conflict itself; there is disagreement with respect to the modes of conflict and the structures of power that created this legislation.[4] Chambliss and Dolinski have both suggested that the changing nature of economic relationships was responsible for anti-opium legislation. Small, Solomon and Madison, and Green have urged rather that pluralist conflict gave rise to Canada's first prohibition of opiate use. These authors have implied that the interactions of various essentially unrelated interest groups produced the laws that would control the "non-medical" use of drugs. While critical of the premises of the anti-drug ideology of the day, these authors appear to imply that the social democratic tradition of pluralist conflict merely misfired in the instance of Canadian narcotics legislation. Small, Solomon and Madison, and Green, while they give us historical data on the process of criminalization, fail to inform us as to what the data say about such a process in theoretical context.

Chambliss and Dolinski make the bold claim that criminalization here was a consequence of purely materialist forces, thereby supporting a culturally

† Dalhousie Law Journal 8, no. 1 (Jan. 1984): 102–36. The author would like to thank John Lowman, Department of Geography, University of British Columbia, for his perceptive research assistance, and would also like to thank Simon Fraser University for the provision of a President's Research Grant, 1979.

materialist, or "Marxist" view of history.[5] Small et al. stand *implicitly* in opposition, suggesting nothing more than that a plurality of interest groups unhappily shaped a statute of repressive character.

The present work seeks to expand, both empirically and theoretically, upon the historical context of the process of criminalization. The empirical data have revealed a theoretical tension — the pluralist conflict view of the process of law creation is challenged by a view that sees economic exploitation as the effective *cause* of criminalization. These two positions represent the poles of highly simplified ideological discourse. The rich tradition of Marxian analytic thought demands interpretation in the context of twentieth-century North America; implicit acceptance of a pluralist conflict model reveals the mighty but problematic Hegelian notion that a contradiction of *ideas* produces a social order in the evolutionary context.

It is suggested that materialist and ideational analyses of the process of criminalization are most appropriately viewed as complementary and not as competing constructions of social reality.[6] As Robert Heilbroner has noted,[7] it can be said that not only did Marx turn the Hegelian construct on its head, but so too, in retrospect, does Hegel dislocate the consistency of Marx.

In the context of the emergence of Canadian narcotics legislation it can be seen that while material life created contradictions that required political decisions, it was ideational life that attempted the resolution of capital's contradictions. It is to an empirical substantiation of this hypothesis that we now turn.

The Evolution of Narcotics Legislation

It is only since 1908 that the social control of altered states of consciousness has been, perhaps unwittingly, a state priority in Canada. The initial two-section statute prohibited the importation, manufacture, and sale of opium and established a penalty of not less than $50 for contravention of the Act.[8] A maximum penalty of three years imprisonment was also provided for. Sale of existing opium stocks was allowed for six months following the statute's enactment, apparently as a concession to the merchants of the industry.[9]

The next twenty-one years would see the institutionalization of the ideology of criminalization, a development which has been the subject of much critical scrutiny.[10] Melvyn Green has most recently said of these "formative years" that

> The process of legislative revision eventually led to a moral redefinition of narcotic drug use. What was once viewed as a private indulgence came to be regarded almost universally as a public evil. Contrary to what might be expected, it was changes in the criminal law that brought about the transformation of public attitudes, and not the converse proposition.[11]

Green, though he surely appreciates the social contexts in which law arises, here presents what might be best characterized as a deceptively attractive hypothesis. While one cannot quarrel with the fact of moral redefinition of opiate use, one is hard pressed to find evidence to support the notion that it is the *law* that has transformed public attitudes. As William Chambliss has noted, "The law may be hallowed but it does not exist in a vacuum."[12] The assertion that law can transform public attitudes is tantamount to a reification of law; it ignores the human medium through which law is both enacted and enforced.

The claim that law can create public attitudes in thus problematic: it too easily excuses human beings for their actions and implies the absence of an often cited dialectical relationship — social life as both a construction of reality, and as a reality in the process of construction.[13] The assertion that law can transform public attitudes is more an attribution of blame than it is a description of events in historical context; there is need to scratch this surface.

The Decision to Criminalize 1870–1908; The Social Control of Consumer Preference

In 1879 one had to pay the city of Vancouver $500 if one wanted to enter the business of dealing in opium.[14] The profits were lucrative and the city felt that it had a right to a certain percentage of the annual take. Federal records indicate that tens of thousands of pounds of crude opium were imported annually into Canada from 1876 to 1908.[15] This opium was principally destined for Caucasian pharmaceutical companies and Chinese opium factories in British Columbia. The Chinese opium factories produced smoking opium; the pharmaceutical companies produced opiated tonics, elixirs, cough syrups, analgesics, and patent medicines.[16] The Caucasian pharmaceutical companies did not pay the $500 licensing fee expected of opium merchants; they were naturally not perceived as such.[17] The Caucasian intake for relief from pain was legally differentiated from the Chinese intake in pursuit of pleasure. The settings and circumstances in which one used opiates were of qualitative importance; the racial origin of the merchant was also naturally a variable of significance. Most important, though, was the international backdrop against which British Columbia opiate use was emerging.

In 1839 and in 1856 Britain had gone to war against China in order to preserve and expand British-India trade in opium.[18] As a consequence of the Chinese defeat in 1856, Britain ultimately managed to obtain from China the legalization of opium smoking and trading within Chinese boundaries in 1858;[19] China, however, managed to obtain the right to impose taxes on opium imported from India. As Chambliss has noted, "Legalization (ironically) . . . planted the seed that would eventually destroy the profits and the British opium monopoly. For with legalization came (a) taxes and (b) the legal right of Chinese farmers to grow their own opium. Competition would shortly ruin the hard-won right to import opium from India into China."[20]

The period of transition was, nevertheless, of some fifty years duration: it was not until the early twentieth century that the opium trade shifted from India to South China and the Golden Triangle. At the time of Canada's first anti-opium legislation, British India's profits from opium were still substantial, though competition from China was obviously increasing. By the 1880s the Chinese province of Szechwan was harvesting an estimated ten thousand tons of raw opium annually.[21]

On the domestic front, the latter half of the nineteenth century saw substantial Chinese immigration into both California and British Columbia. The Chinese of 1870 British Columbia were welcome additions to the owners of west coast industry in a time of labour shortage; the Chinese were industrious workers with few financial expectations.[22] The Chinese opium habit was initially only of financial interest to the municipal, provincial, and federal governments; the new opium business amounted to one more means of raising government revenues.

As Solomon and Madison have pointed out,

> The tolerant attitude towards the Chinese, and Chinese opium smoking lasted only as long as the labour shortage. The decline in railroad construction and the end of the gold rush reduced job opportunities, first in California during the 1870's and subsequently in British Columbia during the 1880's. The Chinese, once welcomed as a cheap source of labour, were now resented for this very reason. White labour could not compete with the Chinese workers, who were unmarried and lived frugally. It was not the white businessman who was blamed, but the Chinese labourers he hired, for they were willing to work for a salary a white man could not live on.[23]

Towards the end of the nineteenth century, then, the British in India were losing control of the lucrative opium trade; the Chinese of British Columbia were finding increasing hostility in the infant nation state of Canada. Chambliss has argued that "As the opium trade became less profitable for Europeans (most importantly the British), anti-opium legislation began to appear in most Western countries. A series of International Opium Conferences . . . were the consequence of the changing economic realities which helped spread anti-opium sentiment and subsequent legislation."[24]

Chambliss has urged the radical hypothesis that criminalization of opium occurred as a *consequence* of its declining profitability in the West. By shutting down potential markets for expanding Chinese opium production, the West could help to minimize the economic gains that China could make as a consequence of its emerging control of the opium market. The Canadian experience of criminalization can lend little support to the Chambliss hypothesis, though, as we shall see later, it does reveal that domestic economic concerns were an integral force in Canada's early efforts.

The year 1885 saw both declining employment opportunities on the west coast and the appointment of a federal royal commission on Chinese immigration.[25] The commission proposed a $50 tax on most Chinese entering the country;[26] the proposal was enacted within the year.[27] In 1901 the tax was increased to $100, in 1904 to $500.[28] This can now be seen as a kind of interference with the labour pool of west coast industry, necessitated by the clamouring of the economically vulnerable white working class.

The Chinese Immigration Act of 1900 had exempted Chinese merchants, Chinese men of science, and Chinese students from payment of the $100 entry tax; it was only the Chinese who would labour for west coast industrialists who would be subject to such a penalty for admission.[29] As the tax on Chinese labourers increased, there was a dramatic decline in Chinese immigration — and a dramatic increase in Japanese immigration. The voice of the white working class had temporarily stemmed the tide of Chinese immigration, but the owners of industry were now managing to acquire the alternative of cheap Japanese labour.[30] Japanese admissions increased from none in 1904 to just under 2000 in 1906 to over 7500 in 1908.[31]

Mackenzie King, appointed in 1908 to inquire into the methods by which Oriental labourers had been induced to come to Canada, revealed a comprehensive understanding of the interactions of labour, government, and the owners of industry.[32] The $500 entry tax, King observed, was having the effect of creating greater bargaining power for the Chinese immigrants already resident in Canada prior to 1904. The tax had effectively cut off Chinese immigration; the "coolie labourer," willing to work for substantially less than the white labourer, was always a highly useful energy source for Canadian corporations. By 1906 the average wage of the Chinese labourer had gone from $30 per month to $65 per month — an increase of over 100 percent in less than two years. The Chinese labourer, while still earning less than the white labourer, had at least marginally diminished the economic power of the owners of industry; there was an acknowledgement of utility.

King was also able to astutely forecast the ultimate irony that the $500 tax would impose. The Chinese labourer, King noted, could save a life's earnings in China after working in Canada for a few years. The newly affluent would then be able to afford to bring over friends and relatives or to return and sponsor the coming of other Chinese. From 1905 to 1913 Chinese immigration would grow from 77 annually to 7445 annually.[33] The $500 entry tax, designed as an appeasement for the fears of white workers, in fact created a labour monopoly of sorts for the Chinese workers already in British Columbia. This labour monopoly, King noted, when coupled with the value of Canadian currency in China, would allow Chinese immigration to continue strongly from 1908 onwards.[34] In fact, it was not until 1923 that an exclusionary immigration policy was finally arrived at.[35]

On the international front, the dawn of the twentieth century saw the Central Government of China beginning to sound the alarm on opium. The Imperial Decree of September 1906 read, in translation:

> Since the restrictions against the use of opium were removed, the poison of this drug has practically permeated the whole of China. The opium smoker waste time and neglects his work, . . . and impoverishes his family, and the poverty and weakness which for the past few decades have been daily increasing amongst us are undoubtedly attributable to this cause . . . at a moment when we are striving to strengthen the Empire, it behooves us to admonish the people. . . . It is hereby commanded that within a period of ten years the evils arising from foreign and native opium be equally and completely eradicated.[36]

Those who had the power of government were telling the people of China to relinquish the indulgence of opium, in order to effect what was perceived as a need for greater economic productivity.

The Manchu dynasty had launched a vast program of reform at the beginning of the twentieth century. As Chesneaux et al. have noted, "Reform was intended to create a modern state by developing centralization, specialization and information."[37] The Imperial Decree of January 1901 announced, "The teachings handed down to us by our sacred ancestors are really the same as those upon which the wealth and power of European countries have been based, but China has hitherto failed to realize this and has been content to acquire the rudiments of European languages or technicalities, while changing nothing of her ancient habits of inefficiency. . . ."[38]

In 1906, an estimated 13 million opium smokers in a population of some 400 million people was seen as symptomatic of such inefficiency.[39] Those in favour of expanding material production in China had the power of government; they had decreed that the social control of a consumer preference was a necessity. The use of a dream-inducing sedative was incompatible with the vision of an emerging industrial state.

Indeed the use of such a sedative could be seen as inimical to the interests of any who might aspire to power. Both the materialist revolutionary and the guardian of the status quo must ultimately prohibit such an alteration of consciousness.[40]

On 27 January 1908, Britain and China entered into an agreement intended to bring about just such a prohibition — the world-wide cessation of the opium trade — an agreement that can now perhaps facetiously be cast as the 10 percent solution.[41] The British would bind themselves to reducing opium exports from India at the rate of 10 percent per year, for a period of three years; China would in turn reduce production of its opium at a similar rate. The ultimate goal of the agreement, if the initial three-year period should prove satisfactory, was to stamp out the "evil" of opium addiction within ten years.

Economic interests most obviously precluded the immediate cessation of the trade. Mackenzie King's correspondence reveals Canadian doubts about the ultimate efficacy of the internationally sanctioned 10 percent solution. King wrote that

> Much has been said about the ten year period being too long. The conviction I reached while in Shanghai, was that if in ten years the traffic were wiped out it would be the most remarkable reform in the matter of time the world had ever known. . . . As it is, it means almost an industrial revolution to effect the change desired in the period of ten years.[42]

The King diaries further reveal King's awareness of the economic interests that necessitated a gradual reduction of the international trade in opium. He noted that,

> So far as the effect in India was concerned it meant of course, the loss of considerable revenue to the Indian Government, but what was the greater problem, it meant the loss of almost the entire revenue to some of the native states. The natives who had been accustomed to this export trade for years could not understand why it should be stopped. The moral aspect of it was not as apparent to them as to us.[43]

The 10 percent solution, then, was necessitated by the fact that entire states in India and entire provinces in China derived almost all revenue from the production and marketing of opium; in an essentially monolithic economy the economic cessation of the trade could not be ignored.

The 10 percent solution, while motivated by a sincere desire to stamp out opium, had the ironic effect of putting yet more money into the pockets of the owners of the industry. As the British Councillor Leech wrote from Peking in June of 1908:

> From various quarters in China it is announced that the price of foreign opium is rising, and this increase is likely to continue in proportion to the reduction of production in China and of importation from abroad, except in the somewhat improbable contingency of the demand for the drug decreasing proportionately to the reduction of supply. There can be no doubt that foreign opium is superior both in quality and strength to the native product, consequently a great stimulus will be given to smuggling in a country where people attach more importance to quality than to price.[44]

The 10 percent solution had given rise to the creation of false scarcity — a mechanism which would ensure British opium merchants a substantial and continuing return from a lucrative market.

Such long-term kindness was not to be visited upon the Chinese opium merchant in British Columbia, for though the 10 percent solution would boost the prices of B.C. opium, the social milieu in which Canadian legislation was to take place would ultimately preclude the possibility of such a lengthy conces- sion. The literature to date on "the formative years" of Canadian narcotics legislation has suggested that the anti-Asiatic riot of 1907 indirectly gave rise to opiate criminalization in Canada; it is to a detailed consideration of this sequence of events that we now turn.[45]

In July of 1907, over 1500 Japanese arrived in the province of British Columbia, more than double the number of such admissions in any of the previous six months.[46] Mackenzie King would later learn that several emigra- tion agencies in Vancouver had accepted contracts to supply cheap Japanese labour for large Canadian corporations.[47] By late July both the provincial press and the Vancouver Trades and Labour Council were greatly agitated. *The Vancouver Province* featured daily articles on the Oriental "invasion"; the Van- couver Trades and Labour Council formed the Asiatic Exclusion League and began to hold public meetings.[48] Through the month of August provincial politicians took to the hustings in support of anti-Asiatic sentiment. The Liberal member for Vancouver, R.G. McPherson, wrote to Laurier, "it is the last thing I want to be, but I can see without any difficulty the Province of British Columbia slipping into the hands of Asiatics and this part of Western Canada no longer a part and parcel of the Dominion."[49]

It was in the context of this rampant paranoia that the anti-Asiatic riot of September 1907 was to take place. The Asiatic Exclusion League, inspired by the economic fears of the white workers, held a large protest rally at City Hall on the night of 7 September. A problem which was essentially of an economic origin was being translated into a problem of racial "domination."

A crowd of 9000 converged on City Hall; an immediate end to all immigration from Asia was demanded. The angry mob drifted from the meeting into the Chinese district and within a period of four hours the Chinese and Japanese quarters of Vancouver had sustained substantial property damage.[50]

The Deputy Minister of Labour, Mackenzie King, was sent to Vancouver in October of 1907 to satisfy Japanese claims for losses incurred; settlement of Chinese claims was not considered a priority at the time.[51] King wrote to Laurier while in Vancouver,

> The feeling in this city and in the other parts of the Province wherever I have been, is very generally strong anti-Japanese. I believe it is no longer merely a labour, but has become a race agitation . . . the fact that the Japanese have proven themselves the equal of the white man in so many ways has caused people of all classes to fear their competition. Nothing has surprised me more than to find, in conversation with persons who have every reason to wish for an increase in the available supply of labour a very decided opinion that other than Japanese labourers must be sought.[52]

King recognized, then, that the impetus for fears of racial domination had an economic origin.

In the spring of 1908 King returned to Vancouver to settle claims for Chinese losses, a settlement for which he had pushed some six months prior. He had been distressed by Laurier's refusal to consider Chinese claims. "It looked as tho' we were afraid of the power of the people [the Japanese] — that fear not justice was the motive," King stated.[53] It was the Chinese, then, who were at the bottom of the social and economic pecking order of 1908 British Columbia; it was the rights of the Chinese that appeared as most vulnerable at this time.

In the course of settling claims from Chinese merchants, King received two requests for compensation from Vancouver opium manufacturers. The dialogue on 27 May 1908, between Lee Theung, manager of the Lee Yuen Opium Company, and Mackenzie King gives some insight into King's concerns. "Question: Many white people buy it? Answer: Some. Q: How many? A: Some buy lots and some buy small. Q: Who are the best customers, white people or Chinese? A: White people. Q: Do you sell more opium to white people than you do to Chinese? A: Yes."[54]

King's general reaction to the opium business was documented in the next morning's *Vancouver Province*. "Prosperous Chinese merchants startle King," said the newspaper of King's first acquaintance with the Chinese opium industry.[55] The day's hearings would see a focus given to Commissioner King's concerns. The *Vancouver Province* of 29 May 1908, reported a perceived need of a better licensing system for Chinese "druggists": "I will look into this drug business," said the commissioner. "It is very important that if Chinese merchants are going to carry on such a business they should do so in a strictly legal way."[56]

At this point, then, King had no intention of making opiate use illegal. On 1 June, the *Province* reported, King received a deputation of local Chinese interested in anti-opium legislation. On 3 June, King made the following statement to the assembled commission: "My own opinion is that it should be made impossible to manufacture this drug in any part of the Dominion. We will get some good out of this riot yet."[57] In the course of three days government policy regarding psychoactive substances was effectively changed.

On 3 July 1908, King presented his "Report on the Need for the Suppression of the Opium Traffic in Canada" to Rodolphe Lemieux, the then Minister of Labour; three weeks later Canada would officially proscribe the importation, sale and manufacturing of opium. The report noted that opium smoking was increasing among young white men and women and that considerable profits were being made by the Chinese merchants.[58] Not surprisingly, the report also noted the support of many Chinese Canadians in efforts to suppress the trade. King led no precise evidence as to the physiological or psychological harm occasioned by opiate use but relied rather upon substantiated claims of "dire influence."[59] The crusade was a moral crusade, to King's way of thinking. King appeared, though, quite unable to unravel the moral logic on which his desire for criminalization was premised.

The literature to date reveals confusion as to how to interpret all of this history — how to interpret the genesis of Canada's first laws prohibiting psychoactive substances. Dolinski has suggested that "it was primarily the necessity to provide an ideological smokescreen to appease the white workers on the west coast that prompted this legislation."[60] Small, Solomon and Madison, and Green have argued rather that not only economic, but also political and cultural conflict gave rise to the 1908 statute: these authors have implicitly rejected a monolithic interpretation of law creation.

Our empirical consideration of the origins of Canadian narcotics legislation appears similarly to reject such a monolithic interpretation. As C. Wright Mills noted in 1959,

> we must always be historically specific and open to complexities. The simple Marxian view makes the big economic man the *real* holder of power; the simple liberal view makes the big political man the chief of the power system; and there are some who would view the warlords as virtual dictators. Each of these is an oversimplified view.[61]

Indeed, it is only when we examine the workings of Canadian industrialists, Canadian politicians and our domestic military — the RCMP[62] — that a clear picture of the genesis and proliferation of "narcotics" legislation begins to emerge.

The owners of west coast industry induced the opium smoking Chinese labourer to come to British Columbia to work for ten times what could be attained for similar kinds of work in China. A particularly rapid climb in Oriental immigration in the summer of 1907 gave rise to an anti-Asiatic riot in Vancouver that fall, a riot initiated by white workers. The Vancouver Trades and Labour Council, perceiving the Orientals as an economic threat, had called for the immediate exclusion of all Asiatics.

When Mackenzie King, then Canada's Deputy Minister of Labour, came to Vancouver to settle Chinese claims arising out of the 1907 riot, he was "startled" by the massive nature of the Chinese opium industry. His initial response was to call for the licensing of these Chinese druggists. King was not about to criminalize the drug intake of a particular race; he had spoken out against unequal treatment of the Chinese. It was only when "the better class of Chinese"[63] requested state intervention that King was moved to legislate. The support of these Chinese then elevated King to the status of "moral entrepreneur"; he moved swiftly and decisively against the use of opium. The clash of white and Chinese workers that was induced and nourished[64] by west coast industrialists had given rise to King's 1908 commission. When affluent and powerful Chinese Canadians spoke out against opiate use, King could see a means of "getting good out of this riot." His demand for the exclusion of opium displayed an unarticulated kind of moral logic.

King could not be seen to be concerned about the mental and physical harm occasioned by opiate use: he had no useful evidence of such harm. Indeed, King's understanding of psychoactive substances was essentially muddled. While travelling to India King wrote approvingly of the practice of eating opium: he was able to distinguish the eating of the drug from the smoking of it. King remarked that "opium was used in India at certain seasons by the natives as a preventative against dysentery. It was taken in the form of pills — one might say for medicinal reasons . . . in much the same manner that spirits would be taken by Englishmen . . . there was little smoking save in these [very northern] parts."[65]

This apparent lack of pharmacological understanding makes clear that Canada's decision to make opiate use illegal was not substantially the product of an ethic of consumer protection. The legislation is better understood as reflecting a fear of socio-economic and socio-cultural assimilation, a fear that was exacerbated by the Chinese who were successfully making their way in the young nation of Canada. These Chinese were already well acculturated to the ideology of upward material mobility; they did not want anti-Chinese sentiments to grow in this plush new land. The practice of opium smoking could serve to differentiate, could provide a focus for a cultural backlash. Mackenzie King, it would seem, could not confront the reality of this paranoia — the reality of his and others' fears of cultural conflict and assimilation.

Dolinksi's claim that the 1908 legislation was "prompted" by the need to appease white workers can now be seen as only partly true: there is a reluctance here to distinguish between intention and effect. While one can assemble evidence to demonstrate that the legislation was, in practice, aimed at the Chinese "coolie" opium smoker,[66] one can find no evidence to suggest that this legislation was *intended* as an appeasement. It *is* fair to say that the legislation was ultimately economic in its origin. Had it not been for the greed of west coast industrialists the Chinese opium smoker would not have come to Canada and competed in a tightening labour market. Had it not been for the lucrative profits to be enjoyed from the trade, the British would never have forced the habit on the Chinese in the mid-nineteenth century.

But it is not historically correct to assert that economic power alone gave rise to this legislation. It is only through regarding the more complex duality of economic and political power that we can understand the 1908 legislation.

It is perhaps then the problematic nature of economic hierarchy, that we need to be sensitive to here. As T.R. Bottomore has remarked,

> This confrontation between the concepts of "ruling class" and "political elite" shows, I think, that, while on one level they may be totally opposed, as elements in wide-ranging theories which interpret political life . . . in very different ways, on another level they may be seen as complementary concepts, which refer to different types of political systems or to different aspects of the same political system.[67]

Our efforts to dissect theoretically are now empirically informed. We are cast back to our original contention. The material life of early twentieth-century Canada produced contradictions that required an ideational resolution. The ideational resolution cannot be divorced from the hierarchy implicit in the materialism[68] of the day and the material conditions cannot be meaningfully detached from an ideational superstructure.

The greed of west coast industrialists inspired the Chinese opium smoker to come to Canada; the "competition" that his cheap labour presented to an established labour movement required political resolution. The government did not choose to regulate the labour-capital relationship but rather compensated the victims of trade unionist anger and quite inadvertently constructed a new criminal law.

In a theoretical context it is a scenario that provides powerful support for a materialist view of history. The scenario virtually confirms a vulgar kind of economic determinism: an economic base dominates and shapes the process of criminalization.

The caveat that can be introduced at this point, though, is one of overwhelming theoretical and empirical significance. There is an important definitional problem inherent in the term "economic." As Heilbroner has noted, "The intermingling of nonmaterial activities with material ones, the suffusion of ideational elements throughout the body of society, the inextricable unity of 'social' and 'economic' life, make it difficult to draw boundaries around the material sphere."[69]

We return to our impasse. The notion of dialectical materialism and the notion of a conflicting plurality of interests are most appropriately viewed as complementary.

The mistake of much sociology of law has been to regard one analysis as *necessarily* a refutation of the other.[70] While the ideological sentiments of these two positions may differ (the optimism of democratic pluralism and the pessimism of materialism) it appears that both are capable of enhancing our understanding of social life and hence of the process of criminalization.

The Social Construction of Criminal Pathology: The Proliferation of Prosecutorial Powers 1908–1929

The year 1908 saw other federal legislation regulating the marketing of psychoactive substances — the deceptively innocuous Proprietary or Patent Medicine Act.[71] This Act required, among other things, that pharmaceutical manufacturers label patent medicines that contained heroin and cannabis. Green has noted of the attached penalty provision here that:

> despite the fact that far more persons were at risk to drug addiction as a result of the indiscriminate marketing of opiate-containing patent medicines than opium smoking — the maximum first and subsequent offence penalties for manufacture, importation or sale of prohibited or unlabelled scheduled drugs were fines of fifty and one hundred dollars, respectively.[72]

The relatively mild nature of the penalties accompanying the improper use of patent medicines has been explained both by the perception of a greater "moral degeneration occasioned by opium smoking, and more simply, by the racial nature of such use."[73] It is perhaps fair to say that the moral degeneration complained of was to be found in the consciousness of the opium-smoking Chinese labourer of early twentieth-century British Columbia.

This individual was not using opium as a means of relieving pain but rather as a pleasurable means of altering consciousness. The opium den functioned in much the same way as did the typically Caucasian saloon. The intake of the drug was perceived by both groups of experientially informed consumers as socially desirable behaviour. Nevertheless, the newly arrived mode of consciousness alteration was never compared with the prevalent use of alcohol — the existent mode of consciousness alteration.[74]

The prohibitive 1908 legislation imposed a heavy burden on smokers of opium. The criminal status of the opium business increased the risk of the enterprise; the increased risk was passed on to the consumer in the form of increased prices. The law had created a false scarcity; the business of smuggling opium was becoming a highly lucrative enterprise.

In 1910, in response to charges that Chinese smugglers were working in collaboration with corrupt customs officials, the federal government established the Royal Commission to Investigate Alleged Chinese Frauds and Opium Smuggling on the Pacific Coast.[75] The commission's conclusion essentially urged draconian measures in an effort to rid Canada of opiate use. The smoking and possession of opium were judged to be in need of prohibition; police powers of search and seizure similarly required expansion.

Without possession being made illegal, then, prosecution of opium use was problematic. The domestic military — the police — required greater powers if they were to be at all successful in their cat-and-mouse harassment of the Chinese opium industry. To the dimensions of economic and political power could now be added the dimension of military power — the power of those whose duty it was to enforce the law.[76] The domestic military would, with the creation of a drug enforcement branch of the RCMP, ultimately exercise a leadership role in the growth of state powers relating to certain forms of drug use.[77]

With the introduction of the Opium and Drug Act of 1911 Canada moved to make criminal the actual use of a psychoactive substance; the state policy of controlling the entrepreneurs of the opium industry had been subverted by customs officials — the state's own agents. Drastic measures were thought necessary. As King noted, in moving second reading of the bill, "The police have found that the present legislation is not drastic enough, or broad enough, to give them the powers of seizure and confiscation which they regard as necessary. One of the objects of the present Bill is to make more drastic the regulations in that regard."[78] The decision to make opiate *use* illegal was not, then, founded on the premise that use leads to crime but rather on the observation that the present methods of control were inadequate. Indeed, section 4(2) of the 1911 Act went so far as to make it illegal to be in a "house, room or place" where opium was smoked.[79]

In explaining the intent of the 1911 legislation to the House of Commons, King read out letters from many prominent Canadians, concerned generally about the non-medical use of psychoactive drugs, and most specifically about the practice of opium smoking. King read letters solicited from the police chiefs of Vancouver and Montreal. The Vancouver chief urged that possession of opium be made illegal, and that there be "close supervision of the waterfront of Vancouver to prevent smuggling";[80] the police chief of Montreal had requested that cocaine be added to the schedule of prohibited substances. The Montreal chief had claimed that "according to the medical men the cocaine produces worse effects than opium."[81] King also read approvingly the following lines from the *Montreal Witness* of November 1910, "Alcoholism and morphine are nothing to cocaine. It is the agent for the seduction of our daughters and the demoralization of our young men."[82]

It was in the context, then, of unknowing paranoia that opium and cocaine use was made illegal. Mackenzie King had become Canada's narcotics "expert"; his presence dominated the House of Commons debate on the appropriateness of the 1911 legislation. Indeed King had rambled on in his introduction to the legislation to such an extent that a member of the opposition was moved to comment, "The minister seems to be giving himself unnecessary trouble in presenting [these] communications to us. I have not heard of anyone opposed to the Bill. The Minister of Labour will soon be as bad as the Minister of Agriculture in taking up the time of the House."[83]

The House of 1911 was not, then, reluctant to endorse the principle of prohibiting cocaine and opium use. What was at issue was the manner in which this goal could be most appropriately effected. King wanted to give the cabinet the power to add substances to the schedule of prohibited drugs: he did not want the subject of adding new drugs to be brought up for discussion in the House of Commons.

The Leader of the Opposition, Robert Borden, argued, "I would like to emphasize the point that the entire pharmacopoeia might be added by order in council to this schedule . . . I think that this is the first time that criminal legislation by order in council has ever been attempted."[84] As a consequence of the urgings of Borden and others, King modified section 14 of the Act. While the section initially allowed the Governor in Council to "add to the schedule to this Act *any substance*, the addition of which is by him deemed necessary in the public interest," King ultimately proposed the more modest "*any alkaloids, derivatives or preparations of the drugs named* in the said schedule."[85]

What the Commons debate here brought to light was the nature of the term "drug." A member of the Opposition had noted, "We might pass this Act just as it is, and the Governor in Council will still be free to add tobacco to that schedule. The Governor in Council are taking a power without any limit."[86] Another member actually invited King to include tobacco in the schedule. King remarked that, "Cigarettes and tobacco have not yet been considered a drug, and it is advantageous to deal with only one class of subjects at this time."[87] He also argued that "in naming the three drugs, cocaine, morphine and opium, parliament makes it plain that it is legislating against what are known as habit forming drugs."[88] The exclusion of tobacco from such a categorization did not represent pharmacological reality, but it nicely represented the socio-political reality of the day. This was, unfortunately, a reality that Parliament was not inclined to explain.[89]

The 1911 statute also did not require the intention of possession to be proven by the Crown: the accused was required to rebut a presumption of guilt if found in physical possession. King justified the shift of onus from the state to the individual with the premise that convictions might be made impossible otherwise. He argued that, "As to the insertion of the word 'knowingly,' I am informed that this is a favourite word with the legal profession, but its insertion here, I fear, would make it practically impossible to secure a conviction, and would have the effect of nullifying the legislation."[90] King's hypothesis here, while in no manner supported by empirical evidence, nevertheless went unchallenged in Parliament: drastic measures were thought necessary to curtail the trade in "drugs." King, too, was highly respected as both a narcotics "expert" and a "moral reformer."[91]

With the initial 1908 legislation, participation in the Shanghai Opium Commission, and presentation of the 1911 statute, Mackenzie King had achieved a position of prominence — he had become, in the words of Small and others,[92] a successful moral entrepreneur. King's commitment to the view of non-medical drug use as morally degenerative is, however, somewhat suspect. There is little doubt the King was a committed entrepreneur: he successfully marketed two statutes that made certain drugs illegal. King's moral vision, however, seems to have sprung more from his instinct of political survival than from strong moral commitment. He wrote of the Indian opium trade while en route to the Shanghai Commission,

> I would learn the part that opium played in the life of the people. Some persons, for example, were of the opinion that opium was used by many of the Sikhs in the same way that he [Lord Morley] was using the cigar which he smoked; that it did not appear to harm them in that climate when used in moderation; that if taken from them it might lead to other drugs being used. . . .[Lord Morley] would give me the names of one or two gentlemen to whom I could speak freely as to conditions in India; they would give me a true statement of conditions, not to be given, for example, to the people in North Waterloo, but which I might impart privately to Sir Wilfrid. I would be informed on the real conditions so that the Government of Canada might be made fully aware of them.[93]

King seemed to recognize that there was more than one side to this story of the morally degenerative effects of opium; the Canadian public could be told one point of view and the Cabinet quite another.

Some twelve years later there would again be a singularity of message delivered to the Canadian people. In the words of Judge Emily Murphy, "every drug-fiend is a liar . . . these ashy-faced, half-witted droolers; these unfortunate cringing creatures."[94] The next decade, however, would see little legislative initiative; it would not be until 1921 that the government would be moved to substantially amend the Opium and Narcotic Drug Act of 1911. Legislative amendments in 1919 and 1920 established more strict controls on the legal trade in opium, but they were not primarily directed towards a more harsh treatment of non-medical use.[95] As Green has said of these amendments, "Parliament . . . seemed concerned to restrict the easy dissemination of opiate-containing nostrums for reasons of public health security, and the major resistance came from those opposed to the 'repressive and restrictive measures' drafted to improve regulation of the medical and pharmaceutical profession."[96] Indeed, the member for Muskoka, a medical doctor, urged that "this Bill is going to work a great hardship to the people . . . the ordinary people still have some rights and . . . these rights ought to be preserved . . . [the Bill] proposes to debar ordinary people from buying, for instance, some tincture of opium to have convenient for medicinal purposes."[97] The member later asked more pointedly, "Has there been any demand from the public for these restrictive measures?"[98] The Minister of Health, the Honourable N.W. Rowell, essentially replied in the negative when he said, "This Bill is rendered necessary only by virtue of the provisions of the International Opium Convention settled at the Hague and brought into force by the ratification of the Treaty of Peace."[99] The 1919 and 1920 amendments, were, then, dictated by international law.

The 1921 and 1922 amendments, and the 1923 consolidation of the Opium and Narcotic Drug Act has been characterized by Green as reflecting a "get tough" approach.[100] The Opium and Narcotic Drug Branch of the Department of Health, and its enforcement arm, the RCMP, had embarked upon anti-"drug" work in 1920.[101] As Solomon and Madison have remarked, "Given their clear mandate, apparent expertise and control over public information, these agencies became the most powerful, well-organized lobby for expansion of the drug laws."[102] During the same period of time anti-Asiatic sentiment in British Columbia continued to swell; the image of the Chinese drug pedlar provoked considerable hostility.[103] With these two forces in action, the proliferation of prosecutorial powers became virtually inevitable.

Prior to the passage of 1921 statute, the Minister of Health had commented in the House, "I think that dealers of these drugs generally have come to recognize the fact that the department means business. The mounted police have been co-operating with the department to the fullest possible extent. . . . Many of the convictions secured during the year have been the result of the operations of the mounted police."[104] The 1921 amendments clearly displayed the fact that the department meant business; the maximum penalty of imprisonment for the importation, manufacture, and sale of narcotics was increased from one year to seven years.[105] An individual simply found occupying the premises in which drugs were found was to be convicted of possession unless there was proof that "the drug was there without his authority, knowledge or consent, or that he was lawfully entitled to the possession thereof".[106] supplying drugs to minors was made exclusively an indictable offence.

In May of 1922, the Minister of Health explained to the House of Commons the need for a substantial increase in budgetary funds allotted to the Opium and Narcotic Drug Act. The Honourable H. S. Beland stated that, "Though the quantity of narcotics entering into Canada through ordinary, permitted channels has immensely decreased during the last three years, I am sorry to convey to the committee the information that the illicit introduction of opium and its derivatives, such as morphine, heroin and cocaine has considerably increased."[107] The Minister's report also noted that 634 of the 853 opium and narcotic convictions in the 1921–22 fiscal year were lodged against "Chinamen."

The 1922 amendments not surprisingly strengthened police powers of search and seizure and took direct aim at the image of the Chinese drug pedlar. Section 7 of the Act now enabled the police officer with "reasonable cause to suspect" to search, without warrant, any premises other than a dwelling house; section 5a(2) of the Act now allowed whipping, at the discretion of the judge; section 10B allowed for the deportation of aliens convicted of drug offences.[108]

The House of Commons, in its discussion of the bill, seemed primarily concerned with the issues of whipping and deportation. The House deferred to the "expertise" of the members from British Columbia in its debate. A member from the city of Vancouver actually introduced the possibility of whipping in the context of the debate. F.L. Ladner, Vancouver South, argued that, "The chief purpose of such an amendment will not be so much in its application as in its deterrent effect upon those men who contemplate engaging in this traffic, for when they know that the law contains a proviso of that kind the dread of being subjected to the lash will effectually deter them from incurring the risk."[109]

There was, of course, no useful empirical evidence led to support this hypothesis of deterrent effect. An Ontario medical doctor who had been unwilling to support the legislative initiative of whipping in 1921 now found himself compelled. He argued, "I believe that the honourable gentlemen who represent British Columbia in this House are more familiar with this question than the rest of us, even those of us who are in the medical profession. . . . While what the Minister says is true, that lashing should be kept for certain crimes of physical violence, I think perhaps moral violence as in this case is a much more serious crime."[110] One member of the House went so far in his support of whipping to assert that, "This crime, in my mind, is even more serious than the crime of robbery with violence. To hold a man up at the point of a gun and take his money away from him is serious of course, but it is not so serious as to give drugs to a minor and take away his future. . . . I would much rather have anyone hold me up, and shoot me for that matter, than sell me drugs and cause me to become a drug addict."[111] This view of the drug as devil revealed that the honourable member had not been checking all his sources: the empirical reality of legalized opium in China of 1906 showed that only 20 million people in a country of 400 million in fact desired to use the substance; of these 20 million users the majority were judged by a British medical doctor to be using in moderation and to have suffered little detriment as a consequence of use.[112]

While this was only the judgement of a single medical doctor, it stood in striking contrast to viewpoints expressed within the House of Commons: the debate of the day was only partially informed. Indeed, we now see that in today's context, Dr. Andrew Weil has remarked that "Dependence on opium if stable can be as consistent with social productivity as dependence on coffee or tobacco."[113]

The amendments passed by the House of 1922 would, however, pay no attention to such information; the minimum penalty for simply being in possession of a prohibited drug was now six months imprisonment and a $200 fine.[114]

The 1922 amendments, as noted before, also catered to the image of the noxious Chinese drug pedlar. H.H. Stevens of Vancouver noted, "I think that the clause the minister is adding providing for the deportation of aliens will very, very materially strengthen the Bill and the arm of the law. I also agree with him in his estimate that a very large proportion of these . . . Chinese would be aliens, and therefore subject to deportation."[115] The concern that some Chinese drug dealers might be naturalized Canadians, and hence not deportable, had been raised in the House; members had been assured that substantial deportation of Chinese could take place as a consequence of the legislation. It was not entirely coincidental, then, that the Chinese Immigration Act of the following year, 1923, constructed for the first time an exclusionary policy with respect to the influx of Chinese into Canada.

The Opium and Narcotic Drug Act, 1923, was both a consolidation and an amendment. Though the Health Minister explained that the bill was "mainly a consolidation of the different acts,"[116] there was in fact one important revision, at least in the contemporary context. Marijuana was added to the list of prohibited substances with the Health Minister's simple assertion, "There is a new drug in the schedule":[117] there was no Commons discussion of the addition here.[118]

Through the early 1920s, then, the social construction of a criminal pathology had flourished. Drug use had been described by members of the House of Commons as "illicit desire . . . unscrupulous, . . . fiendish, . . . low beastly crime . . . and more definitively as a 'living hell.' "[119] The one treatise that documents the ideology of this period of time and no doubt served to shape some of the severity of state response is Emily Murphy's most illuminating *The Black Candle*.[120] Emily Murphy was a police magistrate and judge of the juvenile court in Edmonton; she had been commissioned by *Maclean's* magazine in 1920 to write a series of articles on the problem of drug abuse; the series ultimately formed the basis of *The Black Candle*. As Green has perceptively noted of this effort, "her style tended more to sensationalist rhetoric than impartial reportage, and, from an historical perspective, it is clear that her moral and racial biases compromised her research. . . . The effects of the various drugs were not clearly distinguished, but it hardly mattered as Murphy was convinced that they all produced the same general sequelae: moral degeneration, crime, physical and mental deterioration and disease, intellectual and spiritual wastage, and material loss through drug-induced negligence."[121]

It is instructive to look carefully at the moral logic that Emily Murphy employed. Her very first words in *The Black Candle* nicely set out her argument against drug use. Miss Murphy wrote, "An opium smoker questioned, 'If I should gain heaven for a coin, why should you be envious?' " She responded, "His question is based on two lies. The smoker does not gain heaven, and we are not envious." Murphy was not willing to accord to the drug user the validity of his or her perception. The user, whether imbibing to alleviate the effects of relative poverty, or existential angst, or simply partaking so as to enjoy a pleasurable alteration of consciousness, was in no event to be indulged, let alone tolerated. Murphy asserted that an opium dream ultimately became "a terrible hell, a dwelling deadly cold, full of bloody eagles and pale adders." Murphy was asking the Canadian public to believe that the consumers of smoking opium were in fact masochists — individuals who would repeatedly subject themselves to such torturous visions.

What is most interesting about Murphy's work, however, are the distorted kernels of truth that can be found within it. Murphy argued that "it would be well for the Government to consider whether or not [dealers in drugs] should be given the option of a fine. The profits from the traffic are so high that fines are not in any sense deterrent."[122] Judge Murphy was quite correctly asserting that a fine could be considered by the narcotic entrepreneur as a kind of overhead: while the fine could cut into one's profit margins, it was only an economic cost, to be balanced with the other economic costs of doing business. Murphy seemed unaware, however, of the human consequence of increasing the severity of penalties associated with non-medical drug use. The law would serve to socially construct a criminal pathology. The greater severity of punishment naturally led to increased business risks, risks that were passed on to the consumer in the form of higher prices. The heroin addict became quite literally an individual who had to steal to support a craving. The legal creation of false scarcity was socially responsible for the self-fulfilling assertion — the heroin addict as lowly predator.

Even the use of heroin itself can be seen to have arisen in part as a consequence of the imposition of criminal law. As Solomon and Madison have noted, "Although there was substantial profit to be made in the illicit distribution of smoking opium and morphine, the illicit heroin trade was more lucrative. Since heroin was three times as potent as morphine and more readily capable of being diluted, it provided far greater returns per unit of weight . . . enforcement . . . increased the illicit distributor's costs of avoiding arrest and thus prompted the switch from morphine to heroin."[123] The human cost of the escalation from smoking opium is well described by Dr. Andrew Weil. Weil remarks that,

> Opium forms a relatively harmless habit in that a high percentage of users can smoke it for years without developing troublesome problems with

tolerance. Dependence on opium, if stable, can be as consistent with social productivity as dependence on coffee or tobacco. But when morphine, the active principle of opium is isolated and made available, problems do appear. In particular a significant percentage of users (though possibly still a minority) finds it impossible to achieve equilibrium with habitual use of morphine or with the still more potent derivative, heroin.[124]

The proliferation of heroin use in the United States and Canada can, then, profitably be seen as the result of a conscious decision made by the distributors of the drug industry — a decision necessitated by the risks of increasingly severe sanctions. Emily Murphy's anti-drug ideology had failed to comprehend these unintentional consequences of repressive legislation — the complex relations between the intentions and effects of law.

In her discussion of the different drugs in vogue, Murphy is again revealed as being unable to look at a piece of information through more than a single lens. Murphy wrote of "Marahuana — A New Menace: It appears that in using this poison, the time-sense becomes impaired in such a way that time appears to pass slowly."[125] While Murphy accurately cites a reported phar-macological effect of time distortion in the instance of cannabis use, she un-necessarily ascribes a negative value to this "altered" state of consciousness. As Andrew Weil has noted,

> the phrase disturbance of immediate memory bristles with negativity. Is it
> a negative description of a condition that might just as well be looked at
> positively? . . . the ability to live entirely in the present, without paying
> attention to the immediate past or future, is precisely the goal of
> meditation and the exact aim of many religious disciplines. The rationale
> behind living in the present is stated in ancient Hindu writings and forms a
> prominent theme of Buddhist and Christian philosophy as well: to the
> extent that consciousness is diverted into the past and future — both of
> which are unreal   to that extent is it unavailable for use in the real here
> and now.[126]

Emily Murphy's deprecation of drug induced present-centered awareness can also be seen as extending beyond the boundaries of drug use itself. The culture itself was necessarily linear in its mode of thought; there was a socio-economic and socio-cultural abhorrence of present-centred awareness. There was the delay of gratification that was implicit in the Protestant work ethic, the need for self-control and restraint in the building of the young state of Canada.

The judiciary of this young state were inclined to go along with the visions of non-medical drug use preferred by Emily Murphy, the Department of Health, and the RCMP. While very little case law is available for the period 1908 to 1929, what analysis there is tends to suggest that the judiciary strongly supported the use of repressive measures against the drug use. In *R. v. Vene-gratsky*,[127] a Crown appeal from a six-month term of imprisonment for traf-ficking, the Manitoba Court of Appeal increased the sentence length to three years with the advice that, "The narcotic problem in Canada is a very acute one. . . . The Government is evidently alarmed at the existing conditions and determined, if possible, to stamp out this illegal traffic. In an effort to effect such a laudable object it is entitled to every assistance the Court can legitimately give it."[128]

A Quebec court in a case of possession of opium noted of the Opium and Narcotic Drug Act, "there is no necessity of mens rea, as there is under the Criminal Code. . . ."[129] The court justified the exclusion of mens rea with the statement that, "If such a defence could be admitted, it would be very easy to evade the law and as this law must be, in the public welfare and interest, strictly interpreted, I find the defendant guilty."[130]

In *R. v. Gordon*[131] a medical doctor who gave morphine tablets to a patient for long term self-administration was successfully prosecuted. The decision helped to transform the conception of drug use from a problem for medical pedagogy to an important police priority.

In *Ex parte Wakabayashi*,[132] a fundamental challenge to the constitutionality of the Opium and Narcotic Drug Act was rejected: the court would not accept the notion that the Act merely licensed the running of a particular business. Justice MacDonald of the B.C. Supreme Court argued that, "I have no hesitation in holding that the Act in question is criminal and not licensing legislation. . . . While such legislation constituted a new crime, it was remedial, in order, if possible, to destroy an existing evil. It was for the promotion of public order, safety and morals."[133] These decisions, then, aptly represented judicial sentiments: [134] as was the case with Mackenzie King and Emily Murphy, the judiciary appeared unable to articulate the moral logic on which the repression of "drugs" was based.

The 1920s saw only two other amendments, the first most importantly directed at tightening state control over the medical profession's distribution of drugs. The 1925 amendment allowed the state to prosecute by indictment the medical profession's unlawful prescription:[135] the convicted physician, veterinary surgeon, or dentist would be subject to a mandatory three-month term of imprisonment in such event. The doctor who believed in listening to his patient's expressed interests could lose his liberty for this act of heresy: the state was dictating a mode of "treatment" to its doctors.

The 1929 revision of the Act was essentially a technical revision, dominated by the need to tighten loopholes present in the 1923 Act. Definitional and procedural changes, and a greater control of the postal service, served to accomplish this loophole tightening;[136] the anti-drug philosophy remained unchanged. The 1929 Act did, however, contain the introduction of one rather remarkable prosecutorial weapon: section 22 required a superior court judge to grant an exclusive writ of assistance when requested. The writ of assistance, aptly described as "a blanket warrant authorizing the holder to search for controlled drugs anywhere and at any time," was established in the Opium and Narcotic Drug Act: a substantial and not demonstrably necessary invasion of civil liberty was effected here. The Health Minister, in introducing the bill, had only mentioned in passing, "provision is being made for the issuing of writs of assistance to certain officers engaged in narcotic drug work, as is done under the customs act":[137] there was no debate of this issue in the House.

Conclusion

The past twenty years have seen a refocusing of the academic lens with respect to the subject of criminality. As John Hagan has noted,[138] the 1960s saw a shift in our paradigm of inquiry. Questions about the origins and psychological correlates of deviance were displaced by questions about the origins and development of the process of labeling deviance. The process of "criminalization"[139] became a focus for intensive empirical and theoretical research.

Much of the work of this decade was impressive in its scope. Kai Erikson's study of the construction of deviance in the midst of seventeenth-century New England Puritanism,[140] Joseph Gusfield's thoughtful analysis of the American Temperance movement,[141] and Howard Becker's insightful construction of marijuana use[142] are perhaps the richest examples of this tradition.

In the 1970s the inquiry became more monolithic in its focus. The process of criminalization was often explained by the contradictions created from the labour-capital relationship. From Britain came *The New Criminology*[143] and a host of sophisticated critical analyses of the process of criminal law. In the United States William Chambliss,[144] Richard Quinney,[145] and others broke with pluralist conflict explanations of crime and began to discover the insights of dialectical materialism.

This paper has attempted to demonstrate that the two forms of inquiry represented by these two decades can be viewed as complementary. In the context of the origins of Canadian narcotics legislation, it is suggested that a change in the labour-capital relationship in early twentieth-century British Columbia required a political resolution. The opium-smoking Chinese labourer had been induced to come to Canada by west coast industrialists; his cheap labour was both resented and feared by established trade unionists.

The tendency of west coast capital towards expansion through the medium of cheap labour had perhaps unforeseen consequences. Trade unionists developed anti-Asiatic sentiment to the point of physical violence and property destruction. Such oppressive behaviour required government intervention and hence political resolution.

The interchange of ideas that constructed Canadian narcotics legislation was not a happy reminder of an informed egalitarian expression of shared values. The interaction of powerful Chinese Canadians and the Canadian government forged this political resolution: the criminalization of opium was ultimately urged by both groups as a means of "getting good" out of anti-Asiatic sentiment. With introduction into proscriptive law, certain forms of drug use quickly became intolerable to those whose duty it was to enforce such proscription. The police — the domestic military — urged control-oriented "reforms" in their cat-and-mouse manoeuvring with the drug industry.

It is a scenario that vividly asserts the validity of materialism as a world view. But it is also a scenario that confirms political life as the interchange of ideas. The contradictions of hierarchical relationships require political resolution. And political resolution seeks to reshape or to stabilize the nature of specific power-based relationships.

The emergence of Canadian narcotics legislation reveals a portrait of a reflexive process in historical context. As Berger and Luckmann have said, "such intrinsically biological functions as orgasm and digestion [and drug use][146] are socially structured. Society also determines the manner in which the organism is used in activity; expressivity, gait and gesture are socially structured . . . society sets limits to the organism as the organism sets limits to society." In the context of Canada's prohibition of "narcotics," state control has had the effect of inhibiting awareness of the pharmacological reality of psychoactive drug use: the Canadian citizenry has, however, not been entirely acquiescent; the reflexive relationship of the controllers and the controlled continues into 1983.

Those of us who seek the democratic spirit of egalitarianism cannot take cheer in the origins of Canadian narcotics legislation. The moral logic on which certain psychoactive substances were made illegal is never articulated: empirical study presents a picture of a problem created by economic greed, resolved by the holders of political power, and exacerbated by the perceived need to increasingly repress.

Though the portrait is one that lends strong support to a materialist view of criminalization, there is no power to predict the future; it is the necessary product of a socially and hence ideationally constructed reality. We are catapulted into the present, materially[147] and ideationally, and hence come full circle.

Notes

1. Canada, *Cannabis: A Report of the Commission of Inquiry Into the Non-Medical Use of Drugs* (Ottawa: Information Canada, 1972).

2. These are descriptions culled from the work of M. Green, "A History of Canadian Narcotics Control: The Formative Years," *University of Toronto Faculty of Law Review* (1979): 42-79; Solomon and Madison, "The Evolution of Non-Medical Opiate Use in Canada — Part 1: 1870-1929," *Drug Forum* 5 (1976-77): 237; and S. Small, "Canadian Narcotics Legislation, 1908-1923: A Conflict Model Interpretation" in *Law and Social Control in Canada*, edited by Greenaway and Brickey (Scarborough: Prentice Hall, 1978), 28-42. Those interested in the empirical origins of Canadian narcotics legislation might also want to see C.E. Trasov, "History of the Opium and Narcotic Drug Legislation in Canada," *Criminal Law Quarterly* 4 (1962): 274; S. Cook, "Ideology and Canadian Narcotics Legislation, 1908-1923" (M.A. thesis, University of Toronto, 1964); B. McKeown, "The Development of Canadian Narcotics Legislation, 1907-1950: A Study of Interest Groups and Power Relationships" (M.A. thesis, University of Toronto, 1966); B. MacFarlane, *Drug Offences in Canada* (Toronto: Canada Law Book, 1979); G. Dolinski, "The Development of North American Drug Laws from a Marxist Perspective" (unpublished ms , Osgoode Hall Law School, Toronto, 1979).

3. All of the academic literature to date on the subject of Canadian narcotics legislation supports the conflict model of law creation. One might fairly say that the empirical evidence simply precludes any notion of the legislative emergence of an informed consensus of opinion.

4. W. Chambliss, "The Political Economy of Smack: Opiates, Capitalism and Law," *Research in Law and Sociology* 1 (1975): 115-41, and see Dolinski, "The Development of North American Drug Laws from a Marxist Perspective."

5. The use of the term "Marxist" is problematic. Dialectical materialism, economic determinism, and state communism have all been graced with the label of Marxism, despite their significant theoretical differences. It may be that the term Marxist is simply too nebulous to be of explanatory utility.

6. See P.L. Berger and T. Luckmann, *The Social Construction of Reality* (Baltimore: Penguin Books, 1966).

7. R. Heilbroner, *Marxism For and Against* (New York: Norton Press, 1980), 33–37.

8. 7 & 8 Edward VII, *Statutes of Canada* (hereafter S.C.) 1908, c. 50, s. 1.

9. Green argues that the work of the Senate prompted this concession, a concern for the "legitimate investments of opium manufacturers" (M. Green "A History of Canadian Narcotics Control," 47).

10. See note 2. See more especially M. Green and Solomon and Madison, for amplifications of the exploratory work begun by Shirley Small.

11. M. Green "A History of Canadian Narcotics Control," 43.

12. W. Chambliss, "The Political Economy of Smack," 115.

13. This is a point that is made throughout Berger and Luckmann, *The Social Construction of Reality*. See especially 207–11.

14. See Trasov, "History of the Opium and Narcotic Drug Legislation in Canada"; Green, "A History of Canadian Narcotics Control."

15. Statement Showing the Quantity and Value of Opium Imported into Canada During the Fiscal Years 1867 to 1908 Inclusive, Public Archives of Canada (hereafter PAC), Department of Customs, C.M.G. 26, J–4, vol. 30, Ottawa, 1908.

16. See Solomon and Madison, "The Evolution of Non-Medical Opiate Use in Canada — Part 1," 238. See also the *Vancouver Province*, selected advertisements, 1900–1907, for primary source data.

17. See the City of Vancouver by-laws, consolidated 1879.

18. For a good discussion of China's development in the late nineteenth century, see Jean Chesneaux et al., *China From the Opium Wars to the 1911 Revolution* (New York: Pantheon Books, 1976).

19. See A.W. McCoy et al., *The Politics of Heroin in Southeast Asia* (New York: Harper Row, 1972), 63.

20. Chambliss, "The Political Economy of Smack," 120.

21. McCoy et al., *The Politics of Heroin in Southeast Asia*, 64.

22. The Chinese made a good deal less than the whites in Canada but still some ten times what they could be making, had they remained in China. This differential is documented by the *Report of the Royal Commission Appointed to Inquire Into the Methods By Which Oriental Labourers Have Been Induced to Come to Canada* (Ottawa: Government Printing Bureau, 1908), 70.

23. Solomon and Madison, "The Evolution of Non-Medical Opiate Use in Canada," 70.

24. Chambliss, "The Political Economy of Smack," 192.

25. For a good description of the importance of the federal Commission see Green, "A History of Canadian Narcotics Control"; Solomon and Madison, "The Evolution of Non-Medical Opiate Use in Canada - Part 1"; Cook, "Ideology and Canadian Narcotics Legislation, 1908–1923"; and Trasov, "History of the Opium and Narcotic Legislation in Canada."

26. Chinese merchants, Chinese men of science, and Chinese students would not be required to make such a payment for admission.

27. Chinese Immigration Act, 1885, S.C. 1885, c. 71, s. 4.

28. Chinese Immigration Act, S.C. 1904.

29. Section 6(a), (b), and (c) of the 1900 Act set out the exemptions from entry tax in the case of Chinese immigrants.

30. Chinese immigration decreased from over 5000 in 1903 and over 4000 in 1904 to under 100 in 1905. Canada, *The Canada Year Book, 1932* (Ottawa, 1932).

31. Ibid.

32. While King most often blurred the distinction between "moral" tones and physiological effects in consideration of various drugs, he is often revealed here as an astute practitioner of political economy.

33. See note 30.

34. *Report of the Royal Commission into Chinese Labourers*, 68-73.

35. Chinese Immigration Act, S.C. 1923, c. 38.

36. British Documents to the Shanghai Commission, Mackenzie King Papers, PAC, 1909, c. 136–39.

37. Chesneaux et al., *China from the Opium Wars to the 1911 Revolution*, 345.

38. Ibid., 380.

39. Arnold Taylor, *American Diplomacy and the Narcotics Traffic 1900–1939* (Durham, N.C.: Duke University Press, 1969), 6.

40. Those who are interested in attainment of power must not weaken such resolve. In addition they must shun the possibility of the psychological ambivalence necessarily induced by a non-ordinary consciousness. As Harvard-trained physician Andrew Weil has noted, "when we enter nonordinary reality, our relationship to the pairs of opposites changes. Instead of trying to hold one and shun the other, we are able to transcend both, to experience them as two phases of manifestation of a single reality. . . ." Weil, interestingly enough, argues against drug use, viewing it as premised upon the erroneous belief that there need be a chemical ingestion for mental and emotional highs. Weil argues compellingly that a more humanly ambitious society might try to find its own highs, independent of chemical stimulation. There is a need to realize the possibility of a mental basis for chemical events. Andrew Weil, *The Natural Mind* (Boston: Houghton Mifflin, 1972).

41. The 10 percent solution was, of course, anything but a solution. It merely documented the existence of a tension between the owners of the industry and the Chinese government — a tension that is still being played out today in somewhat altered form (different state, different sets of consumers).

42. Letter to Mrs. W. Cummings, 31 Dec. 1909, Mackenzie King Personal Correspondence, 1909, PAC, 10243–45.

43. Mission to the Orient, 1907–1909, King Diaries, Mackenzie King Papers, PAC, 202–3.

44. Letter from Peking, June 1908, British Documents to the Shanghai Commission, Mackenzie King Papers, PAC.

45. Melvyn Green uses the term "formative years" to apply to the period 1870–1929. It is within this period that we see the ideology of criminalization of "drug" use. See Green, "A History of Canadian Narcotics Control."

46. *Report of the Royal Commission into Chinese Labourers.*

47. Ibid.

48. The history of the 1907 anti-Asiatic riot is especially well documented in W.P. Ward, "White Canada Forever: British Columbia's Response to Orientals 1858–1914" (Ph.D. dissertation, Queen's University, 1973), 194–217.

49. Letter to Laurier, quoted from Laurier papers in "White Canada Forever," 196.

50. Ward, "White Canada Forever," 202.

51. Ward has argued that "While Laurier felt compelled to reimburse the Japanese for their losses, he felt no similar need to meet Chinese claims. Evidently China's lack of international prestige, her less aggressive efforts to protect the welfare of her citizens overseas, and her more distant relations with Canada and the Empire led him to conclude that they could be treated with less respect and charity" ("White Canada Forever," 211).

52. Letter to Laurier, 9 Nov. 1907, Laurier Papers, PAC, 131662–64.

53. 12 Oct. 1907, King Diaries, Mackenzie King Papers, PAC, C2108.

54. Minutes of the Settlement of Chinese Claims, Mackenzie King Papers, PAC, c. 31592–98.

55. *Vancouver Province,* 28 May 1908, 1.

56. Ibid., 29 May 1908.

57. Ibid., 3 June 1908.

58. W.L.M. King, "The Need for the Suppression of the Opium Traffic in Canada," *Sessional Papers,* 1908, no. 36b.

59. King spoke of "ugly and horrible *evidence*" of dire influence — a "pretty and young" woman found in an opium den.

60. Dolinski, "The Development of North American Drug Laws from a Marxist Perspective," 41.

61. C. Wright Mills, *The Power Elite* (New York: Oxford University Press, 1959), 277.

62. It might be argued that the RCMP is simply an arm of the political power of the state. While this can be seen to be in large measure true, it can also be seen that the RCMP may have disagreements with Parliament that tend to reveal the force's own unique perspective. Consider, for example, the interaction of the RCMP and the Liberal government [under Trudeau].

More importantly, by viewing the RCMP as the "domestic military" here, we can see the particular interests of those who are actually charged with the duty of enforcing law. Narcotics legislation requires anticipatory policing; the strategy of control, as we shall see, is largely determined by the outcomes of such cat-and-mouse manoeuvring. A failed attempt at control brings a demand for greater severity of punishment and increased certainty of apprehension.

63. In a letter to Prime Minister Laurier, Chinese clergyman S.D. Chown responded to a request for information on the opium trade in B.C. Chown argued that "the better class of Chinese in Canada are strongly in favour of putting an end to it" (Personal Correspondence, Mackenzie King Papers, PAC, 7294–97). [Editor's note: S.D. Chown is incorrectly identified here as a Chinese clergyman. Samuel Dwight Chown was a Methodist clergyman from Ontario. He was secretary of the Department of Moral and Social Reform of the church and later its General Superintendent. - R.C.M.]

64. We must remember that, with the imposition of the $500 head tax, Chinese immigration dramatically declined. The industrialists' replacement of cheap Chinese labour with cheap Japanese labour tended only to nourish anti-Asiatic sentiment. It was perhaps ironic that the frustrations of the white workers were directed at their lesser paid brethren, the Asiatic workers.

65. Mission to the Orient, 1907–1909, King Diaries, Mackenzie King Papers, PAC, 203.

66. In the *Vancouver Province* of 1907 and 1908 one finds much talk of the Chinese "coolie" labourer. Virtually every issue of the paper in this period contains an article with expressions of anti-Asiatic sentiment. Most of this hostility is directed against the "Chinese coolie" labourer.

67. T.B. Bottomore, *Elites in Society* (Middlesex, England: Penguin Books, 1964), 44.

68. See Heilbroner, *Marxism For and Against*, 82.

69. Ibid., 84.

70. This is a pitfall encountered by both pluralists and materialists. See R. Quinney's *Class, State and Crime* (New York: David McKay, 1977); and Hagan and Leon, "Rediscovering Delinquency. . . ," *American Sociological Review* 42 (1977): 587.

71. Proprietary or Patent Medicine Act, S.C. 1907–08, c. 56.

72. Green, "A History of Canadian Narcotics Control," 48.

73. Ibid. Green has suggested that these two explanations of statutory distinction are "alternative" explanations. In fact it may be more appropriate to view the explanations as complementary.

74. This is perhaps ironic, in light of the fact that most dismissals from the Vancouver police force came as a consequence of being drunk on duty (there were no indications of dismissal for opium use; there was no indication of police opium use). Board of Police Commissioners 1905–1911, Vancouver City Police, Vancouver City Archives.

75. "Proceedings of the Royal Commission to Investigate Alleged Chinese Frauds and Opium Smoking on the Pacific Coast," *Sessional Papers*, 1910–11.

76. This analysis would tend to be consistent, then, with that of C. Wright Mills in *The Power Elite*, though a word of caution from Bottomore seems appropriate here. Bottomore argues that the concept of pluralistic elites, in eliminating the idea of a ruling class, "also excludes that of classes in opposition and so . . . arrives at an extremely pessimistic account of [North] American society."

77. In 1920 the federal Department of Health was given the responsibility of supervising the enforcement of the Opium and Narcotic Drug Act. Later in that year the drug enforcement branch of the RCMP was created.

78. Canada, House of Commons, *Debates*, 1910–11, 2519.

79. An Act to prohibit the improper use of Opium and other Drugs, 1 & 2 George 5, c. 17, s. 4(2).

80. House of Commons, *Debates*, 1910–1911, 2523.

81. Ibid., 2524.

82. Ibid., 2525.

83. Ibid., 2527.

84. Ibid., 2534.

85. Ibid., 2532, and see the Opium and Drug Act, 1 & 2 George 5, c. 17.

86. House of Commons, *Debates*, 1910–11, 2540.

87. Ibid.

88. Ibid., 2549.

89. King's exclusion of tobacco from the category of drug begs pharmacological and political explanation; the House's lack of political pharmacological sophistication would seem to have precluded the necessity for such.

90. House of Commons, *Debates*, 1910–11, 2537.

91. Ibid., 2539-40. (Note the lengthy tribute to King's role as "moral reformer.")

92. The term "moral entrepreneur" was first envisioned by Howard Becker in his well-known sociological treatise, *Outsiders* (New York: The Free Press, 1963). The moral entrepreneur can be described as an individual whose commitment to a "correct" mode of social behaviour is highly intense. This commitment is successfully marketed when "communicated" to the people through the medium of law.

93. Mission to the Orient, 1907–09, King Diaries, Mackenzie King Papers, PAC, 85–86.

94. Emily Murphy, *The Black Candle* (Toronto: Thomas Allen, 1922), 16.

95. An Act to amend the Opium and Drug Act, S.C. 1919, c. 25; An Act to Amend the Opium and Narcotic Drug Act, S.C. 1920, c. 31.

96. Green, "A History of Canadian Narcotics Control," 52.

97. House of Commons, *Debates*, 1920, 1746.

98. Ibid., 1748.

99. Ibid., 1749.

100. Green, "A History of Canadian Narcotics of Control," 56. Green describes only the 1921 amendments in this light. It might be more appropriate to view all legislative changes between 1921 and 1923 as reflecting a "get tough" approach; the following text attempts to support this contention.

101. The word "drug" ought to be placed in quotations when used in the context of substance criminalization. To do otherwise is to leave the reader with the impression that nicotine, caffeine, and alcohol are not properly conceived of as drugs.

102. Solomon and Madison, "The Evolution of Non-Medical Opiate Use in Canada — Part 1," 258.

103. See most especially House of Commons, *Debates*, 1922, 3013–19.

104. Ibid., 1921, 3131.

105. An Act to amend the Opium and Narcotic Drug Act, S.C. 1921, c. 42, s. 1(e).

106. Ibid., s. 1(d).

107. House of Commons, *Debates*, 1922, 2017.

108. An Act to amend the Opium and Narcotic Drug Act, S.C. 1922, c. 36.

109. House of Commons, *Debates*, 1922, 3015.

110. Ibid., 3016.

111. Ibid., 3018.

112. Letter from Dr. W. Gray, Peking, 1906, British Documents to the Shanghai Commission, Mackenzie King Papers, PAC.

113. Weil, *The Natural Mind*, 91.

114. Opium and Narcotic Drug Act, S.C. 1922, c. 36, s. 2(2).

115. House of Commons, *Debates*, 1922, 3017.

116. Ibid., 1923, 2114.

117. Ibid., 2124.

118. The specific reason for the inclusion of marijuana is not clearly discernible. The LeDain Commission has commented that "a decision was made in 1923, without any apparent scientific basis nor even any real sense of social urgency." See *Cannabis: A Report of the Commission of Inquiry into the Non-Medical Use of Drugs*, 230.

119. See House of Commons, *Debates*, 1921, 3130; *Debates*, 1922, 3013–19; *Debates*, 1923, 2114–24.

120. See note 94.

121. Green, "A History of Canadian Narcotics Control," 53.

122. Murphy, *The Black Candle*. For a good indication of the severity of Murphy's response, see 190–99.

123. Solomon and Madison, "The Evolution of Non-Medical Opiate Use in Canada — Part 1," 254.

124. Weil, *The Natural Mind*, 102.

125. Murphy, *The Black Candle*, 334.

126. Weil, *The Natural Mind*, 91.

127. *R. v. Venegratsky* (1928), 49 C.C.C. 298 (Man. C.A.).

128. Ibid., at 300.

129. *R. v. Sung Lung* (1923), 39 C.C.C. 187 (Q. Dist. C.).

130. Ibid., 189.

131. *R. v. Gordon* (1928), 48 C.C.C. 272.

132. *Ex parte Wakabayashi, Ex parte Lore Yip* (1928), 49 C.C.C. 392 (B.C.S.C.).

133. Ibid., 400–1.

134. For a good discussion of the technical changes imposed by case law from 1908 to 1929, see Green, "A History of Canadian Narcotics Control."

135. An Act to amend the Opium and Narcotic Drug Act, S.C. 1923, c. 20, s. 5.

136. To see this point most clearly compare the Opium and Narcotic Drug Act, R.S.C. 1927, c. 144, with An Act to amend and consolidate the Opium and Narcotic Drug Act, S.C. 1929, c. 49.

137. House of Commons, *Debates*, 1929, 61.

138. J. Hagan, "Rediscovering Deliquency," 587.

139. "Criminalization" here is used in a context that includes both pre-state designations of deviance and state labels of criminality.

140. K.T. Erikson, *Wayward Puritans* (New York: John Wiley and Sons, 1966).

141. J.R. Gusfield, *Symbolic Crusade: Status Politics and the American Movement* (Urbana: University of Illinois Press, 1963).

142. H.S. Becker, *Outsiders*.

143. I. Taylor, P. Walton, and J. Young, *The New Criminology* (London: Routledge and Kegan Paul, 1973).

144. See, for example, W. Chambliss, *On The Take: From Petty Crooks to Presidents* (Bloomington: Indiana University Press, 1978).

145. R. Quinney, *Class, State and Crime*.

146. Berger and Luckmann, *The Social Construction of Reality*, 203; "[and drug use]" my own addition.

147. Andrew Weil has ironically argued that "drugs are merely means to achieve states of nonordinary awareness and must not be confused with the experiences themselves. They have the capacity to trigger highs; they do not contain highs. Moreover, the experiences they trigger are essentially no different from experiences triggered by more natural means . . . the real risk of using drugs as the primary method of altering consciousness is in their tendency to reinforce an illusory view of cause and effect that makes it ultimately harder to learn how to maintain highs without dependence on the *material* world" (Weil, *The Natural Mind*).

SECTION 4

PRISONS, PUNISHMENT, AND REHABILITATION

Those who are unfamiliar with the history of criminal justice are usually astonished to find that in Canada, as in most western countries, rehabilitation has been the dominant philosophy in the prison system since the early nineteenth century. There is a persistent tendency among those who write about corrections to make past efforts seem cruder and less humane in intent than was actually the case, perhaps because this perspective helps make current problems seem more tractable. The gloomy fact is, however, that every major approach to the rehabilitation of criminals has been tried at least once in the past. The more obvious ones have been tried numerous times. None have worked. Some writers will admit individual failures but find the reasons for those failures in faulty planning and execution or lack of funds. The overall pattern is so consistent, however, that these explanations lack conviction.

The persistence of efforts to reform criminals in the face of repeated failures over a century and a half is dramatic illustration of the power of ideas. The idea in question, that behaviour can be altered by a relatively simple manipulation of the environment, derived its potency from its origins in two of the most powerful forces of the nineteenth century, industrialization and evangelical Christianity. From the latter came the notion of a sudden, dramatic change in behaviour through penitence and recognition of sin. From the former came a faith in the efficacy of standardization and repetition. John Howard, Jeremy Bentham, and the other theorists of the penitentiary in the late eighteenth century sought to create institutions which would reproduce on a massive scale the external conditions associated with Christian conversion. Each convict would live an austere existence, denied access to liquor and to the company of the evil companions, forced to spend his time at hard labour or silent contemplation.

The imposition of these conditions would, it was assumed, draw the criminal inevitably to the right path. When the idea was put into practice and found not to work, all sorts of excuses were found, mostly on the theme that the conditions were not being imposed with sufficient rigor. In some places discipline was tightened to the point that many prisoners were driven to insanity, but there was no noticeable improvement in the number of convicts reformed. Governments spared no expense to achieve such a highly desirable goal and Canada was no exception. The Kingston Penitentiary was designed with elaborate care that each room, almost each block of stone, should contribute to the rehabilitation of the prisoners. No other public building in nineteenth-century Canada was as specialized or as expensive. C.J. Taylor is quite correct in labelling it "moral architecture."

What went on inside the prisons was at least as important as their architecture. In the early nineteenth century the programs for convicts consisted of isolation, silence, hard labour, and religion. The first three elements remained fairly constant well into the twentieth century but religion declined in relative importance largely through the addition of secular programs designed to supplement the reforming influence. Much effort and ingenuity was devoted to developing schemes for classifying prisoners. If the environment was crucial to changing the criminal, it followed that a newcomer to the life of crime should be easier to change than an older and more hardened criminal. Penitentiary authorities therefore attempted, as a minimum, to segregate first offenders from repeaters. Often more elaborate plans with several categories emerged. Whether or not classification had any effect on rehabilitation is impossible to prove.

Proponents of classification never attempted to provide proof; for them the importance of segregating different types of prisoner was self-evident. In retrospect doubts must be permitted to creep in. The assumption that moral contagion was a leading cause of crime seems dubious at best. Even if it was valid, classification on the basis of offences known to authorities was quite artificial. Contemporary students of criminal careers point out that many offences are typically committed for every one punished by imprisonment. There is no reason to believe that nineteenth-century criminals differed in this respect. The enthusiasm for classification was not confined to the federal penitentiary system, which after 1867 looked after all prisoners serving sentences of two years or more. Donald G. Wetherell's article shows that the Ontario prison system was just as committed to classification of short-term prisoners.

In the late nineteenth century the nature of work in prisons and penitentiaries began to change. Instead of repetitive, economically meaningless tasks like breaking stone, valued only for their supposed contribution to teaching discipline, the ideal became work that taught the convict usable skills. Although the rhetoric of advocates of this new kind of work did not differ greatly from that of their predecessors, the change marked an important alteration in the concept of the criminal. He or she was no longer simply a person who through ignorance or perversity had made wrong moral choices. The decision to teach skills that would help the convict to retain an honest job on the outside implied that criminality was at least in part the result of economic necessity. Society had failed the individual and must now make up for it. The same set of assumptions underlay the programs of secular education designed to reduce illiteracy and give the inmate a grasp of basic arithmetic. As Wetherell points out, these programs in practice were almost always underfunded and understaffed, but there is no evidence that they would have had any greater effect with unlimited resources.

As soon as religion ceased to be the primary means of rehabilitating the criminal, incarceration lost much of its logic. The search for secular cures for criminality led directly away from the prison in all its forms. The goal, after all, was to produce individuals who could function in society normally. How could they be taught to do so in a highly artificial environment like the penitentiary? In the late nineteenth century attention began to turn to a variety of alternatives to imprisonment. Most of these involved some form of release under supervision. Parole was the earliest of these, and dates from the passage of the Ticket of Leave Act in 1899. Early release from prison for good behaviour was a useful disciplinary tool for wardens but it did not go far to resolving the contradiction that was increasingly apparent between the goals of punishment and rehabilitation.

Probation, in which supervised release in the community was substituted for incarceration, took the process a step further. In Canada, probation originates with the Juvenile Delinquents Act of 1908. Young persons were presumed to be uniquely vulnerable to external influences. The law therefore made provision for keeping them out of institutions if possible. Later the same provisions were extended to adult offenders. The article on probation by D.W. Coughlan is interesting because it was written by an active participant in the system. It was also written at a time (1963) when faith in the power of social agencies to rehabilitate criminals was at its height.

The ultimate logic of rehabilitation in its secular phase is to do away with imprisonment altogether. Deinstitutionalization is currently popular and is promoted as a new approach but its roots are much older. In Canada, as Andrew Jones shows, the first attempt in this direction took place shortly after the beginning of the twentieth century. A movement led by J.J. Kelso, the Ontario Superintendent of Neglected and Dependent Children, resulted in the closure of Penetanguishene Reformatory in 1904. Kelso sought to place the juvenile offenders who would have been incarcerated, in foster homes instead. He also confidently predicted that this was just the beginning of a movement that would see the closure of all juvenile institutions. At first it appeared that the deinstitutionalization was working as its proponents had said it would, but after several years it became apparent that the bulk of juvenile offenders were ending up in the industrial schools instead.

The history of attempts to rehabilitate criminals both within and outside institutions is so consistently dismal that one can only marvel at the persistence of its advocates through the years. The process is strongly reminiscent of the cargo cults that appeared in the South Pacific at the end of the Second World War. The war had brought military bases and airstrips to many remote island communities. When the soldiers departed the supply of modern goods naturally dried up. The islanders reacted by constructing shrines whose central features were large reproductions of the airplanes that had brought the soldiers. They were attempting to influence their environment by creating the externals of the situation that had existed during the war years. In a somewhat more sophisticated manner, this is what the advocates of rehabilitation have been doing. Without understanding the underlying process involved, they have attempted to change people in fundamental ways by manipulating the externals of their environment.

THE KINGSTON, ONTARIO PENITENTIARY AND MORAL ARCHITECTURE†

C.J. TAYLOR

> The expression of the purpose, for which every building is erected, is the first and most essential beauty; and should be obvious from its architecture, altogether independently of any particular style; in the same manner as the reasons for things, are altogether independent of the language in which they are conveyed. As in literary compositions, no beauty of language can ever compensate for poverty of sense; so, in architectural composition, no beauty of style can ever compensate for the want of purpose. Every reasonable mind must feel this; for, as we have said before, the foundation of all true and permanent beauty is utility.
>
> — J.C. Loudon (1833)

The grey stone walls of the Kingston Penitentiary enclose about nine acres of a point of land jutting into Hatters Bay in the old village of Portsmouth. Today, "the big house" serves as a receiving centre for prisoners entering the federal penitentiary system; many of its buildings stand vacant, scarred by prisoner disturbances over the last quarter-century. Its architecture, hidden from public view by the high walls and mystery of a penal institution, has not attracted much study, yet here lies the key to a former glory. When planned in 1832, the Kingston Penitentiary was to be the largest public building in Upper Canada, pre-dating other large institutional buildings such as asylums and colleges. The original design devised a complex of structures on a massive scale which allowed for planned expansion well into the nineteenth century. As prison architecture the penitentiary was, when first planned with its cruciform plan, dome, and elaborate interior arrangement, one of the more advanced prison designs in the world, more sophisticated than the American penitentiary buildings at Auburn and Sing Sing, institutions which had inspired its creation. It remained impressive for decades afterward, attracting many visitors and comment in popular journals.[1]

Just as remarkable as the design itself are the ideas which promoted the Kingston Penitentiary and justified its expense: the penitentiary was created in response to particular concerns for the more rational punishment of deviant behaviour as well as a response to more general concerns about disorder in society. The design reflected these interests by incorporating particular ideas about the proper treatment of prisoners and more general ideas about order and morality. The result was "moral architecture," a concept with which the originators of the penitentiary were familiar and which gave the particular and

† Histoire sociale/Social History 12, no. 24 (Nov. 1979): 385–408.

general concerns about penal reform and society architectural expression. In order to appreciate how this was done it is first necessary to know something of the events leading up to the ideas behind the penitentiary's construction. It will then be possible to understand the original design in the context of these concerns. The result will be an appreciation of the Kingston Penitentiary as an expression of Upper Canadian thought and feeling.

The basic history of the penitentiary is well documented and the details of its origin are readily available.[2] The idea of a provincial penitentiary was first presented to the Upper Canada House of Assembly by the member from Frontenac, Hugh C. Thompson, in 1826.[3] Although a committee was appointed to look into the matter, the idea was let drop and nothing further happened until 1831. By this time Thompson had visited, among other institutions, the Bridewell at Glasgow and the Auburn Penitentiary in New York State. When Thompson reintroduced the motion to look into the matter, he was made chairman of a committee to "consider the propriety of establishing a penitentiary within this province" in January 1831.[4] By February the report was complete. It recommended the building of a penitentiary for five negative reasons: the death penalty was not being executed for crimes less than murder, fines were unjust, local gaols were bad because they lumped young offenders together with seasoned criminals, corporal punishment was improper and degrading, and banishment was unenforceable and often no punishment at all. For Thompson, the virtue of a penitentiary was that

> a penitentiary, as its name imparts, should be a place to lead a man to repent of his sins and amend his life, and if it has that effect, so much the better, as the cause of religion gains by it, but it is quite enough for the purposes of the public if the punishment is so terrible that the dread of a repetition of it deters him from crime, or his description of it, others.[5]

Prior to Thompson's suggestion, gaols had been considered places either for holding prisoners for trial or as a means of punishment. The originality of the penitentiary idea was that it believed that the criminal could be reformed by separation from his formerly vicious environment and imposing on him a routine of hard labour. Thompson recommended Kingston as the site of the provincial penitentiary because of the presence there of large quantities of stone for quarrying by the convicts and the British garrison which could provide extra security if needed.

The report of 1831 led to the acceptance by the House of Assembly of the principle of a penitentiary. Two commissioners were appointed the following year to procure appropriate plans for its building:[6] Hugh Thompson and another Kingston member, John Macaulay.[7] They began their search early that same year.

The commissioners toured part of the eastern United States in June, to gather plans, estimates and other information pertaining to the running of a penitentiary. In all, they visited institutions at Auburn, Sing Sing, Blackwell's Island, New York, and Weathersfield, Connecticut.[8] These prisons were all managed on the congregate or Auburn system whereby prisoners were confined separately at night while being made to work together in absolute silence during the day. Meals were also taken together but the prisoners were arranged so that they could not see the faces of those opposite. The commissioners were prevented by the cholera epidemic from visiting the Eastern State Penitentiary in Philadelphia, an institution run on an alternative method known as the separate system, whereby prisoners were kept in solitary confinement at all times even when they worked. Both systems were described in the report presented by the commissioners to the legislature in 1832 as well as the features of their respective buildings. The penitentiary at Auburn had in 1820 developed the idea of cell blocks where units of cells were arranged in tiers separated by a central gallery. The distinguishing feature of the Eastern Penitentiary as described in the report was its radial plan where lines of single storey cells radiated from a central inspection rotunda. Although different in application, both systems were based on the principle of a strict discipline through hard work and enforced silence. Both prison designs stressed the importance of supervision and isolating the prisoners in individual cells. The 1832 report recommended the Auburn system and attached a preferred design drawn by the deputy keeper of the Auburn penitentiary, William Powers.

The Auburn penitentiary system had been known to Thompson before the report of 1831 and it is possible that Powers discussed the planning of a penitentiary with him at that time. Certainly the plans included in the report of 1832 were produced fully conceived in a short time. It is also apparent from the report of 1832, that Powers had some influence on the minds of the commissioners; his design and ideas were accepted without criticism by them. The design was central to the report of 1832 and to the subsequent development of the penitentiary, so before the ideas behind it can be discussed its essential parts must be examined.

Although the original drawings have been lost, Powers' description of these plans in the report of 1832,[9] as well as amendments which appeared in the report of the following year, have survived.[10] Furthermore, the annual report of the Boston Prison Discipline Society, published in 1836, reproduced a plan which is probably a facsimile of one of Powers' drawings (figure 1). These, taken along with Powers' notes and contemporary newspaper accounts permit a fairly accurate reproduction of what the plans looked like. Figure 1, situated with south at the top, shows the configuration of the main building, workshop to the south, female prison to the northwest, and surrounding grounds. The cruciform shape of the main building utilized the principle of the radial plan noticed in the Eastern Penitentiary and had four wings, each ninety feet long. The main entrance is at the end of the north wing, described by Powers as having Grecian Doric columns. Inside this wing there is a main entrance hall flanked by living quarters for the keepers. Originally it was intended to have a flanking building containing kitchen and dining hall for the prisoners with a hospital above but the 1833 revisions placed these facilities in the north wing of the main building. The other three wings were each to contain 270 cells. Figure 2 shows the south wing, which was built under Powers' direction, as it appeared in the 1880s. The axis for the four wings formed a rotunda forty-six feet in diameter, designated by the letter "R" in figure 1. It was to provide access to the wings and contained additional cells. It also functioned as a centre

FIGURE 1

Plan of Kingston Penitentiary, 1836

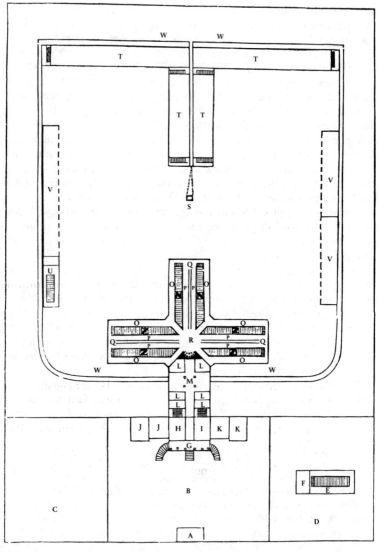

A, lodge; B, entrance court; C, warden's garden; D, female prison yard; E, female prison; F, kitchen, with work room above; G, portico; H, warden's office; I, clerk's office, J, J, warden's house; K, K, deputy warden's house; L, L, store rooms; M, keeper's hall; O, O, area in rear of cells 8 ft. wide; P, P, the same in front; Q, Q, inspector's avenue; R, centre of rotunda; S, vault; T, T, T, T, workshops; U, cells for "lunatics"; V, V, lumber sheds; W, W, inspector's avenue from keeper's hall.

SOURCE: *Reports of the Prison Discipline Society of Boston*, vol. 6, p. 889

for inspection both within and without the walls. This was topped by a large dome providing light and ventilation to the building as well as forming an aesthetic anchor to the external design. This effect can be seen from the 1919 air photo which shows the actual plan as it came to be built (figure 3).

The workshop building situated to the south of the main building is shown in figure 1 as being "T" shaped, but Powers' commentary described it as being "on the same plan" as the main building, implying a cruciform shape.[11] As figure 3 shows the workshops to have been built to this latter plan, it can be assumed that the plan of the workshop shown in figure 1 is a temporary building which existed before the erection of a permanent structure in 1845. Both buildings would have housed shops for blacksmithing, carpentry, tailoring and shoemaking as well as a rope walk, a long narrow area for prisoners to walk while twisting strands of hemp into rope. Power describes his shop building as having a corridor around its perimeter for the guards to watch the prisoners undetected in the work areas. The workshops were linked to the main building by a main avenue, called the "inspector's avenue" in figure 1. The female prison, shown as letter "E" in the same illustration, was set apart in a corner of the grounds and was designed to be completely self-sufficient, having its own workshops, eating facilities, and yard.

The general impression given by figures 1, 2 and 3 is one of order and symmetery. The main building, designed on a massive scale, with its cruciform shape and central dome, is neoclassical in mode, its arms neatly organizing the surrounding space. In a sense this symmetry reflects the almost mathematical interior design of the main building, which was based on the individual cell and expanded outward by multiples: in the south, east and west wings the cells were organized in blocks of five tiers, each tier containing twenty-two cells; two blocks arranged side by side and surrounded by a corridor formed a wing: three cell-block wings plus the service wing surrounded the rotunda to form the building.

The cell-block principle was modelled on similar arrangements at the Auburn and Sing Sing penitentiaries but in an improved fashion that reflected the functionalism of the design. The overriding concern of the penitentiary for Powers was silence, as he explained in a letter to Thompson and Macaulay.

> You are aware that the particularly excellent and distinguishing characteristic of the Auburn system is non-intercourse among the convicts, while at the same time, they are employed by day, in active useful labor. This is the grand foundation on which rests the whole fabric of prison discipline. The security of the convicts, the safety of the keepers, the profits of labor, the hope of reformation, all depend on this one feature of the system.[12]

It was the function of the penitentiary design according to Powers to promote silence by isolating the inmate and providing for his undetected surveillance: "therefore, any arrangements that can be made to facilitate *inspection*, must be considered as improvements of no small importance."[13] It was this criterion, along with concerns for security and sanitation, that governed the execution of the plan.

FIGURE 2

South Wing, Kingston Penitentiary, ca. 1880

SOURCE: Queen's University Archives

FIGURE 3

"Penitentiary, Kingston, Ontario, Taken from an Aeroplane, ca. 1919"

SOURCE: Public Archives of Canada, National Photography Collection, PA-39472

Entry to the cell block wings was gained from the outside through a double set of doors at the end of each wing, described as being "very thick, studded with nails, and strongly fastened with bars and locks, within and without."[14] Once inside the three-story wing the prisoners were organized into one of the two parallel cell blocks. These blocks, designated by the letter "N" in figure 1, were five tiers high, separated from the exterior walls by a space of two and one half feet. Facing inward the cells were reached by means of galleries running along each tier, designated by the letter "P" on figure 1. Each cell had a grilled door which opened onto the gallery. At the rear of each was a small window which provided for the circulation of air inward from the outer area between the cell block and the exterior wall. Each cell was two and one half feet wide and nine feet long[15] and was probably furnished only with a cot that folded down from the wall and filled most of the space. Clearly the intended function was for the inmate to sleep, contemplate and perhaps study the Bible. The cells at the Auburn penitentiary were three and one half feet by seven but Powers saw the longer cells in his design as being superior for they provided more useful space for the prisoner while the narrowness permitted compression of the cells to facilitate surveillance.

Powers believed that while the prisoners were at rest in their cells or engaged in labour in the shops they were controlled by the system. While the prisoners were in motion between these two areas of rigid control, filing out in the morning or back at night down the long galleries, the potential for illicit talk or non-directed behaviour was great. The architect partly compensated for this defect by shortening the length of the corridor but mostly by an ingenious idea: the parallel galleries would be separated by an inspection avenue (designated by letter "Q" on figure 1) whose floors would be staggered between the tiers of cells.

> It will be observed, by looking at the drawing, that the space between the two ranges of cells is 20 feet wide — an avenue of three feet in width, through the centre, would leave a space on each side between it and the cells, of eight and a half feet — now by raising the floor of the avenue four feet higher than the floor of the lower tier of cells, a keeper in the avenue could distinctly see, through the apertures above mentioned into *two galleries on each side*. . . .[16]

In order to eliminate the problems that a single keeper would have in supervising a long row of inmates, Powers designed the inspection avenue to have walls between it and the galleries. These would allow the keeper to observe the prisoners through apertures even when they were in their cells but would prevent the prisoners from knowing whether or not they were being watched, giving the impression of continuous surveillance. By having the cell blocks separated from the outside walls and the central inspection avenue by walls and the position of the stories, Powers had essentially designed a five-story structure within a three-story building, thereby organizing the inmates in a completely separate space from that of their keepers.

The interior of the rotunda was lined with tiers of cells encircling an open space five tiers high. As with the cell blocks, access to these cells was by galleries, and a photograph of the interior of the rotunda taken in the 1880s shows the galleries as they would have appeared in the wings as well as the rotunda (figure 4). Facility of inspection was one of the intended functions of the rotunda although visibility down the wings must have been limited. Figure 4 illustrates its potential for watching prisoners as they filed down the stairs and as they assembled in the central area below. Probably it was the *idea* of surveillance and control which was more effectively implemented than the actual function itself.

Powers allowed for the gradual realization of his design as it would be many years before the province required an institution for the incarceration of 800 felons. He proposed that the south wing be built first to meet the immediate needs of Upper Canada, to be followed by the other components as need dictated. On this basis the legislature accepted the plans presented in the 1832 report and authorized the expenditure of £12 500 to complete the initial phase of construction.[17] Henry Smith was appointed warden and William Powers was made superintending architect, a position he held until about 1840. John Mills, also from Auburn, was appointed master builder but he was replaced in 1834 by the English-trained builder William Coverdale. Coverdale gradually took over from Powers and effected some design changes as can be seen by comparing the fenestration and roof styles between the south and east wings in figure 2.[18] The south wing was finished by about 1836 and in 1839 the north wing was commenced, with the main floor intended for the much-needed dining hall and kitchen. The west wing was begun in 1840 and, after the union of the provinces increased the potential number of prisoners, the east wing was commenced in 1842. By 1845 the commissioners had initiated the building of permanent workshops, the female prison and a separate hospital building and overseen the completion of the surrounding stone wall. Some of the features of prison discipline were changed as a result of the report of Charles Duncombe presented to the legislature in 1836 and the Royal Commission of 1849 headed by George Brown, but the Auburn system and Powers' design, although modified, were not replaced until after Confederation.[19]

In the context of the development of the Kingston Penitentiary the report of 1832, which recommended the Auburn system and presented Powers' plans, is of primary importance and it is to the sources of this document that we must return in order to understand the significance of the institution which it engendered. The prison commissioners Thompson and Macaulay and architect Powers did not derive their ideas solely from a knowledge of the penitentiaries at Auburn and Sing Sing although these were obviously important influences. Rather, their philosophies on penitentiaries relied much on the works of two great champions of prison reform, John Howard and the Boston Prison Discipline Society, and the report of 1832 is full of references to both.

The earliest of these influences, the Englishman John Howard, had visited many European penitentiaries in the eighteenth century and formed conclusions about the possible reform of the prisons in England. Howard was responsible for introducing the idea in Britain and North America that it was possible to reform criminals as well as punish them by a method of incarceration involving a rigid regime of behaviour control. In volume one of his work *Prisons and Lazarettos*, entitled *The State of the Prisons in England and Wales*, first published in 1777, Howard proposed the rudiments of what became known as the congregate system arguing the benefits of separate confinement and a highly structured routine as having some moral benefit on inmates.

> The hours of rising, of reading a chapter in the Bible, of prayers, of meals, of work, etc. should all be fixed by the magistrates, and notice of them given by a bell. . . . To reform prisoners, or to make them better as to their morals, should always be the *leading* view in every house of correction, and their earnings should only be a *secondary* object.[20]

This view, which stemmed in part from the idea that criminals were a product of their environment, aimed at artificially creating a morally superior routine.

Howard had influenced the English parliamentarian Sir William Eden and the jurist Sir William Blackstone to push through the Penitentiary Houses Act of 1779. This Act stated in part:

> And whereas, if many offenders, convicted of Crimes for which Transportation hath been usually inflicted, were ordered to solitary Imprisonment, accompanied by well-regulated Labour and religious Instruction, it might be the means, under Providence, not only of deterring others from the Commission of the like Crimes, but also of reforming the Individuals, and inuring them to habits of industry. . . .[21]

The Act provided for the appointment of three persons to oversee the construction of new penitentiaries and Howard was subsequently appointed to this commission. Unfortunately the three appointees could not agree on a final decision and after two years of deadlock Howard resigned from the commission. This action effectively delayed prison reform in Britain for many years.[22]

Both Howard's survey of European prisons and his proposals for reform in Britain were cited by Thompson and Macaulay to give credence to their report. They were thus able to provide European precedents to the congregate system described at Auburn.

> The mode of punishment by solitary confinement with labour, appears to have been adopted in the Netherlands as early as the year 1770; and at Ghent in particular, the great Philanthropist, Howard, found a penitentiary called the Maison de Force, conducted in the year 1776 on the principle of seclusion, each convict occupying a separate cell at night, and the whole of labouring and eating in company but in total silence. . . .[23]

The report also drew attention to the English Act passed in 1779 which had not as yet borne fruit.[24] The influence of this Act on the legislation of Upper Canada is evidenced by the fact that the Act enabling the management of the Kingston Penitentiary used the above-quoted passage in its preamble.[25]

Even more apparent than Howard in the report of 1832 is the influence of the Boston Prison Discipline Society, whose annual reports were included with the original presentation as well as being cited in the body of the text.

FIGURE 4

Interior of Rotunda, Kingston Penitentiary, ca. 1880

SOURCE: Queen's University Archives

"The Commissioners would request special attention to the reports of Gentlemen, chiefly resident at Boston."[26] Founded in 1825 by the Reverend Louis Dwight, the Boston Prison Discipline Society became a major proselytizer of the Auburn system in North America through its chapter organizations and its reports.[27] The principles of the Auburn system, its many applications and the architectural designs compatible with this system were described at length in the pages of the reports. Here prisons built upon the new system were praised and their plans and rules discussed and copied; prisons operated by the old method which lumped inmates together in large rooms were condemned. The society, for example, supported the construction of the Kingston Penitentiary, as figure 1 attests, and recommended the building of a similar institution in Lower Canada.[28] The rival new method used at the Eastern Penitentiary in Philadelphia was dismissed as being unproven although its design was viewed with interest and its plan reproduced in the reports.

Rev. Dwight was greatly influenced by John Howard for he saw the penitentiary's ability to reform criminals by correcting the cause of their deviant behaviour. It was the view of the Boston Prison Discipline Society that crime was caused by poor parental discipline, loose living, or intemperance. "Among the causes of crime," wrote Dwight, "the neglect of family government stands next to intemperance: it is in fact, not infrequently the cause of intemperance."[29] Both Howard and Dwight saw the penitentiary's need to re-create a positive environment in which crime was impossible to thrive. To Dwight and the Boston Prison Discipline Society go the credit of spelling out in detail how this could be achieved. Labour and vigilance became the keywords of their philosophy. "In the reformed prisons, where labour has been systematically introduced, and industriously prosecuted, under a vigilant inspection, a vast amount of moral evil has been prevented."[30] For the Boston gentlemen, the penitentiary introduced a necessary factor into the felon's hitherto immoral life: disciplined control from above.

Both Howard and the American reformers considered the architecture of prisons crucial to their effectiveness. This is why Howard illustrated his book so profusely with European examples and commented on their respective merits, although he did not arrive at a clear design for a penitentiary himself. The Boston Prison Discipline Society also believed that prison design was very much a part of the corrective environment and devoted much space in its *Reports* to the discussion of preferred prison design. Paramount to the American reformers' ideal prisons were small cells for the separate confinement of prisoners at night coupled with an overall security system for constant supervision. The elements of their model prison — enabling solitary confinement at night and hard work during the day, with regular and strict supervision — they abstracted into a concept which they termed "moral architecture."

Although the phrase "moral architecture" was coined by the Boston Prison Discipline Society, the principles of its philosophy had been articulated much earlier by the English utilitarian Jeremy Bentham. Bentham is not mentioned in the report of 1832 but his influence is implicit, especially for a building called a Panopticon. The original design was of a circular building with tiers of cells around the perimeter and a central hall with an observation post at the centre (figure 5). The method of discipline described by the utilitarian was essentially the separate system where prisoners worked and slept alone in their cells. While different in application from the system advocated by the Boston

Society and the Kingston commissioners, the chief concern, vigilance, was at the heart of both systems. Bentham wrote of the plan: "The essence of it consists, then, in the *centrality* of the inspector's situation, combined with the well-known and most effectual contrivances for *seeing without being seen*."[31] The idea was that even if the prisoners were not actually being observed at every moment, they should be made to think that they were. The Panopticon was a forerunner of Powers' design in two ways: it introduced the concept of the rotunda, organizing cells around a central observation post; and it emphasized a system of undetected surveillance by designing separate passages for prisoners and keepers, in effect, as a close scrutiny of figure 5 reveals, one building within another. Powers utilized the principles of the central rotunda in the design of his central dome lined with cells. The idea of undetected surveillance was also used by Powers in his design for the observation avenue between the cell blocks.

Specific influences on the establishment of the penitentiary at Kingston then, were that the penitentiary solved problems of justice, for as Thompson noted in his report of 1831, capital punishment was not being consistently carried out for crimes other than murder, banishment was ineffective, flogging barbaric, and fines inequitable. The potential for reforming the transgressor in the penitentiary was an added bonus. This movement for the reformation of punishment echoed earlier trends, and legislation in England and Upper Canada was modelled on English precedents. The particular system of prison management chosen was influenced by the writings of John Howard but more so by the zealous propaganda of the Boston Prison Discipline Society. This system made sense: solitary confinement helped prevent escape, prison labour helped finance the institution and reform the criminal, forced labour and confinement were deterrents to crime. Powers' design was certainly influenced by his intimate knowledge of the penitentiaries at Auburn and Sing Sing, as seen in his use of the cell blocks. The radial plan could have come indirectly from Howard's book but more probably was influenced by the design of the Eastern Penitentiary which had been publicized in the reports of the Boston Prison Discipline Society. Yet another influence was Jeremy Bentham's Panopticon (figure 5) which emphasized the importance of architecture in undetected surveillance. All of these factors are the particular causes for the construction of the Kingston Penitentiary and yet there are deeper, more general concerns which motivated its creation.

A clue to the general concerns leading to the establishment of the penitentiary can be found in the universal application which the early reformers saw for prison architecture. It was a simple step for Bentham and later the Boston Prison Discipline Society to effect a broader application of prison architecture than the reformation of criminals. The principle of the Panopticon, allowing constant vigilance, was intended by Bentham to apply not only to prison but, as he says in the title of his pamphlet on the subject, to "houses of industry, work-houses, poor houses, manufactories, mad-houses, lazarettos, hospitals, and schools." The Panopticon was an example of moral architecture of general application for a universal benefit.

FIGURE 5

"A General Idea of a Penitentiary Panopticon in an Improved but as yet (January 23rd, 1791) Unfinished State"

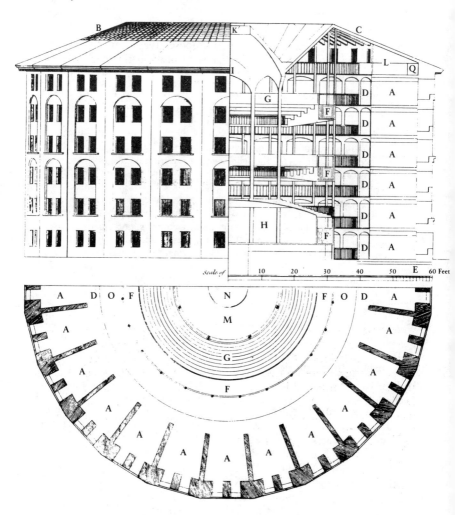

A, cells; B to C, great annular sky light; D, cell galleries; E, entrance; F, inspection galleries; G, chapel galleries; H, inspector's lodge; I, dome of the chapel; K, sky light to chapel; L, store rooms, etc., with their galleries, and immediately within the outer wall place for an annular cistern Q; M, floor of the chapel; N, circular opening in chapel (open except at Church times), to light the inspector's lodge; O, annular wall from top to bottom, for light, air, and separation.

SOURCE: Jeremy Bentham's Panopticon, from *Works*, vol. 4, edited by J. Bowring, 173.

What would you say, if by the gradual adoption and diversified application of this single principle, you should see a new scene of things spread itself over the face of civilized society? — morals reformed, health preserved, industry invigorated, instruction diffused, public burdens lightened, economy seated as it were upon a rock, the gordion knot of the poor-laws not cut but untied — all by a simple idea in architecture.[32]

The Boston Prison Discipline Society also proposed that ideas of prison architecture be applied to other public buildings such as boarding schools, almshouses and seminaries.

If there are principles in architecture, by the observance of which great moral changes can be more easily produced among the most abandoned of our race, are not these principles, with certain modifications, applicable to those persons who are not yet lost to virtue, but prone to evil? If it is found most salutary to place very vicious men alone at night, and give them opportunities for thought, without interruption, is not the principle applicable to others subject to like passions? If old offenders corrupt juvenile delinquents, in buildings so constructed as to make it necessary to lodge them in the same room, will not vicious youths of seventeen, in similar apartments, corrupt innocent boys of eight, or nine? If a night room in a prison containing ten to twenty convicts, presents to an invisible spirit, profaneness, obscenity, histories of past and design for future mischief, and generally contagion in sin, what will be presented in the same spirit, in a night room occupied by five or six unruly apprentices? If females, in prison, crowded together in a room at night, and left to themselves, dishonor their name, is there no tendency to a similar result among factory girls, lodged in the same manner?[33]

The tract goes on the describe a model plan of a boarding school, similar in design to the new wing of the Auburn Penitentiary. It is interesting to note that the society saw the application of moral architecture particularly relevant for the habitation of the lower ranks of society such as factory girls and apprentices.

While the Boston Prison Discipline Society identified moral architecture as a design that organized its inmates into individual units and then permitted a system of undetected surveillance, there also existed a broader understanding of the moral qualities of architecture. Harmony and order in architectural planning had long been associated with the ideal of classical architecture but by the beginning of the nineteenth century these attributes were thought to affect the people experiencing the design. Timothy Dwight, president of Yale, wrote in 1812 a passage quoted by J.C. Loudon in his widely read *Encyclopedia of Cottage, Farm and Villa Architecture and Furniture*:

There is a kind of symmetry in the thoughts, feelings, and efforts of the human mind. Its taste, intelligence, affections, and conduct, all so intimately related, that no preconcertion can prevent them from being mutually causes and effects. The first thing powerfully operated on, and, in its term, proportionally operative, is the taste. The perception of beauty and deformity, of refinement and grossness, of decency and vulgarity, or propriety and indecorum, is the first thing which influences man to attempt an escape from a grovelling, brutish character; a character in which morality is effectively chilled, or absolutely frozen. In most persons, this perception is awakened by what may be called the exterior of society, particularly by the mode of building. Uncouth, mean, ragged, dirty houses, constituting the body of any town, will regularly be accompanied by coarse, grovelling manners. The dress, the furniture, the equipage, the mode of living, and the manners, will all correspond with the appearance of the buildings, and will universally be, in every such case, of a vulgar and debased nature. . . . Of Morals, except in the coarsest form, and that which has the least influence on the heart, they will scarcely have any apprehensions.[34]

The ideal design, then, would impose order on its inhabitants by facilitating separate confinement and surveillance embodying principles of order and harmony which would be imparted to those who contemplated it.

By identifying the concept of moral architecture as it was understood by the late eighteenth- and early nineteenth-century prison reformers, we are provided with an important clue to the general concerns surrounding the establishment of penal institutions and the broader function of the new prisons themselves besides the reformation of criminals. The importance of the penitentiary as a corrective to a malignant environment suggests that penitentiary promoters had more general concerns than just the punishment of crime. Studies of nineteenth-century American reformers have pointed to the conservative ideology behind the movement. W. David Lewis and David J. Rothman both argue that the Boston Prison Discipline Society responded to a fear of rapid social change caused by a level of immigration and urbanization which threatened traditional values. Lewis argues that American conservatives looked to established institutions to impose order and conformity on individuals.

These institutions, however, were not enough, they had to be supplemented by a powerful effort to develop within the individual person strong inner controls which would compensate for the wide economic and political freedoms which had been granted him and guarantee that conformity without which no orderly society could exist.[35]

In responding to these general concerns, institutions themselves took on a broader meaning. Rothman points out that the institutions — penitentiary or lunatic asylum — would not only control deviant behaviour by imposing order, but serve as a symbol of order and control on the whole society. "The institution would become a laboratory for social improvement. By demonstrating how regularity and discipline transformed the most corrupt persons, it would reawaken the public to these virtues. The penitentiary would promote a new respect for order and authority."[36] Michel Foucault, in a recent book on prisons, arrives at a similar interpretation of Bentham's Panopticon, which he describes as a laboratory of power. He argues that the Panopticon was intended to impart principles of behaviour through society by creating a kind of utopia.

Dans la fameuse cage transparente et circulaire, avec sa haute tour, puissante et savante, il est peut-être question pour Bentham de projeter une institution disciplinaire parfaite; mais il s'agit aussi de montrer comment on peut désenfermer les disciplines et les faire fonctionner de façon diffuse, multiple, polyvalente dans le corps social tout entier.[37]

Foucault argues that prisons are much more than places for the incarceration of felons; they symbolize a whole code of values.

Moral architecture as a conservative response to a society whose values were no longer unquestioned — a utopian panacea for real and imagined ills — is an interesting phenomenon in European and American intellectual history, but to what extent was it connected with the Kingston Penitentiary? Before the relationship between the concept of moral architecture and the Kingston Penitentiary can be understood it is first necessary to examine the context of attitudes surrounding the construction of the Upper Canadian institution. We have seen the particular rationale given by the Kingston promoters for the penitentiary and the influence of British and American reformers on the type of prison system they argued for; but the extent to which the prison was a reponse to general concerns about the nature of society is at first problematic. The argument subordinates, for instance, the obvious reason that the penitentiary was accepted as a solution to rising crime. Therefore, before facilely transferring this explanation to Upper Canada, it is necessary to determine just what Upper Canadian concerns were when the idea of the penitentiary was accepted.

It is difficult to ascertain objectively whether or not crime was a problem in Upper Canada. Recent studies have suggested that crime was perceived as such. Gerald Bellomo has written: "In the early 1830s the increase in crime and the overcrowding of the gaols of the province made the construction of the penitentiary a legislative priority."[38] This perception stems from the association of crime with social disorder, a condition generally agreed to have been prevalent in Upper Canada in the 1830s.[39] Crime as an actual problem in this period has been disputed by J.M. Beattie who avers: "Serious crime was not a problem in Canada in the 1830's and 1840's. It was not uncommon for the criminal calendar at the assizes in Upper Canada, for example, to be very light indeed when the court met for its annual session in the various Districts of the Province."[40]

Given the imprecision of available statistics, hard evidence as to the crime rate is lacking.[41] One source that provides an impression of the nature and degree of crime in Upper Canada is the return of convicts in the Kingston Penitentiary provided annually by the penitentiary warden. This return gives the name, district, crime, date of sentence, and length of sentence of each prisoner.[42] From these returns one discovers that between October 1835 and October 1836 the prison received forty-six convicts.[43] The population of Upper Canada in 1833–34 was comprised of 77 471 males over sixteen years of age.[44] In 1838 there were 145 convicts in the penitentiary[45] while the number of males in Upper Canada over the age of sixteen at this time was 97 326.[46] It is obvious that the rise in the number of convicts does not reflect the overall growth in population. This can be explained by factors such as more convictions carrying penitentiary terms and a greater tendency for district gaols to transfer felons to the Kingston institution. Still the number of convicts in the penitentiary at the end of the decade is small compared to the total adult male population and their crimes were usually not very serious. In 1841 after the south wing was complete and the east and west wings begun, there were still sixty vacant cells.[47]

While actual crime affected a small proportion of the population, perceived crime was of general concern. Here again Beattie is helpful in his conclusions drawn from a study of Upper Canadian newspapers between 1830 and 1850.

> [T]here is no doubt that punishment of crime — how it should be dealt with — was a frequent topic of public discussion. And this was principally because crime was regarded not simply as acts of theft or violence, but more broadly as one aspect of a much larger social question. Criminality, indeed, provided evidence of much deeper and more serious evils — evils that threatened the moral and social fabric of the society, and that called for powerful measures of defence.[48]

The way is clear, then, for transferring the broader implications of the penitentiary to Upper Canada.

But what were these "deeper and more serious evils"? My own survey of the Kingston newspapers between 1830 and 1832 as well as other literature for this period found that while there was widespread interest in the building of the penitentiary there was little concern specifically with crime. There was a great concern over a more general sort of disequilibrium. Immorality, idleness, drunkenness and disrespect for social ranks caused obvious anxiety to contemporary writers, who perceived in such disorder a threat to their own values. Susanna Moodie's reaction to the immigrant peasants throwing off social and moral constraint as they disembarked in the new world in 1832 is an eloquent expression of the fear felt by the upper classes, although Moodie herself was an immigrant.

> And here I must observe that our passengers, who were chiefly honest Scotch labourers and mechanics from the vicinity of Edinburgh, and who while on board ship had conducted themselves with the greatest propriety, and appeared the most quiet, orderly set of people in the world, no sooner set foot upon the island than they became infected by the same spirit of insubordination and misrule, and were just as insolent and noisy as the rest.[49]

This kind of scene was unsettling to the higher ranks of Upper Canadian society and often repeated. While the educated Upper Canadian believed that idleness, riotous behaviour, drunkenness, and licentiousness led to crime, he or she was just as disturbed by this threatening situation in itself.

The reason that this fear of disorder was so profoundly felt by the educated Upper Canadian was because it affected his world view. This world view can only be simply stated here, based on evidence implied in contemporary commentary. While this epistemology was probably only fully perceived by a few, fragments of it were held by many in the higher ranks of Upper Canadian society. In its fullest form this philosophy saw the universe as a rationally ordered system whose parts were interconnected in a rational and harmonious fashion. The underlying principle of the organism was an order and symmetry that connected the lowliest forms with the highest and kept the whole intact.

Order was both a moral and a rational principle related to divine and scientific knowledge. By contrast disorder was both irrational and immoral, a threat to universal harmony, worse still it was exportable, a contagion that could soon spread. Rapid change was causing disorder not only in North America at the beginning of the nineteenth century but also in Britain as a result of the industrial revolution.

The threat of change and disorder to the natural balance of society is implicit in editorials and comments in the Upper Canadian press. An editorial which appeared in the Kingston *Chronicle* in 1831 on the English Reform Bill then passing through the House of Commons stated:

> Above all we hope that this event will bring not only REFORMATION but INFORMATION sufficient to instruct the minds of the people of the extent to which it can be carried with safety; and without placing bounds to human affairs, convince the rational portion of Society that the greatest danger to be apprehended by a Nation would, by the permanence of such a spirit, created by a succession of new and violent minds who would by a supposed increase of knowledge and a certain perpetuity of presumption, change the wholesome and self-purifying efforts of Nature to recover its proper tone and powers, into permanent disorder and disease.[50]

Comparing the body politic to the physical health of the individual is more than a metaphor here; there is a direct correlation implied between order on one level and health on another in the overall structure of the world.

Aberrations in normal behaviour, crime, lunacy, and sickness, were seen as manifestations of disorder, indications that the universe at large was not in harmony. Individual deviancy threatened the social order. Disharmony in the world threatened the individual. With such a world view, great emphasis was placed on conformity. The Rev. H.C. Knight, in a sermon quoted by the Kingston *Herald* in 1833, said: "Actions to be right, must proceed from right motives. Were all classes of the community sober and moral, hospitals and asylums would be almost emptied of their unhappy inmates."[51]

If crime itself was not an overwhelming problem in Upper Canada in the early 1830s, there were other signs, especially the cholera epidemic of 1832, that the order of the universe was imbalanced. An address given by the chief Justice in Upper Canada, John Beverley Robinson, to the Grand Jury of the Home District in 1832 illustrates the way in which the world view lumped together social problems as manifestations of a larger disorder:

> The increasing population of this province demands attention to all that is connected with public justice and police. The inhabitants of this District alone now number more than 40 000 and to say nothing further of the importance, on ordinary grounds of maintaining the efficacy of the law among so large a body of people, the melancholy events of the last summer [i.e. the cholera epidemic] have placed, in a striking point of view, the indispensible necessity of a due vigilance on the part of the magistracy, and courts of justice in enforcing, as far as the law enables them, the duties of order, cleanliness and sobriety.[52]

This statement would be mystifying without knowing the way in which the Upper Canadian mind interrelated signs of disorder. But accepting this we can see that is was quite plausible to Robinson that the regulation of social order would have an effect on disease.

To the Upper Canadian world view, as exemplified by Moodie and Robinson, institutions were obvious bulwarks against disorder, imparting education, obedience, religion and constraint on the individuals who made up society. The Kingston Penitentiary was the largest institution established in the 1830s and the enthusiasm of its reception can only be explained by the ideals associated with it. In Kingston, especially, these ideals were discussed at length.

Though it was noted how the penitentiary enabled the better administration of justice, more attention and approval was given to the particular method of running the penitentiary and to its promise to modify deviant behaviour. The congregate system imposed habits of industry on the disordered element of society, and virtues such as hard work, sobriety, and obedience were enforced. John Beverley Robinson observed in 1832:

> When a convict finds himself engaged in hard labour within the walls of a prison, and under the compulsion of a legal sentence, it is scarcely possible but his situation must force upon him the obvious and salutory reflection that he had much better have been applying the same exertion in gaining an honest living himself.[53]

In order to impress upon the prisoner the relation between habits forced upon him inside and habits to be followed on the outside, certain aspects of prison life had to be related to life on the outside as well. For this reason it was argued that the prisoner should perform useful work and not merely move a treadmill.[54] Useful work was rational in its productivity and its ability to teach a trade. The convict was to work in a group, imitating in a perverse fashion the grouping of shop workers or labourers. To middle class Upper Canadians, the penitentiary was an ideal society.

The idea of the penitentiary was much more than a system of dealing with transgression of the law; it became a projection of the world as it should be. The penitentiary represented a community, although an artificial one, where the old values of obedience by the lower orders to a higher power were implicit. In their 1832 report, the commissioners wrote:

> at Auburn, Sing Sing & c. we have, as the Boston Society remarks, "a beautiful example of what may be done by proper discipline, in a prison well constructed." Here it is said of officers as well as men, that "there is a place for every man, and that every man is in his place" — we regard it, they add, "as a model worthy of the world's imitation."[55]

The commissioners and the Boston Prison Discipline Society were not just suggesting that all the world have prisons like Auburn and Sing Sing, but were advocating that the world be run on the same principles.

Although the chances of permanently reforming all, or even most, criminals must have seemed slight even to the Kingston enthusiasts of the congregate system, what was generally reassuring was the sight of a model society being forced to behave in an ordered manner. The idealism expressed by the penitentiary greatly impressed Susanna Moodie who visited the Kingston institution about 1850. The reassurance of the society described here contrasts remarkably with her anxious impression of the Scottish and Irish settlers in 1832 quoted above:

> I was surprised at the neatness, cleanliness, order and regularity of all the arrangements in the vast building, and still more astonished that forty or fifty strong active looking men, unfettered, with the free use of their limbs, could be controlled by one person, who sat on a tall chair as overseer of each ward. In several instances, particularly in the tailoring and shoemaking department, the overseers were small delicate-looking men; but such is the force of habit, and the want of moral courage which generally accompanies guilt, that a word or a look from these men was sufficient to keep them at work.[56]

Though the guards were armed, it was an important point that the prisoners seemed to be free yet remained constrained and acted just as they were supposed to behave on the outside, respecting authority and working hard. This is subtle point, but one which the commissioners were well aware of in 1831. In this way not only was the prisoner impressed, but the upper classes of society were as well.

Seen as an ideal microcosmic community, the architecture of the penitentiary assumed a great degree of importance as it had to Howard, Bentham and the Boston Prison Discipline Society. It was necessary that the prison be designed to allow constant close supervision by a minimal staff, allowing order and discipline in a seemingly natural fashion, if possible, like a self-regulating machine. It was the architecture that should constrain and organize the inmate rather than the guard. In this way the penitentiary system would seem to embody an abstract moral principle which the inmate was supposed to adhere to when he was released. To support an ideal community, the design had to appear rationally ordered and effectively regulate physical problems such as santitation, ventilation, and heat. Finally, as the penitentiary was an important symbol of order to the community at large the design had to embody qualities reflecting this function. People had to be able to view the penitentiary and feel reassured or cowed depending on their natural inclinations. It was these factors influencing the design of the penitentiary that made it the most sophisticated piece of architecture in Upper Canada.

At this point we can form some conclusions about why the Kingston Penitentiary was designed the way it was. The penitentiary responded to particular and general concerns: particular concerns about the punishment of crime; general concerns about the state of disorder in the world, resulting from the industrial revolution, urbanization, and immigration, and which led to deviant behaviour and disease. The idea of the penitentiary was presented as an answer to both of these concerns through the writings of John Howard, Jeremy Bentham, and the Boston Prison Discipline Society. These antecedents legitimized the idea of an effective mode of punishment as well as a possible method of reforming behaviour. The philosophy of these penologists was based on principles of order, routine, control, hard work, and reflection enforced by strict supervision. Architecture was crucial to implementing this prison discipline that controlled behaviour, theoretically with minimal personal intervention. But, as the philosophy of prison discipline reflected ideals of how societal behaviour, implicit in the penologists' writings was the idea that the prison community could serve as a model for all society. This aspect is quite explicit in Bentham and the Boston Prison Discipline Society with their articulation of the concept of moral architecture. Thus, the solutions provided by the penologists suggested means of dealing with the uncertainties in the world, offering, as they did, a system of rigid control from above for a society where behaviour was no longer certain.

The architecture of the Kingston Penitentiary was an admirable response to the influences which brought about the institution. Planned far in excess of any conceivable needs for the incarceration of prisoners, it was a model society, a laboratory of controlled behaviour, a visible panacea for many of Upper Canada's real or imagined ills.

Notes

1. For example, Charles Dickens, *American Notes* (London: Oxford, 1957), 207; *Canadian Illustrated News* (Montreal), 25 Sept. 1875, 195.

2. Rainer Baehre, "The Origins of the Penitentiary System in Upper Canada," *Ontario History* 69, 3 (Sept. 1977); J. Beattie, *Attitudes Towards Crime and Punishment in Upper Canada, 1830-1850: A Documentary Study* (Toronto: Centre of Criminology, 1977); J. Gerald Bellomo, "Upper Canadian Attitudes Towards Crime and Punishment (1832-1851)," *Ontario History* 64, 1 (Mar. 1972): J. Edmison, "The History of Kingston Penitentiary," *Historic Kingston* 3 (1954).

3. Province of Upper Canada, House of Assembly, *Journal, 1826* (York: King's Printer, 1827), 3. Thompson was the editor of Kingston's *Upper Canada Herald* as well as being a politician. His public life is treated by H. Pearson Gundy, "Hugh C. Thompson: Editor, Publisher, and Politician, 1791-1834," in *To Preserve and Defend, Essays on Kingston in the Nineteenth Century*, edited by Gerald Tulchinsky (Montreal: McGill-Queen's University Press, 1976), 203-22.

4. Province of Upper Canada, House of Assembly, *Journal, 1831* (York: King's Printer, 1831), 6.

5. Province of Upper Canada, House of Assembly, *Appendix to the Journal, 1831* (York: King's Printer, 1831), 211 (hereafter cited as "Report," 1831).

6. Province of Upper Canada, *Laws and Statutes*, 2 William 4, c. 30.

7. Politician and former publisher of the Kingston *Chronicle*, Macaulay's public life is described by S.F. Wise, "John Macaulay: Tory for All Seasons," in *To Preserve and Defend, Essays on Kingston in the Nineteenth Century*, 185-202.

8. Province of Upper Canada, House of Assembly, *Appendix to the Journal, 1832-1833*, "Report of the Commissioners appointed by an Act of the last Session of the Provincial Legislature, for the purpose of obtaining Plans and Estimates of a penitentiary, to be erected in this province" (York: King's Printer, 1833) (hereafter cited as "Report," 1832), 26.

9. Ibid., 39.

10. Upper Canada, House of Assembly, *Appendix to the Journal, 1833-1834* (Toronto: King's Printer, 1834), "Report of the Commissioners appointed to superintend the erection of the Provincial Penitentiary. . . ," 101ff.

11. "Report," 1832, 39.

12. Ibid., 33.

13. "Report," 1832.

14. *Chronicle and Gazette* (Kingston), 6 Sept. 1834.

15. The following year the plan was amended to make the cells eight feet, four inches long. "Report," 1833, 102.

16. "Report," 1832, 34.

17. Province of Upper Canada, *Law and Statutes*, 3 William 4, c. 44. Powers' estimate for the total cost for building the penitentiary came to approximately £55 000.

18. For Coverdale's career see *Dictionary of Canadian Biography* (Toronto: University of Toronto Press, 1976), 9: 164–65.

19. Rainer Baehre, "The Origins of the Penitentiary System in Upper Canada," 207.

20. John Howard, *Prison and Lazarettos*, vol. 1, *The State of Prisons in England and Wales*, introduction by Ralph W. England (Montclair, N.J.: Patterson and Smith, 1973), 40.

21. Great Britain, *Statutes at Large*, 19 George 3, c. 74.

22. John Howard, *Prisons and Lazarettos*, 1: xix.

23. "Report," 1832, 26.

24. Ibid., 30: "It is indeed full time that England should act truly in the spirit of the Statute passed in the year 1779. . . ."

25. Upper Canada, *Laws and Statutes*, 4 William 4, c. 37.

26. "Report," 1832, 36.

27. A summary of the founder's life and the work of the society can be found in the introduction by Albert G. Hess to the *Reports of the Prison Discipline Society of Boston*, vol. 1 (Montclair, N.J.: Patterson and Smith, 1972).

28. *Reports of the Prison Discipline Society of Boston*, vol. 2, eighth annual report, 1833, 740, and ninth annual report, 1834, 824.

29. Ibid., vol. 1, fourth annual report, 1829, 298.

30. Ibid., vol. 1, fourth annual report, 1829, 295.

31. Jeremy Bentham, "Panopticon; or Inspection-House: containing the idea of a new principle of construction applicable to any sort of establishment, in which persons of any description are to be kept under inspection. . . ," *Works*, edited by J. Bowring (New York: Russell and Russell, 1962), 4: 44.

32. Ibid., 295.

33. *Reports of the Prison Discipline Society of Boston*, vol. 1, fourth annual report, 1829, 289.

34. Timothy Dwight, *Travels in New England and New York*, edited by Barbara Miller Solomon (Cambridge, Mass.: Harvard University Press, 1969), 2: 347, quoted by J.C. Loudon, *An Encyclopedia of Cottage, Farm, and Villa Architecture and Furniture* (London: Longman, Brown, Green and Longmans, 1846), 3.

35. W. David Lewis, *From Newgate to Dannemora, the Rise of the Penitentiary in New York, 1796–1848* (Ithaca, N.Y.: Cornell University Press, 1965), 72.

36. David J. Rothman, *The Discovery of the Asylum* (Boston: Little, Brown, 1971), 107.

37. Michel Foucault, *Surveiller et Punir, naissance de la prison* (Paris: Gallimard, 1975), 210.

38. Bellomo, "Upper Canadian Attitudes Towards Crime and Punishment (1832–1851)" 16.

39. Robert D. Wolfe, "The Myth of the Poor Man's Country: Upper Canadian Attitudes to Immigration, 1830–37" (M.A. thesis, Carleton University, 1976), 139.

40. Beattie, *Attitudes Towards Crime and Punishment in Upper Canada, 1830–1850*, 1.

41. For a discussion of the problems of measuring the rate of crime in nineteenth-century England, see the introductory chapter in J.J. Tobias, *Crime and Industrial Society in the Nineteenth Century* (Harmondsworth: Penguin Books, 1972).

42. Upper Canada, House of Assembly, *Appendix to the Journal, 1836–37*, "Report of the Penitentiary Inspectors," 3.

43. Ibid., 7.

44. Based on returns of districts in Upper Canada, House of Assembly, *Appendix to the Journal, 1833* (Toronto: King's Printer, 1834), 142.

45. House of Assembly, *Appendix to the Journal, 1839–40*, "Annual Report of the Inspectors of the Provincial Penitentiary" (Toronto: Queen's Printer, 1840), Warden's Report, 61.

46. Based on district returns in Upper Canada, *Appendix to the Journal, 1838* (Toronto: Queen's Printer, 1840), 446.

47. House of Assembly, *Appendix to the Journal, 1840*, vol. 1 "Report of the Board of Inspectors of the Provincial Penitentiary" (Kingston: Queen's Printer, 1841).

48. Beattie, *Attitudes Towards Crime and Punishment in Upper Canada*, 2.

49. Susanna Moodie, *Roughing it in the Bush* (Toronto: McClelland and Stewart, 1923), 29.

50. *Chronicle* (Kingston), 11 June 1831.

51. *Herald* (Kingston), 16 Jan. 1833.

52. Ibid., 31 Oct. 1832.

53. Ibid.

54. "As instruments of punishment merely, Tread Mills are very effectual; but they are ill adapted to *reform* the offender, the system does not speak to his mind — does not instruct him by moral principles and duties, or in mechanical arts — does not assist him to recover his standing among honest and honourable men, by qualifying him to obtain his living as an honest man" (*Herald*, 18 Dec. 1833).

55. "Report," 1832, 28.

56. Susanna Moodie, *Life in the Clearings* (Toronto: Macmillan, 1959), 153.

TO DISCIPLINE AND TRAIN:
ADULT REHABILITATION PROGRAMMES IN ONTARIO PRISONS, 1874–1900†

DONALD G. WETHERELL

Incarceration in the Central Prison in Toronto was not, claimed the warden, James Massie, simply a matter of punishment "as some seem to think." Rather it was to "bring out penitence for the past and purer motives for the future."[1] During the term of imprisonment, the inmates would be put "under the necessary discipline and training to help them enter upon and lead proper lives."[2] This ambition had been a major force behind the establishment of the Central Prison in 1874 and the Andrew Mercer Reformatory for Women in 1880.[3] A further example of this contemporary concern was the organization in 1874 of the Prisoner's Aid Association of Toronto. The PAA was a government-subsidized voluntary body which lobbied for prison reform and, as well, worked directly with the inmates of the Toronto prisons to supplement and complement the institutions' rehabilitation programmes. Thus, in respect to prisons, 1874 marks the beginning of a new phase of state social policy in post-Confederation Ontario.

This is not to suggest that rehabilitation was a novel ambition in 1874. The establishment of Kingston Penitentiary in 1835 had been in part justified on the grounds of rehabilitation.[4] Many of the ambitions of prison reformers and administrators in pre-Confederation Canada were repeated and elaborated during the last quarter of the nineteenth century. Confederation had created new jurisdictions in criminal justice, and it is natural to see the Ontario developments after 1874 as in part being a response to the new constitutional arrangement.

In the last quarter of the nineteenth century Ontario penal institutions were one element in the struggle to preserve social order by deterring deviance and by changing the behaviour of those who had been imprisoned. The analogy in the latter instance between parents and their children and prisons and their inmates was frequently made and even more frequently implied. The techniques which were applied inside the institutions to change behaviour were the same ones which were believed to be effective in socializing children.[5] In this context the penal institutions were obviously acting as agents of social control. The inmates had to be socialized to the norms which the state endorsed. The wider implications of social control as illustrated, for example, through the public deterrence function of prisons, falls outside the scope of this paper. Nevertheless, reference to a wider study is useful, the most notable being David Rothman's *The Discovery of the Asylum*. Rothman argues that early

† *Histoire sociale/Social History* 12, no. 23 (May 1979): 145–65.

nineteenth-century American penitentiaries sought not only to reform criminals, but through example the whole society.[6] In the United States these notions soon broke down in the face of recidivism and the institutional needs for order and security. The end result was that American penitentiaries had become merely custodial institutions by the middle of the nineteenth century.[7]

The disillusionment with penal institutions was not characteristic of Ontario thinking, even though American penology provided the main model for Ontario theorists. Long after many Americans had become dissatisfied with their institutions as places of reform, many concerned Ontarians still placed substantial faith in penal institutions as the locale of rehabilitation. The reasons for this dissimilarity between the model and its imitator lay both in the relative newness of the Ontario system and the type of inmates with whom it dealt. Ontario provincial inmates all had sentences of less than two years, for any with longer sentences were confined in a federal penitentiary. Thus the majority of prisoners in the Ontario prisons had been convicted of relatively minor offences. Nevertheless, Ontario prison reformers and officials agreed that a number of abuses were present in their system, but they assumed that through certain reforms the system could be made more effective. More importantly, rehabilitation and institutional integrity were most often see as compatible. Though between the actual and ideal of many prison activities there were a number of tensions, in general these activities were held to be consistent with both rehabilitation and institutional order. Thus prison labour reformed the inmates but at the same time made money for the state. Prison discipline was necessary for institutional order but it also reformed. The various rewards kept order but as well created character change. The melding of objectives was enhanced by the relatively strong strain of authoritarianism in Ontario legal and political thinking during this period.[8] Consequently it was natural to see the various objectives of the penal institutions as being symbiotic.

After 1874 there were three categories of prisons to which adult offenders were sentenced in Ontario. At the lowest level were the county or common jails, where both men and women convicted for minor offences or awaiting trial were held. At the next level was the Central Prison for men and after 1880, the Mercer Reformatory for Women. The latter two institutions were known as intermediate prisons and held those persons sentenced to between two months and two years. They were the most important prisons in the provincial system and carried out the most comprehensive rehabilitation schemes. Anyone who was sentenced for a term longer than two years was confined to one of the federal penitentiaries and was thus removed from provincial jurisdiction. The funding of the provincial prisons was divided between the counties and the province. County jails were partially funded out of local rates,[9] and the two intermediate prisons were wholly financed by the province.

Though the county jails were in part funded by the local government, the province theoretically had substantial control over them.[10] Through the Office of the Inspector of Prisons and Public Charities, the provincial government exercised its authority to frame regulations, supervise the organization and inspect all prisons in the province. In cases where the provincial regulations were flouted by the county, the inspectors could recommend action to the

Department of the Provincial Secretary. However, this system of control was not easily enforced. The province's only effective resource in the face of county intransigence was first to negotiate with the county for compliance, and failing that, to take the county to court. Since the two intermediate prisons came under a different administrative category in the provincial network, they were under more effective control by the provincial authorities.

The inmates of the provincial prisons were incarcerated for a wide variety of reasons. The most common causes were drunk and disorderly conduct, vagrancy, larceny, and in relatively fewer cases other offences against property, the person, the peace and public morals. In addition, those awaiting trial were held in the county jails, which meant in effect that all convicted criminals initially passed through the local jails. Roughly 40 to 45 percent of those awaiting trial were subsequently acquitted. Thus the jails held both the innocent and the guilty. The total number of commitments to the various jails and prisons was relatively high, and the numbers tended to rise slowly for the Central Prison and the Mercer Reformatory, while they lessened for the common jails. For example, in 1874, 366 men were committed to the Central Prison. By 1886 the number had risen to 579 and to over 600 annually for most of the 1890s. The number of yearly commitments to the Mercer Reformatory was much less, and generally stood between 100 and 150, again tending to rise over the years. As for the county jails, the total number of commitments was 7589 in 1877 and 6171 in the following year, but by the 1890s had declined to the mid-four-thousand range.[11]

The cause of crime was the subject of much contemporary discussion. It was of course necessary to arrive at a conclusion about the reasons for crime in order to implement successful rehabilitation schemes. The majority opinion on this matter appears to have centred mainly around the institution of the family and its importance in the formation of good character in children. It was the lack or perversion of parental duties that produced the greatest number of criminals. The family was seen as the basic factor in socialization and subsequently in social control. Hence negligence in a child's upbringing could have disastrous results.

In the framework of the family the child should be taught thrift, self-control, industry, habits of regularity and be encouraged to acquire a trade or profession. It was essential that these values and attitudes be formed in youth so that they would develop into habits in later life.[12] As well, it was assumed that Christian precepts should be imparted through the example and encouragement of the parents. The results of a neglected upbringing could be manifest in many forms: in poor work habits and idleness; in poor self-control and drunkenness and violence; in avarice and a general weakness in controlling one's passions.[13] It was also reasoned that other factors such as urbanization, drunkenness, poverty and uncontrolled immigration were sometimes responsible for crime. However, the latter also were generally grounded in an implicit belief that a good family was the first bulwark against the development of criminals. The foundations of social order lay in the family.[14] When that system of control failed, and fears were expressed that it was failing in increasing numbers, it was the obligation and duty of the state to step in and try to correct the resulting evils.

Ontario prison officials often voiced these arguments about the link between the family and character formation. Mrs. O'Reilly, the superintendent of the Mercer Reformatory claimed that "a large number of those now in the reformatory have drifted into criminal ways through not having been trained to habits of industry in their own homes."[15] When in 1890 the number of juvenile commitments to the Central Prison increased over the previous year, Warden Massie stated that "it shews that the number of neglected and improperly trained youths is on the increase." The parents of these prisoners often showed "great anxiety" about their sons, but Massie was unsympathetic. The prisoners "often" told him that they had "received no training from their parents, were not sent to school, nor taught anything good at home, but allowed to run the streets" and consequently, the parents' "assumed anxiety. . . is but mockery and comes too late." The Warden ominously concluded that it was "no uncommon thing to hear young lads curse their parents for their neglect and blame them for being here."[16]

These fruits of neglect were not considered in all cases to be permanent. After the individual had been imprisoned, the state began to attempt his rehabilitation. The methods used were closely related to those which were advocated for rearing children. Thus the prisons utilized work and the instruction in a trade, discipline, education, religion, a number of positive and negative reinforcements and a tightly controlled environment. These techniques would theoretically create new habits and behaviour in the prisoners.

The first stage of the rehabilitation programme was to ensure that the prison environment would not lead to further corruption of character. This was especially important for first offenders, youths and those awaiting trial for it was believed that the recidivists or "hardened" criminals would inevitably corrupt them. Finlay Spencer of the PAA warned in his report in 1882 that:[17]

> no one can have any conception of the amount of moral strength that is requisite to enable prisoners who desire to reform to withstand the incessant efforts to make foul and keep foul which the hardened criminals put forth. The one thing which these do with their might is the corruption of the young (and, in many cases, more sinned against than sinning) prisoners.

To prevent such occurrences, the prison had to be physically structured and organized so that the novices were separated from the "hardened" criminals. These classification systems meant that the inmates were graduated and separated from each other on the basis of sex, age, crime and as far as known, criminal record. Theoretically, each class would be confined to a corridor totally separate from the other classes.

Classification was in Inspector Chamberlain's opinion of such great significance that it was the "most important factor in the prevention of crime."[18] Proof of this contention had been presented in the "Report" of 1888 in which the Ottawa jail had been condemned as a school of crime. In Ottawa no proper system of classification was used. As a result, "young girls have started out on the most dissolute courses of life after associations formed while temporarily incarcerated for trifling offences and ultimately graduated as matured criminals."[19] Such occurrences gave impetus to the drive to classify the provincial jails, especially when it is recalled that the jails also held those awaiting trial.

In respect to the common jails, classification was, by the 1880s one of the most ardently pursued objectives of the inspectors. It had been said in the 1870s that the county jails were, because of "faulty arrangement and improper classification. . . nurseries of crime and bad morals."[20] It had been hoped that the newly created Central Prison would draw from the county jails the most serious and therefore potentially the most corrupting inmates. However, it was becoming apparent by the 1880s that that ambition had failed and that the jails were still a source of corruption.

Accordingly, the government began seriously to promote a classification system for all county jails in the province; especially those located in areas with high urban population. In 1887 the provincial secretary issued a memorandum informing the counties in which Toronto, Ottawa, Hamilton and London were located, that the province expected them to implement proper systems of classification in their jails. If the counties refused this demand, the provincial government would "compel" them to "make proper provision for classification" even if it necessitated major renovations or the erection of additional buildings.[21]

The system which the government wanted the counties to implement was based on seven categories. Each jail should establish adequate and separate facilities for the insane who were temporarily committed, for juveniles committed for the first time for "trivial offences," for prisoners committed for default of sufficient distress or non-payment of fines, for old and infirm inmates committed under the Vagrant Act, for those awaiting trial, for people convicted of serious offences, and for those committed for capital offences.[22]

There were, however, a number of obstacles to the proper classification of the county jails which were not surmounted during the period under consideration. In the first place, many of the county jails were old buildings which had been constructed in the years before classification. Chamberlain noted in 1891 that many of the jails had been built when "little, if any, attention was given. . . to such arrangement of cells and corridors as would best facilitate a proper classification of prisoners. This faulty structural arrangement is now difficult to remedy. . . ."[23] It was not, though, only the county jails that suffered from poor design. The Mercer Reformatory, which had been designed to permit proper classification was criticized by a grand jury only eight years after its opening as being poorly arranged, for young girls were allowed to associate with "lunatics and hardened criminals." This was denied by the superintendent,[24] and no immediate action was taken on the jury's findings. However, in 1899 it was found necessary to renovate completely the reformatory to permit the proper arrangement of prisoners in classes.[25]

The same situation developed in respect to the classification system at the Central Prison. The building had been designed with classification as a priority, but by 1894 the system was breaking down because of overcrowding.[26] The overcrowding subsequently became worse, and some prisoners were forced to sleep two in a cell. This was an occurrence, it was said, which would "engender vices the most odious, to neutralize all reformatory efforts, and to cause a pestilence destructive to all morals to overspread the prisoners."[27] By 1898, some prisoners sentenced by the courts to the Central Prison were held for their full term in the county jails instead of being sent to the overcrowded Central Prison.[28]

A further factor which caused overcrowding and inhibited classification in the common jails was the unfortunate committal of aged, infirm and indigent persons as vagrants. It was the duty of the county to build and maintain refuges and poor houses, but rather than suffer the expense, many counties used their jails not only for the normal function but as poor houses as well. This was in part a continuation of practices of earlier years, but the inspectors had no patience with old-fashioned approaches. It was a "disgrace" to use the jails for such purposes, thought Chamberlain, "for in most cases these people have lived honest and respectable lives," but due to events "over which they had no control have lost children, property and health." To commit such people to jail as vagrants was "unhuman, unchristian, and unpatriotic" and it "should be prevented by the most stringent legislation, if not immediately remedied by the authorities of the various counties."[29] To stop this abuse, the province offered the counties subsidies to build poor houses. That was not a sufficient incentive in all cases and consequently in 1891 the province went a step further and framed regulations requiring the local authorities to provide better food and clothing for the indigent inmates.[30] In the same year the commission examining the Ontario penal system advised that all counties be compelled to build poor houses to relieve the prisons of their destitute inmates.[31] Neither this recommendation nor the provincial regulations were very effective. In 1893 it was reported that the regulation was not receiving proper attention in some counties for indigents were still clothed in prisoner uniforms and were eating prisoner food. Chamberlain warned that he would be "compelled to make the counties build additions to the gaols for the special care and comfort of these indigent people" for they were taking up room that was required for the "criminal classes."[32] By 1896 these conditions were reported to be improving in the county jails, but the issue was an indication of the respect with which some of the counties approached their social welfare responsibilities. It is not an exaggeration to say that in many cases the counties' prime concern was expense.[33]

Despite the impediments to classification that have been noted, it remained one of the pillars of late nineteenth-century penology and was judged as the first and indispensable step towards rehabilitation. Classification was in part a reflection of the contemporary assumptions about the importance of environment in affecting behaviour. If for certain individuals the socialization process had not been effective or had broken down, and crime was considered to be proof of that, the individual was at the mercy of not only his passions but his environment. Thus it was imperative that an environment be created which would mitigate as far as possible this vulnerability and such a created environment was only possible within an institution.[34]

The creation of the uncorrupting environment was only the beginning of the rehabilitation programme. All the prisons, especially the intermediate ones, used work as a rehabilitative device, though in many county jails this was more honoured in the breach. It was believed that work was an activity which would help the inmates to learn habits of industriousness, self-discipline and ultimately, a trade. Warden Massie explained several of these advantages when he noted that "as a factor in the preservation of good order, for the elevation and fitting of the prisoner for his place in the contest for an honourable living, labour in its several pursuits stands next to Christianity, first and indispensable; without it reformation of character may be said to be impossible."[35]

The advantages of work were not only of a moral nature. It was a widespread belief that prisoners should help defray the cost of their imprisonment and thus be made, in theory at least, responsible for their past actions. The ultimate in this line of reasoning was the occasional demand that the prisons be made self-sustaining from the production of the inmates' labour. These notions fitted nicely with the contemporary emphasis upon inexpensive government. In accordance with this fiscal ambition, some prison labour at the Central Prison was done under the contract system. Contract labour was an arrangement whereby a capitalist would rent the inmates' labour for a fixed per diem rate and carry out a manufacturing operation on the prison property. This system was justly criticized as both an unwarrantable interference with the state's authority over the prisoners and as a hindrance to rehabilitation.[36]

Not all the complaints about the contract system were based on a concern for the inmate's rehabilitation. It was sometimes contended, often by labour spokesmen, that contract labour as well as any prison labour was an interference with the rights of free labourers. It was argued that prison labour lessened the work available in the society as a whole, and also that prison manufactures were sold on the open market at low prices which undercut the efforts of honest and free workers. This issue was never resolved to the satisfaction of the concerned parties during these years. In reality a solution was impossible, for the prisons insisted upon utilizing work as an economic and rehabilitative device, and their critics refused to believe that prison labour was not a threat. The government was concerned nevertheless with the resulting public resentment. In 1882 Inspector Christie asserted that an "important consideration" when planning prison labour was the selection of work projects which would interfere "in the smallest degree" with that of free workers and yet still have some rehabilitative benefit for the prisoners.[37] An example of the depths to which debate over this question could go was given in the legislature in 1895. During the debates of that year MPP George Ryerson asserted that any form of productive prison labour was an unjust interference with free labour. Therefore he thought it would be best to "keep the prisoners employed in carrying balls and chains or digging holes in the sand and filling them up again." He subsequently amended his proposals for unproductive labour by recommending that the prisoners be employed in doing the printing of the legislature.[38]

Such ideas about unproductive labour had been dismissed previously by Warden Massie as old-fashioned and "far behind in what this progressive age requires." He believed instead that the inmates should work on useful and productive projects.[39] This was not simply a justification for money-making work. It was also an assertion of the contemporary belief in usefulness as an indispensable factor in human activity and in the creation of self-confidence and self-respect. It was pointed out in 1891 that work which did not force the inmate to acquire manual and mental dexterity could not rehabilitate. Consequently, it was observed that "many may be said to begin life anew and on truer principles from the time they enter the workshops."[40] Inspector Noxon argued that there would be no "improvement" in the Mercer Reformatory inmates[41]

> until habits of industry have been formed and skill in the use of hands acquired as foundation upon which to build a confidence in their ability to maintain themselves in the honest pursuits of life. This once given it is not difficult to arouse the moral sense to a hope that there may yet be for them the reward of a better life.

Accordingly, an important aspect of work was teaching trades. To this end the workshops at the Central Prison were gradually enlarged so that by 1892 the manufacture of bricks, shoes, brooms, and wooden-wares was carried out. In addition the inmates were employed in the prison's tailor shop, the machine shop, the small woolen mill and the farm. It was stated that these various activities offered the inmates seventeen occupational choices.[42] This variety of work entailed high capitalization which reduced possible profits, but Warden Massie contended that the rehabilitative benefits were a "sufficient offset to any lessening of the revenue which might be averted by throwing the whole energies of the management into one of two lines of manufacture."[43] Despite this variety of training though, the inmates' occupational aspirations were firmly limited to trades. In the Mercer Reformatory the occupational choices were considerably less, and reflected the contemporary image of women's work. The women were employed at sewing, knitting, mending clothes and doing laundry;[44] all of which would fit them to be either housewives, domestics or workers in the needle and thread trade.

All these work programmes were based on the ambition to reintegrate the prisoner into the wage economy. However, it was soon realized that the possession of a skill was not the only requirement for that integration to be successful. In addition, the inmates had to be given a reason to acquire proficiency in a trade, and the reason they were eventually given was money.

In 1881 it was discovered that the workers in the contract broom shop at the Central Prison were producing only one and a half dozen brooms per day, as compared to the three dozen which free labourers normally produced. Thus an incentive payment was instituted and the contractor paid $0.10 per dozen brooms produced over three dozen per day.[45] The advantages soon became apparent, for payment not only increased productivity but also served as a device which had both immediate and long-term impact on the prisoner's behaviour. The payments were held in trust by the Warden until the inmate was released from prison, and the collection of these earnings was made conditional upon his past good behaviour and observation of the prison rules.[46]

By 1890 the system of overwork payments had been extended to the other industrial pursuits of the prison. Warden Massie found the system invaluable for encouraging good behaviour, as well as for promoting rehabilitation. He observed in 1896 that "there are some prisoners who have never earned honest money, and these people have been made to feel that honest labour has its rewards."[47]

The payments did not prove to be sufficient incentive for all the Central Prison inmates. It was said that some of the men were so physically debilitated through "intemperance and unclean habits," that they were incapable of doing any work until they had been "physically built up." Others were so lazy and without self-discipline that they had shunned work "by every conceivable device when at liberty, and they bring the same arts into practice here, and if deceitful pretences, lying, shamming could avail, they would not do a stroke of work."[48] In any case, the payments which the inmates received were generally quite small. In 1896 the total amount paid to the men was $2478, and the average payment was $4.00; though it was reported that some inmates earned as much as $2.00 to $4.00 per month. However, these latter amounts were only within the reach of those men who "possessed mechanical skill, great aptitude for work and who have borne themselves well in point of conduct."[49]

Overwork payments were available only to inmates of the Central Prison. Neither the Mercer Reformatory nor the county jails used such a system, though the superintendent of the reformatory urged that a "trifling sum be given to each woman who does her work well, thus giving her an interest in her own work."[50] This recommendation was not acted upon. As for the county jails, such a system of payments would have been pointless, for work was scarce. This was the result of several factors. First, there was an extremely limited market for any prison manufactures in Canada, and many counties were in any case reluctant to make the necessary capital investment for machinery and material. Another factor was that since most inmates were being held on short sentences, the teaching of trades or any employment which required the development of skill was impossible. An added complication was local politics. In 1877 the federal government had passed a permissive statute on public works.[51] This was, however, nullified by the issue of free versus prison labour. Inspector Langmuir noted that "the fact that the prisoner's labour would conflict with that of free men, has an influence upon the elections for the members of municipal councils. . . ."[52]

This lack of work in the jails constantly irritated the inspectors, and they urged and threatened the county authorities to provide facilities for work in the jails. Generally, the work available for the jail inmates was splitting wood for the jail stoves, breaking stone for the county streets, whitewashing and cleaning the jail and sometimes picking oakum. In 1893 the inspector observed that the jails had at least recognized the necessity of labour "on account of the beneficial effect that work produces. . . both physically, morally and mentally."[53] Recognition however, did not lead to a change in practice. In 1900 it was again reported that work in the jails was almost non-existent, and the inmates were being "allowed to spend their time idly and worse than use-lessly. . . ."[54] As with classification, so it was with work: the jails did not oper-ate in a fashion that was consistent either with provincial government policy or with the opinions of contemporary penologists.

Work was only part of the rehabilitation programme. In addition the pris-oners received regular religious and secular instruction. For Protestant inmates of the Mercer Reformatory, the Central Prison and the Toronto Jail, the reli-gious efforts were handled by the Prisoner's Aid Association. Roman Catholic inmates were ministered to by a priest who was assisted by "young men of the Christian Doctrinal Society." As well as saying mass, the priest and his helpers visited with the inmates on Sunday evenings.[55] Secular instruction, however, was handled by the PAA for all inmates.

When the Central Prison was opened in 1874, the Toronto Jail Mission was approached by the then Inspector John Langmuir to assume the respon-sibility for the religious work with the inmates. Later that year they reorga-nized themselves as the Prisoner's Aid Association.[56] When the Mercer Reformatory was opened, the PAA took on the additional charge of working with the inmates of that institution. In return for their efforts with the inmates, the association received a yearly grant from the provincial government. This enabled the association to conduct regular long-term programmes in the Toronto prisons. Accordingly they employed an agent, a school teacher, several Bible readers and recruited voluntary ministers to preach at the prisons. The recruitment of ministers did not prove to be easy. In 1873 the PAA sent a circular to the Toronto Ministerial Association asking for volunteers to lead the Sunday school and to conduct regular religious services.[57] The work was undenominational and the PAA gave assistance in the form of cab fares and hints on how best to approach the inmates. The PAA appeal was not as successful as they had expected it to be, and consequently they were able to have compulsory Sunday school and service only on alternate Sundays. This lack of workers was eventually corrected, and by 1879 both Sunday activities were being held weekly.[58]

There was never any doubt expressed about the efficacy of Christianity as an agent for the rehabilitation of prisoners. W.H. Howland, Superintendent of the Mercer Reformatory Sunday School, remarked that "we [the PAA] are satisfied that the Word of God is the best means for the reformation of the fallen. The steady persistent teaching of this Word bears more fruit than any other method."[59] Maude Keith, one of the PAA Bible readers, testified that the gospel had given new life to some of the inmates. One of the Mercer Reformatory inmates reputedly told her that "I praise the Lord that I was ever sent to the Mercer Reformatory." Keith found, however, that some of the Central Prison inmates were tougher to convert, but nevertheless the reli-gious readings often inspired hope and ambition for a changed life. She claimed that "often as we tell the simple story of the cross, I have seen tears course down the bruised and battered faces and have felt that there is still something good left in them."[60]

The PAA believed that the Sunday school was one of the most important aspects of their work in the prisons, for it presented the pulpit preaching as "personally applied to the heart and conscience of the prisoners." The key to this effectiveness was that the Sunday school teacher:[61]

> looks with a kindly interest into the eyes of the individual man in his class, and reasons with him "of the righteousness and a judgment to come," while he, at the same time, in various forms, puts these questions substantially and directly to him: "Do you desire to flee from the wrath to come?," "Will you accept the blessed Saviour as your Saviour?" Few men, with even so hard a heart, can long resist the kind, loving appeal of an earnest devoted Christian man who talks to him thus.

The timetable of the Sunday school shows that it primarily consisted of the hymn singing, reading Bible verses and studying the Bible. In 1877, the PAA reported that the attendance of the Sunday school had averaged thirty-five, and throughout the year forty different individuals had conducted the school.[62]

The association employed a full-time agent at the Central Prison to supplement the regular Sunday activities. He individually counselled the inmates in their cells each Sunday, and visited each Thursday afternoon at which time he conducted a service in the corridor. During these visits he distributed bibles, New Testaments and tracts, all of which the PAA obtained from the Bible and Tract Society.[63] A further responsibility of the agent was to assist the men at the time of their release. More will be said about this activity later.

In addition to the overtly religious work that it carried on at the Toronto institutions, in 1883 the PAA began to operate a night school four times a week at the Central Prison. The establishment of this school was one of the conditions of its annual government grant. The school aimed at giving an elementary education which would prepare the inmates to earn an "honest" living after their release.[64] The curriculum consisted of mathematics, writing, reading, "current events," and occasionally geography.[65] Current events was designed to give the inmates "something healthy to think about. . .thus diverting their thoughts into more healthy channels." As well, every third lesson included a lecture by the teacher on topics of concern such as temperance, masturbation, discipline and "self-control." The teacher, E.A. Stevens, noted that he was "more and more convinced that these subjects should be frequently brought before them. My motto is: 'The poorest education that teaches self-control is better than the best that neglects it.' "[66] A further example of the school's role in rehabilitation was the teacher's boast in 1896 that "every opportunity is seized to inculcate moral lessons, and develop an ambition to rise to a useful, pure and noble life."[67]

The school was thus designed to teach the inmates those ideal attributes that had apparently been neglected during their youth. Since contemporary theory held that lack of education was often a cause of crime, it followed that education could also reverse the process. To increase the lessons of self-control which the inmates received in the school, and at the same time better organize the prison, attendance at the school was made a "privilege" which was "forfeitable for any misconduct in or out of school." The inmate had to obtain the Warden's approval before he could enroll in the school, and this was granted only if he was considered a "fit subject for the school" and there were "no bad reports recorded against him in the prison books." This ruling was often rescinded if the prisoner pleaded long and convincingly enough, and after a "couple of refusals the man is usually allowed to attend."[68] In 1889 both Warden Massie and the PAA recommended that schooling be made compulsory for all inmates.[69] This recommendation was doubtless due to the increasing emphasis which was being placed on literacy as a marketable skill and on the power of the written word to shape character. Nevertheless, that schooling was made a reward is suggestive of the manner in which institutional needs were identified with rehabilitation.

Literacy was difficult to encourage in the prisons because books were not available in sufficient quantities in either the jails, the Central Prison or the Mercer Reformatory. The Central Prison library consisted of 840 books which were insufficient for the number of users. These volumes consisted of "carefully selected books of the best authors in the various branches of literature."[70] The Mercer Reformatory library was small but was even more inadequate than that of the Central Prison. It was noted in 1898 that more books were needed at the reformatory because the ones they had were falling to pieces since they had been of a "cheap" variety.[71] The women who were able to read were allowed to take these books out and read them in their cells. The policy at the Central Prison was that the men were allowed to have, in addition to a Bible and a prayer book, one library book at a time in their cells. This was only allowed if the inmate's "conduct has been good."[72]

Books for prisoners could be a mixed blessing. In keeping with the controlled environment which it was believed essential to establish in the prisons, it was necessary to keep undesirable books away from the inmates. In 1881 one of the prisoners in London Jail was discovered reading "flash novels," an occurrence which Langmuir found alarming.[73] It was believed to be of little use to attempt to wean men from their past habits if they were only reinforced through tales of murders, crimes and passion. This was a recurrent problem with books. Since it was accepted that the written word could shape minds, conversely it was felt that it could corrupt if the content was of an inappropriate nature. The same issue was at stake when the Central Prison warden had pictures, some of which had religious motifs, taken down from the cell walls, because "there were writings and drawings of an obscene character drawn by the prisoners on the backs of some of these pictures."[74]

To help fill this gap in approved reading and at the same time impart knowledge to the inmates, the PAA School Teacher established in 1886 a small newspaper for the prisoners in the Central Prison. It was called the *Echo*, and as the teacher explained, "by this means I endeavour to stir up a taste for wholesome reading and bring before them things which it may be useful to know."[75] Unfortunately the *Echo* seems to have been a short-lived enterprise, for there was no subsequent mention of its publication. An additional means of imparting knowledge to the inmates was through lectures given by people from outside the prison. In 1886 for example, a "number of gentlemen" gave lectures to the prisoners of the Central Prison on "various topics." This too was a privilege, for attendance was conditional upon good behaviour.[76] Again, the needs of the institution were combined with the need for rehabilitation.

It would be misleading to suggest that the encouragement of discipline through a system of privileges in return for good conduct was a matter which only marginally concerned rehabilitation. Discipline was necessary to preserve order in the institution, but that order and discipline would, it was believed, also lead to personal habits of restraint, regularity and decorum. Through the tightly regulated prison life which was reinforced through various punishments and rewards, the inmates' former habits would be broken and replaced by more conventional and repressed ones. Massie believed that discipline was "highly beneficial in its effects towards reform" because many of the prisoners had never been "put under proper restraint. . .and were accustomed to follow only the dictates of their depraved and vicious natures. . .they have to be educated and comply with order, and be submissive to authority."[77]

Many of the prison rules were designed to further this process of trans-formation of habit.[78] For example, in 1884 the use of tobacco by the inmates at the Central Prison was forbidden. In addition to teaching the men denial, though perhaps for many it only taught deviousness, the non-use of tobacco helped in the struggle against rum. In 1882 Hamilton Cassels of the PAA had urged the abolition of tobacco, for it "to a large extent, keeps alive and satisfies for the time being that desire and appetite for the excessive use of intoxicating liquor, indulgence in which it is well known, is the cause, in the majority of cases, for which the men are committed. . . ." Consequently, if they were denied tobacco their rehabilitation would be furthered and strengthened.[79]

The abolition of tobacco was only a single example in the overall picture. In addition, the rigid timetables, silence and restraint which were part of the prison rules were intended to aid rehabilitation. Rules provided an external form of discipline which would in time affect the inmates' personal habits. In this manner the older habits would be replaced with more desirable ones. In that connection, Inspector Langmuir explained that "the regularity, order and decorum" that "should prevail" if the prisoners ate together instead of in their cells "cannot fail in having a good moral effect." In addition, "good discipline and complete subordination, two of the most important lessons that prisoners have to learn — are practically inculcated." He concluded that the act of "sitting down together — although in silence" would have a "humanizing and elevating effect" upon the inmates.[80]

The creation of new personalities and habits by such means as have been outlined above obviously required a great deal of time. This was recognized at the time and consequently there was a continual and bitter stream of com-plaint directed by prison administrators and reformers against the existing sys-tem of sentencing. The maximum sentence of any inmate in an Ontario prison was two years, though the average sentence imposed upon inmates in the Central Prison was between six and nine months.[81] The sentences in the jails were of course less. These sentences were considered to be much too short to achieve any lasting and effective transformation of character. Therefore, demands were made for longer fixed sentences or for the implementation of indeterminate sentencing. Under an indeterminate sentence the prisoner would be committed for a minimum but not a maximum term, and release would be conditional upon rehabilitation being achieved.[82] Mrs. O'Reilly of the Mercer Reformatory wanted longer sentences, especially for recidivists and drunkards. She argued that "much greater good would likely result, owing to the more permanent influences which Reformatory discipline and training would have."[83] John Langmuir had made the same argument in 1873 when he wrote that society received no benefit from short sentences for recidivists, and suggested that "when a person, by repeated petty offences, evidences a proclivity to crime, his term of imprisonment should be made so long that his idle and vagrant habits may be broken up, and replaced by habits of industry and usefulness."[84] Later in the century Massie flatly stated that short sentences were in fact an encouragement for crime. He argued that the prisoners served only short sentences after which they were released to "resume their depredations on society, . . . with invigorated health, acquired at the expense of the province. . . ."[85] In 1890 Mrs. O'Reilly visited several female reformatories in the United States and she returned to Canada even more enthusiastic about long sentences. The American inmates, because of their long sentences of up to ten years, "look upon the Reformatory as their home" she reported, and consequently they found it in their "best interests" to behave in a "quiet orderly manner."[86] Similarly, the PAA in its various annual reports made demands for the implementation of either the indeterminate sentence or at least longer fixed sentences. Institutionalization had not yet become a concern for prison theorists.

The demands for longer fixed sentences were in large part the result of a feeling that the existing rehabilitation schemes were inadequate, especially for those inmates who were "incorrigible" or recidivist. However, criminal records were not kept until 1900, and prior to that date only occasional statistical counts were made. One such tabulation for the common jails in 1876 revealed that 30 percent of the inmates were recidivists.[87] The same percentage of inmates of the Central Prison were discovered to be recividists in 1900 when regularly collected figures were published.[88] Despite these figures, which were considered to be alarmingly high, there were many references made to the examples of men and women who had been rehabilitated in the province's prisons. These were very subjective impressions, and were based upon word of mouth reports or letters from former inmates.

In order to counter recidivism, the PAA and the Salvation Army provided the inmates with assistance at the time of their release. It has already been noted that the PAA employed an agent who in addition to his other duties assisted the released inmates. The scope and amount of aid granted by the PAA is shown in the table below. It was a remarkably comprehensive set of benefits, and was a credit to the efforts of the association. Many of the necessities that were distributed were obtained from public donations. In 1875 the association stressed in its annual report that it welcomed any "donation of cast off clothing for discharged prisoners many of whom are destitute and have no friends."[89] The PAA was not the only source of clothing, for the prisons distributed clothing to the inmates at the time of their release. At the Mercer Reformatory all the women received, at the time of their discharge, a suit of clothes. Those who had been confined for longer than twelve months and who had been well behaved were "provided with an outfit of better material."[90] The association also made loans to former prisoners, and as is reported in the table a considerable portion of these loans were repaid.

The PAA also helped the released prisoners to find jobs, and they reported in 1883 that "it is remarkable how willing the great majority of employers of labour are to give them [former prisoners] an opportunity to retrieve their character and position."[91] However, in 1898 it was reported that it was more difficult to get employment for these people because the employers showed "preference to others than prisoners."[92] The latter condition was in fact the normal state of affairs, and consequently the availability of jobs for former prisoners was closely tied to current economic conditions.[93] The inmates of the Mercer Reformatory were sometimes placed in positions by the reformatory.[94] Through that system the women were more closely watched and controlled after their release, but there was no legal authority for the reformatory to regulate their behaviour. Further assistance was provided in the form of two PAA shelters, one for females and another for males, in which

TABLE 1

Aid Granted to Prisoners By the PAA: 1885–1894

	1885	1886	1887	1888	1889	1890	1891	1892	1893	1894
Work found for	384	311	291	301	319	181	174	128	71	120
Prisoners' families aided	n/a	40	37	43	71	84	140	75	26	25
Articles of furniture given	68[a]	105	93	68	39	32	21	81[a]	n/a	1
Rent paid for	24	33	21	14	9	14	18	15	4	1
Articles of clothing given	339	428	362	274	193	226	160	183	50	222[b]
Number given tools and materials	59	33	24	31	53	40	52	36	4	6
Fares paid (Rail)	29	39	28	17	26	40	72	51	31	21
Number of meals given	380[d]	3066	2118	2835	4343	n/a	n/a	n/a	n/a	229[d]
Lodgings given to	250	500	547	625	1344[c]	n/a	n/a	n/a	n/a	n/a
Money loaned	$522	$593	$615	$304	$313	$350	$338	$167	$42	$26
Money repaid on loans	$417	$507	$518	$222	$219	$240	$204	$115	$37	n/a
Total number assisted by PAA	726	841	673	715	723	761	796	506	271	457

a Number of families.
b Number to whom clothing was given.
c Nights of lodging given.
d Includes lodgings.

SOURCE: Compiled from "Reports," 1886–95.

the released prisoners could stay for a short time. In 1900 the Salvation Army established a farm just outside of Toronto to which the men could go after their release.[95] The Army also operated a shelter in Toronto.

The Salvation Army had become involved in prison work towards the end of the century and operated under the name of the Prison Gate Movement. It was directed by W.P. Archibald, who later became the first Dominion parole officer. Archibald had a deep faith that the gospel could reform men, but at the same time he rejected the "twaddle of many people" who preached at the prisoners about the "Prodigal Son or some other wild character of the Bible." He believed that former prisoners needed not more tracts but realistic programmes of assistance. He argued that "if the criminal classes are to be transformed into new men. . . Divine life must be transfused into them through human agencies or channels." It was essential however that "this be done by practical methods adapted to meet the requirements as the individual case may need." These practical methods included visiting and giving necessities to inmates and their families both before and after release, assistance in finding a job and temporary shelter when needed.[96]

Archibald's insistence upon practical help was not, as can be seen in the table, confined only to the Salvation Army. The PAA assistance was largely predicated upon the same assumption. As extensions of the institutonal programmes they gave tools and materials to encourage wage employment and self-employment, provided household goods to re-establish or create homes and gave loans for the same general purposes. The rail fares were provided either to return ex-prisoners to their homes or to send them to places where employment was available. The objects of the PAA and the Salvation Army were therefore the same: to normalize through various means, the former prisoner's relationship with society.

This policy of reintegration began to be more closely associated with the institution by the close of the century. Throughout the 1890s various demands had been made for a parole system, and a parole or ticket of leave Act was finally passed in 1899 for the inmates of federal penitentiaries.[97] In the following year this Act was extended as well to the inmates of provincial prisons. J.T. Gilmour, the new Central Prison Warden, thought that the Act was an "excellent one." However, he felt that the "mode of enforcing it was so very imperfect that we derive but little benefit from it."[98] He was probably referring to the lack of centralized supervision of the parolees.

The Parole Act can be seen as a first tentative step away from the previous reliance upon programmes carried on within institutions to effect rehabilitation. During the nineteenth century institutions had become integral and assumed factors in the treatment of many forms of deviance. Parole was not a rejection of those methods, nor was it intended to be. Rather it was envisaged as a consistent development of those programmes which gave rewards in return for good behaviour. Nevertheless, it was significant that the state had begun offering the ultimate reward. It signaled a slowly developing change in Canadian correctional thought, and a recognition that there were alternative programmes with which to attempt rehabilitation.

Notes

1. "Report of the Inspector of Prisons and Public Charities for the Year 1888," Ontario, *Sessional Papers*, 1889, no. 2, 90 (hereinafter cited as "Report").

2. "Report," 1891, no. 7, 78.

3. See "Report," 1874, no. 2, 1–2, and "Report," 1879, no. 8, 81–82.

4. J.M. Beattie, *Attitudes Towards Crime and Punishment in Upper Canada, 1830–50* (Toronto, 1977), 15ff; and R. Baehre, "Origins of the Penitentiary System in Upper Canada," *Ontario History* 69, no. 3 (1977): 185–207.

5. Alison Prentice, *The School Promoters* (Toronto, 1977), 25–41.

6. David Rothman, *The Discovery of the Asylum* (Boston, 1971), xix and 84.

7. Ibid., 235–46.

8. See, for example, Bruce Hodgins, "Democracy and the Ontario Fathers of Confederation," in *Profiles of a Province*, edited by Edith Firth (Toronto, 1967), 83–90.

9. The province paid for the maintenance of those prisoners in the county jails who were "criminal prisoners"; the remainder of the inmates in local jails were supported by the county. "Report," 1884, no. 8, 11.

10. Richard Splane, *Social Welfare in Ontario* (Toronto, 1965), 158.

11. Compiled from figures cited in "Reports," 1874–1901.

12. For an example of one theory on "habit" see: "Early Formation of Habits," *Journal of Education* (Mar. 1874), 45, where habit is described as follows: "after he has repeated them frequently [a given action], each single action suggests the following one so instantaneously that he cannot distinguish them in his knowledge, but is conscious of them only as a comprehensive whole. This is to be explained by several laws of suggestion, and. . . by the law of frequency of occurrence." The implication of such a theory of character development made the importance of environment and youth obvious.

13. Egerton Ryerson, *First Lessons in Christian Morals for Canadian Families and Schools* (Toronto, 1871). See especially 20–43.

14. Some of the contemporary theories about the cause of crime can be found in various numbers of: Ontario, "Report of the Inspectors of Prisons and Public Charities"; Canada, "Report of the Minister of Justice as to Penitentiaries in Canada"; and the annual reports of the various prisoner's aid associations. See also: "Report of the Commissioners Appointed to Enquire into the Prison and Reformatory System of Ontario," 1891, 34–47; and the various proceedings of the International Prison Congress and the National Conference of Charities and Correction. Reports from the latter two organizations were often quoted by Canadians concerned with the problems of crime and rehabilitation.

15. "Report," 1887, no. 12, 102.

16. "Report," 1891, no. 7, 77.

17. "Report," 1882–83, no. 8, 79.

18. "Report," 1892, no. 8, 5. See also: "Report of Commissioners Appointed to Enquire into the Prison and Reformatory System of Ontario," 1891, 222. Hereinafter cited as "Commissioner's Report," 1891.

19. "Report," 1889, no. 2, 59.

20. *Asylums, Prisons and Public Charities — Ontario — 1876* (Toronto: Printed for the Government of Ontario for the Centennial Exhibition, Philadelphia, 1876), 18.

21. "Report," 1889, no. 2, 12.

22. "Report," 1889, no. 2, 46.

23. "Report," 1892, no. 8, 3.

24. "Report," 1888, no. 11, 101.

25. "Report," 1889, no. 35, 77.

26. "Report — Central Prison," 1895, 11, 13.

27. "Report — Central Prison," 1898, no. 11, 13

28. "Report," 1899, no. 12, 16.

29. "Report," 1892, no. 8, 5.

30. "Report," 1893, no. 9, 4.

31. "Commissioner's Report," 1891, 220.

32. "Report," 1893, no. 9, 5.

33. See "Report," 1894, no. 27, 4 and "Report," 1897, no. 11, 2.

34. Rothman, *The Discovery of the Asylum*, 82–83.

35. "Report," 1889, no. 2, 90. A further disadvantage of idleness in poorly classified prisons was that it gave "the older and more hardened criminals full opportunity to teach the younger ones all the varied devices for committing crime" ("Report," 1893, no. 9, 4).

36. See: "The Prison Labour Question. History of the Contract System in the Toronto Central Prison. A Record of Continuous Failures. The Outlook for the Future." (a speech of the Hon. W.J. Hanna delivered in the Ontario legislature, 26 Feb. 1907). The problem was not only interference with the prison's direct authority. In one short-lived case at the Central Prison, the contractor employed free labourers to work alongside the inmates. Langmuir protested against this practice, and demanded that the outside workers be forbidden to give tobacco to the inmates, as well as stop "the practice of expressing sympathy with the prisoners" ("Report," 1874, no. 2, 208).

37. "Report," 1882–83, no. 8, 55.

38. *Globe*, 10 Apr. 1895.

39. "Report," 1888, no. 11, 78.

40. "Report," 1892, no. 8, 85.

41. "Report — Andrew Mercer Reformatory," 1899, no. 12, 3.

42. "Report," 1892, no. 8, 84.

43. "Report," 1894, no. 27, 139.

44. "Report," 1892, no. 8, 109.

45. "Report," 1882, no. 8, 160.

46. "Report," 1891, no. 7, 75. In earlier years it had been the practice to give to discharged prisoners who had been well-behaved, a small gratuity to assist them in the first few days of freedom. "Report," 1875, no. 4, 66.

47. "Report — Central Prison," 1897, no. 11, 14. Another system which was often advocated but never implemented was remission of sentence. Under that arrangement, the inmate would receive a given number of days per month off his sentence in return for good behaviour. As with payment of wages, he could forfeit the whole through bad conduct. "Commisioner's Report," 1891, 331.

48. "Report," 1882–83, no. 8, 66.

49. "Report — Central Prison," 1897, no. 11, 14.

50. "Report," 1884, no. 8, 145.

51. House Of Commons, *Debates*, 29 Mar. 1877, 1062. The Act was: An Act to Provide for the Employment without the Walls of Common Gaols, of Prisoners sentenced to the Imprisonment therein, *Statutes of Canada* 1877, 40 Vict., c. 36. Edward Blake was not certain of the benefit of this statute. He agreed with the need for hard labour in the county's jails and prisons, but feared that public labour, except for the most "Hardened" criminals would tend "to degrade any prisoner so employed in the presence of the free people of the country." He did not think such work would be "likely to be productive of improving results to the prisoner" as would be if the prisoner worked "on a farm or something of that kind more in the country" (*Debates*, 29 Mar. 1877, 1062).

52. "Report," 1879, no. 8, 76.

53. "Report," 1894, no. 27, 3.

54. "Report," 1901, no. 36, 9.

55. "Report," 1878, no. 4, 364. There is little information provided in the reports on religious efforts for Roman Catholic inmates. In 1885, however, a number of charges were laid against Warden Massie, some of which included allegations of anti-Roman Catholic bias. A commission was held to examine these charges. Massie was charged with taking down Roman Catholic pictures from Catholic inmates' cells, refusing admittance to the prison to Catholic chaplains who had come to preach, and among other things, that those "in authority" had spoken disparagingly about Catholics and their institutions. None of these charges were authenticated due to a lack of evidence. "Report of Evidence of Wardens of Prisons etc. in the United States and Canada, Taken Before the Royal Commission Appointed to Enquire into Certain Charges Against the Warden of the Central Prison and into the Management of the Said Prison," in Ontario, *Sessional Papers*, 1886, no. 26, 4–6 and 61–63 (hereafter cited as "Central Prison Inquiry — 1885").

56. "Report," 1874, 217–18.

57. Ibid., 218–19. Attendance at both Sunday school and church service was compulsory for all inmates.

58. "Report," 1879, no. 8, 391.

59. "Report," 1892, no. 8, 121.

60. "Report," 1894, no. 27, 104.

61. "Report," 1874, no. 2, 219.

62. "Report," 1878, no. 4, 365.

63. "Report of the Toronto Prisoner's Aid Society for the Year 1875–76," 6.

64. "Report," 1894, no. 27, 162.

65. "Report," 1889, no. 2, 101–2.

66. Ibid.

67. "Report — Central Prison," 1896, no. 12, 32.

68. "Report," 1885, no. 12, 103.

69. "Report," 1890, no. 11, 91.

70. "Report — Central Prison," 1896, no. 12, 14.

71. "Report — Andrew Mercer Reformatory," 1899, no. 12, 8.

72. "Report," 1874, no. 2, 46.

73. "Report," 1882, no. 8, 105.

74. "Central Prison Inquiry — 1885," 61. See also: "What to Read," *The Journal of Education for Ontario* 29 (1876): 63.

75. "Report," 1887, no. 12, 93.

76. Ibid., 81.

77. "Report," 1889, no. 2, 91.

78. For rules of the county jails see: "Report," 1882, no. 8, 77–91. A timetable for the Mercer Reformatory is in: "Report," 1889, no. 2, 103.

79. "Report," 1882–83, no. 8, 79.

80. "Report," 1874, no. 2, 47.

81. "Report — Central Prison," 1898, no. 11, 18–19.

82. James Massie, "Prison Reform in Ontario," *The Canadian Law Review* 2 (1902–3): 394–96.

83. "Report," 1889, no. 2, 105.

84. "Report," 1874, no. 2, 45.

85. "Report," 1890, no. 11, 88.

86. "Report," 1891, no. 7, 103.

87. "Report," 1876, no. 2, 67.

88. "Report," 1901, no. 36, 46.

89. "Report of the Toronto Prisoner's Aid Society for the Year 1874–75," 10.

90. "Report — Andrew Mercer Reformatory," 1899, no. 12, 7. In 1885 it was recommended that clothing for discharged prisoners at the Central Prison be used as a reward. If an inmate had behaved badly in prison then he should receive clothes only sufficient "to protect him from the severity of the season." Well behaved inmates would receive clothing of a better quality. "Central Prison Inquiry — 1885," 55.

91. "Report," 1884, no. 8, 111.

92. "Report — Central Prison," 1898, no. 11, 35.

93. "Report," 1901, no. 36, 64.

94. "Report," 1894, no. 27, 88.

95. "Report," 1901, no. 36, 67. The use of farms for released inmates was a common theme. In 1877 the Roman Catholic archbishop of Toronto urged Langmuir to establish an "industrial farm" for released men, or alternatively put them to out-door public works in the free-grant districts. "Report," 1878, no. 4, 364–65. Likewise the myth of agricultural pursuits, or at least rural ones, appealed to the PAA who discouraged newly released inmates from staying in Toronto, presumably to avoid urban-caused corruption. "Twelfth Annual Report of the Prisoner's Aid Association of Canada for the Year 1886," 4. See also note 44 above.

96. "Report," 1901, no. 36, 66.

97. The Act was: An Act to provide for the Conditional Liberation of Penitentiary Convicts, *Statutes*, 62–63 Vict., c. 49. Under this Act the inmate was supervised only insofar as he had to regularly report to the local police.

98. "Report," 1901, no. 36, 46.

THE HISTORY AND FUNCTION OF PROBATION†

D.W.F. COUGHLAN

It is commonly supposed that probation began in August 1841 when John Augustus, a Boston cobbler, "put his hand to the plough" as he expresses it, in the Boston police court by standing surety for a drunkard and taking him under his protective wing. Actually the idea behind probation is much older than this and had its origin in the English common law process of "binding over."

In the Records of the Court of Assistants of the colony of Massachusetts Bay for 1630–92 in New England, you will find illustrations of the seventeenth century use of what looks remarkably like probation. For instance, the General Court respited the case of Mrs. Harding until the next court, and ordered that in the meantime she be dealt with by Mr. Cotton, Mr. Wilson and the church, to see "if she may be convinced and give satisfaction." Mr. Ambrose Martin was fined ten pounds and ordered to go to Mr. Mather for instruction, for the offence of trying to found a new church. John Cooper, was for some offence, "committed to his father for correction." (In a lighter vein, there existed in England in 1693 vulgar probation — this was a trial by ordeal for witchcraft and consisted of immersing the accused in water — the terse comment was made "we found he sank like other people").

In 1927 the Young Offenders Committee in England made an ingenious attempt to claim Athelstane, an Anglo-Saxon king (A.D. 895–939) who made his mark in legal reform, as the father of a rudimentary probation system. Athelstane enacted that: "men should slay none younger than a fifteen winters' man," and provided that, "If his kindred will not take him or be surety for him, then swear him as the bishop shall teach him, that he will shun all evil, and let him be in bondage for his price. And if he steal again, let men slay him or hang him as they do his elders." (Rather a rugged penalty for violating one's probation!)

Whatever may be the merits of this intriguing controversy as to the origin of probation, there can be no doubt that the release of offenders under supervision as an alternative to punishment first developed as a legal system in the United States of America and that the term probation was first applied to the new system in that country. Even if America borrowed from English common law a valuable legal instrument (binding over), we gratefully acknowledge that it was returned tempered by imaginative insight and forged to new purposes!

In reviewing the history of probation in Canada, two interesting factors emerge, which are probably common to all countries where probation has developed. The initial interest in probation appears to stem mainly from concern over children who have broken the law, and the initial work in probation

† *Canadian Bar Journal* 6 (1963): 198–213.

appears to have been done by private citizens and private societies. After this task of demonstration and interpretation has been accomplished, the various levels of government become interested in probation, as a means of dealing with adult offenders as well as juvenile offenders. Further, it is interesting to note that in twenty of twenty-three countries which have probation systems, the legal profession added great impetus in the early stages of development by its interest in, and outspoken advocacy of probation. This has yet to happen in Canada!

Probation first became available in Canada as a legal alternative to incarceration in 1908 with the passage of the Juvenile Delinquents' Act (Canada). It was one of the nine ways in which the judge of a juvenile court could dispose of a child adjudged to be delinquent. Enabling legislation to implement this act was passed in Ontario in 1910 — the Juvenile Courts Act.

This provincial statute was revised in 1914 and again in 1916 and, after several more revisions, emerged in its present form as the Juvenile and Family Courts Act, 1960.

The original Act in 1910 was the means whereby the federal legislation was implemented and made possible the establishment of juvenile courts in Ontario. It was not until 1921, by amendment to section 1081 of the former Criminal Code, that probation became available to the criminal courts of Canada. Prior to this, the criminal courts were limited to "suspended" sentence which also had its roots in the ancient procedure of "binding over."

In 1942, by a further amendment to the Criminal Code, following an Ontario appeal case, probation became available to the appellate courts as well as the trial courts. The present pertinent section of the Criminal Code is 638. It is interesting to note that under this section there has been a subtle but extremely important change of which many courts and most lawyers have not taken cognizance. Suspended sentence as such is no longer possible, only probation through the medium of suspended sentence can now be granted. Such probation may be with or without supervision. Probation without supervision could have adverse results for probation generally, a factor of which the legislators did not seem aware. Such a procedure also signifies a lack of appreciation of the historical development of probation on the part of the draftors of the present Criminal Code.

Historically, probation means release *with supervision*. To grant probation *without supervision* is to empty it of its historical content and connotation!

In 1961, section 637(2) of the Criminal Code was amended and a close study of this presents some "rather startling ramifications." A court may now order a convicted person placed on probation for a period of two years *after* he has served his prison sentence. In cases of indictment and in cases of summary conviction this can either be in lieu of or in addition to the court's sentence. An even wider implication is that the chafing collar of limiting probation to first or selected second offenders is circumvented. For a more detailed discussion of this matter the reader is referred to the *Criminal Law Quarterly*, vol. 4, March 1962, an article by A.K. Gigeroff of Ottawa. Mr. Gigeroff is a lawyer working as a probation officer.

The 1921 federal legislation on probation was implemented in Ontario by the enactment of the Probation Act in 1922. The draftors of this Act were extremely progressive thinkers; unfortunately its implementation since then has been the converse of progressive.

The present Probation Act is chapter 308, R.S.O. 1960 and in section 6 of this Act it will be noted that the court has power to release on "probation of good conduct" a person *charged* (not necessarily convicted) with an offence under any statute of Ontario. That this was the intent of the legislators is beyond question because the Act proceeds to stipulate a specific penalty for any violation of probation thus granted, a fifty-dollar fine for the violation and the relaying of the original information. As to whether this is "good" law is surely a matter that should be left for the appellate courts!

The use of probation in Canadian courts since 1921 has been greatly retarded by the lack of Canadian literature on the whole field of penology. Until 1952, no Canadian university had any facilities for proper research into the subject of criminology or offered any specific training to people interested in the correctional field. Such courses are now available in only a few Canadian universities and only the University of Montreal has a department of criminology leading to a master's degree in this subject. It is interesting to note that most civilized countries have had criminology departments in their universities for many years.

Because of the lack of literature and research in this field, there has been very little professional or public enlightenment on the subject of probation. The fact that many professional people engaged in the area of law enforcement still think of probation as a "letting-off" of the convicted person, a way in which he escapes the "just" desserts of his actions, is illustrative of our ignorance in matters penological.

David Dressler, a former chief of probation for New York State, once said, "The probationer must realize that the probation officer is there to do at least one thing: prevent further depredations on society. This he must accept whether the realization is pleasant or not, and this must be the framework within which any other treatment operates."

In 1936, the chief probation officer for New Zealand said,

> Although by comparison, probation must be admitted to be a lenient form of treatment, it is quite wrong to assume that it is equivalent to being "let off." This deep-rooted misconception, no doubt arising from the genesis of the scheme, which originally applied to first offenders only, for offences more or less of a venial character, has been to some extent responsible for probation not being utilized as extensively as it might be. There is definitely a disciplinary purpose in probation, and usually strict compliance with the terms of the recognizance makes exacting demands upon the probationer.
>
> It is, in effect, conditioned liberty, but the positive feature of it is that, although in some cases the restrictions on liberty may be irksome, they are imposed not so much as punishment as with the object of assisting the probationer in habituating himself to a more ordered and disciplined mode of living. Right living is largely a matter of acquiring good habits.

Consider further that no country is receiving the protection to which it is entitled from its law enforcement system until the majority of offenders are *permanently* reclaimed as useful citizens. It follows that any mode of procedure which will permanently reclaim offenders as useful citizens enhances the administration of justice providing that procedure is not illegal. Probation achieves this goal in 70 percent of the cases it deals with, whereas incarceration falls short of this objective in an almost direct inverse ratio; over 75 percent of the people admitted to Canadian penitentiaries each year have been incarcerated before, and between 65 and 75 percent of those admitted to provincial reformatories each year have been incarcerated previously! At the present time, there are fewer than 350 full-time probation officers to serve the criminal courts and the juvenile and family courts of Canada! Two hundred of these are officers in Ontario.

Another illustration of Canada's backwardness in matters of penology may be seen in the new Criminal Code. The use of probation is still very restricted in the first instance. It is available to any first offender where there is no mandatory penalty; it is available to certain selected second offenders, the method of selection being either that the second offence shall occur over five years after the first offence or that if it occurs within the five years it shall be of a different nature, providing that once again, in both cases, there is no mandatory penalty. This procedure is tempered to a degree by the 1961 amendment to section 637(2) of the Code which has already been discussed.

In the former Criminal Code, the consent of counsel acting for the Crown was necessary before a first offender could be placed on probation if the penalty could be two years or more, and such consent was necessary for all eligible second offenders before they could be placed on probation. Much ado was made about removing this consent in the new Code but the more basic restrictions were completely overlooked by the legislators and by the many learned people appearing before them.

This is very difficult to understand in the light of the specific recommendations of the Archambault and Fauteux Reports in this connection. It was strongly urged that the matter of probation should be left entirely at the discretion of the presiding judge thus leaving the only restriction on the granting of probation the several mandatory sentences. The Archambault Commission stressed the apparent contradiction in our present procedure; we have enough confidence in the ability of the bench to weigh evidence leading to conviction, should it not follow that we have enough confidence in their ability to dispose of a convicted person in the best interests of society and of the convicted person? Most other countries have had such confidence and leave the matter of probation to the sole discretion of the bench. After fifty years of probation in these countries, there is no evidence to show that this confidence has been misplaced. In the last analysis, there is always the safeguard of appeal. This illustration is significant of the whole field of penology in Canada. Where there is a dearth of knowledge, and hence little expert opinion, everyone becomes an expert!

Another gap in the efficient functioning of probation could be closed by a simple amendment to the Criminal Code and although this has been recommended by the Canadian Bar Association nothing has been done about it. In Canada, seasonal employment requires a certain mobility in the labour forces, thus it often become necessary for a probationer to be transferred from one jurisdiction to another. Sometimes the distance thus entailed can be considerable even within the confines of one province. If he violates his probation in the distant jurisdiction and further court proceedings are indicated, it can involve a very costly process. Sometimes to avoid the expense thus incurred, no action is taken. This in turn tends to bring both probation and the administration of justice into disrepute. Authority to transfer the case as well as the probationer in toto so that the distant court becomes solely seized of the case would save money and enhance the administration of justice. This move has been accomplished in other countries without ill effect.

In Ontario, probation had its inception and early growth in the juvenile courts. Through the demonstration of its usefulness in these courts, it gradually became acceptable in the criminal courts (ten county court judges and twenty-three magistrates also sit in juvenile court).

Following the enactment of the Juvenile Delinquent's Act (Canada) in 1908, the first juvenile court for Canada and Ontario was established at Ottawa on 24 July 1909; the Toronto juvenile court followed in 1912 but, in the interim, such courts had been established in Vancouver and Winnipeg. In the thirty-four years between 1908 and 1942, twenty-one juvenile courts were established in Ontario and, in the twenty-one years between 1942 and 1963, thirty more juvenile courts came into being giving a present total of fifty-one juvenile and family courts in Ontario which at the same time achieves total coverage of the province by these courts.

There are three separate methods by which a probation officer may be appointed in Ontario:
1. Under the Juvenile Delinquents' Act (Canada) such an officer may be appointed by the judge of a juvenile court;
2. Under the Juvenile and Family Court Act (Ontario) such an officer may be appointed by the Attorney General;
3. Under the Probation Act (Ontario) such an officer may be appointed by the Lieutenant Governor in Council.

The first two methods limit the probation officer to working in the specific juvenile and family court for which he is appointed and, under the second method he becomes a municipal employee; the third method makes the probation officer available to *all* courts (supreme, county, magistrate's and juvenile and family) in the county or district for which he is appointed and he becomes an employee of the provincial government, a civil servant. Recently, the Probation Act has been further amended so that officers thus appointed become probation officers "in and for the Province of Ontario" and the authority rests with the Attorney General for designation of specific areas.

At the present time there are 200 probation officers in Ontario; 160 of these are appointed under the Probation Act and are thus available to all courts; forty officers are appointed under the Juvenile and Family Courts Act and thus limited to the juvenile and family courts for which they are appointed (Ottawa and Toronto).

Significant once again of the dearth of knowledge about probation and hence its sparse use in Ontario are the following figures: from 1922, when the Probation Act was passed, until the end of 1952 — thirty-one years — only four areas had availed themselves of its provisions and there were thirteen probation officers serving the criminal courts of Ontario and they were stationed in Ottawa, Toronto, Hamilton and London.

There is a general lack of understanding about probation, of both its content and its function. So often one hears the term "probationary" officer used which is a complete misnomer; quite frequently, the terms probation and parole are glibly interchanged and substituted for each other with fine abandon! Probation comes *before* prison; parole comes *after* prison. Probation is a legal alternative to imprisonment and is a means whereby a convicted person serves a period *outside* of prison under supervision; parole is the means whereby a person is released *from* prison under supervision before completing the full prison sentence imposed by the court if he has behaved himself during the earlier part of his incarceration.

Probation derived from a Latin verb *probo* — to prove; you probate a will by bringing it into the right surroundings, a court, and proving it; you probate a person by helping that person to get into the right surroundings where he will have a chance to prove himself. Parole is derived from the French term *parole d'honneur*, word of honour, which was a means of releasing a martial prisoner during the One Hundred Years' War.

The National Parole Board has jurisdiction over any adult inmate serving a sentence under any federal statute in either a federal or provincial institution. It has no jurisdiction over a child under the Juvenile Delinquents' Act (Canada), or an inmate serving a sentence for a breach of a provincial statue, e.g., Liquor Control Act. In Ontario and British Columbia, provincial parole boards have jurisdiction to grant parole for the "indeterminate" or "indefinite" portion of any sentence if such is imposed by the court.

The National Parole Board has jurisdiction to revoke or suspend any sentence of corporal punishment, or any order made under the Criminal Code prohibiting a person from operating a motor vehicle.

In countries which have a well-rounded penal system, the number of people granted probation exceeds the number of people granted parole by a ratio of about seven to one. In many enlightened countries the use of probation has become society's first line of defence in dealing with the criminal element.

In Great Britain (England and Wales) in 1953, there were 18 000 people in prison on 31 December and there were 49 911 people on probation and 6 512 people on parole on 31 December. Neither Canada nor Ontario have developed their probation or parole services to a point there this is possible.

Indeed, it is very doubtful whether there were 12 000 adult people on probation and parole in Canada even on 31 December 1961, although there were many more people sentenced to prison than in Great Britain, even though our population is only one-third as large.

In 1953, Great Britain sent 34 000 people to prison and Canada sent 98 000 people to prison! In order to make probation the first line of society's defence against the criminal element in Ontario, so that as many people could be placed on probation each year as are sent to prison, as is the case in Great Britain, it would be necessary to double the staff of probation officers devoting their time entirely to the criminal courts of the province. A decade would then have to elapse before the prison population could be substantially reduced to the point where some penal institutions could be closed. That probation makes for better law enforcement than prison by reclaiming a greater percentage of persons permanently as useful citizens, that it accomplishes this at a far smaller financial expenditure than through the procedure of prison, are both recognized and accepted facts. It is hardly necessary . . . to mention the intangible but very real humane values accruing to probation that are impossible through the venue of imprisonment. Probation in the juvenile and the criminal courts has two main facets: the pre-sentence report and supervision. After a finding of delinquency or guilt is registered, the court may then order a pre-sentence report before pronouncing sentence. It is greatly to be desired that the court would make use of this facet for, without it, probation must inevitably be harmed. It is very doubtful whether any court would refuse the request of defence counsel for such a report. It is, therefore, very disturbing to realize that many lawyers are not cognizant that such a facet is available to their clients! This is even more puzzling when it is further realized than in nine cases out of ten, such a report has a mitigating influence upon sentence! This pre-sentence report is actually a social history of the person before the court. The accepted modern theory of penal punishment is, as the late Lord Samuel stated, "The disposition of a case should fit the *character of the criminal* not less than the character of the crime."

Upon conviction, the court knows the character of the crime and through the medium of the pre-sentence report it comes to know the character of the criminal. It is devoutly to be wished that no one would be placed on probation without the guidance such a report supplies. The pre-sentence report to the judge is the same as the X-ray and the scalpel to the surgeon. No physician would prescribe medicine or treatment without a diagnosis and yet, in England, where they have had probation for over fifty years, difficulty is still encountered in getting some judges to make use of the pre-sentence report. This perversity is hard to understand. It perhaps accounts for R.M. Jackson's remark in *The Machinery of Justice in England*: "An English criminal trial, properly conducted, is one of the best products of our law, providing you walk out of court before the sentence is given; if you stay to the end, you may find that it takes far less time and inquiry to settle a man's prospects in life than it has taken to find out whether he took a suitcase out of a parked motor car." The pre-sentence report supplies guidance to the probation officer for the conduct of the probation period as well as assisting the court to reach an equitable and just disposition of the case. Another fallacy that is quite common is the proposition that only matters advantageous to the convicted person should appear in this report. *All* possible facts pro and con should be entered into such a report for precisely the same reasons that *all* facts are used during the trial.

Further, it should be remembered, especially by counsel, that the report is prepared by an officer of the court who must by the very nature of his work and position remain objective and impartial. His opinion as to disposition is given only if requested by the court. (The officer should always have a "plan" for the probation period in case such information is requested by the court).

The pre-sentence report should be available to counsel for the Crown and to counsel for the defence, as well as to the bench (if there is no defence counsel then it should be read to the convicted person), in order that all parties concerned may have an opportunity to agree or disagree with its contents.

Anything of an adverse nature to the convicted person *must* be made known to him before sentence is passed so that he may have the opportunity of questioning such material if he so desires! Any procedure less than this brings us perilously close to "star chamber" justice. The material in this report is in the general nature of character evidence and therefore does not have to be proved with the same weight as evidence leading to conviction or acquittal; it is, however, essential that it should be open to "the purifying crucible of cross-examination."

The court now decides whether it will order the convicted person fined, incarcerated or placed on probation. If he is to be placed on probation, the *passing* of sentence is "suspended" and the convicted person signs a recognizance to abide by such conditions as the court lays down for the conduct of his life during the period of probation. Note well at this juncture that the court may only delegate its authority in this regard specifically — not generally, such terms as "to faithfully obey the directions of the probation officer as to his conduct and mode of life during the probation period" have been held not valid: such terms as "he will be in his own home by ten o'clock every evening and remain there until he goes to work the following morning" are valid.

In the drawing of these conditions, the only safe guide the court has is the material in the pre-sentence report. Unless the conditions of the recognizance are realistic, it is very probable that the probationer will fail in fulfilling them. They can only be realistic if the court has a thorough knowledge of the convicted persons' background. Failure by the bench to appreciate this point has led to some very bizarre "conditions."

In Britain, in the early days of probation, such "conditions" as the following appeared: for creating a disturbance in a theatre, an eighteen-year-old boy was forbidden to enter any theatre for three years; for stealing a package of cigarettes, a nineteen-year-old youth was forbidden to smoke for two years; a man and a woman, both in their late twenties, who had been courting for eight years, were placed on probation for two years for a first offence of "attempted break and entry," and they were ordered not to speak to each other during the two-year probation period; inside of three months they were married to each other!

Quite recently, in a large Ontario city, a . . . [man], about thirty-eight years old, was placed on probation for a year after a conviction for theft. As in the above cases, no pre-sentence report was ordered by the court. The probationer reported to the senior probation officer of that area immediately upon his release from custody. This experienced officer, while taking the probationer's initial social history, asked him if he had ever been in trouble with the law before. The rather vehement denial aroused some doubt in the officer's mind. As the man was not working, he was asked to report back after lunch. Within an hour, the officer learned that the probationer had three previous criminal convictions, two of a serious nature, and that he was in arrears of over $2000 on a support order drawn by the family court of that area for the support of his children, having made no attempt to make any payments for three years.

Due to an oversight, these matters were not called to the attention of the bench; in fact, it was stated in court that he was the first offender. In addition to this, it was ascertained that he was an inveterate alcoholic. As might be expected, he violated the terms of his recognizance within a few weeks and was returned to court and sentenced on his original offence and credited a failure of the probation system. The court could have had the above information had it requested a pre-sentence report.

Further, in the last two years, the Appellate Court of Ontario has had to order eight pre-sentence reports which were not originally ordered by the trial courts and, in six of these cases, in the light of the pre-sentence report, the appeals have been allowed and probation substituted for prison sentences. In two of these cases the prison sentences were for "two years less one day definite . . . ."

The pre-sentence report may constitute about 10 percent of the probation officer's work but it is the lifeblood of probation without which probation becomes haphazard in many cases and even dangerous in others!

When a person is released on probation, the second facet comes into play, namely, *supervision*. This supervision is probably the most exacting of all social work because it is social work undertaken in an authoritarian setting: terms that as recently as a decade ago were held to be mutually exclusive. If the probationer abides by the terms of his recognizance, the probation officer becomes his friend and counsellor; if he violates those terms, the probation officer has a mandatory duty to report such violation to the court. It then rests with the court whether or not the probationer will be charged with a violation. This is another "danger point" in a developing probation system, especially in the adult offender field.

If the courts, through lack of interest or through overwork, fail to hold hearings on such violations, then the whole system is undermined and weakened. If the probationer is charged with a violation and found guilty, then he becomes liable to the penalty which could have been imposed for the original offence. In other words, the suspended sentence may now descend. However, the court can, if it wishes, extend or vary the terms of probation and continue the probation period. If the violation is constituted through the commission of another overt offence, then any penalty imposed for the violation must be *consecutive* to the penalty for the recent offence. (It would be most helpful if the Criminal Code contained a similar provision to the Probation Act (Ontario) for a violation of probation — a fifty-dollar fine.)

If the probationer completes the period of probation successfully, he is completely discharged but the conviction remains on his record — if the conviction was under the Code. As stated earlier, if the offence charged is against a provincial statute in Ontario, the offender may be placed on probation without conviction. It was no doubt to obviate the stigma of a "record" that the legislators formulated this procedure. It is unfortunate that it has not been implemented by the courts, at least in selected cases.

Much thought and discussion has occurred during the past decade as to whether a person with a criminal record should, after five years of subsequent good behaviour, be allowed the expunging of that record. Perhaps some such provision is needed in the Criminal Code. This is dealt with in England by the procedure of an "unconditional discharge" for first offenders and thus obviates a "record." It hardly seems just that after a man has paid his debt to society he should be punished for the rest of his life. We make the proud claim that, under our system, when a man has paid his debt to society he is a free man. This, of course, is an unconscious hypocrisy on our part. He is not "free" and he really begins to pay his debt to society the day the prison gates swing open. Any person who has tried to help a man with a "record" get employment is made only too aware of this! It is felt by many authorities that this situation contributes greatly to our problem of recidivism in Canada.

The work of the probation officer in family court differs from his work in the juvenile or criminal court. Invariably, he enters the scene in marital conflicts before any charges are preferred and his efforts are directed along the line of counselling, an attempt to help the parties resolve their difficulties without recourse to court action.

If court action is necessary, theoretically his task is at an end in these cases. Unfortunately it does not work out that way in practice! The writer knows of one family case that has been carried on probation files for twenty-five years. Every so often the embattled couple flare into open conflict and both run to the probation office so that they may be the first one to recount their own side of the argument. After several interviews they appear pacified and content for several more months; the spirit could be willing for separation but perhaps the flesh is weak! Good probation staff should be able to prevent about seven out of every ten family cases from going to trial.

In 1961 there were 9980 convicted adults on probation in Ontario, considerably more than in the rest of Canada for any other given year. Each one of these people was costing the taxpayers sixty cents a day for probation rather than four dollars a day for prison; they were supporting their own families, thus saving public expenditure through relief and mothers' allowances; they paid $49 000 in restitution; they poured over $18 000 000 of earnings back into the national economy and there is a far better chance that they will be reclaimed permanently as useful citizens through probation rather than prison!

In 1961 there were also 5226 juveniles on probation in Ontario costing the taxpayer sixty cents a day rather than four dollars and fifty cents a day for training school. The probation officers also counselled over 17 300 family disputes in 1961 without the subsequent necessity of them going to trial, which usually means a permanently broken home. Over $3 000 000 was collected on behalf of deserted wives and children in the province in 1961. It must be stressed that with the above "case loads" the present probation staff is working with a maximum load. Any further developments will require an expansion of probation personnel.

Quo Vadis?

The basic thinking of the Archambault Commission and the Fauteux Committee could be summed up as follows — in Canada, in matters penological, equity can only reside in unity. We must be sure that exactly the same facilities are available to deal with an offender in Prince Rupert as there are in St. John's. Then, and only then, can we safely state from a penological viewpoint, that there is equality for all offenders in Canada.

This will require a major move that was sensed by the Archambault commissioners but completely overlooked by the Fauteux Committee. In essence their argument was as follows: there are four main elements in a country's penal system, its courts (and all that leads up to the courts), its probation system, its prisons, and its parole system. In Canada the courts are set up uniformly by the Criminal Code; the Canadian government has never hesitated to legislate upon prisons and reformatories (although the latter do not belong to them); and there is a Canadian parole system. Thus these three elements of the penal system are all legislated upon in a uniform fashion by the central government. Even greater uniformity will be achieved when federal prisons receive every offender who receives a sentence in excess of six months, a present commitment. However, up to this time, probation has been left at provincial level. If each province had a probation system, there would be ten different types of gasoline flowing into this "penological Cadillac" and hence there would be ten *different* performances. Thus the basic philosophy of the two reports — unity — would still be obviated.

Unfortunately there are several provinces where there will never be probation systems until financial help is forthcoming from Ottawa. Thus it becomes apparent that in order to have equity in our penal system there *must* be a national Probation Act.

At one time it was argued that this was not constitutionally possible. Without going into the merits of this argument pro and con, it is sufficient to state that several years ago Ottawa decided that it was quite constitutional and proper that they should legislate upon probation if they desired to do so, as indeed that have already legislated upon it in the Criminal Code. Having given legitimate birth to the child it seems a somewhat fatuous argument, to this layman's mind, to hold that the parent can have no say in the child's upbringing *providing he supports it!*

The writer envisages a "National Probation Act" in the form of permissive legislation with the smallest unit for which it can be proclaimed not less than a whole province, with considerable financial support (perhaps 51 percent) being paid by the central government. The probation systems could remain on the same administrative basis provincially as they presently are but would have to meet the standards set out in the "National Probation Act" in order to qualify for financial support under the Act. In turn the National Parole Board could quite easily and with good precedent become the "National Probation and Parole Board" and the officers could be termed probation and parole officers with equally good precedent. Indeed the Archambault Report of 1938 spelled this out quite clearly: "Probation Officers should be given supervision of prisoners who are released on ticket-of-leave and they should make the necessary investigations of persons with whom prisoners wish to communicate" (recommendation no. 73). Further, "The pay and duties of probation officers should be the subject of an agreement between the provincial and federal authorities" (recommendation no. 74). This arrangement would enable a far wider use of parole and would be the *most economical* method of developing the parole system. It would also put the operation of the National Parole Board on a non-charitable basis. At present the several provincial probation systems are performing a considerable task for the National Parole Board on a gratis basis: it is time that this work should be performed under a more business-like agreement!

From probation, the community lifeblood, so necessary to the success of a penal system, is poured into the three other elements of our penological system — courts, prisons and parole. To the courts probation provides the services of pre-sentence reporting and supervision of the probationer if required; to the prisons the pre-sentence report follows the offender as a social history which is essential to a practical system of classification in the prison — (some day it is going to be recognized that *all* inmates should arrive with an up-to-date social history even if a pre-sentence report has not been ordered for only thus can a classification system become efficient — when this day arrives it is very likely that the probation staffs will be called upon to perform this task); to the parole board the probation staffs supply pre-release reports and supervision of the parolee. It is essential that these services which supply this very vital community link should be uniform throughout the country.

Someday there will be a National Probation Act! Whether it comes sooner or later in point of time depends entirely upon the vision of our leaders!

The greatest need of probation at the present time and for the future is professional and public awareness, an awakening from the all-pervading apathy that made possible the committal of over 100 000 Canadians to prison in 1954!

If this article has a moral, it is a heartfelt plea that the legal profession will accept its share of the responsibility and support probation; that it will assist in interpreting probation to the general public. The day is not too far distant when the recommendations of the Archambault Commission (nos. 70, 71 and 72) and the Fauteux Committee will be a fait accompli, "that there should be a nation-wide system of trained probation officers in Canada."

The outspoken support of the public and of the legal profession in particular could hasten the advent of that day!

"Closing Penetanguishene Reformatory": An Attempt to Deinstitutionalize Treatment of Juvenile Offenders in Early Twentieth-Century Ontario†

ANDREW JONES

From 1882 to 1903, The Ontario Reformatory for Boys at Penetanguishene was an institution in decline. The clearest indication of this was the steady fall in the number of inmates, from 263 boys in 1882 to a mere 86 at the end of 1903.[1] In 1897, following a particularly sharp drop in numbers, the Inspector of Prisons and Public Charities, James Noxon, observed that "the same causes continuing to operate to the same extent, and in a few years the reformatory will be almost without occupants."[2] The point was not lost on the Ontario government. Believing at first that a major reason for the gradual reduction in the number of inmates was the unsuitability of its building and location, the province in 1900 set aside $80 000 for the construction of a new reformatory.[3] Concerns over the eventual cost of a new building and haggles as to where it should be located, however, led to delay, and prompted consideration of completely doing away with the reformatory, an alternative in the form of industrial schools being at hand. In 1903 this plan was adopted, and legislation was passed empowering the provincial government to abolish the reformatory and to transfer the inmates either to the central prison or industrial schools.[4] On 4 April 1904, by order in council, the Ontario Reformatory was officially closed down.

Although the means of disposition of the inmates of the reformatory was specified in the legislation, their placement presented a major short-term problem for provincial officials. An immediate addition of some one hundred boys to the industrial school population would have created serious problems of overcrowding, even with the extra allocation of $10 000 provided in the 1904 provincial budget to the industrial schools to meet the anticipated influx.[5] The problem was referred to J.J. Kelso, Superintendent of Neglected and Dependent Children for the province and Inspector of Industrial Schools.[6] A long-standing opponent of institutional care for delinquent or deprived children, Kelso put forward a radical solution. He proposed that his office assume the guardianship of all the boys at Penetanguishene, and undertake to provide them with foster homes or jobs. After some hesitation, the responsible provincial ministers agreed to Kelso's scheme and during February to April 1904 Kelso personally placed the reformatory boys in community situations. By

† *Ontario History* 70 (1978): 227–44.

May 1904 all the inmates of the reformatory had been released and were living with family, friends or foster parents in various parts of the province.

Kelso never doubted that his experiment would be successful, and in the short term his faith seemed to have been vindicated. Three years later he proudly reported that of the ninety-five boys who were in the reformatory in February 1904, only six subsequently had spent time in industrial schools and only three in the central prison.[7] To Kelso the 1904 amnesty was conclusive evidence that institutionalization of juvenile offenders was unnecessary and, indeed, harmful. In his 1905 annual report he claimed that, "the closing was a great success — so great that one feels like exulting in the possibilities opened up for future efforts with so-called incorrigible boys. Clearly it has been demonstrated that lads, however degraded, can be reclaimed and restored to good citizenship if only the right methods are used."[8] In a detailed, forty-page report on the closure he outlined the methods which had been used to place the boys and facilitate their adjustment to normal community living, and he expressed his hope that the report would "exercise a widespread educational influence." "If good people everywhere would direct their attention more than ever before to this neglected class of children there are illimitable opportunities for effective social service — service that will tell, not only in young lives saved to happy and useful careers, but, in the greater safety of the community from crime, and in greater economy in the administration of public institutions."[9]

The closing of Penetanguishene Reformatory is a very early example of an attempt to abolish institutions for juvenile offenders. It was the climax of a hotly contested debate over the most appropriate means of dealing with young offenders, carried on during the latter half of the nineteenth century in Ontario. In this paper the early history of Penetanguishene Reformatory will be briefly outlined, followed by an account of the three major reactions to the perceived ineffectiveness of the institution: reform of the reformatory, the industrial school movement, and the "home finding" movement led by J.J. Kelso. The events leading to the closure of the reformatory will be recounted in detail. Finally, the resurgence of institutional care of juvenile offenders in the years after 1904 will be outlined. Institutionalization of juvenile offenders in Ontario was merely thwarted, not ended, in 1904. In the form of industrial schools, boys' welfare homes, and training schools the incarceration of juvenile offenders has continued in the twentieth century.

Prior to 1859, children found guilty of criminal offences in Upper Canada served prison sentences at the provincial penitentiary at Kingston. This practice came under increasing criticism, and there was considerable pressure exerted on the government to establish a separate institution for children. In 1858 a decision finally was taken to establish two juvenile reformatories, one on the Isle aux Noix on the Richelieu River to serve Canada East, and the other near the village of Penetanguishene on Georgian Bay to serve Canada West. The first boys transferred to Penetanguishene arrived there in 1859.[10]

Penetanguishene was chosen as the site of the Upper Canada reformatory principally because of the availability of unused military barracks remaining from the defence of the upper Great Lakes in the war of 1812. The barracks were used as temporary accommodation until a new permanent building was completed circa 1866. During the 1860s the population of the reformatory steadily grew. There were only 40 boys in the original contingent of 1859, but by 1870 the reformatory had 193 inmates. This expansion reflected the high level of public confidence in the institution during the early years. However, the appointment of J.W. Langmuir as the first Inspector of Prisons, Asylums and Public Charities for Ontario in 1867 resulted in far closer public scrutiny of the reformatory's activities than had previously been undertaken. Langmuir performed his duties as inspector with thoroughness, and in his reports drew attention to the poor physical conditions of the reformatory, the tight security and rigid discipline imposed by the warden, the lack of educational facilities, and the arduous work routine imposed on the boys. The crux of his criticism was that the reformatory had become indistinguishable from an adult prison: "the appearance of the building is that of a prison; the interior construction is that of a prison; the discipline is that of a prison; the dress is that of convicts."[11] Faced with the intractable opposition of the warden of the reformatory to even minor reforms. Langmuir mounted a sustained but ineffective attack on the administration of the reformatory throughout the 1870s. The retirement of this warden in 1879, however, provided Langmuir with his opportunity. At Langmuir's behest, the provincial government in 1880 announced its intention to bring

> the management of the Reformatory for Boys at Penetanguishene more thoroughly in harmony with the original design and intention of such an institution. The system it is proposed to pursue is modelled on the improved method adopted at the most successful establishments of this kind elsewhere, and with the view of substituting for penal discipline treatment and influences of a strictly reformatory character.[12]

The reform of the reformatory was underway.

In 1880 Penetanguishene Reformatory was given a new charter and a new administrator. The name of the institution was changed by legislation from "reformatory prison" to "reformatory for boys," and the "warden" became a "superintendent."[13] The new appointee to the superintendency, Thomas McCrossan, was sent by Langmuir to visit some of the most modern reformatories in the United States prior to commencing his duties. Upon his return to Penetanguishene he set about the implementation of the long overdue reforms. Changes were made to the physical structure of the reformatory, most notably the substitution of two dormitories in place of individual cells and the provision of adequate bathing and heating facilities. Greater stress was placed on the education of the boys, and their working hours, which during the 1870s had been mainly spent in the manufacture of cigars, were now spent on more worthwhile tasks.[14] Langmuir insisted that the boys be given individual treatment and that all officials "exercise the greatest kindness, patience, forbearance and well-directed zeal in the performance of their duties."[15] McCrossan fully supported Langmuir's aims and within three years the reforms were well underway.

One immediate result was a marked increase in the number of boys committed to the reformatory. The police magistrates and judges showed their renewed confidence in the institution by sentencing a record 96 boys in 1881, and by the end of 1882 there were a record 263 boys at Penetanguishene. During the following decade the numbers declined somewhat, but in 1890 the population still numbered over 200 boys. Langmuir, however, had retired in 1881, and with him went the driving force for reform of the institution. The momentum of the 1880 reforms gradually slowed, and by the late 1880s the reformatory was once again coming under sharp criticism. Langmuir came out of retirement to chair the 1890 Royal Commission on the Prison and Reformatory System, and resumed his role as chief critic and reformer of the reformatory. The commissioners found that while the reformatory was "equal if not superior to any they had seen in the best institutions visited by them in the United States," it was, nevertheless, essentially a prison for boys. They recommended that it be moved to a more suitable location, that it be reorganized into a number of smaller "cottages," and that its atmosphere be changed from that of a prison to a school. The commissioners also proposed that boys should be sentenced to the reformatory for an indeterminate period so that a boy "by his industry, his diligence, and general good conduct" had the opportunity to secure an early release.[16]

The release of the Royal Commission's findings in 1891 began a period of great difficulty for the administrators of the reformatory. Although they believed strongly in the efficacy of their institution as a reforming agency, they were nevertheless aware that there were some grounds for criticism of the system. McCrossan's annual reports repeatedly drew attention to the constraints within which he and his staff were working. A recurring theme was the unsuitability of the physical structure. "Our building is not up-to-date and it could not be made so without tearing down the building completely," he told the Ontario Conference on Child Saving in 1894.[17] A further concern was the administrative difficulty associated with the release of a boy for good behaviour before his term was complete. In most cases reliance had to be placed on the pardoning power, a prerogative of the federal government. Applications to Ottawa for pardons were subject to considerable delays and were by no means automatically granted; allegedly this "caused the boys to become disheartened and distrustful of the sincerity of the officers of the Reformatory."[18] In report after report, McCrossan called for the pardoning power to be granted to the provincial government.[19] Apart from these matters, however, McCrossan and his staff felt that most of the criticism levelled against them was unfair or mistaken. McCrossan's reports stressed the religious, educational and industrial training the boys were receiving, and the high ideals of the reformatory.[20] He frequently complained that outsiders still were judging the reformatory as if the reforms of 1880 had not been undertaken.[21] The Protestant chaplain at the reformatory, Reverend Stephen Card, had no doubts regarding the value of the work: "my experience here for six years fully satisfies me that the best thing that can be done with an incorrigible or a criminal boy is to send him for a term of from two to five years to this Reformatory. The remedy is severe, but in most cases it is effective."[22]

Throughout the 1890s, the number of inmates steadily declined. This reflected in part the unwillingness of magistrates to commit boys to the institution, in view of the criticism it had received. However, the declining numbers also reflected an attempt by McCrossan to stem criticism by placing many of the boys as apprentices, and by obtaining pardons for those who showed good behaviour. Between 1893 and 1902 McCrossan placed sixty-four boys as apprentices, and despite the administrative difficulties, obtained pardons for 272 boys. Altogether, almost 60 percent of those committed during this period were apprenticed or pardoned before finishing their sentences.[23] However, the reformatory received little or no praise for this. Indeed, by thus reducing the number of boys, it drew even greater criticism. Ever since the 1860s the maintenance costs had caused concern, and now that the inmate population was rapidly declining, this issue again came to the fore. The total annual expenditure of the reformatory in the late 1890s was around $30 000, a yearly cost per boy of between $230 and $250. This was considered by many to be excessive, and the provincial government came under pressure to reduce the appropriation for the institution.[24] This presented a dilemma for McCrossan. He pointed out in his report for 1897 that "given that the rate per capita is seemingly the standard in respect to efficiency and good management one might be tempted to criminally overlook, or rather ignore, the claims of the meritorious and thus lead to their detention until the termination of sentence."[25] Although McCrossan claimed to have resisted the temptation of such "unholy action," the provincial government was unsympathetic to his difficulties. In 1898 the reformatory was forced to cut back on staff and limit fuel supply in an effort to reduce costs. By 1900 the provincial government's intention to close the reformatory was plain, and in 1903 those who had hoped to reform the reformatory were forced to concede political defeat. The faith of McCrossan and his colleagues in the value of their work was, however, undiminished. In his final report, McCrossan concluded that "we can comfort ourselves with the reflection that notwithstanding all our disabilities and drawbacks . . . a decided majority of our past inmates, who are still in the flesh, are leading honest and useful lives."[26] Reverend Card was more forthright:

> I point with proud satisfaction to the fact, unchallenged and undeniable, that with all our discouragements and limitations, seventy five per cent of the boys and young men committed to the Provincial Reformatory have been reformed. In all fairness, all reasonable persons ought to be satisfied with this showing, for we can neither work miracles nor cast out devils.[27]

The main criticisms levelled at the Penetanguishene Reformatory during the 1890s were that its location and physical layout were unsuitable, that its educational and other training facilities were inadequate, and that the administratively awkward pardoning procedures deterred individual reforms.[28] On this last point the administrators of the reformatory were in complete agreement with their critics, and repeatedly advocated change. With regard to the criticisms of their educational and training facilities they were in partial accord, claiming lack of funds as their excuse. Concerning location and layout they also agreed that their buildings were in many ways unsuited to the task of reforming boys, but nevertheless claimed that the "dormitory system" of the reformatory was preferable to the more fashionable "cottage system."[29] This last question was the only major matter of principle which distinguished McCrossan from his major critics, most of whom in the 1890s shared his belief that in certain circumstances institutionalization of delinquent children was necessary. Most of these critics were associated with the industrial schools movement.

The first school in Ontario was established by the Industrial Schools Association in Toronto in 1887. Named the Victoria Industrial School for Boys, it admitted some fifty boys during its first year of operation. In 1892 the Alexandra Industrial School for Girls was opened in Toronto, followed later in the decade by the St. John's School for Catholic Boys in East Toronto, and the St. Mary's School for Catholic Girls. By 1894 there were almost two hundred children resident in the province's industrial schools. The schools were developed as an alternative means of treating neglected and delinquent children; their rapid development in the early 1890s was a major factor in the declining intake of the Penetanguishene Reformatory.[30]

The industrial schools differed from the reformatory in structure, clientele and sentencing provisions. Although in structure they resembled the reformatory in that they were residential, custodial institutions, their internal organization was distinctive. Central to the concept of the industrial schools was the "cottage system," in which the children resided "in a cottage home, under the care of a matron and guard" who acted as "mother" and "father" of the "family."[31] Within each of these "cottages" the boys were taught housekeeping tasks, attended day and Sunday school, were trained in trades, and took part in drill and sports. This system was viewed as a highly significant advance in children's institutions, representing the most modern thinking and practice.

The clientele of the industrial schools differed from the reformatory with respect to both age and offence. After 1890 it was established by legislation that no child below the age of thirteen could be sentenced to the reformatory, and it was laid down that offenders in this younger age group should be sent to the industrial schools. Some magistrates, particularly in rural areas, ignored this provision and continued to send nine, ten and eleven year old boys to the reformatory.[32] But generally the age distinction was maintained. As well as being younger, children sent to the industrial schools were sentenced on somewhat different charges. Underlying the industrial school movement was a strong belief that neglected children were potentially delinquent children, and that society therefore had a responsibility to take preventative action to save both the child and the community from the likely consequences of neglect. Therefore, the legislation under which the industrial schools were established provided that children could be sent to the schools not only for committing crimes but also in circumstances in which there was evidence of neglect.[33] Similar concerns underlay the terms under which a child was sentenced to the industrial schools. After 1900 all children committed to industrial schools were given indeterminate sentences, the timing of their release being based solely on an assessment of their potential to lead honest, upright lives.[34] Once committed to an industrial school, a child automatically remained under the guardianship of the school until reaching eighteen years of age. In this way it was hoped to prevent graduates from the schools from drifting into crime before attaining adulthood.

The industrial schools were perceived by their supporters as more progressive, up-to-date, humane, and effective institutions for the reform of delinquents and "predelinquents" than the Ontario Reformatory, and they welcomed the reformatory's demise. However, despite their differences, the industrial schools and Ontario Reformatory shared an "institutional" approach to the treatment of young offenders. Both believed, in the words of D.J. McKinnon, Superintendent of the Victoria Industrial School, that "the quickest and safest way" to reform a young offender was "to put him in some well disciplined institution where every boy must obey."[35] The 1903 statute proposing the transfer of the reformatory boys to the industrial school was based on a recognition of this similarity. The "home finding" movement, under the leadership of J.J. Kelso, presented an alternative and a challenge to both systems.

Although the industrial schools were successfully challenging the Ontario Reformatory during the 1890s, their own position and methods were in turn under attack. From the mid–1880s there was widespread interest in Ontario in the foster home method of caring for neglected children, which had been practised by a number of public authorities and private societies in the United States since the 1870s. The Ontario Royal Commission of 1890 spoke approvingly of the foster home system, and although its central recommendation was an extension of the industrial schools, it did recommend that wherever possible industrial school children should be placed "in a private family, either as apprentices or boarders." The formation of the Toronto Children's Aid Society in 1891, an organization deeply interested in the foster home method, gave further impetus to the movement to care for neglected children in family settings. This movement achieved success in 1893 when the provincial government passed the Children's Protection Act establishing foster homes as an official means of caring for neglected and dependent children, alongside the industrial school system.[36] The Act also provided for the establishment of children's aid societies throughout the province, with wide powers to take neglected children into their custody and place them in foster homes. To implement the new policy, the Act created a new official position, the Superintendent of Neglected and Dependent Children. J.J. Kelso was appointed to this position in July 1893.[37]

From 1893, therefore, the industrial schools and the reformatory had to compete with the children's aid societies for jurisdiction over juvenile offenders and those children considered potential offenders. The challenge had an immediate impact on the industrial schools. Between 1894 and 1897 their population declined from 196 to 168; in the same period 603 children were provided with foster homes by the children's aid societies. Kelso had no hesitation in attributing the decline in the industrial school enrolment to "the popularity of the Children's Aid movement, and the simplicity and economy of newer methods." In 1894 he raised the question "whether many of the boys now in our industrial schools and some in the reformatory would not do better in a good foster home, and be better prepared there for the real work of life than they could possibly be in the best reform school ever established?"[38] By 1897 he was clear and adamant that "the homefinding movement is recognized . . . to be the only true and correct principle in dealing with dependent youth. Many children who would formerly have been committed to the industrial schools for a term of years are now happily provided for without that necessity." He described the industrial schools as institutions "where no permanent attachments can be formed, and where the highest incentives to nobility of life and conduct are lacking."[39]

Kelso's criticisms of the industrial schools brought him into conflict with the members of the Industrial Schools Association, several of whom had been Kelso's colleagues in reform work since the mid–1880s. He was accused of having "flopped over from being an advocate of the schools to becoming an opponent,"[40] a charge not without substance as Kelso had strongly supported the establishment of industrial schools prior to his appointment as superintendent. Kelso responded to this criticism by moderating his opposition to the industrial schools during the late 1890s. In 1899 he affirmed that the industrial schools were filling a "very necessary and important place in the general work of child saving. There will always be children who have been neglected too long and for whom a course of training is necessary before they can be placed in family homes. There are, too, children who are guilty of repeated offences and as a punishment their temporary commitment is decided upon."[41] In his official reports as inspector of industrial schools, Kelso lavished praise on the staff of the schools, stressing their "motives of compassion and love," and expressing the view that they were "fully in touch with child life."[42] However, despite these basic expressions of support, Kelso did not attempt to disguise his basic antipathy towards all forms of institutionalization of children. He continued to criticize certain features of the industrial schools, such as the grey and red uniforms worn at the Victoria Industrial School: "however successfully disguised it may be, the distinctive dress is a prison badge; the boys realize this, and it is a stumbling block in their reformation."[43] He also expressed concern with the lack of supervision of children after they left the industrial school, and with the continued association of a child at the schools with his "former companions in wrongdoing."[44] When the number of children in the industrial schools rose to 246 at the end of 1901, Kelso resumed his stance of strong opposition to the schools: "the natural tendencies of all institutions is to increase both in size and numbers, but there should be a constant effort put forth to decrease the number of those who have to be placed under restraint and discipline."[45]

Between 1893 and 1900 Kelso paid comparatively little attention to the issue of the future of Penetanguishene Reformatory, appearing to be far more concerned with the problems posed by the industrial schools. This was understandable given that the schools overlapped more closely with his responsibilities for neglected children, and that he was officially responsible for their annual inspection. However, as criticism of the reformatory grew in the late 1890s Kelso once again directed his attention to that institution. In 1898, together with the warden of the Central Prison in Toronto, he became involved in a scheme, almost certainly illegal, to intercept children before they were sent to the reformatory. Despite the legislation of 1890 prohibiting the sentencing of boys under thirteen to the reformatory, many magistrates in rural districts continued this practice throughout the 1890s and into the twentieth century. They were encouraged in this practice by the fact that the upkeep of the reformatory was the responsibility of the provincial government only, whereas the municipalities were required to pay two dollars per week for the upkeep of any child sent to an industrial school.[46] Kelso drew attention to the magistrates' violation of the law in his annual reports, but the committals of underage boys continued unabated. Late in the decade an opportunity arose to intervene. Boys from the country who were sentenced to Penetanguishene usually were brought first to Toronto, where they spent some weeks in the Central Prison before being conveyed to the reformatory. The warden of Central Prison frequently contacted Kelso to come and see his "kindergarten class," and the two officials agreed to combine efforts to keep these young boys from the reformatory. In 1898 two boys, one nine and one eleven, under sentence to five years in the reformatory, were unofficially removed from the Central Prison by Kelso with the warden's approval and placed in farm homes. Kelso "waited with baited breath. . . but no one showed the least concern or even inquired as to what had become of the children." Over the next four years Kelso claimed to have intercepted over forty boys in this way.[47] By 1902 the practice had come to official attention, and Superintendent McCrossan complained about Kelso's interceptions in his annual report.[48] However, by this time it had virtually been decided that the reformatory would be closed, and although the provincial Attorney General was asked to stop Kelso's actions, he "kindly consented to shut his eyes as to what was going on."[49]

The 1903 announcement of the provincial government's intention to close Penetanguishene Reformatory presented Kelso and the "home finders" with an ideal opportunity to prove the superiority of their methods over all forms of institutionalization of children. For if the boys at Penetanguishene, allegedly the most incorrigible juvenile criminals in the province, could be restored to good citizenship without resort to institutions, of what further use were any institutions for juvenile offenders? Given this chance, Kelso pressed hard to be given the responsibility for the placement of the reformatory boys. When informed by the Inspector of Prisons, James Noxon, in late 1903 that the task was his, Kelso immediately began work on the assignment. His first step was to gather as much information as possible on each of the hundred or so boys remaining in the institution. He wrote letters to constables, parents, and friends of the boys in their home towns, and visited Penetanguishene to review the whole situation and discuss the prospects of each boy with reformatory officials. On the basis of the information gathered, he compiled special history forms for each boy.[50]

By February 1904 there were only eighty-seven boys left in the reformatory, as a number whose terms were nearing completion had been allowed to leave. In that month Kelso began to visit Penetanguishene regularly to begin the process of releasing the boys. He began by privately interviewing each of the boys "to inspire them with absolute confidence in the new policy and to secure their loyalty in the plans that were about to be made for them."[51] Kelso recounted that he stressed to each boy that his liberation was a matter of personal favour and responsibility, that he would be fully trusted and helped, and that he would always have a friend to whom he could turn.

> This promise and this appeal made a deep impression. In some cases tears flowed down their cheeks at the thought of somebody being willing to trust them and to give them an opportunity to show that they were not entirely lost to the sense of goodness and honour. . . .With all these boys, each with his own broken life and early misfortunes to contend against, it was impossible not to sympathize deeply, and these touching interviews gave an added incentive to help and befriend them.[52]

Each time Kelso visited Penetanguishene he conducted five or six of these interviews, beginning with those boys whose families or relatives had indicated willingness to have the boy returned home. During February and March approximately twenty-five such boys were sent home. Attention was then directed towards boys who were acquainted with farm life and willing to accept situations in the country. This comprised the majority of the remaining boys. Next, a number of city boys were found suitable jobs and lodging in Toronto or elsewhere, and finally the most difficult cases were given special consideration. On 5 May Kelso informed J.M. Gibson, the Attorney General, that all the boys had been removed from the reformatory, and that each boy was being closely supervised, and that his progress would be followed for at least one year. Kelso explained that his aim was to "thoroughly interest the boys in their own reclamation and rehabilitation in good society, first of all by showing them kindness and friendship, dressing them well, and drawing out their self-respect, letting them feel that someone was interested in them, and providing them with good surroundings and employment."[53] He drew Gibson's attention particularly to the point that as yet none of those released had been apprehended by the police for committing any offence.

Kelso's claim that he was exercising close supervision over the released boys was not exaggerated. When each group of five or six boys was released they were first brought to Toronto by train, where they were met by Kelso, provided with a good supper, and shown around the city. Before being sent off to their new homes, the boys were provided with a valise, extra clothing, a Bible, and stamped envelopes so that they could write to Kelso of their progress. Kelso's log book on the boys shows that he maintained contact with some of them up to six years later. Correspondence was also kept up with the boys' employers or foster parents for over twelve months after the closure.[54] In almost all cases, according to Kelso, the reports of the boys' progress were favourable, and it was not until late November that any boy got into any trouble with the police.

"Personally I regard the part I have had in bringing about these results as the greatest pleasure in life," Kelso wrote in December 1904 of his work in closing the reformatory.[55] His enthusiasm was shared by Gibson who expressed "extreme satisfaction" with the job that had been done, and described the results as being "of more than ordinary significance and importance." Support also came from Inspector Noxon, the other senior government official involved in the closure. Noxon's support was particularly valuable in April 1904 when a query was received from the acting Under-Secretary of State in the federal government about the general release of the inmates of Penetanguishene Reformatory. As recently as November 1903 the Ottawa authorities had refused to grant pardons to several of the boys in the reformatory, and they were in consequence anxious to have the new policy clarified. Noxon wrote a soothing, and not altogether frank, reply stating that subsequent to the closing of the reformatory it had been decided "to select a number of the best behaved youths for situations that were freely offered."[56] No further queries were received from Ottawa.

Not everyone shared Noxon's and Gibson's favourable evaluation of the release of the boys. Although Kelso stated that he had received good co-operation from the officials of the reformatory, they were very skeptical of the wholesale release. McCrossan expressed his doubts concerning the scheme in a letter to Noxon: "Of course the best possible has been and is being done for all the lads; yet I am not over hopeful that the majority of them will stay where placed. I will indeed be pleased should the future show that my fears have been groundless."[57] Kelso noted that nearly all the opposition to the undertaking came from officials whose business it was to deal with criminals, a matter he attributed to their "constant association with the derelicts of society which has evidently made them thoroughly pessimistic."[58] The other group which expressed concern about the release of the reformatory boys were the industrial school administrators. In mid-April the superintendent of Victoria Industrial School wrote an angry letter to Kelso complaining that he had purchased extra furniture to the value of several hundred dollars on the understanding that at least twenty boys from Penetanguishene would be sent to the school. "Personally, I was never anxious to have the management of the boys from Penetanguishene," he wrote, "But once it had been settled that they should come here, and preparation for their accommodation having been made, then I think in all fairness to the school they should be sent here." Kelso's reply showed no concern for the predicament of the industrial schools. Hardly surprising given the effort he expended in keeping the ex-reformatory boys away from the industrial school's control.[59]

As a result of his experience with the boys from the Penetanguishene Reformatory, Kelso's belief in the reforming power of good homes and kindly influences was in 1904 at its highest point ever. "There is only one way of reforming a boy," he wrote in December 1905,

> and that is by securing his friendship, his goodwill, his
> co-operation. . . .Get into friendly sympathetic relationship with the boy,
> learn his wishes and aspirations, show that you trust and believe him, visit
> and encourage him from time to time, and if he fails to respond you can
> put it down that he is deficient and that his proper place is in an asylum
> for the feeble-minded. Normal boys like to be regarded as rational human
> beings and they have a great depth of loyalty for the man who knows how
> to treat them right and rely upon their honor.[60]

Kelso was convinced after his experiences with the boys from Penetanguishene that "large and expensive institutions are not indispensible in dealing with homeless or delinquent youth. By proper organization and a helpful and sympathetic attitude on the part of good people, it is possible to readjust these unfortunate children in society in such a manner as to avoid long institutional confinement while at the same time ensuring for the children a happier and better environment."[61]

The hopes of the "home finders" that the experimental release of the boys from Penetanguishene would lead to the closing of all institutions for juvenile offenders in the province were boosted when in 1905 Kelso was requested to similarly dispose of the inmates of the Mercer Industrial Refuge for Girls. The refuge had been established in Toronto in 1879 as an institution for young female offenders and young girls who were considered potentially delinquent. Most of the seventy or so girls in the refuge were committed on account of parental neglect or for vagrancy, immoral or disorderly conduct, or prostitution. After the passage of the 1893 Children's Protection Act, and the establishment of the first industrial school for girls in 1891, the refuge assumed a role similar to that of the reformatory for boys in that it served the older population of delinquent and neglected children. In the late 1890s and early 1900s most of the girls in the institution were committed between the ages of sixteen and eighteen. The refuge stressed educational aims and instruction in domestic matters, and an active system of apprenticeship was pursued. Nevertheless, the institution's work was hindered by poor facilities and its location adjoining the adult women's prison. It was decided in 1905 that the refuge should be closed, and Kelso supervised the placing of some forty girls in foster homes and other situations. Once again he was able to report that this method was in most cases successful.[62]

The closing of the refuge did not, however, result in pressure for further closures of juvenile institutions. The legislation which abolished the Penetanguishene Reformatory also extended the age at which a child could be committed to an industrial school from fourteen to sixteen, and despite Kelso's apparent success in placing juvenile offenders in foster homes, magistrates now began to commit to the industrial schools children who formerly would have been sent to the reformatory. In the year after the reformatory was closed, the number of children in the industrial schools jumped from 267 to 320, and the remainder of the decade saw a continuing steady increase in the industrial school population, which reached 545 by 1911.[63] This last figure can be compared with the 442 children resident in the reformatory, refuge and industrial schools combined in 1901. In effect, the industrial schools had taken over the functions previously performed by the reformatory and the refuge.

Kelso's attitude to this resurgence of institutionalization of juvenile offenders was surprisingly equivocal. His annual reports from 1904 onwards continued to state that the industrial schools were doing a "necessary work in the training of wayward children," and in 1907 he went so far as to claim an 80 percent success rate for the schools.[64] His opposition to the industrial schools may have been moderated by the fact that the schools were between 1904 and 1910 sending approximately one third of their children to foster homes or farms under apprenceticeship arrangements. Kelso regularly called for the continuation and further extension of this practice.[65]

Although he thus seemed to accept, with reluctance, a continuing role for the industrial schools, Kelso still found plenty to criticise in their operation. Some of his themes were by now well worn, such as the danger of crowding delinquent children together in the same building, and the need to remove a child completely from his former harmful environment.[66] He also objected to the per capita method of funding the industrial schools, which he described as "fundamentally wrong, ignoring as it does the policy of prevention, and putting a premium on the accumulation of inmates."[67] The tendency for magistrates to commit children as young as eight, nine and ten to the industrial schools also raised his ire. Most of his criticism in this period, however, was directed towards the steadily deteriorating conditions within the industrial schools which, as their population grew, began to suffer from chronic overcrowding. Some extensions were made to the schools' buildings between 1904 and 1916, but these lagged far behind the increasing number of inmates. In 1916 Kelso estimated that the 558 industrial school children in the province were being maintained in accommodation which at most should accommodate 400 children, and he stressed that this was a severe impediment to the work of the schools.[68]

This concern over deteriorating conditions led Kelso in 1913 to a position directly contrary to his stance in 1904. In his annual report in that year he advocated the establishment of a new reformatory for youths aged sixteen to twenty-one years. His concern was that the presence of older boys in the industrial schools was making it impossible for the school to meet the needs of the younger boys, particularly in a situation where some of the cottages were operating at twice the desirable capacity. He reaffirmed his belief that young boys should not be kept in institutions for long periods, but adopted a different attitude to older, "more hardened" boys, claiming that "in spite of various social preventative measures there will always be boys who escape observation and drift on in dissolute and criminal ways until at fifteen or sixteen these are in a fair way to become habitual idlers and criminals. They require a special institution, and a longer period of training to overcome and eradicate the neglect of years."[69] The following year he advocated the replacement of the Victoria Industrial School with a new institution with more adequate facilities and built on modern principles.[70] Two years later, in 1916, he advocated the establishment of two or three more industrial schools to meet their increased population.[71] Co-existence with, rather than abolition of, institutions for juvenile offenders had now become the theme of the "home finding" movement.

The closure of Penetanguishene Reformatory in 1904 was, therefore, the high point of the "home finders" efforts to deinstitutionalize treatment of juvenile offenders. After 1904, the home finding movement gradually became reconciled to the idea that there would always be some delinquent and potentially delinquent children who would need institutional care. In the years following the closure of the reformatory, the focus of efforts to keep delinquent children out of institutions shifted to the campaigns for separate judges for children, detention homes, and probation officers, and the most important result of which was the passage of the federal Juvenile Delinquents Act in 1908.[72] Meanwhile, the institutions became more entrenched. Under the provisions of the Boys' Welfare Act of 1925 and the Boys' Welfare Home and School Act of 1931, institutions for juvenile offenders were given new names and new terms of reference which, it was felt, were more in keeping with up-to-date methods. Institutionalization of juvenile offenders has remained a feature of the Ontario child welfare and correctional systems to this day.

The child-welfare reformers of late nineteenth-century Ontario were split into three groups in their approach to the Penetanguishene Reformatory. Some wished to reform the reformatory, others to create alternative institutions, and others to abolish institutions for juvenile offenders altogether. These three groups shared several common attitudes and beliefs. All stressed the relationship between neglect and delinquency; all wished to save the children from their unfortunate circumstances, both for the child's own benefit and for the welfare of society as a whole. The differences amongst the three groups primarily were concerned with emphasis and method. Kelso's faith in the therapeutic power of kindness, compassion and a good home was unbounded: for his less visionary colleagues, thorough education, vocational training and firm discipline in an institution were the primary needs of the wayward boy. The closure of Penetanguishene Reformatory in 1904 represented a defeat for those who had worked to reform the reformatory. The apparent victory of the "home finders," however, was short-lived. Despite the apparent success in placing the boys in fosters homes and community situations, most government officials, as well as magistrates and judges, continued to believe that institutions reformed delinquent boys, and that they should be retained for that purpose. Kelso's willingness to remove the reformatory boys from institutional life solved an administrative problem for the provincial government: it did not presage a more general policy of deinstitutionalization. Ten years later even Kelso had abandoned his belief that institutions for juvenile offenders should be abolished.

Notes

1. Ontario, *Sessional Papers*, 1904, no. 27, 50.

2. Ibid., 1897–98, no. 11, 3.

3. Ontario, *Hansard*, 10 Apr. 1901.

4. *Statutes of Ontario* 1903, c. 37.

5. Public Archives of Canada (hereinafter PAC), Kelso Papers, MG30, C97, vol. 6.

6. J.J. Kelso was a prominent figure in the field of child welfare in Ontario in the late nineteenth- and early twentieth-century. He was a key figure in the formation of the Toronto Humane Society in 1887, and the Toronto Children's Aid Society in 1891. He held the position of Superintendent of Neglected and Dependent Children from 1893 until his retirement in 1934.

7. Ontario, *Sessional Papers*, 1907, no. 35, 11.

8. Ibid., 1906, no. 43, 83.

9. Ibid., 120.

10. Early nineteenth-century attitudes and policy towards juvenile offenders and the early history of Penetanguishene Reformatory are discussed in detail in Richard B. Splane, *Social Welfare in Ontario, 1791–1893* (Toronto, 1965), 149–51 and 172–76; Jerard J. Bellomo, "Upper Canadian Attitudes Towards Crime and Punishment (1832–1851)," *Ontario History* (1972): 11–26; and Susan E. Houston, "Victorian Origins of Juvenile Delinquency: A Canadian Experience," *History of Education Quarterly* (1972): 254–69.

11. PAC, Kelso Papers, vol. 6.

12. Splane, *Social Welfare in Ontario, 1791–1893*, 174–75.

13. *Statutes of Ontario* 1880, c. 34.

14. PAC, Kelso Papers, vol. 6.

15. Splane, *Social Welfare in Ontario, 1791–1893*, 176.

16. Neil Sutherland, *Children in English-Canadian Society: Framing the Twentieth Century Consensus* (Toronto, 1976), 105 and 110.

17. Ontario, *Sessional Papers*, 1894, no. 47, 36 (appendix).

18. Ibid., 1894, no. 27, 110.

19. See, for example, ibid., 1897–98, no. 11, 98.

20. Ibid., 96.

21. Ontario, *Sessional Papers*, 1898–99, no. 12, 5.

22. Ibid., 1897–98, no. 11, 105.

23. Based on figures presented in the annual reports of the Inspector of Prisons and Public Charities in Ontario, *Sessional Papers*, 1894–1903.

24. Ontario, *Hansard*, 8 Mar. 1899. The leader of the opposition called for a $10 000 reduction in the vote for the reformatory.

25. Ontario, *Sessional Papers*, 1897–98, no. 11, 3.

26. Ibid., 1904, no. 39, 48.

27. Ibid., 52.

28. There were also suggestions that McCrossan's leadership and management were inadequate. See Ontario, *Hansard*, 8 Mar. 1899.

29. Principally on the grounds that closer supervision was possible in dormitories, thus facilitating the prevention of masturbation. Sutherland, *Children in English-Canadian Society*, 105–6; Ontario, *Sessional Papers*, 1894, no. 47, 36 (appendix).

30. The early history of the industrial school movement is recounted in Splane, *Social Welfare in Ontario, 1791–1893*, 248–254, and Sutherland, *Children in English-Canadian Society*, 99–100.

31. Sutherland, *Children in English-Canadian Society*, 107.

32. Ontario, *Sessional Papers*, 1901, no. 43, 80–81.

33. From 1880 boys had been sent to the reformatory if judged to be beyond the control of their parents "by reason of incorrigible or vicious conduct," even if not guilty of any other charge.

34. Ontario, *Statutes* 1900, c. 56. To avoid abuse of this provision, it was also laid down that after a maximum of three years in the school, a child had to be given a chance in the community, either by being returned to his parents or by being placed in a foster home or apprenticeship.

35. Sutherland, *Children in English-Canadian Society*, 100.

36. The Act also gave magistrates the power to judge that a child charged with an offence was "neglected," and to place such a child under the care of a children's aid society.

37. The early history of foster care in Victoria is described by Splane, *Social Welfare in Ontario, 1791–1893*, 259–60 and 268–277.

38. Ontario, *Sessional Papers*, 1895, no. 29, 11.

39. Ibid., 1897–98, no. 16, xviii.

40. PAC, Kelso Papers, vol. 24.

41. Ontario, *Sessional Papers*, 1898–99, no. 17, 65.

42. Ibid., 1901, no. 43, 78.

43. Ibid., 80.

44. Ibid.; see also PAC, Kelso Papers, vol. 29.

45. Ontario, *Sessional Papers*, 1902, no. 43, 105.

46. Ibid., 1901, no. 43, 81.

47. PAC, Kelso Papers, vol. 6; see also Sutherland, *Children in English-Canadian Society*, 117–118.

48. Ontario, *Sessional Papers*, 1903, no. 39, 61.

49. PAC, Kelso Papers, vol. 6.

50. Ibid.

51. Ibid.

52. Ontario, *Sessional Papers*, 1904, no. 43, 86.

53. PAC, Kelso Papers, vol. 1.

54. Many of these letters are reproduced in Ontario, *Sessional Papers*, 1904, no. 43, 93–96.

55. Ibid., 118.

56. PAC, Kelso Papers, vol. 1.

57. Ibid.

58. Ontario, *Sessional Papers*, 1904, no. 43, 119.

59. PAC, Kelso Papers, vol. 1

60. Ontario, *Sessional Papers*, 1904, no. 43, 120.

61. Ibid., 7.

62. Ibid., 1906, no. 43, 8–10.

63. The increase was partly due to the reduction in the contribution required from municipalities for the upkeep of the industrial schools, thus lessening the disincentive to the local magistrates to commit to the schools. Ontario, *Sessional Papers*, 1905, no. 43, 63.

64. Ibid., 1907, no. 35, 101.

65. For example, ibid., 1909, no. 35, 84.

66. Ibid., 1905, no. 43, 63; and ibid., 1907, no. 35, 102.

67. Ibid., 1912, no. 26, 81.

68. Ibid., 1916, no. 27, 63–64.

69. Ibid., 1913, no. 26, 100.

70. PAC, Kelso Papers, vol. 5.

71. Ontario, *Sessional Papers*, 1916, no. 27, 63.

72. See Sutherland, *Children in English-Canadian Society*, 118–123.

FURTHER READING

No general study of the history of criminal justice in Canada exists at the present time. Some criminology textbooks such as C.T. Griffiths, J.F. Klein, and Simon N. Verdun-Jones, *Criminal Justice in Canada* (Toronto, 1980), and R.A. Silverman and James Teevan, Jr., *Crime in Canadian Society* (Toronto, 1975) contain brief historical introductions. W.T. McGrath, *Crime and Its Treatment in Canada* (Toronto, 1965), is now somewhat dated but has some useful sections.

Two collections of proceedings of conferences held at the University of Calgary contain a number of significant articles: David J. Bercuson and L.A. Knafla, eds., *Law and Society in Canada in Historical Perspective* (Calgary, 1979); and L.A. Knafla, ed., *Crime and Criminal Justice in Europe and Canada* (Waterloo, 1981).

André Lachance, *La justice criminelle du roi au Canada au XVIIIe siècle* (Quebec, 1978); L.A. Knafla and Terry Chapman, "Criminal Justice in Canada: A Comparative Study of the Maritimes and Lower Canada, 1760–1820," *Osgoode Hall Law Journal* (1983); and Charles K. Talbot, *Justice in Early Ontario, 1791–1840: A Study of Crime, Courts and Prisons in Early Upper Canada* (Ottawa, 1983), present reasonably comprehensive surveys of various regions for limited periods.

Historical writing on criminality in Canada has tended to concentrate almost exclusively on particular crimes or categories of crime. Some of the better examples include: Michael Cross, "The Shiners' War: Social Violence in the Ottawa Valley in the 1830s," *Canadian Historical Review* (1973); T. Crowley, " 'Thunder Gusts': Popular Disturbances in Early French Canada," Canadian Historical Association, *Historical Papers/Communications historiques* (1979); Susan E. Houston, "The Victorian Origins of Juvenile Delinquency: A Canadian Experience," *History of Education Quarterly* (1972); and Lori Rotenberg, "The Wayward Worker: Toronto's Prostitutes at the Turn of the Century" in *Women at Work: Ontario 1850–1930*, edited by Janice Acton, Penny Goldsmith, and Bonnie Shepard (Toronto, 1974).

The only approach to a comprehensive history of police in Canada is Charles K. Talbot, C.H.S. Jayewardene, and T.J. Juliani, *The Thin Blue Line: An Historical Perspective of Policing in Canada* (Ottawa, 1983).

There is an enormous popular literature on the history of the North West Mounted Police and its successor, the Royal Canadian Mounted Police, much of it badly done. The best popular history is Ronald Atkin, *Maintain the Right: The Early History of the North West Mounted Police* (Toronto, 1973). Scholarly books on the subject include: R.C. Macleod, *The North West Mounted Police and Law Enforcement* (Toronto, 1976); William R. Morrison, *Showing the Flag: The Mounted Police and Canadian Sovereignty in the North, 1894–1925* (Vancouver, 1985); and Keith Walden, *Visions of Order: The Canadian Mounties in Symbol and Myth* (Toronto, 1982). No one seriously interested in the history of the mounted police can ignore the article by S.W. Horrall, "Sir John A.

Macdonald and the Mounted Police Force for the North West Territories,"
Canadian Historical Review (1972).

The historical literature on other police forces in the country is disappoint-
ingly sparse. Some works worth reading include: Arthur Fox, *The Newfound-*
land Constabulary (St. John's 1971); Jean Turmel, *Le service de police de la cité*
de Montréal (1909–1971) (Montreal, 1974); and Nicholas Rogers, "Serving
Toronto the Good: The Development of the City Police Force 1834–1880"
in *Forging a Consensus: Historical Essays on Toronto*, edited by V.L. Russell
(Toronto, 1984). Desmond Morton's article "Aid to the Civil Power: The
Canadian Militia in Support of Social Order, 1867–1914," *Canadian Historical*
Review (1970), is a good introduction to the history of non-police alternatives
to enforcement.

The Osgoode Society has sponsored the publication of two volumes edited
by David J. Flaherty, *Essays in the History of Canadian Law* (Toronto; vol. 1,
1981, vol. 2, 1983), both of which contain a number of articles on Canadian
criminal law and the courts. Most of the articles by Martin Friedland in his
collection *A Century of Criminal Justice: Perspectives on the Development of Cana-*
dian Law (Toronto, 1984), are historical in their approach. The Law Reform
Commission of Canada published a useful summary of the development of
criminal law entitled "Our Criminal Law" in the *Canadian Journal of Cri-*
minology (1976).

More limited aspects of the history of the criminal law are covered in R.C.
Macleod, "The Shaping of Canadian Criminal Law, 1892–1902," Canadian
Historical Association, *Historical Papers/Communications historiques* (1978), and
Graham Parker, "The Origins of the Canadian Criminal Code," in Flaherty,
Essays in the History of Canadian Law, vol. 1.

Courts at very different levels are examined in: James G. Snell and Frederick
Vaughan, *The Supreme Court of Canada: History of the Institution* (Toronto,
1985); Paul Craven, "Law and Ideology: The Toronto Police Court, 1850–
1880" in Flaherty, *Essays in the History of Canadian Law*, vol. 2; and Thomas
Thorner and Neil Watson, "Keeper of the King's Peace: Colonel G.E. Sanders
and the Calgary Police Magistrate's Court, 1911–1932," *Urban History Review*
(1984). Desmond Morton in *The Queen vs. Louis Riel* (Toronto, 1976) repro-
duces the complete transcript of the most famous Canadian criminal trial of
the nineteenth century.

The beginnings of the penitentiary in Canada are well covered in the J.M.
Beattie, *Attitudes Towards Crime and Punishment in Upper Canada, 1830–1850:*
A Documentary Study (Toronto, 1977), and Rainer Baehre, "Origins of the
Penitentiary System in Upper Canada," *Ontario History* (1977). A more spec-
ialized aspect of imprisonment is examined in Simon N. Verdun-Jones and
Russell Smandych, "Catch–22 in the Nineteenth Century: The Evolution of
Therapeutic Confinement for the Criminally Insane in Canada, 1840–1900,"
Criminal Justice History: An International Annual (1981). The only full-length
history of a provincial prison system is Shirley Skinner, Otto Driedger, and
Brian Grainger, *Corrections: An Historical Perspective of the Saskatchewan Experi-*
ence (Regina, 1981).

Two of the better pieces of work on juvenile justice are: Rebecca Coulter,

"Not to Punish but to Reform: Juvenile Delinquency and the Children's Protection Act in Alberta, 1909–1929," in *Studies in Childhood History: A Canadian Perspective*, edited by Patricia T. Rooke (Calgary, 1982), and Susan E. Houston, "The 'Waifs and Strays' of a Late Victorian City: Juvenile Delinquents in Toronto," in *Childhood and the Family in Canadian History*, edited by Joy Parr (Toronto, 1982). The recent history of capital punishment in Canada is reasonably well covered in David Chandler, *Capital Punishment in Canada* (Toronto, 1976).

An honest attempt has been made to secure permission for all material used, and if there are errors or omissions, these are wholly unintentional and the Publisher will be grateful to learn of them.

André Lachance, "Women and Crime in Canada in the Early Eighteenth Century, 1712–1759." This essay was originally published in Louis A. Knafla, editor, *Crime and Criminal Justice in Europe and Canada* (Waterloo, Ontario: Wilfrid Laurier University Press, 1981, for the Calgary Institute for the Humanities). Reprinted by permission of the publisher.

John Weaver, "Crime, Public Order, and Repression: The Gore District in Upheaval, 1832–1851," *Ontario History* 78, no. 3 (1986): 175–207; Michael S. Cross, "Stony Monday, 1849: The Rebellion Losses Riots in Bytown," *Ontario History* 63 (1971): 177–90; Gene Howard Homel, "Denison's Law: Criminal Justice and the Police Court in Toronto, 1877–1921," *Ontario History* 72 (1980): 171–86; Andrew Jones, " 'Closing Penetanguishene Reformatory': An Attempt to Deinstitutionalize Treatment of Juvenile Offenders in Early Twentieth-Century Ontario," *Ontario History* 70 (1978): 227–44. Reprinted by permission of the Ontario Historical Society.

Judith Fingard, "Jailbirds in Mid-Victorian Halifax," in *Law in a Colonial Society: The Nova Scotia Experience*, edited by Peter Waite, Sandra Oxner, and Thomas Barnes, The Dalhousie/Berkeley Lectures in Legal History (Toronto: Carswell, 1984), 81–102. Reprinted by permission of The Carswell Company Limited.

Elinor Kyte Senior, "The Influence of the British Garrison on the Development of the Montreal Police, 1832 to 1853," *Military Affairs* 43, no. 2 (Apr. 1979):63–68. Reprinted by permission of the journal and the author.

Carl Betke, "Pioneers and Police on the Canadian Prairies, 1885–1914," Canadian Historical Association, *Historical Papers/Communications historiques* (1980): 9–32. Reprinted by permission of the Canadian Historical Association and the author.

Patricia E. Roy, "The Preservation of the Peace in Vancouver: The Aftermath of the Anti-Chinese Riot of 1887," *BC Studies* 31 (Autumn 1976): 44–59. Reprinted by permission of the journal.

S.W. Horrall, "The Royal North-West Mounted Police and Labour Unrest in Western Canada, 1919," *Canadian Historical Review* 61, no. 2 (1980): 169–90. Reprinted by permission of the author and University of Toronto Press.

Alan W. Mewett, "The Criminal Law, 1867–1967," *The Canadian Bar Review* 45 (1967): 726–40. Reprinted by permission of *The Canadian Bar Review*.

Martin L. Friedland, "A Century of Criminal Justice," in *A Century of Criminal Justice: Perspectives on the Development of Canadian Law*, edited by Martin L. Friedland (Toronto: Carswell, 1984), 233–45. Reprinted by permission of the author and The Carswell Company Limited.

Neil Boyd, "The Origins of Canadian Narcotics Legislation: The Process of Criminalization in Historical Context," *Dalhousie Law Journal* 8, no. 1 (Jan. 1984): 102–36. Reprinted by permission of the journal and the author.

C.J. Taylor, "The Kingston, Ontario Penitentiary and Moral Architecture," *Histoire sociale/Social History* 12, no. 24 (Nov. 1979): 385–408; Donald G. Wetherell, "To Discipline and Train: Adult Rehabilitation Programmes in Ontario Prisons, 1874–1900," *Histoire sociale/Social History* 12, no. 23 (May 1979): 145–65. Reprinted by permission of the journal.

D.W.F. Coughlan, "The History and Function of Probation," *Canadian Bar Journal* 6 (1963): 198–213. Reprinted by permission of the *Canadian Bar Journal*.

1 2 3 4 5   135529   92 91 90 89 88
0-7730-4681-X